Not Your Father's Antisemitism

Not Your Father's Antisemitism

Hatred of the Jews in the
Twenty-first Century

Edited by Michael Berenbaum

Paragon House
St. Paul, Minnesota

First Edition 2008

Published in the United States by
Paragon House
1925 Oakcrest Ave, Suite 7
St. Paul, MN 55113
www.paragonhouse.com

Library of Congress Cataloging-in-Publication Data

Not your father's antisemitism : hatred of the Jews in the 21st century /
edited by Michael Berenbaum.—1st ed.
     p. cm.
  Summary: "Essays by sixteen prominent scholars from diverse disciplines
investigate antisemitism in the contemporary world debunking the fear that
the 1930s is being revisited and discussing what is unique about 21st
century antisemitism"—Provided by publisher.
  ISBN 978-1-55778-874-0 (pbk. : alk. paper)
  1. Antisemitism—History—21st century. I. Berenbaum, Michael, 1945-
DS145.N68 2008
305.892'4—dc22
                              2007043884

The paper used in this publication meets the minimum requirements of American National Standard for Information Sciences— Permanence of Paper for Printed Library Materials, ANSIZ39.48-1984.

Manufactured in the United States of America
10 9 8 7 6 5 4 3 2 1

For current information about all releases from Paragon House, visit the
website at http://www.paragonhouse.com

In Memory of Nathan Shapell
1922-2007
Survivor, Builder, Philanthropist, Public Servant,
Visionary and Witness

Contents

Acknowledgments

Words of gratitude are in order.

This work resulted from a conference sponsored by the Sigi Ziering Institute: Exploring the Religious and Ethical Implications of the Holocaust at the American Jewish University, my academic home for the past half dozen years. It was made possible through the generosity of a wonderful benefactor my friend Nathan Shapell, with whom I worked for almost thirty years on the creation and development of the United States Holocaust Memorial Museum before his demise as this work was nearing completion. Nathan was a survivor, a builder, a public servant of enormous dedication and talent. His death reminds all that we are the last to live in the presence of survivors, how much they have given and how deep our loss at their passing.

My gratitude to the leadership of the American Jewish University, its President Robert Wexler, Academic Vice President Mark Bookman and his predecessor Lois Oppenheim and Dean Sam Edelman who have enabled me to work and to teach in an atmosphere conducive to scholarship.

I am grateful to Marilyn Ziering and the Ziering Family Foundation, to Lou Colen and his late wife Irma and to Maxwell and Janet Salter for their generosity in establishing the Sigi Zeiring Institute and to the inspiring memory of Sigi Ziering. He was a survivor, a brilliant scientist and a creative philanthropist dedicated to the memory of the Holocaust and to the highest standards of ethics and learning.

Ruthie Small, who was my assistant through the planning of the conference, was skilled and dedicated. She handled so many details well and my current assistant Tosha Petronicolos takes much off my plate so that I can work. She is competent and seemingly unflappable.

I would like to thank Ron Petrisca for coming to my rescue and resolving so many computer glitches in both a skillful and a timely manner.

My wife Melissa pursues her own high pressured career and still manages to do so much to make our home life warm and inviting, a gathering place and a place of joy. Our children Joshua Boaz and Mira Leza are a constant blessing. My daughter Rabbi Ilana Grinblat and her husband Tal are an engaging presence in my life and their son, my first grandchild, Jeremy Judah is a source of marvel and delight. Thanks also to my son Lev.

As this work was reaching conclusion my first granddaughter was born, Hannah Leah, named after my late mother. May Hannah know of a world of less hatred and less venom! May she and her brother, along with their young aunt and uncle, live without the anxieties of her parents and grandparents and the generations before that antisemitism is resurgent and the world is descending into madness.

Michael Berenbaum
Los Angeles, California
The Eve of Passover 5767

Foreword

John K. Roth

This work is an effort to understand antisemitism as it is manifested in our times—nothing less, nothing more.

Michael Berenbaum

The Holocaust was in the news on January 27, 2005. On that date, death camp survivors and a few of their Russian liberators joined heads of state and Jewish leaders at a snow-covered Auschwitz-Birkenau to observe the sixtieth anniversary of that killing center's liberation by the Red Army. The aging and dying of the survivors and liberators meant that such a gathering is not likely to take place again.

The speeches at the Auschwitz-Birkenau commemoration underscored twin themes: First, the mass murder of Jews at that place was a warning—not only for Jews but also for all humankind. Second, never again should humanity permit such atrocities. Even as those words were uttered, however, awareness of more recent genocides, such as the 1994 slaughter in Rwanda and the devastation in the Darfur region of Sudan were on the minds of many who heard them.

That late January commemoration at Auschwitz-Birkenau took place under another ominous shadow as well. It was identified on January 5, 2005, when the US Department of State issued its Report on Global Anti-Semitism. The report documented and analyzed what it called "the increasing frequency and severity of anti-Semitic incidents since the start of the 21st century."[1]

One might have thought that the Holocaust, awareness and education about it, would have a significant ethical impact that, in particular, would reduce if not eliminate antisemitism. Such hopes were not entirely wrong, but unfortunately they proved far too optimistic.

In fact, Holocaust educators currently have to deal with an ironic development, namely, that teaching about the Holocaust can inflame antisemitism because critics (1) indict Holocaust education as special pleading to cover up or to justify Israel's alleged human rights abuses, a strategy that is often accompanied by Holocaust minimalization or denial; (2) use Holocaust images to portray Palestinians and other non-Jews as victims; and (3) depict Israelis and other Jews as akin to Nazi perpetrators.

Antisemitism has aptly been called the longest hatred, but it is more than hatred of Jews. As the French president Jacques Chirac stated in his January 25, 2005, address on the occasion of the opening of a Holocaust memorial in Paris, "antisemitism is not an opinion. It is a perversion . . . rooted in the depths of evil."[2] Antisemitism's intensity has waxed and waned, but as the State Department's Report on Global Anti-Semitism testified, its frequency and severity have been on the rise again. The 2005 report underscored four main sources for this upsurge. Forming much of the context in which this book appears, they remain very much in play.

First, traditional anti-Jewish prejudice never went away entirely. It enjoys new popularity among ultra-nationalists, especially in Europe, who, as the State Department report put it, "assert that the Jewish community controls governments, the media, international business, and the financial world." Second, inflamed by the Israeli-Palestinian conflict and reaching far beyond objective criticism of some Israeli policies, there is demonization of Israel and vilification of Israeli leaders. Third, in both Europe and the Middle East, specifically in Muslim communities, opposition to "developments in Israel and the occupied territories" intensifies anti-Jewish feelings. Fourth, there is "criticism of both the United States and globalization that spills over to Israel, and to Jews in general who are identified with both."[3]

In the twenty-first century, antisemitism is widely and easily spread by diverse media outlets, including the internet. Many governments, the State Department report found, have spoken out against antisemitism, but law enforcement against hate crimes and protection for their targets has been "uneven," to use the report's understated word.[4] Noting that antisemitism is "an intolerable burden" in our "increasingly interdependent world," the report saw Holocaust education as "a potential long-term solution to anti-Semitism" but acknowledged that "the problem is still rapidly outpacing the solution."[5]

In one sense, then, the answer to the question "Why has anti-semitism surged in the twenty-first century?" is neither surprising nor difficult to locate: Despite the Holocaust, antisemitism never went away. Current developments in the Middle East expanded and re-intensified it, advances in communication technologies facilitated its spread, and responses have been insufficient to thwart, let alone eliminate, the threat.

Michael Berenbaum has titled this important book appropriately. Like viruses that morph into more resistant strains, twenty-first century antisemitism is related to and yet significantly different from that used by and inflicted upon previous generations. Its end-game is no longer the gas chamber and crematoria of Auschwitz; the eventual specter of a nuclear-armed antisemitism, aimed particularly—but not only—at Israel, is scarcely unthinkable.

As Berenbaum's introduction rightly warns, an effective strategy against, let alone a cure for, this century's newly infectious antisemitism has yet to be found. Such a strategy will remain elusive and even illusory unless contemporary antisemitism is well understood, which means that what has previously passed for understanding will have to be carefully scrutinized in the light of twenty-first century developments.

The aim of *Not Your Father's Antisemitism* is to advance such inquiry—in Berenbaum's words, "nothing less, nothing more" than that. Far from being modest, the standard set by his "nothing less, nothing more" is demanding and even daunting. If analysis of contemporary antisemitism comes up short, the findings can be dangerously misleading. That difficulty makes it imperative to do the best one can to "get it right" where understanding of current antisemitism is at stake. Only then will the best strategies for combating it come into clearest view.

It would be naïve to think that the twenty-first century will be the one in which antisemitism ceases to exist. Unfortunately, even after the contributors to this book are gone, there may be a need for second, third, or fourth editions with the same title. Although scholarship of the kind found in these pages will not be sufficient to eliminate those grim possibilities, there is not likely to be an effective check against them without it. Neither individually nor collectively do this book's chapters bring closure and finality to the inquiry that is needed, but they contribute to sound analysis in ways that are lucid and insightful, well-informed and penetrating, timely and urgent. To say that study of this book can be a matter of life or death is no exaggeration.

Notes

1. US Department of State, "Report on Global Anti-Semitism, July 1, 2003–December 15, 2004," submitted by the Department of State to the Committee on Foreign Relations and the Committee on International Relations in accordance with Section 4 of PL 108-322, December 30, 2004, and released by the Bureau of Democracy, Human Rights, and Labor, January 5, 2005. See p. 1. Available online at: http://www.state.gov/g/drl/rls/40258.htm. All references are to the online version, which is designated hereafter as Report on Global Anti-Semitism.

2. Jacques Chirac, "Discours a l'occasion de l'inauguration du memorial de la Shoah," Paris, January 25, 2005. I owe this reference to Paul Shapiro, director of the Center for Advanced Holocaust Studies, United States Holocaust Memorial Museum.

3. Report on Global Anti-Semitism, pp. 1-2.

4. Ibid., p. 4.

5. Ibid., pp. 1, 2.

Introduction

Michael Berenbaum

This is not a book I had once thought I would edit, not a conference I once thought would be needed. Like many of my generation, I once thought antisemitism was a problem of the past, one resolved in my lifetime by my parents' generation. It was their great achievement. I believed my children could grow up without knowing its reality. Sadly, I was wrong.

In the early 1990, when I published *After Tragedy and Triumph: Modern Jewish Thought and the American Experience,* I argued that the two defining questions of contemporary Jewish life would be the questions posed by European philosophers Jean-Paul Sartre and Friedrich Nietzsche. Sartre asked: Would it take the antisemite to make the Jew? In the absence of antisemitism, could Jews sustain themselves internally without the external pressures? Sartre was not alone; the undisputed religious leader of mid-twentieth-century modern Orthodoxy, Joseph B. Soloveitchik, advanced the concept of the two covenants; the covenant of fate and the covenant of faith. In the absence of a covenant of fate—a commonality of destiny imposed by external situation of the Jewish people—would a second covenant, a covenant of faith, bind the Jews?

Nietzsche asked: Was Judaism the religion of the powerless? Would an empowered people affirm the same values, maintain the same traditions, champion the same causes? We live in a time of the empowerment of the Jewish people, and it was presumed that with adequate power the problem of antisemitism could be resolved. Even political Zionism's founder, Theodor Herzl, whose vision was shaped by the antisemitism he experienced at the trial of Alfred Dreyfus, presumed that antisemitism could be ended with the normalization of the Jewish condition, with sovereignty and a state. For a while, Israel offered precisely that promise, but it now seems quite illusory.

The answers were uncertain then; they remain uncertain now, yet, I had underestimated the degree to which more than a decade later we would still be confronting antisemitism, now in very different manifestations.

The late Milton Himmelfarb, the pithy commentator of American Jewish life, gave us two memorable characterizations of American Jewish life. He said: "Jews live like Episcopalians and vote like Puerto Ricans"—at least at a time when Puerto Ricans voted like Puerto Ricans. His second comment is somewhat less well known but nonetheless no less true: "The easiest way to get booed by a Jewish audience is to tell them that antisemitism is less severe a problem than they think it is."

I am not sure that throughout this book, we will tell you antisemitism is less severe of a problem, but I am quite certain readers will see its shape, contour, and context quite differently after reading this work, which will offer insights into the scope of the problem and a considered understanding of its dimensions.

A brief word of history: In the 1980s, Jonathan Woocher published an important work on the American Jewish community entitled *Sacred Survival*. His argued that the American Jewish community was united in its mission of survival, which expressed itself in three areas of activity: working on behalf of the survival of the State of Israel; freeing and protecting endangered Jews—Soviet Jews, Ethiopian Jews, Latin American Jews; and remembering the Holocaust, which endowed all postwar Jewish life with a special quality of triumph over our oppressors. "Do not give Hitler a posthumous victory" became Emil Fackenheim's and the Jewish people's 614th commandment, a commitment shared by all Jews, secular and religious, Conservative, Orthodox, Reform, Reconstructionist, Humanistic, Zionist and non-Zionist alike.

Within fifteen years Woocher's work no longer resonated with the younger Jews who looked inwardly, not outwardly, to define their Jewishness. They had seen the barriers to advancement of Jews within the United States disappear; there was nothing they could not be, nowhere they could not travel, and nothing they could not achieve, from the chairman of the board to the presidency of Harvard, Princeton, and Yale, to nomination for the vice presidency of the United States. More important, they could achieve what they sought to achieve as Jews, without changing their names, masking their identity, or even limiting their observance of Jewish rituals in private or in public. Indeed, American Jews had broken the unwritten rule of postemancipation

Jewish life: "Be a Jew in your home and a man in the street!" One now has the freedom to be Jewish everywhere.

In the mid 1990s, after the Oslo Accords and all the barriers to American Jewish participation in the larger society were broken, many Jews thought antisemitism was a malaise of the past, and the major challenge to Jewish survival was solely internal. They wondered: Was there enough within Judaism, Jewish history, Jewish thought, Jewish tradition, Jewish memory, and the Jewish community to command the allegiance of a new generation of Jews who had every opportunity —even the opportunity to leave without a sense of betrayal—and for whom no barriers existed? Could Judaism thrive without antisemitism, without the common fate of collective animus to fuel communal allegiance?

In the 1990s, it seemed as if peace in Israel was but a matter of time and Jews could be a "normal" people, a nation whose survival was granted and who could thrive with opportunity and without being the target of hatred. Israel was productive and prosperous, secure and stable, and Jews everywhere were experiencing the joys of freedom.

A personal story: Each year at our Passover Seder, just prior to the cup of Elijah, we recount what must be done in our world at this time to liberate the Jews from slavery. One year in the late 1990s the conversation was blessedly brief; Jews were free virtually everywhere, so the conversation was fully spiritual.

Enter the new millennia!

The peace process collapsed; the hope of Oslo was replaced by the dismal reality of Intifada II, which now seems tame in comparison to the activities of militant Islam. Antisemitism has exploded within the Muslim world. Debunked myths alien to Islam, painstakingly discredited over the past half century within the Christian world, have been absorbed in the Muslim world. *The Protocols of the Elders of Zion*, the Russian forgery that purports to show Jewish world domination, has been made into a television series in Egypt. Islam has borrowed the Blood Libel and the desecration of the Eucharist, which makes psychological sense within Christianity but should not have resonated within the Muslim world. Political anti-Zionism has fueled hatred within the Arab world, and religious anti-Judaism has propelled political opposition to Israel. The results have been bad; the trends are worse.

Religious extremism has reared its head within each of the major monotheistic faiths and with the greatest intensity within the Muslim world, where the balance of secularism and Western liberalism does not hold sway. In Judaism, religious extremism is a minority phenomenon. Abhorred by the majority, Jewish extremism still resulted in the Purim Days massacre at Hebron, the assassination of Israeli prime minister Yitzhak Rabin, and thwarted attempts to blow up the Al Aksa Mosque, on the Temple Mount in Jerusalem. Contemporary religious extremism is intemperate, either by lack of exposure to outside thought or by principled rejection of all outside thought. It is fueled by the certitude of the assent of God and the demonization of one's enemies as God's enemies.

In Europe, antisemitism has been on the rise as country after country throughout the Continent faces a demographic situation that can only make things worse. The European population is aging and a new working class must be imported to take their place and to work, in part to provide the social safety net the European workers have come to expect.

As we learn from Richard Rubenstein, for three centuries after the Industrial Revolution, Europe produced a surplus population that was exported to settle the New World or to exploit and colonize the Third World; and now Europe is unable to reproduce itself. The result has been the importation of large Muslim populations: Turks in Germany and Arabs in many other countries.

And unlike the United States, where immigration was followed by assimilation and Americanization—or at least it should be—these populations reside in the countries of Europe but do not become Europeans. French president Jacques Chirac could say with all confidence "that antisemitism is not France," by which he meant that antisemitism is alien to the values of liberty, equality, and fraternity even as populations living in France increase their antisemitic activities. They reside in France but *are not of France.* Only belatedly has French officialdom begun to recognize that these differences will spell the doom of France —as we know it—unless these populations assimilate French values and become part of French culture. Only after the riots in the streets of Paris and elsewhere has the French government started to change its orientation, but the transformation may be clumsy and too little, too late.

As we shall see time and again in this book, European opposition to Israeli policies, whether legitimate or excessive, only exacerbates the situation. Frenchmen and other Europeans easily distinguish between their native Jews, whom they regard as fellow citizens, and their denunciation of Israeli policies. And yet local inhabitants, Arab residents of the European countries, regard the intensity of European opposition to Israel as license to attack indigenous Jews. Any talk of the illegitimacy of the state of Israel is translated as the illegitimacy of Jews—everywhere.

To the degree that European nationalism is coupled with anti-Americanism, or at least with the rivalry between the Old World and the New World—a rivalry intensified by the language used by some American officials—opposition to the Jews also intensifies. Jews are seen as agents of globalization and shapers of American policy, a privileged constituency within the American power structure. Efraim Zuroff contrasts antisemitism in Western Europe with antisemitism in Eastern Europe, where it was seemingly more pervasive and more dangerous—but not so today.

As Jerome Chanes and Fred Jaher argue, the picture in the United States is dramatically different. Non-Jews regard Jews in a manner that Jews do not regard themselves. Jews are seen as privileged, empowered members of the white majority and not as a minority population. Other antagonisms—based on race, country of origin, or language—seem more central. All the while, American Jews anguish over local threats, which have not materialized—at least to date. Still, as Mark Weizman and Sam Edelman document, there is antisemitism at the fringes of American society—right and left.

As opposed to other countries where antisemitism thrives without Jews, in the United States antisemitism is comparatively tame despite the prevalence of Jews in the areas where traditional anti-Jewish conspiracy theorists sought to explain Jewish domination. Over the past decades there has been ample opportunity for an increase in antisemitism.

Jews were recognizable in the banking crisis of the 1980s and in the insider trading scandals. Jews led the economic policy of the Clinton administration, from Robert Rubin and Lawrence Summers at the Department of Treasury to Alan Greenspan at the Federal Reserve and James Wolfenson at the World Bank (the latter two were succeeded by Jews Ben S. Bernake and Paul Wolfowitz). Dominant players at the center of American economic policy were Jews.

Jews—but not only Jews—were also among the strongest voices calling for the invasion of Iraq and conducting the war, from Paul Wolfowitz and Doug Feith at the Department of Defense to William Kristol and

Charles Krautheimer in the press. Jews are prominent in the neocon-servative movement, and indeed there was widespread talk of a back-lash against Jews precisely as casualties mounted and the war seemed to be going badly. Indeed, some feared political support for the state of Israel might diminish because of the war. Such concerns were confined to fringe elements in American politics, yet the fear was widespread among American Jews. Are the fears justified? Despite the publication of a scathing piece of quasi-journalistic scholarship by the University of Chicago's John Mearsheimer and Harvard's Kennedy School's academic dean Stephen Walt that accuses the Israel lobby of thwarting America's security interests, support for Israel remains strong and bipartisan. Mel Gibson's *The Passion of the Christ* was a blockbuster success in bringing to the theater Christians who seldom saw R-rated movies. Their reli-gious experience in the theater was profound, so profound that Chris-tian believers were blinded to Gibson's portrayal of the Jews. Jews who saw the very same film were so chagrined by the portrayal of the Jews that they could not see the majesty of the passion. Jewish opponents of the film, Jews who expressed concern about its content, from Abraham Foxman to Marvin Hier, were depicted as anti-Christian by elements of the religious and political right. And for the first time in a very long time, Jews experienced themselves as cultural outsiders, unable to understand what was a major cultural event to their neighbors. Yet the results were neither pogroms nor a dramatic rise in antisemitic incidents. It seems that Americans can readily distinguish between the historical depic-tion of first century Jews and their Jewish neighbors, and even between ancient Jews living in the land of Israel and contemporary Israelis. Amid all the talk of resurgent antisemitism ADL published its findings which show that for the second year in a row, in 2006, antisemitic incidents were on the decline in the United States.

Frankly, America is different. After more than 350 years on this soil, the arrival of the first Jews forced Peter Stuyvesant, much against his will, to forge a pluralistic *multireligious* society in the New Land, and not a pluralistic *Christian* society, and that sense of America has continued for more than three centuries, into the third millennia. America has only become more diverse in the past half century. In the mid-fifties, Wil Herberg could define the American religious experi-ence as Catholic, Protestant, or Jew. Jews constituted 3 percent of the American community but 33 percent of the American religious expe-rience. This is no longer the case and will never again be true of the

United States as our religious experience is more diverse. The Muslim population has grown dramatically; so too the number of adherents to Eastern religions and confirmed secularists. Still, the place of the Jews in the United States is secure, at least for the foreseeable future.

We have heard some reckless talk: the all too common—and all too unchallenged—comparison between the Jewish condition of today and the Jewish condition during the Holocaust. The vulnerability of the 1930s cannot be compared with contemporary Jewish vulnerability. It was different and we are different.

The Holocaust was unique. It bears reiteration: Not every Jewish vulnerability is the vulnerability of the Holocaust, and not every enemy is Adolf Hitler. As Leon Wieseltier wrote, "Hitler is dead." Hitler ruled most of Europe, but Arafat in his last years could not move more than 150 yards from his battered headquarters.

In a fine book on *Power and Powerless in Jewish History*, David Biale summarized the Jewish predicament:

> From biblical times to the present day, Jews have wandered the uncertain terrain between power and powerlessness, never quite achieving the power necessary to guarantee long-term security, but equally avoiding, with a number of disastrous exceptions, the abyss of absolute impotence. They developed the consummate skill of living with uncertainty and insecurity.[1]

The Holocaust was the paradigmatic example of near absolute Jewish impotence. Today, Jews are an empowered people. Israel is ranked as the third or fourth most powerful army in the world. And by any scale of power, the American Jewish community is a powerful community, not quite as powerful as the antisemites proclaim, but far more powerful than Jews sense themselves to be.

Jews have wealth, power, and influence. They can be seen in the corridors of power in government and industry, in academia and in the media. They face virtually no barriers to career advancement, and they can advance without having to abandon or mute their commitment to Jewish faith and their proud membership in the Jewish people. Twenty-first-century Jews are not the Jews of the thirties and forties, and they are not hesitant to advance Jewish issues to the very center of the American national agenda. In fact, they are quite skilled at it; so skilled that American administration after administration has been responsive to Jewish issues, large and small and supportive of Israel.

After the Yom Kippur War, Jews mistakenly feared that power in the last third of the twentieth century would be in control of natural resources—in Arab oil, the great addiction of the West. In fact, it turned out that over the past four decades power was in the management of information, and Jews both in Israel and the United States were ideally positioned to benefit from the information revolution.

The much heralded antisemitic address by the prime minister of Malaysia underscored the degree to which Muslims feel disempowered and socially unprepared for this information revolution, and the way they have not built their societies from the newfound wealth of oil. Islam, which had been at the center of philosophy and science, in partnership with the Jews living creatively under Islam, had brought forth classical thought to what was termed "the Dark Ages." It had shut itself off from science and closed itself to outside ideas. It is only in dialogue with these new ideas that power is found in the twenty-first-century world.

In the aftermath of World War II and the experience of powerlessness during the Shoah, Jews learned a fundamental lesson: Powerlessness invites victimization. Jews had presumed with Theodor Herzl and the Zionists that the Jewish state would become a normal state and end the problem of antisemitism. And for a time it seemed that it might. Jews assumed that power would end victimization and that a land and state would end vulnerability. They have not.

The painful lesson of this time, taught again in the first years of the twenty-first century as it was demonstrable during the oil crises of 1973 and 1979, is that Israel can fuel the flames of antisemitism and not only quench its fires. Empowerment has not ended Jewish vulnerability; it has merely given us alternate means with which to grapple with our ongoing vulnerability.

In the 1930s, racial antisemitism became the dominant philosophy of an expansionist Germany that soon conquered country after country, and wherever it ruled it imposed that racial antisemitism and the policies that led to the annihilation of the Jewish people. The Jewish people were powerless to combat it and unable—perhaps not willing enough—to marshal the support of the United States and Great Britain, those with power, to adequately respond to the genocide.

The most extreme antisemitism is found today in countries where Jews no longer reside, and however bad the situation is in France, its Jewish community is not vulnerable to state-sponsored systematic murder. It is far less vulnerable to antisemitism than it was in the late nineteenth century when Frenchmen were chanting in the streets of Paris "death to the Jews," and extraordinarily less vulnerable than when French policemen and Vichy officials participated in the roundup and deportation of French Jews to transit camps in France and from transit camps to Auschwitz.

Still, the times are depressing. I belong to the generation that lived through the Six-Day War, saw Israel emerge as a military power and a potential economic powerhouse, and experienced the collapse of antisemitism as a factor in American life. My peers were illprepared for its resurgence and unable to explain why the Jewish state became the place where Jews are most vulnerable.

Jews on the right see it as more of the same, ongoing antisemitism that seems seamless from Hitler to Hezbollah, Hamas and Mahmoud Ahmadinejad. And Jews on the left can only blame Israel for its occupational policies, and because of that blame seem silent when antisemitism is manifest.

Still, comparing the contemporary situation to the 1930s as Jewish organizations seemingly are prone to do is to cede to our enemies a power they do not have, an intent they may not share, and to disparage the great achievement of the Zionist revolution when the Jews become actors in history rather than its passive victims.

It is to invite upon ourselves not only nightmares of our own times, but the absolute darkness of another time and another place that is not our own and bears no resemblance to our own. Those who do so manifest considerable ignorance of those times and misinterpret our own.

I neither wish to condone or to minimize contemporary antisemitism nor to presume for a moment that Jews are not vulnerable today. Anyone who hears the statements of Iranian president Mahmoud Ahmadinejad speaking of death to Israel and contemplates him and those of his fellow countrymen to whom he appeals in possession of nuclear arms must think of the heightened vulnerability of our age. To state that something is not the Holocaust or that a second Holocaust is not pending is merely to restate the obvious, not to prescribe complacency.

The contemporary feeling of powerlessness may be explained by our own paralysis. We have heard time and again from Israeli military leaders that the Jewish-Palestinian struggle does not lend itself to a military solution, at least not one commensurate with democratic norms and with values most Jews—and I would argue, though others would certainly disagree, that Judaism also—holds dear. We have employed many tactics in our contemporary struggle, but it seems blatantly clear that we are without a strategy. We don't quite know what we want to achieve or how to achieve it and consequently we have empowered extremists who alone seem able to determine the agenda. Because we can't decide what to do, we are reactive and not proactive.

A word about the shape of this book, which is the result of a conference convened by the Sigi Ziering Institute: Exploring the Ethical and Religious Implications of the Holocaust at the American Jewish University (formerly the University of Judaism), my academic home for the past six years. The work is divided into six parts, preceded by an introduction: antisemitism in contemporary Europe; in classical and contemporary Islam; the migration of discredited myths from the Christian West to Islam, namely the *Protocols of the Elders of Zion* and Holocaust denial; the argument for American exceptionalism; an exploration of antisemitism on the right and the left in the United States today, and, finally, the question of Israel and contemporary antisemitism.

My colleague and friend Robert Wistrich termed antisemitism "the longest hatred," the reality of which is in little dispute. For this hatred to end, perhaps even for it to be diminished, it must be understood. This work is an effort to understand antisemitism as it is manifested in our times—nothing less, nothing more.

Notes

1. David Biale, *Power and Powerlessness in Jewish History* (New York: Schocken Books, 1985.)

SECTION I

Antisemitism in Contemporary Europe

The situation in France is a microcosm of European antisemitism. France is home to the fourth-largest Jewish community in the world, but also home to a Muslim immigrant community that is at least ten times the size of its Jewish community, a community that dwells in France but is not—or is not quite part—of France. Since the famous confrontation with President Charles de Gaulle on the eve of the Six Day War in June 1967, France has also been at best muted in its support of Israel. More frequently, it has been highly critical of Israeli policies on the West Bank and especially critical during Israel's two incursions into Lebanon, in 1982 and 2006. Government statements and press criticism has been harsh toward Israel and tilted strongly toward the Arabs. Sympathy for the Palestinians is deep, and the upsurge in antisemitism is directly correlated with events in the Middle East: the beginning of Intifada II, the Passover massacres, the events in Jenin, and the summer 2006 war in Lebanon. In the runup to and the aftermath of the American-led invasion of Iraq, France has also been deeply critical of American policy and a leading force in the tension between the "old world" and the "new world." Anti-Americanism and antiglobalism present in France are also linked to an increase in antisemitism.

Le Monde journalist Nicholas Weill contends that there has been a qualitative change in the Jewish situation in France. Antisemitic incidents are on the rise. In the past they were a small part of the total number of racist or xenophobic incidents. In the past antisemitism was ascribed to the right wing and neo-Nazis, but not so today. Anti-Jewish hate is acted out by new protagonists, immigrants and their descendants, but it is tolerated by antiglobalism protesters and fed by the media and the press. And perhaps even more important, antisemitism is not opposed by large segments of French society. The social stigma

1

of the expression of antisemitism is gone, and social antisemitism is on the rise as well, and the well-integrated Jewish community is feeling a much greater degree of discomfort.

The impact of the increase of antisemitism on the Jews has been significant. Some have left, gone to Israel or the United States. Students have been moved from public to Jewish schools because they have feared for their safety, and there has been a process of estrangement, interior emigration, or discreet marginalization.

Unlike the Holocaust period where antisemitism was sponsored and fueled by government, what Weill calls not a new antisemitism, but a new tolerance for antisemitism, is not governmentally inspired but rooted in certain areas of society, and the government seems inept or uneasy in its efforts to deal with this new hatred. Society, polite, tolerant French society, seems unwilling to fight it with much conviction.

As Weill argues, Holocaust fatigue has set in in France, a desire to rid oneself of the moral burdens and the guilt for the Holocaust. While in Germany consciousness of the Holocaust has been used to defend the institutions of democracy and to fortify tolerance, in France there is a sense that the memory of the Holocaust obscures the efforts to fight other evils such as colonialism, and there has been an effort to equate in images and rhetoric Israel with the Nazis.

Richard L. Rubenstein offers a powerful and provocative essay on "Antisemitism and the Contemporary Jewish Condition." His own work has been influenced by Freud and Weber, and his essay picks up on some of the issues he raised in his masterful brief work of some thirty-five years ago, *The Cunning of History*. Rubenstein insists we must examine the demographic changes in Europe. For centuries Europe was an exporter of superfluous population, but due to the aging and graying of its population it now has to import a working population, of non-Christians, who are invited in to European countries but not made a part of the countries that they inhabit but do not make their home.

European civilization—even in its most secularized form—is Christian, Rubenstein argues, and a potential clash is brewing with its Islamic minority. "For over fourteen hundred years Islam has been Christianity's most important competitor and dangerous adversary. By its very nature, the triumph of Islam in any western country would have revolutionary consequences for that country's non-Islamic population, and most especially for its Jewish minority."

To understand contemporary antagonism to the Jews, Rubenstein suggests we turn to the Freudian concept of "the return of the repressed." Dislike of the Jews had been repressed in the post-Holocaust world. Some elements within post-Holocaust Europe have made genuine efforts not only to repress this hatred but to transform it and eliminate it, but the return of the repressed has come with a vengeance.

Rubenstein explores the shifting of Europe into the Arab-Islamic sphere of influence and its important implication for the Atlantic alliance, dominated by the United States. He follows Bat Ye'or's contention of the Eurabia alliance, which has a double target, the United States and the state of Israel, a theme that will become central to Weill's second essay on antisemitism in France. Rubenstein argues that Jews have a degree of influence in the United States that is unparalleled in any other country other than Israel, a reality that is fully understood in Europe.

He argues: "Simply stated, deep religious antagonisms have resurfaced in contemporary Europe in secular guise—the 'return of the repressed.' "

In this respect it is important to see that from the Six-Day War of 1967 onward, "an antisemitic response was formulated that was capable of salving some Christian consciences and beginning the process of eliminating the stench of the Holocaust. The Palestinian is the new Jew, and the Jew the new Nazi." In some cartoons the Palestinians are depicted as the new Christ and the Israelis as their crucifiers. Themes that were religiously deemphasized by the *Nostra Aetate* have found new expression in the popular imagination of French cartoonists and intellectuals. Cartoons in particular are effective precisely because they don't need commentary; they must be widely understood.

In a reportorial manner, I sketched the dimensions of antisemitism within France in the years since 2000, seeing it as a critical part of an important demographic shift. France is now the home of at least six million Muslims who live in France but are not of France, not assimilated into French culture and French values and who thus are responding directly to events in the Middle East by attacking local Jews. French policy toward these immigrants, its inability and/or unwillingness to assimilate them and acculturate them to French values, allows the problem to linger. French law did not distinguish between hate crimes and petty vandalism and hence it was slow to comprehend the scope of antisemitic violence. French politicians were intimidated or reluctant to confront antisemitism for fear of alienating a larger segment of the society, and French political attacks on Israel—warranted or excessive as they may be—were regarded as license to attack the vulnerable Jews who lived in proximity to the Muslim populations. Where the French government did not act, other segments of French society were also slow to respond, and thus the problem was allowed to fester. Only when it spilled over into the streets of Paris, Marseilles, Lyon, and other French cities did it draw the attention of the political and cultural establishments, which have not as of this writing coherently responded to an all-pervasive problem.

In a second essay, Weill considers the situation of French Jewry and the meeting place between anti-Zionism and anti-Americanism. As Rubenstein has argued before, part of the untold dimension of anti-Americanism is the French perception of Jewish influence in the United States.

An amalgam of Jews and American imperialism is prevalent in progressive groups and widespread within left-wing circles. He traces the etiology of this Judeophobia and Americaphobia in French intellectual life and sketches the cultural code that has become central to the identity of some French intellectuals.

Weill argues that the post-Shoah taboo in expressing antisemitism has ironically contributed to strengthening it. Like Rubenstein, he sees the metamorphosis of the Jew as victim into the tormentor, a move that has been most effective in ridding French society of the burdens of the Holocaust. Still, Israel does not operate alone. American Jews have become the embodiment of globalism and American imperialism. The Jew who had been in the post-Shoah world the "absolute victim" is now displaced by the Arab. This image is persuasive and pervasive among those opposed to globablism and not just among the Muslim inhabitants of France.

Weill argues that French intellectuals interpret the Israel-Palestine conflict on the mode of the eschatological struggle between the forces of good and the forces of evil. He concludes with somber words:

> Such is the invisible wall that renders the atmosphere intolerable for the Jews of France and makes them outcasts by depicting them again in the form of racist and potentially totalitarian white conservatism, dark face of the modernity. ...The Jews of France lead a harsher life because of such letdowns, which at bottom could really carry a regression, if not a betrayal of the promises of emancipation.

It is an irony of contemporary times that as antisemitism intensifies in Western Europe, it seems under control in Eastern Europe, where for so long antisemitic vitriol ran deep within the population. Efraim Zuroff, perhaps the last of the Nazi hunters, suggests that we must look beneath the surface to the rallying points of Eastern European antisemitism, which can be seen in their response to the Holocaust, a response that was held in check for almost half a century by communism. He explores the first four of six dimensions of the response to the Holocaust:

- Acknowledgment of the Crime

- Commemoration of the Shoah

- Prosecution of its perpetrators

- Documentation of the crime

- Introduction of Holocaust education

- Restitution

He then examines popular and governmental responses to each of these efforts over the past fifteen years. Antisemites opposed each response and have employed several strategies to neutralize them, including the equation of Nazi and communist crimes, speaking of their own history as a double genocide, the exaggeration of the number of righteous rescuers, the minimization of and amnesia toward local, native perpetrators, and finally blaming Jews for the Holocaust, blaming politicians for apologizing to the Jews and intellectuals for exploring these issues.

1

Antisemitism in France and "Holocaust Fatigue"
Nicolas Weill

Since the autumn of 2000, the wave of antisemitism in Europe and France seems to have gone on longer than at any period in the last decades. The trigger of this epidemic is usually associated with the beginning of Intifada II in the fall of 2000, associating the antisemitism with the events of the Israeli/Palestinian conflict. However, the outburst of recorded anti-Jewish violence can be traced to 1999, significantly before the intensification of the conflict. Whereas violent antisemitic incidents were cataloged in 1995 as constituting 5 percent of the global racist and xenophobic violence, they reached 23 percent in 1999.[1]

What does this mean? First, the increase recorded in the official statistics are significant, bearing witness to a qualitative change. Earlier, the proportion of recorded antisemitic incidents was minor compared with racist and xenophobic acts. Today it prevails in considerable proportions over the latter categories, reaching on occasion a rate of 80 percent (2000) for a Jewish population representing only one-tenth of the population affected by racism or xenophobia.

Some figures need no further comment:

- In 2001 antisemitic violent incidents declined, but still amounted to 45% of racist violence in France;

- In 2002: 62%;

- In 2003: it amounted to over 72% of recorded acts of racist violence in France.

According to the French Home Office, the antisemitic, racist, or xenophobic acts recorded in France have been more numerous between January 1 and June 30, 2004, than during the entire year 2003,[2] when the proportion was almost as high as during the 2000 peak. A total of 135 antisemitic acts were recorded over this period, against 127 in 2003. The police also recorded 375 threats against Jews (466 in 2003) and 161 racist and xenophobic threats (140 in 2003).

The authorities and the press used to issue reassuring statements every time the graph of incidents receded, hoping to see the light at the end of the tunnel. Some Jewish leaders in France, such as Theo Klein, former chairman of the Conseil représentatif des institutions juives de France (CRIF), find comfort in attributing the reduced outbursts of violence to some marginal groups and outcasts who have no other means of expression. It should be remembered that amid the ocean of delinquencies flooding modern societies, the proportion of racist violence remains minor. But one also ought to remember that the graph of antisemitism does not follow a continuous line but a broken one. And in the past few years—this tendency is confirmed by all the records, however diverging the figures—the peaks have always grown higher.

This new tendency may be further characterized by another difference: Whereas antisemitism used to be systematically ascribed to right-wing extremists and neo-Nazis, nowadays anti-Jewish hatred is acted out by new protagonists, primarily by immigrants or descendants of immigrants of African or North African origins, and tolerated by some antiglobalization protesters, Another characteristic, constituting the most "massive" factor and a more troublesome phenomenon, is not only the relative passivity of the elite, but also society's general familiarization and acceptance of the phenomenon. We shall simply note that the first organized demonstration in France against this antisemitism, on May 16, 2004, attracted only 9,000 to 30,000 people. By comparison, the demonstrations that followed such spectacular assaults or desecrations as the bombing of the Rue Copernic synagogue in Paris in 1980 or the profanation of the Jewish cemetery of Carpentras in the south of France in 1990 attracted tens of thousands of people in the streets, and even the then-president, François Mitterrand.[3]

Worse than the recurrent incidents, it is this relative lack of reaction that renders the current situation hardly bearable for the Jews of France. Some of them, a minority, feel an urge to leave the country; the number of candidates for aliyah has undeniably grown. The number of Jews leaving for other destinations is not known, but is often not taken into account. The fact that the term "time of departure" is now heard underscores the increasing disarray experienced by the Jews of France.[4]

This insidious disarray is expressed through an increasing feeling of "estrangement," "interior emigration," or "discreet marginalization," which is in no way counterbalanced (as it is sometimes claimed, especially abroad) by the success of a few individuals or by the number of politicians of Jewish origin who achieve power[5] and prominence. The specific, more recent marginalization of Jews may be further illustrated by the difficulties encountered by history teachers lecturing on the subject of the Shoah in districts with a majority population of immigrants (but not only there). The situation is particularly painful in schools for Jewish students, constituting a major threat to future generations.

This phenomenon does not apply to the suburban fringes only, as we will see later on. In the French school system, expression of antisemitic feelings became part of the everyday routine, even infiltrating the pupils' slang (the Jewish schools are overwhelmed with applications). This appears to be a particularly troubling development. In a word, without any excessive alarmism, it could be said that at the beginning of the twenty-first century one can note the reemergence of a social antisemitism expressed through innumerable daily humiliations, and not only by violence. There may be answers to such antisemitism, but civil mobilization remains weak.

We have *not* reverted back to the Europe of the 1930s, as is sometimes said. Several factors account for the singularity of the present time. First, antisemitism today emanates not from the government, but from certain areas of society. Second, and by way of consequence, any attempt to undermine the vested rights of emancipation now seems quite impossible—there are neither Nuremberg laws nor questions of Jewish status in view. Third, the Jewish communities, and certain national or European authorities, now have a better grasp of the phenomenon. Last but not least, although certain forms of antisemitism, among extremist groups in particular, tend to sing a genocidal tune (expressed, for example, in the famous Durban slogan "One Jew, one bullet"), and although the recurrent condemnation of Israel leads to more frequent condemnations of Jews who are held collectively responsible for the most controversial aspects of Israel's policy, yet we fortunately do not witness a "cumulative radicalization" to the Shoah, which led to the destruction of the majority of the Jews in Europe.

Should we therefore speak of a "new" antisemitism, as many French specialists do? I think not.

A New Tolerance to Antisemitism ?

In a recent discussion of the issues,[6] I tried to sketch a general theory of antisemitism by proposing a method explaining how, through the notion of "cultural transfer," and without considering antisemitism as an "eternal" phenomenon, we could understand its transmissibility from one context to another, sprouting from an original violence whose background dates back to the oldest antiquity.[7]

My demonstration is aimed at refuting a thesis commonly held in France to account for the present surge of antisemitism. According to this thesis, the traditional sources of anti-Jewish hatred, which were racial, Christian, and xenophobic, have petered out and been replaced by a "new antisemitism," fostered by the alliance of radical militant Islam, antiglobalization protesters, and left-wing extremists. According to this view, it is virtually inevitable that globalization would create globalized antisemitism. In his lengthy study dedicated to the *Preachers of Hatred*, Pierre-André Taguieff, the French defender of this theory, deems it necessary to coin a new concept to account for this phenomenon, the concept of "new judeophobia."[8]

While looking at the graphs of the present situation, I often noticed that the analysis was almost exclusively based on the most extreme forms of antisemitism, those that make their way into the official statistics recording incidents and threats sufficiently serious to be denounced (to the police or to the institutions of the French Jewish community). Although we may appreciate the fact that the authorities use this graph, which is much more reliable than the public opinion polls, which only estimate the *expression* of anti-Jewish opinions, this approach has a major flaw: It does not account for the depth of a *climate*. We know how dangerous a situation can be in which the antisemitism of some groups is on the one hand radicalized and diffused and on the other hand, public opinion is apathetic toward the anti-Jewish activism of minorities. In his innovative study of public opinion in Bavaria in the late 1930s, Ian Kershaw concluded that the twisted road to Auschwitz was paved with indifference.[9] My motive for considering that the reality and the efficiency of antisemitism ought to be ascribed to this mass of indifference (whether it has or has not criminal consequences) is that I remain convinced this critical mass of antisemitism, which grants it its very possibility and makes it a national phenomenon, lays right there, in the depths of the general public opinion. This interpretation spares us the outdated paradigm, which inefficiently opposes right-wing and left-wing antisemitism, focused on the activists and extremists. Applied to the antisemitism of Holocaust denial, which used to be so loudly expressed in France and is now echoed throughout the Arab world, we may easily admit the uselessness of this dichotomy. As we know, Holocaust denial, even though it has been nurtured in the postwar French far right, has been launched by a former socialist, Paul Rassinier, and defended by groups favorable to the left-wing extremists, who were bold enough to appeal to Noam Chomsky and include one of his essays in a book by Robert Faurisson.[10] We must confess that antisemitism tends to blur the division between right and left, however important it is for the French political mentality.

The signs through which antisemitic violence is expressed in its most extreme forms does not present any genuine novelty: Synagogues are still set on fire, Jews are still blamed for their supposed excessive money or power, and the cartoon and newspaper caricatures revive the oldest clichés of antisemitism: vampirism, ritual murder, and so on.[11] What is worrysome is thus not only the fact the synagogue is on fire, but also that society tolerates such incidents and confronts them with more indifference.

The difficulty in grasping this shadowy zone of indifference, which nonetheless gives its full weight to this phenomenon, is due to the fact that antisemitism belongs to a category that can be defined as "non-public opinions."[12] Here are recorded not the assaults or the beatings, but the signs of connivance with the intolerable. As a matter of fact, it was right on the West Coast of California that the famous sociological investigation on the "authoritarian personality" was launched just after World War II by the Institute for Social Studies led by Max Horkheimer. This major study in antisemitism proposed to denounce the prejudice and "fascist" potential where they were least expected: at the core of a democratic American society, which had just vanquished Nazism.[13] This concern may also be illustrated by Elia Kazan's first film, in the late 1940s, *Gentlemen's Agreement*, which exposed a latent antisemitism.

I mentioned earlier the popular theory that systematically associates the cause of the present crisis to the events in the Middle East and to the Israeli-Palestinian conflict. In my book *Une Histoire personnelle de l'Antisémitisme* [Paris, Robert Laffont, 2002], I tried to show that those events represented in fact only one trigger among others liable to provoke, on occasion, a tremendous spike in the curve (as was the case in the autumn of 2000, at the beginning of Intifada II). It is true the participants in the most spectacular incidents (the only ones to be taken into account by the official statistics), are not the traditional perpetrators of antisemitism, but yet this does not justify the theory of the novelty of the phenomenon.[14]

Thus the violent conflict opposing Jews and Arabs in Belleville (a popular district in northern Paris) after the 1967 war remained confined.[15] And since 1945, many of the waves of antisemitic incidents have borne no connection to the Israel/Arab or Israeli/Palestinian war, whatever you may call it. However slow was the authorities' and the media's reaction, the weak mobilization succeeded by protest demonstrations: Here are the real new elements. In today's France we are not faced with an antisemitism modeled on a politico-administrative machinery serving an enterprise of destruction or genocide as in the 1930/40s, not even with the official anti-Zionism of the communist bloc after 1945. The French government finally decided to take the matter seriously. But today this government and its institutions (justice, national education) seem to deal uneasily with the hatred emanating from society.

On Some Reverse Dreyfus Cases: Strategies of Minimization

If the analysis of the present surge of antisemitism requires that we focus on society's reactions or on its absence of reaction, we have to shift our perpespective. The weltanschauung of the perpetrators of antisemitic acts may sometimes be prompted by what some call "Islamo-progressism." We thus have a scenario consistent with the major features of the predominant discourse: Antisemitism is a function of the events in the Middle East and generally stems from causes external to French society. Society is thus spared an embarrassing self-examination by exteriorizing the cause of evil. But if we look toward the social network in the largest possible sense, the motives for antisemitism become much more difficult to pinpoint, because we are there confronted with a landscape characterized not only by violence or activism but by lethargy. The causes of such apathy are evidently far more diverse than those that account for the outrage of arsonists and extremists. We must account for the passivity, but the evidence to estimate its importance is far more difficult to gather. Anyway, it implies that we take into account the old forms of antisemitism that had been prematurely discarded by the upholders of the "Islamo-progressist" theory. I would like to illustrate this change in French public opinion by quoting a few examples of how and why public opinion now tolerates, or at least does not fight with much conviction, what it used to fight before.

The divisions among the antiracist party, that is, among the groups that would be expected to take the leading role in the fight against the anti-Jewish prejudice, is a determinant factor. Many associations, whose influence is not to be exaggerated and which used to demonstrate together against discrimination, are now divided on that subject, loosening little by little this front that used to protect Jews in France. It is symptomatic that the Human Rights League (la Ligue des droits de l'homme, LDH) founded in 1898, precisely during the turmoil caused by l' *Affaire Dreyfus,* is now one of the most reluctant groups in cases of antisemitism while the Mouvement contre le racisme l'antisémitisme et pour la paix (MRAP), seems to strive now to minimize antisemitic aggressions in order to avoid "Islamophobia," which they put at the top of their political agendas ever at the expense of the fight against antisemitism. It is Islamophobia they tend to put on the same footing with antisemitism. On the contrary, groups like the SOS Racisme or the Ligue contre le racisme et l'antisémitisme (LICRA) still consider antisemitism as a particular phenomenon that should be distinguished from racism and xenophobia. Undoubtedly the Palestinophilia of part of the left-wing extremists—from where many of the present leaders of some antiracist associations stem from—and of the antiglobalization protesters contributes to such minimizations, while anti-Zionism tends to settle as a "cultural code" in such political environments.

A recent example illustrates the scale of the disastrous effects of the division of the antiracist side. At the beginning of the school year in September 2003, a young student attending the Lycée Montaigne, a high school in the center of Paris, complained of being insulted and assaulted on a regular basis by two students of Arab origins. The headmaster let a month go by before filing a complaint and expelling the two aggressors from the school. But the Human Rights League, backed by several teachers, launched a counterinvestigation, which put the aggressors and the victim on the same footing and minimized the anti-Jewish dimension of the incident. In a similar way, at the beginning of the surge of antisemitism, authorities had ascribed to plain delinquency acts of demonstrably anti-Jewish character. The result was pitiful: The two aggressors at the Lycée Montaigne were reintegrated into the school and it was the victim who was compelled to change schools. This sorry ending shows how the lack of unanimity of the antiracist associations, often attributable to diverging political agendas, especially on the matter of Israel, casts discredit on the fight against antisemitism, which is more and more left to Jewish organizations.

Another sign indicating the lack of a reaction to antisemitism as well as the weakening of some traditional poles of resistance to the phenomenon is the increasing numbers of what we could call "reverse Dreyfus cases," widely advertised in the media, where French society acts out the following comedy: We thought there was antisemitism, but *ouf!* it was all an illusion and the bad guy turns out to be innocent. It looks as if French society when facing antisemitism needed more to be comforted than to struggle against it.

Such was the scenario of a much advertised case during the summer of 2004: that of a fake antisemitic incident in which a young girl, Marie Leblanc, claimed to have been the victim in the RER (a train that links Paris to the suburbs). Marie Leblanc pretended that swastikas were painted over her body by a bunch of African and North African individuals. In the course of the investigation, the young woman confessed that she had made it all up. What lesson can we learn from this affair, which fascinated the French news media at a time when the number of genuine antisemitic acts was actually increasing?[16] On the one hand, the emotion the first version of the affair raised shows that public opinion seems to identify more easily with non-Jewish victims taken for Jews than with the usual victims of such violence. On the other hand, it shows that public opinion enjoys a perverse collective catharsis when it is given the opportunity to discard as imaginary or exaggerated one of those many serious incidents.

However, the fact that a disturbed not to say psychotic woman in her late teens, coming from a Roman Catholic background, should blame antisemitism to express her personal disarray was in itself worth considering. Wasn't it the sign of the transformation of antisemitism into a "cultural code?" The most striking detail in her fantasy was her insistence on the apathy of the other passengers on the train. This is proof that antisemitism is now commonplace and has spread throughout French society, in particular in schools, and that every-one may easily imagine that the most brutal aggressions should not provoke any reaction. All the better, since that young woman candidly admitted she had hoped to be granted a loan by her bank after this assault (the association of Jews with money assures its place in the psy-chological elaborations of this young mythomaniac). Such events thus act as revealers of our age, which prefers, once more, to be reassured about the reality of antisemitism rather than a willingness to fight it.[17]

Holocaust Fatigue

I would like to conclude by mentioning a point that to me seems to shed some light on the present situation and to explain this social apathy, which could appropriately be styled "Holocaust fatigue." A short detour through the history of studies on antisemitism may be useful to clarify the matter. In 1959, Theodore Adorno asserted in a famous conference on "What does working on the past mean?"[18] The central intuition of this major text, which was to set the basis for the whole movement of confrontation of the young German generations with the Nazi past, is that in the late 1950s, Adorno found the Germans were not yet genuinely attached to democracy. According to his views, they still considered this regime to be interchangeable with other ones and it only satisfied them insofar as it was linked to a certain economic prosperity. They didn't cherish it for itself but for their own base interest. At the same time, Adorno judged that the factors that had fostered the rise of what was then called fascism were still at work: namely, the weakening of the individual crushed by a society that compelled him to act as an object rather than as an autonomous subject. Collective narcissism (nationalism) progressively and dangerously replaced individual autonomy.

According to Adorno, this was the means to restore the very pos-sibility of the experience of reality. Adorno established a close link between the work on the past and the restoration of democracy. It is from such considerations that after 1968, Germany focused its re-acclimatization to democracy on the *Vergangenheitsbewältigung*, or the confrontation with the Nazi past, thus aiming at considering the past not in the conservative sense of exalting traditions, but in the hope of establishing a critical relation with it. Jürgen Habermas, Adorno's suc-cessor in the Frankfurt School, repeated it in his *laudatio* in honor of Daniel Goldhagen, who was granted the Democracy Prize in 1997: The way we conceive culpability and innocence in a retrospective relation also reflects the norms according to which we intend to live together as citizens. Without idealizing Germany, which also has its own tradition of Holocaust fatigue (the so-called *Schlussstrichmentalität*), we cannot but observe that Germany was able to prevent the extremist parties, especially the right-wing extremists, from reaching important electoral success (as happened in France). It isn't directly the memory of the Shoah that acts as a guarantee against the surge of antisemitism. In fact, the "Judeonazi" equation or the comparisons between the Jenin Palestinians and the Warsaw ghetto may even be perceived as an instrumentalization of the memory of the genocide. But insofar as the memory of the genocide serves the improvement of democratic education—democracy thus becoming a true conviction and not the result of a base calculation of interest—it can represent the best safeguard against anti-Jewish hatred.

Even for the third generation, the Shoah remains a sensitive topic in Germany while it serves as a safeguard for democracy.

What about France?

I mentioned earlier the difficulties encountered by teachers evoking the Shoah in classes mainly composed of pupils from the immigration (though not only in such classes). This phenomenon is typically French. Why? It may be explained by a certain competition between victims. It is sometimes suspected in France that the Jews have had their share of the Shoah memory and it is high time for them to yield their place to the memory of colonization. And I must here, with no offense to the laws of hospitality, utter a warning against the Americanization of French society, since a theory is spread according to which the real genocide is the slave trade orchestrated by Jewish traders. Hence, the idea that the excessive memory of the genocide prevents, for the greatest interest of Israeli politics, the sufferings of slavery and colonialism from being given due consideration is quite prevalent.

I do not intend to come to a decision on that kind of ideological and historical debate. Nevertheless, its effects are obvious. When they fail to deprive Jews of their supposed claims to the status of victims, they indubitably contribute to weakening the feeling of solidarity toward them in the event of an antisemitic aggression. Holocaust fatigue is essentially a discourse, with pernicious effects.

Without going any further into that subject, this discourse may have been reinforced by the lengthy trial of Maurice Papon, one of the last great trials for crimes against humanity and one of the longest trials in French legal history. Its awesome and spectacular dimension may have led some to think it would suffice to turn the page of the Shoah memory. It rapidly turned out to be a kind of psychodrama staged to free French society of its guilt complex and to rid it of the past. Some Jewish leaders, such as Serge Klarsfeld, didn't hesitate to say at the end of this long judicial choreography that we were done with antisemitism. The present crisis seems to belie those observations.

What Can Be Done?

If the situation is worrisome, it is not so much because of its most spectacular aspects than because of the slow erosion of the barriers, which up to now had impeded the development of antisemitism. First, the dispersion of the Dreyfusist coalition, which had for a century united the French left wing as the major supporter of the fight against antisemitism. Of course, the Left has not reverted to the antisemitism of Fourier or Proudhon, but its generosity has been blurred by its Palestinophilia, the temptation to turn the Palestinian into a symbol for the lost proletariat. This is clearly indicated, on the mode of the camera osscura, by the recurrence of reverse Dreyfus cases. The traditional sources of anti-Jewish hatred like the Christian one have generally petered out (although they may awaken on occasion in the course of such enterprise as Mel Gibson's *Passion of the Christ*). But it is to be feared that this evolution will not suffice to compensate the losses. On the other hand, the good side that can be secured from the Judeo-Christian dialogue lies in its spontaneous character, prompted by a few groups of Catholics at odds with the "teaching of contempt" formerly practiced by the church and imposed on its hierarchy. Confronting a surge of hostility that is not supported by the government, the traditional attitude of the Jewish communities, depicted by the historian Yosef Yerushalmi as "servants of kings and not servants of servants," is nonetheless seemingly out of date.[19] It used to define the Jews' tendency to hide behind the emperor's or the government's power in order to seek protection against the sufferings society imposed on them, insofar as the government itself was not animated by criminal intentions. At the beginning of the crisis, we saw that the Jewish institutions—the CRIF in particular—tried to appear more republican than the republicans and to fit in the traditional mold. However, contacts were made with various elements of society deemed hostile, such as the Islamist organization UOIF or with spokesmen of the union of magistrates (Syndicat de la magistrature) whose rather lax attitude toward antisemitism had been denounced. This kind of dialogue can be condemned as another compromise between institutions that are unsure, or even suspicious, as to what they stand for. It may be said that they represent a risk of political instrumentalization, which its protagonists may have cause to regret. We may prefer—and this is my case—informal meetings, closer to the field. But it would be wrong not to admit that such approaches nonetheless take a step in the right direction: that of the reconciliation of the Jews with the society they live in.

Notes

1. See on this issue the reports of Commission consultative des droits de l'homme (CNCDH), an agency dependent on the prime minister since 1990 : *Rapports d'activités*, Paris, La Documentation française.

2. The Department of Justice (AFP, October 6, 2004) had counted 322 antisemitic actions since the beginning of the year. In only 22 percent of the events has a guilty person been identified.

3. See on this specific issue see Nicolas Weill, *Une Histoire personnelle de l'Antisémitisme*, Paris, Robert Laffont, 2002, and *La République et les antisémites*, Paris, Grasset, 2004.

4. See for example the book by Raphaël Drai, *Sous le signe de Sion, l'antisémitisme nouveau est arrivé*, Paris, Michalon, 2001, « Comme si les Juifs n'étaient déjà plus là. Le signal de la sortie ? », p. 227 sq ; see also, by Cécila Gabizon an Johan Weisz, *OPA sur les Juifs de France, enquête sur un exode programmé 2000–2005*, Paris, Grasset, 2006.

5. For example, in *Tikkun*, November/December 2003. For an analysis of the American perception of nowadays French antisemitism, see Weill *La République et les antisémites*, p. 89 sq.

6. Weill, *La République et les antisémites*.

7. For such a conception my debt is great to the works of the German Egyptologist Jan Assmann. See especially his *Moses the Egyptian: The Memory of Egypt in Western Monotheism*, Cambridge, Harvard

University Press, 1997, and *Die Mosaische Unterscheidung oder Der Preis des Monotheismus*, München, Carl Hanser Verlag, 2002.

8. See his *Prêcheurs de haine, traversée de la judéophobie planétaire*, Paris, « Mille et une Nuits », Fayard, 2004.

9. *Popular Opinion and Political Dissent in the Third Reich: Bavaria, 1933–1945*, Oxford, Oxford University Press, 1983.

10. Robert Faurisson, *Mémoire en défense contre ceux qui m'accusent de falsifier l'histoire. La question des chambres à gaz*, Paris, La Vieille Taupe, 1980 « précédé d'un avis de Noam Chomsky ».

11. See Joël et Dan Kottek, *Au nom de l'antisionisme, l'image des Juifs et d'Israël dans la caricature depuis la seconde Intifada*, Bruxelles, Complexe, 2003.

12. This expression, which stems from Franz Böhm, is taken back by Adorno in his famous conference of 1959 "Was heißt die Vergangenheit aufbearbeiten," in *Bericht über die Erzieherkonferenz*, Wiesbaden, 1959.

13. Theodor Adorno, Else Frenkel-Brunswik, Daniel J. Levinson, and Sanford R. Nevitt, *The Authoritarian Personality*, New York, Evanston and London, Harper & Row, 1950.

14. It may be noticed that the European authorities themselves, in spite of their political cautiousness and their constant effort to spare the minorities, finally had to admit reluctantly that many of those perpetrators had an "arabo-muslim background." See "Manifestation of Antisemitism in the EU, 2002–2003," published by the European Monitoring Centre on Racism and Xenophobia (EUMC).

15. *Le Monde*, June 4, 5, 17, 18, 20, and 25, 1968.

16. On meeting the Israeli prime minister Silvan Shalom on August 24, 2004, the French minister Dominique de Villepin stated that 135 antisemitic acts had been recorded over the first seven months of 2004, compared to 127 in 2003.

17. That the cases of "pseudologia" (mental disease of people claiming to have been victimized) are full of lessons, especially concerning antisemitic studies, is shown by the fascinating case of Binjamin Wilkomirski, a Swiss clarinet player who claimed to have been a Holocaust survivor in the late 1990s, whose claim was usurped, whether or not he was sincere in such a claim. See Stefan Mächler, *The Wilkomirski Affair: A Study in Biographical Truth*, New York, 2001 and, directed by Irene Diekmann and Julius Schoeps, *Das Wilkomirski-Syndrom: Eingebildete Erinnerungen oder von der Sensucht, Opfer zu sein*, Zürich, Pendo, 2002.

18. Adorno, "Was bedeutet: Aufarbeitung der Vergangenheit" in Ders., Ges. Schriften, vol. 10.2, Frankfurt, 1977.

19. Title of a conference delivered by Yosef Hayim Yerushalmi for the Carl Friedrich Siemens Foundation, October 19, 1993. The text has been published in a German version in *Themen,* under title "Diener von Königen und nicht Diener von Dienern: Einige Aspekte der politischen Geschichte der Juden," München, 1995, and in French: « Serviteur des rois et non serviteurs des serviteurs. Sur quelques aspects de l'histoire politique des Juifs », *Raisons politiques,* n°7, août-octobre 2002, p 19–52. No English version was available in 2002.

2

Antisemitism and the Contemporary Jewish Condition
Richard L. Rubenstein

In reviewing the literature on the "new antisemitism," one is struck by the surprise many writers express at the resurgence of antisemitism and genocide. In reality, there should be little reason for surprise. Latent attitudes and emotions can often surface after relatively long periods of dormancy. Moreover, persistently hostile emotional patterns such as antisemitism are more likely to emerge when violence and hatred are deemed permissible and even problem-solving than when such behavior is regarded as yielding no benefit. One does not have to be a doctrinaire Freudian to see the "return of the repressed" at work in the so-called "new antisemitism."

What was it that may have been more or less repressed for decades? I would like to suggest that it was *the darker side* of Christian ambivalence toward Jews and Judaism that resulted from knowledge of and horror concerning the Holocaust. That is, of course, not the whole story of Christian ambivalence. Another aspect of that ambivalence is the strong support given to Israel by the American Christian right.

Moreover, the "return of the repressed" cannot be divorced from the unparalleled transformations that have occurred in the relations between Europe, especially Western Europe, and the world of Islam since the end of World War II. These changes have, of necessity, had a profound impact on Jews, Judaism, and Israel. Of these changes, the most important have been demographic. Throughout much of its history, Europe has been a net exporter of people as the United States has been an importer. In Western Europe the situation began to change in the 1950s with the importation into Germany of Turks and Kurds as *Gastarbeiter*, guest workers, during the *Wirtschaftswunder*, the

"economic wonder" period of postwar German economic development. As we know, Muslim emigration into Western Europe has accelerated since then.

Until January 1, 2000, the *Gastarbeiter* and their families were
denied the one right that is the foundation of all other rights, citizenship. German citizenship was based on blood kinship (*ius sanguinis*)
rather than place of birth (*ius soli*), as in the United States, Britain, and
France. Under Social Democratic chancellor Gerhard Schröder, new
laws have been enacted enabling non-Germans, whether born in Germany or elsewhere, to acquire citizenship through naturalization.[1] This
constituted a significant improvement in status for many of Germany's
7 million non-German residents. The new laws did, however, create
other serious long-term problems that Germany shares with the rest
of Europe.

I became mindful of some of those problems in January 1993 when I
visited Germany to study the situation of minorities in the newly reuni-
fied nation. At the time, there was much neo-Nazi violence directed
against minorities, especially Turks. During my stay, I interviewed a
number of well-informed, responsible Germans in and out of government, including Gustav Schmidt, a Roman Catholic priest, university
professor, and longtime friend.[2] Professor Schmidt expressed the view
that over time Germany could absorb *Christian* immigrants from Eastern Europe as it had the descendants of Polish miners who had emi-
grated to the Ruhr in the nineteenth century. On the other hand, he
believed Muslim immigrants neither wanted to assimilate nor could
they be integrated. Eventually, he said, they would have to leave. He
could not conceive of Germany as a genuinely pluralist country even
though Islamic extremism had yet to become a major worldwide problem. In all likelihood, absent a violent right-wing reaction, Germany's
Muslims will not be compelled to leave. They are already too numerous, and the German economy is too dependent upon them. Nevertheless, Schmidt's views are instructive. They are based on the conviction
that there is a fundamental incompatibility between the civilization in
which he had been nurtured and to which he ministers as a priest, and
that of the Muslim immigrants. He is neither a racist nor a right-wing
nationalist. He is, however, a Christian who cannot envisage his civilization, even in its secularized form, as other than Christian.[3]

Europe's Christian identity was a function of what it was not: Europe was neither Jewish nor Muslim. There was, however, a difference.

Christianity has no Muslim roots. Save for Gnosticism and the so-called National Socialist German Christian movement, the Christian churches had traditionally acknowledged their Jewish roots. Moreover, Judaism had neither the power nor the aspiration to displace Christianity as does Islam. In the past, whenever and wherever it could, Islam challenged Christianity militarily, politically, and religiously, and there is little if any evidence that its aspirations, especially among Islamic radicals, have changed fundamentally. Wherever possible, Muslims were instructed that they were obliged to spread the dominion of Islam throughout God's creation, granting to Jews and Christians who submitted to Islam, the privilege, not the right, to practice their religion provided they abided by the terms of their inferior *dhimmi* status.

For over fourteen hundred years Islam has been Christianity's most important competitor and dangerous adversary. By its very nature, the triumph of Islam in any Western country would have revolutionary consequences for that country's non-Islamic population, and most especially for its Jewish minority. And, it is entirely possible that, given Europe's decreasing Christian and increasing Muslim birth rate, one or more Western European nations will have a Muslim majority during the twenty-first century, France, in all likelihood, being the first.[4] In the early 1990s, Professor John Kelsay observed that "the rapidity of Muslim migration… suggests that we may soon be forced to speak not simply of Islam *and*, but of Islam *in* the West."[5] That day has arrived. In an interview in *Die Welt*, July 28, 2004, Professor Bernard Lewis, an eminent authority on Islam, asserted that Europe will be Islamic by the end of the twenty-first century.[6]

When Europe's political elites made the historically unprecedented decisions to permit large-scale Muslim immigration, did they take cognizance of the religious, social, and cultural consequences of their policies, or were they primarily motivated by the economic and perhaps the political advantages that would ensue from the immigration? According to Bat Ye'or, an internationally recognized scholar on Islam's relations with the non-Islamic world, the fundamental decisions concerning Europe's relations with the Arab world were taken in the aftermath of the Arab oil embargo of 1973 when the European Community (EC), the forerunner of the European Union, created a structure of cooperation and dialogue with the Arab League (EAD).[7] The EC agreed wholeheartedly to support the Arab anti-Israel policy in exchange for extensive commercial agreements. Moreover, the collaboration fostered by the EAD was actually far more extensive than an agreement on policy toward Israel. As Bat Ye'or points out, the shifting of Europe into the Arab-Islamic sphere of influence undermined the Atlantic alliance, dominated by the United States, and created a very real but unstated European Union–Arab partnership, identified by Bat Ye'or as Eurabia, as well as the seeds of a new balance of power.[8] We discuss that issue below.

According to Bat Ye'or, Eurabia "is essentially a political project for a total demographic and cultural symbiosis between Europe and the Arab world..." in which Israel is destined eventually to dissolve and in which America would be "isolated and challenged by an emerging Euro-Arab continent that is linked to the whole Muslim world and invested with tremendous political and economic power in international affairs."[9] It is this vision that motivates Jacques Chirac, whose multilateralist policies are expressions of the deepening symbiosis. Bat Ye'or further argues that the Euro-Arab agreements are also based on a vision of Christian-Muslim reconciliation that has been strongly advocated by some Christian religious groups.[10] Given the nature of this agreement, it should be obvious that for the Europeans, Israel, if not European Jewry, is expendable. In that regard, we do well to recall the fate of the *pieds noirs,* the European Christians and Jews domiciled in Algeria until 1962. Having concluded the situation in Algeria was untenable for France, on March 18, 1962, Charles de Gaulle signed the Evian Agreement with Algeria's Provisional Government in which France acknowledged Algerian independence. For their part, the Algerians offered assurances in the agreement both sides knew they could not keep: The Algerians agreed that Europeans living in Algeria would have the choice of taking up Algerian citizenship, remaining in Algeria as foreigners, or departing. Jews were regarded as Europeans inasmuch as French citizenship had been bestowed upon them in 1870.[11] The overwhelming majority of Europeans, close to 1 million, elected to depart. They could not afford to ignore the threat implicit in the slogan of the Algerian People's Party that Europeans had the choice of "the suitcase or the coffin" (*la valise ou le cercueil*), i.e. pack up or be killed.[12] It is hardly likely that were Israel "dissolved," Israelis would have the choice of the "suitcase." Ironically, the millions of Muslims who followed the Europeans to France encountered no such harsh choice.

To assert that the Europeans regard Israel as expendable is no more than a reading of long-standing European policy toward Israel

and Zionism. Even during World War I, the pro-Zionist policy of
Lloyd George and Lord Balfour never achieved a consensus in British government circles. To a certain extent, the British decision to go
ahead with the Balfour Declaration was motivated by an unrealistic
overestimation of Jewish influence in the United States and Russia.
In the autumn of 1917, Britain's leaders mistakenly believed Jews had
the power to influence Russia's revolutionary government to remain
in the war in spite of the Bolshevik Revolution.[13] Nevertheless, within
little more than a decade an explicitly pro-Arab posture was deemed
consistent with the larger imperial interests of Great Britain.[14] That
attitude culminated in the British White Paper of 1939 that know-
ingly and effectively enabled Adolf Hitler to fulfill one of the principal objectives of British policy for Palestine, namely, obstruction of
the emigration of Europe's Jews to Palestine. Nor did British policy
change when the facts of the Holocaust became public knowledge.
When the niceties of diplomatic language were stripped away, Britain
had no use for Jews in Palestine.

Nor did France evince enthusiasm for Zionism during World War
I and the subsequent negotiations over the dismemberment of the
Ottoman Empire. The French attitude has been described by historian
David Fromkin:

> French officials were not prepared to support Zionism in a postwar
> Palestine—and did not envisage allowing Jews to achieve a separate
> national status—but they saw no harm in offering the Zionists words
> of encouragement so long as they were meaningless.[15]

We need not review the history of French policy in the Middle East
save to take note of a widely reported incident that took place shortly
after 9/11 at a gathering in the London home of newspaper magnate
Lord Conrad Black, then publisher of London's *Daily Telegraph* and the
Jerusalem Post. One of the guests, the late Daniel Barnard, ambassador
of France to the United Kingdom, declared that the current troubles
in the world were all because of "that shitty little country Israel." The
ambassador asked rhetorically, "Why should the world be in danger of
World War III because of those people?" The incident was first reported
by Barbara Amiel, Lady Black, in her *Daily Telegraph* column, without
revealing the ambassador's identity, but word quickly got out.[16] Commenting on the incident, the editors of the *Wall Street Journal* wrote:
"We'd like to think that Mr. Barnard's remarks have made him an

embarrassment in European circles. Perhaps the greater scandal here is that they haven't."[17]

Neither Barnard nor his government was embarrassed. Overwhelmingly, the British press faulted Ms. Amiel for having made the incident public. Moreover, implicit in the ambassador's remarks was the desirability of the elimination of the State of Israel.[18] If, as he stated, the world is in danger of World War III "because of those people," then world peace requires the elimination of that danger. We ought not to regard such a suggestion as far-fetched. In spite of the façade of humanitarian rhetoric, genocide, either directly or indirectly, has been the preferred option of the Great Powers when it was perceived to serve an important national interest. To take but one of many examples, on March 23, 1943, William Temple, archbishop of Canterbury, pleaded in the House of Lords for immediate steps to rescue the Jews. To quiet the public outcry, the Foreign Office proposed to the Department of State that "an informal United Nations Conference" be held to consider what steps could be taken for refugees from Nazi terror, but that *no special preference* be given to Jewish refugees. Confident of a sympathetic response, the Foreign Office candidly informed the State Department of the reasons why it did not want to pressure the Germans to stop the slaughter:

> There is the possibility that the Germans or their satellites may change over from the policy of *extermination* to one of *extrusion,* and aim as they did before the war at embarrassing other countries by flooding them with alien immigrants.[19]

Better to let genocide proceed than to suffer embarrassment. Moreover, the Foreign Office was well aware that the real danger Britain might face was not the flooding of England but of Palestine by the survivors. In recent years, we have seen in Darfur, Rwanda, the Sudanese campaign against Christians and animists, Cambodia, Bosnia, and Saddam Hussein's Iraq not only the persistence of genocide as state policy, but the unwillingness or inability of the UN or the major powers to intercede. Our times have aptly been characterized by one informed observer as "the age of genocide."[20]

Whether the issue is genocide or antisemitism, do we not perhaps delude ourselves when we think that somehow the behavior patterns of nations can be altered by some newly discovered set of moral values, arising, for example, from the horror or the moral indignation aroused by catastrophic events? In the column cited above, Barbara Amiel quotes columnist Petronella Wyatt's observation in *The Spectator* that "since September 11 antisemitism and its open expression have become respectable at London dinner tables."[21] Amiel tells of a private lunch at which the hostess, described as the "doyenne of London's political salon scene," made a remark to the effect that she "couldn't stand Jews and everything happening to them was their own fault." When the remark met with shocked silence, the hostess chided her guests on what she took to be their hypocrisy. "Oh come on," she said, "you all feel like that."[22] The hostess was, of course, on target. She could not have become an acknowledged social leader of her community if she did not know well the unspoken sentiments of her community. Wyatt also reveals she was told by a Liberal member of the House of Lords, "The Jews have been asking for it, and now, thank God, we can say what we think at last."[23]

In saying "what we think at last," many Europeans are returning to a tradition of hostility to Jews and Judaism that was not only the province of Nazi ideologues but for centuries an accepted part of the European mainstream. In his book on antisemitism before the Holocaust, William Brustein comments that Jew-hatred is more multidimensional and intense than other forms of prejudice. As such, it "incorporated religious, racial, economic, and political forms of hatred." Brustein also observes that Jews were feared as well as disliked.[24] Few observers have better characterized the pervasiveness of this antipathy than Helen Fein. In her book *Accounting for Genocide,* Fein observes that many of Hitler's orders, such as the extermination of the Poles, the burning of Paris, and the destruction of Germany, were "averted, subverted, or countermanded" by subordinates. By contrast, the order to exterminate the Jews was never checked. It was taken for granted that riddance was a legitimate German and European objective.[25]

Much has been written concerning the complicity of the churches and the European right in creating a climate of opinion in which genocide became a plausible outcome.[26] Nevertheless, anti-Jewish hostility and contempt were by no means restricted to right-wing extremists. In spite of a strong tendency of secular, non-Zionist Jews to identify with the parties of the left in the latter decades of the nineteenth and the early decades of the twentieth century, left-wing identification of Jews as an alien group that either competed with or exploited the indigenous population was a persistent theme in European politics long before the Holocaust.[27] In France in the 1930s, for example, anti-Jewish hostility was also expressed by many celebrated writers, preeminently respectable philosophers, academic intellectuals, and journalists. Negative Jewish stereotypes were to be found in the works of such literary personalities and filmmakers as Nobel Laureates André Gide, François Mauriac, and Romain Roland as well as Paul Morand, Marcel Arland, and Jacques Feyder.[28] Other writers explicitly portrayed Jews in racial terms and as a threat to French society. These included Georges Bernanos, Pierre Drieu de la Rochelle, Jean Giraudoux, Robert Brasillach, and Louis-Ferdinand Destouches (Céline).[29] After the war, when awareness of the full horror of the Holocaust became widespread, it was not so easy to say of the Jews, as did the London hostess cited by Barbara Amiel, "everything happening to them was their own fault." Nevertheless, the newly repressed anti-Jewish feelings, so deeply embedded in the culture of Christian Europe, were destined to rise to the surface sooner or later, as is evident in the British lord's remark to Petronella Wyatt cited above, "The Jews have been asking for it, and now, thank God, we can *say what we think* at last" (italics added).

Another potent example of this "return of the repressed" is evident in the enormous success of Mel Gibson's film *The Passion of the Christ*.[30] From the time of the pioneering work of Jules Isaac (1877–63) in the late 1940s, there has been an increasing understanding among Christian leaders and scholars of the role of the "teaching of contempt" and the characterization of the Jews as "a deicidal people" in creating a hatred and antipathy so profound it could instill in the peoples of Europe an indifference to, if not an approval of, the extermination of Europe's Jews.[31] After seeing the Oberammergau Passion Play in 1934, Adolf Hitler praised it as a "precious tool" in the fight against Jews and Judaism.[32] In reluctant cooperation with American Jewish organizations, the postwar producers of the Oberammergau play have made efforts toward somewhat mitigating the harshness of the original narrative's anti-Jewish sentiments. By contrast, in spite of the pleas to Gibson by a group of distinguished Jewish and Christian biblical scholars, there was no such mitigation in his film, which is now available for rent or purchase worldwide in inexpensive DVDs. Gibson apparently understood that times had changed and that the darker lineaments of Christian ambivalence could once again be given overt expression.

For decades the stench of Auschwitz had imposed severe constraints on the public expression of overtly antisemitic statements. In his 1993 book on violent extremism in newly unified Germany, German journalist Michael Schmidt quotes Ewald Althans, a leading neo-Nazi at the time, as saying: "Auschwitz must fall before man can accept what we want. The people all say, hey, that Althans, that's a nice guy, but Auschwitz...This is *the* problem."[33] One way to overcome "*the* problem" has been mendaciously to reinterpret the history of the Third Reich. Denying that there ever was a deliberate Nazi plan to exterminate all Jews appealed to those who would, if they could, repeat the Nazi performance. These include neo-Nazis, their fellow travelers, and a critical mass within the Arab and Islamic world.[34]

There is yet another response that carries with it greater potential danger to Israel and the Jewish world, the likening Israel and Zionism to Nazism and Ariel Sharon to Adolf Hitler. This pervasive demonization is given expression in cartoons, posters, and political rhetoric, especially in Europe. Cartoons in the mass media have long been one of the most effective means of demonizing Jews and fostering antisemitism. David A. Harris of the American Jewish Committee has published a sampling of such cartoons in which some of the most vicious images of traditional antisemitism have once again surfaced in mainstream European journals such as *The Guardian* (UK), *Le Monde* (France), and *El Pais* (Spain).

The cartoons were published in 2000 and 2001.[35] In one cartoon, two Israeli policemen are depicted beating up a Palestinian. One officer says to the other, "There's no time for me to reflect on the Holocaust" (*La Razón*, Spain, June 9, 2001). The Holocaust theme also appears in a cartoon depicting three completed buildings and one under construction. The signs in front of the completed buildings read "Museum of the Jewish Holocaust," "Museum of the Bosnian Holocaust," "Museum of the Chechen Holocaust." The sign on the building under construction reads, "Future Museum of the Palestinian Holocaust" (*La Vanguardia*, Spain, May 25, 2001). In one image worthy of Julius Streicher's *Der Stürmer*, Sharon is depicted as a fat, ugly, hook-nosed Jew wearing a *kippah* (skullcap) and saying, "From bad can come good. At least, Hitler taught me to invade a country and exterminate every living vermin." Sharon is depicted as wearing a swastika within a star of David on his chest (*Cambio 16*, Spain, June 4, 2001). *El Pais*, arguably Spain's most influential newspaper, published a cartoon depicting a small figure flying toward Sharon. The caption reads, "Clio, the muse of history, placing the mustache of Hitler on Sharon" (May 22, 2001).

One of the most venomous cartoons appeared in *The Independent* (UK) on January 27, 2003, the week of Ariel Sharon's reelection. It depicts a fat, slovenly, naked Sharon, his private parts covered only by a small sign that reads "Vote Likud," voraciously biting off the head of a Palestinian baby. In the left-hand corner four Israeli helicopters are attacking a bombed-out Palestinian town. Sharon is depicted as saying, "What's wrong? You've never seen a politician kissing babies before?" In the lower right-hand corner is the phrase "After Goya," an indication that the cartoon is modeled after one of Francesco Goya's most gruesome paintings, *Saturn Devouring His Children*. Both the cartoonist, Dave Brown, and the editor of the *Independent,* Simon Kellner, are Jewish and denied any antisemitic intent.

If indeed there is a new antisemitism, one of its defining characteristics has been the willingness of deracinated Jews on the left to foster it. The *Independent*'s cartoon image elicited powerful associations with one of the most durable of all antisemitic canards, the blood libel that Jews allegedly require the blood of Christian boys for their religious rites. And, indeed, blood libel cartoons appear frequently in Muslim newspapers and journals. What is shocking was its appearance in a respectable, mainstream British newspaper. Inevitably, the crucifixion of Jesus is assimilated to the Palestinian struggle, as if the Palestinians were a Christ among the nations and the Jews once again Christ's crucifiers. One cartoon depicts a young, innocent Palestinian boy nailed not to a cross but to a Star of David (*El Periodico de Catalunya,* Spain, October 6, 2000). There is no caption. None is needed.

There is a subtext to the equation of Israel to Nazi Germany and Sharon to Hitler: The Israelis deserve no better fate than Nazi Germany: utter destruction. As Hillel Halkin has pointed out, American support of Israel involves risk and the expenditure of human and financial resources that could be curtailed if Israel is seen as "morally undeserving."[36] This is a major objective of the manifold propaganda attacks on Israel. Implicit in the demonization is the legitimation of a potentially genocidal assault on the State of Israel. When the demonization is linked with the widespread distribution of *The Protocols of the Elders of Zion,* it becomes a potent legitimation of the destruction of the Jewish people worldwide. On November 6, 2002, at the beginning of the holy month of Ramadan, Egyptian state television channel 2, Dream TV (a privately owned Egyptian satellite network), Abu Dhabi TV, Hezbollah's al-Manar TV, Yemen TV, and others, all began screening

Horseman without a Horse, a forty-one-episode "historical" series covering the Middle East from 1850 to 1948. The entire series emphasizes *The Protocols of the Elders of Zion* as "proof" of an alleged Jewish plot to dominate and enslave the world and depicts the founding of the State of Israel as a major step toward that end. The unprecedented use of the *Protocols* in a television series reaching perhaps as many as 200 million Muslims continuously for forty-one days constitutes a radical escalation of both the scope and intensity of anti-Jewish propaganda in the Muslim world. No scholarly essay or newspaper article exposing the lie can possibly match the power of a widely promoted, prime-time TV series scheduled immediately after the nightly meal that breaks the fast of the holy month of Ramadan. Earlier antisemites and the Nazis used only widely circulated print editions. The producers of *Horseman without a Horse* possess a far more potent propaganda medium combining visual and dramatic power and capable of influencing millions of varying degrees of literacy.

From 1919 to 1945 the *Protocols* were taken as "proof" by German right-wing nationalists that (a) the Jews were the hidden force that had betrayed Germany and brought about her defeat in World War I and that (b) the Bolshevik Revolution was the result of a Jewish conspiracy to enslave the world and destroy Christianity.[37] These beliefs gave a delusional coherence to Germany's shattering experience of World War I defeat as well as to the conviction that genocide was a *moral* necessity.[38] For example, in his diaries Joseph Goebbels reported a conversation about the *Protocols* with Hitler on May 13, 1943. Hitler expressed the conviction that "the *Protocols* were absolutely genuine" and drew the conclusion that "there is therefore no other recourse left for modern nations except to exterminate the Jew...." (*Es bleibt also den Modernen Völkern nichts anderes übriges, als die Juden auszurotten.*)[39] Now again in our era, the *Protocols* have been put in the service of a radical assault on Jews, Judaism, and the State of Israel. This time on TV throughout the Arab and Muslim world, and the subtext is the same: Jews, Judaism, and Israel must be destroyed.

If the revival of antisemitism can be characterized as a return of the repressed, it can also be characterized as a revival of *historic amnesia* concerning the birth of Zionism and the founding of the State of Israel. The birth of Zionism cannot be divorced from Europe's dangerously intensifying antisemitism in the last decades of the nineteenth and the first decades of the twentieth century; the birth of the State of Israel cannot be divorced from the Holocaust and its aftermath. For the vast majority of Europe's surviving Jews, that continent had become a charnel house. Inevitably, this led to a tragic and enduring conflict between Jews and Arabs in the aftermath of the Holocaust. Unfortunately, for the vast majority of Europe's Jews the options were either escape or death.

We have come to expect widespread Muslim insistence, both on political and theological grounds, that Israel's existence lacks legitimacy and should never have come about. Unfortunately, the Muslim voices have been joined, often stridently, by all too many Europeans who are either indifferent to or want to repeat the circumstances that made the post–World War II outmigration of Europe's Jews a necessity. We take note of the widely publicized comments of British historian A. N. Wilson and Oxford poet Tom Paulin.[40] The import of their remarks is that the destruction of Israel would be a benefit to world peace. That such an outcome could not occur without genocide or something approximating it does not disturb such people. They can clothe their malevolence in the rhetoric of antiracism, human rights, and an outraged sense of injustice. Nevertheless, the outcome would be the same.

Although I have suggested that we are witnessing a historic exemplification of the return of the repressed, that alone would not suffice to explain the phenomenon. As is well known, according to the early theories of Sigmund Freud, painful memories and feelings are repressed because their overt expression is understood to entail too great a cost. Something like that has been at work in the repression of antisemitism in the aftermath of World War II. The war ended with Europe in ruins and the balance of power shifted from the traditional European players to two non-European powers, the United States and the Soviet Union. For several decades, official expressions of antisemitism carried few, if any, benefits and hence were kept under control. In addition to the stench of Auschwitz, the military forces of the Soviet Union were poised in the heart of Germany, and Western Europe was heavily dependent for its survival upon the United States, with its large and influential Jewish population. Nevertheless, hostility toward Jews and Judaism persisted, albeit as a somewhat underground stream. The situation began to change with the collapse of the Soviet Union and the alteration of the balance of power between Europe and the United States. Only one superpower remained, a situation France and other European powers have found unacceptable.

If, as this writer believes, Bat Ye'or is on target in seeing the seeds of a potential new balance of power in the unstated European Union-Arab partnership she identifies as Eurabia, that alliance has a double target, the United States and the State of Israel. In his frequent comments on the evils of "unilateralism" President Jacques Chirac has been quite explicit in his rejection of what he considers the present absence of a suitable balance of power. On July 21, 2003, in Putrajaya, Maylasia, Prime Minister Mahathir Mohammad awarded President Chirac the Kuala Lumpur World Peace Award for his "resolute opposition to the war in Iraq and the courage he demonstrated in placing himself on the side of the oppressed." According to Agence France-Presse, M. Chirac was quoted as saying that the world could no longer submit to the "law of the jungle" and needed to create an international organization that could eliminate unilateralism. What was required instead "is an international structure, an international mechanism that can do away with unilateralism and bring multilateralism."[41] Without explicitly mentioning the United States, American policy was clearly identified with the "law of the jungle."

There are many reasons for European dislike of the United States. They have been amply discussed elsewhere. At least one is relevant to our topic: Jews have a degree of *influence* in the United States that is unparalleled in any other country other than Israel, a reality that is fully understood in Europe. Undoubtedly, that factor influenced considerably the perceptions of Germany's postwar leaders concerning the desirability of some degree of normal relations with Israel and the outreach efforts of the German government toward American-Jewish leaders and writers in the early decades after the war. That, of course, is not the whole story. Many Germans wanted sincerely to wash away the stench of Auschwitz, but it is not an unimportant part of the story. Given the attempt of the European Union to create a coalition with the Arab Muslim world as a balance against American power, Euro-Arabian hostility toward America has a definitely anti-Jewish component primarily formulated in anti-Israel rhetoric.

One of the most puzzling aspects of the resurgence of anti-Jewish hostility in Europe, especially in its guise as opposition to Zionism and Israel, has been the degree to which the objective threat to European civilization and culture from radical Islam has been downplayed or ignored while Israel's conflict with the Palestinians and the wider Arabic and Islamic world has taken center stage as *the* greatest threat to world peace and international stability. We need not take the word of non-Muslims concerning the profound danger Islamic extremism poses to Western civilization. According to Bassam Tibi, professor of political science at Germany's Göttingen University and one of the world's leading authorities on Islamic fundamentalism and himself a Muslim, "The goal of the Islamic fundamentalists is to abolish the Western, secular order and replace it with a new Islamic divine order....The goal of the Islamists is a new imperial, absolutist Islamic power."[42] Their methods have included the viciously depraved murder of 344 civilians at Beslan in the Russian republic of North Ossetia, at least 172 of them children and hundreds more wounded by 30 Chechen and Arab jihadists employing rigged explosives and sniper fire.[43] Their targets have also included the nearly simultaneous bombing of four commuter trains in Madrid on March 11, 2004, at the peak of the morning rush hour, killing 191 and grievously wounding more than 1,000, the bombing of a Bali nightclub primarily patronized by vacationers, killing 187 and wounding 300, not to mention the dead and wounded in New York and Washington on 9/11. We could cite many more but these will suffice.

Nevertheless, in spite of the *real damage* perpetrated against Westerners and their institutions by Islamic extremists, according to an EU survey of 7,500 people randomly chosen across the European Union, almost 60 percent regard Israel as a greater threat to world peace than North Korea, Iran, or Afghanistan. The EU poll is consistent with an earlier poll conducted by the *International Herald Tribune* and the Pew Research Center in which British, Italian, French, and German respondents said they sympathized more with the Palestinians than the Israelis.[44] The survey has been criticized by Dalia Dassa Kaye, a Council of Foreign Relations International Fellow based in the Hague, as an unnuanced example of "shoddy polling practices." Kaye argues the problem is not "Israel per se" but the Arab-Israeli conflict that threatens to spill over into the entire Middle East to the detriment of political and economic stability in Europe.[45]

Undoubtedly, there is fear in Europe of the conflict spilling over, but that would hardly explain the depth or the severity of the venomous antagonism directed toward Israel and, in many quarters, against all Jews. I would like to suggest an alternative hypothesis to account for the deep and profound hostility toward Jews, Israel, and Zionism that pervades much of contemporary Europe. I stress that I can only offer a hypothesis, that is, a tentative theory that attempts to explain certain phenomena. Such a theory would be falsifiable if credible contrary evidence were to be discovered. I know of no such evidence. Simply stated, deep religious antagonisms have resurfaced in contemporary Europe in *secular guise*—the "return of the repressed" to which we refer in this essay. Taken literally, if Christ is the fulfillment and "end" of the Law, then Jews are in error in maintaining fidelity to their religion. If, as all branches of Judaism must assert, he is not, then the belief system of Christianity is devoid of the cosmic legitimation the Church claims for itself. Although we speak of the "Judeo-Christian tradition," historically there has been far greater offense in Christianity over Jewish "unbelief" than Islam's supersessionary claims vis-à-vis the Church. From a Christian perspective, Jesus' mission was first and foremost to the Jews who rejected him in a violently deicidal act, if the Gospel accounts of the Crucifixion are taken literally. The issue of Jewish "unbelief" has been central to Christianity from the time of the Gospels and the Letters of Paul to modern times. Christianity does not claim to be a religion entirely distinct from Judaism, but the completion and perfection of what God had originally intended Judaism to be. This is a claim Jews cannot possibly accept. Christianity makes no comparable claims that it is the completed or perfected Islam. Elsewhere, I have referred to the Jew as the "discomfirming other" par excellence for Christianity. Almost from its inception that "unbelief" has been explained away or discredited by claims of Jewish villainy, betrayal, and the lack of credibility. Indeed, one can argue that a fundamental motive for Christian antisemitism has been to discredit the credibility of the Jewish narrative concerning the circumstances of Jesus' life and death. If Jews are deicides, Satan's spawn or congenitally untrustworthy, that narrative is devoid of credibility. Moreover, in Christian theology, Jewish defeat and suffering have consistently been cited as proof of Christian truth and irrefutable evidence of the falsehood of Jewish claims. As James Carroll has put it, Jews were supposed to "survive but not thrive," and indeed to survive in unhappiness and misery.[46]

In spite of the perennial antagonism resulting from Jewish "unbelief," the stench of Auschwitz introduced a new mood within much of Christendom. Without Auschwitz, Vatican II and Pope Paul VI's declaration *Nostra Aetate* (October 28, 1965) that "…Jews should not be presented as rejected or accursed by God, as if this followed from the Holy Scriptures" would have been unthinkable. The motive for the changed Christian attitude was largely grounded in guilt over a crime that was completely contrary to the self-image of twentieth-century Christian civilization. The unremitting extermination of millions of helpless, unarmed men, women, and children might take place in other, less "civilized" parts of the world, but not where it did, in the heart of Christian Europe. Moreover, in cold-blooded, methodical thoroughness, the world had never before witnessed any slaughter remotely comparable to what took place in Christian Europe. Nevertheless, guilt is an unsustainable emotion in the relations between communities. Not long after the war ended, some survivors had a saying, "The Germans will never forgive *us* for Auschwitz." Put differently, those survivors intuited that as victims they would sooner or later be blamed for the crimes of the perpetrators.

When the deed was done, there were a number of attempts to cope with the guilt engendered by the Holocaust. The healthiest response was honestly to confront the facts and seek for ways to lessen the hostile component in Jewish-Christian relations. And, there is no doubt that honest, epoch-making attempts have been made to that end. Unfortunately, there have also been less felicitous responses. One was that the Jews received their just deserts for having rejected Christ. In a "Statement on the Jewish Question" dated April 1948, the Reich Council of Brethren of the Evangelical Church reminded Israel that it "had crucified the Messiah, Israel's sole hope," and added "that God will not be mocked in the silent sermon of the Jewish faith, a warning to us, a reminder to the Jews about whether or not they want to convert to Him in whom alone their salvation stands."[47] Put differently, "the Darmstadt Declaration ultimately blamed the Holocaust on the Jews' refusal to become Christians."[48]

Another response was simply to deny that the Holocaust had ever taken place, that it was a monumental fraud perpetrated by Zionists and other Jews to induce Christian guilt and to build up the State of Israel.[49] Not surprisingly, Holocaust denial has also been exceedingly popular throughout the Muslim world.[50] The import of denial is simple: If there was no Holocaust, there is no guilt and Israel has no moral claim. The establishment of the State of Israel was not an act of rescue of the remnants of a people unwanted in the charnel house of Europe or the world of Islam, but the rapacious act of a settler colonialist band aided and abetted by an imperialist United States.

Nevertheless, save for a small number of cynical propagandists and their gullible followers, the stench of Auschwitz was too great to be covered up by so patently false a claim. Not until after the Six-Day War of 1967 was an antisemitic response formulated that was capable of salving some Christian consciences and beginning the process of eliminating the stench. The response was: "The Palestinian is the new Jew, and the Jew the new Nazi."[51] In some cartoons the Palestinians are depicted as the new Christ and the Israelis as their crucifiers. As we have seen, Israel has been equated with the Third Reich and Ariel Sharon with Adolf Hitler. This is the most obscene form of Holocaust denial. Throughout Europe and the Muslim world, this canard has been widely circulated in cartoons, articles, and speeches. Its objective is to delegitimize Israel and Israelis so that destroying them entirely can become a legitimate object of the world's so-called "peace-loving peoples." And once again, the cry of "Death to the Jews" has been uttered in the streets of Europe." Since approximately 40 percent of the world's Jews live in Israel, one can hardly claim that this kind of opposition to Israel and Zionism is other than antisemitic.[52]

In order to complete the circle and return to the status quo ante of the 1930s, both the extreme right and the extreme left have, in concert with radical Muslims, once again accused Jews of attempting to dominate the world through commerce, capitalism, and, most especially, globalization. The fundamental thesis of *The Protocols of the Elders of Zion* has been given renewed life by the antiglobalization movement, which has succeeded in uniting left and right in an improbable but effective alliance with Muslim extremists in claiming that globalization is a conspiracy by Jews and Jewish-dominated Americans for world domination.[53] As in the 1920s and '30s, vast economic and social disorganization is being "explained" as a result of a monumental Jewish worldwide conspiracy. If the extremists cannot agree on a common program, they can at least agree on a common enemy.

Admittedly, globalization is not without very serious problems.[54] At least in the short term, there are arguably as many losers as winners, and no single solution will solve the complex disorientations it has produced, save in the minds and propaganda of radical antiglobalists. Their "solution" is the destruction of the State of Israel and the elimination of Jewish influence, if not Jews altogether. But this monocausal solution of a complex problem is magic thinking rooted in religion and myth, and it is to religion that we must turn to uncover its roots.

In all likelihood, many, if not most, of the antiglobalists are undeceived about the efficacy of their solution, but that hardly matters. What they really seek is a target upon which to vent their resentment and aggression and, in the case of the Islamists, their impotent rage.

In the Christian West, that target has historically been the Jews. No other target has been so durable as the object of Christian anger, and it is the one target on which Christian and Muslim anger can unite. Given the numerical difference between the world's Jewish and Muslim populations, there are powerful practical motives for taking the side of the Muslims against the Jews, but such motives cannot explain the exclusive focus on Israel's alleged mistreatment of Palestinians while ignoring the hundreds of thousands murdered recently in other parts of the world or the vehemence with which Israel alone has been condemned. Only the contemporary revival of an ancient hatred rooted in religion can offer an explanation that *begins* to partake of adequacy. The repressed has returned and has once again garnered much of its full force in the public sphere from religion.

Nor has the secularization of Europe's civilization and culture diminished religion's underground potency in defining and targeting the outsider. Nonbelievers of Christian inheritance seldom, if ever, abandon Christmas and Easter, nor are they likely to fail to take note of those depicted as villains in the New Testament and in much of European literature throughout the ages. In the decades following the Holocaust, the power of that tradition to demonize Jews was largely repressed. As we have seen, antisemitism was for a time not *Salon fähig*. That time has now passed. In stressful situations, one need not be a believer to become enraged at those characterized as the classical villains of one's historic inheritance. On the contrary, secularization can often weaken or remove the constraints against terminal violence that Christianity had traditionally placed upon itself in dealing with its most significant "disconfirming other."

Finally, although the West's opponents of Israel have joined together with radical Islam in positing Israel as its real enemy, they ignore at their peril the very real threat to their civilization and culture posed by the adherents of radical Islam who make no secret of the fact that they regard Islam's return to Europe as opening a new chapter in the millennial struggle between Christendom and Islam for the domination of Europe.

Notes

1. Details of the citizenship reform, "Reform of Germany's Citizenship and Nationality Law," are posted on the web page of the German embassy to the United Kingdom, http://www.german-embassy.org.uk/reform_of_germany_s_citizenship.html.

2. I have changed his name.

3. Even its secularization, which has no Islamic counterpart, is derived from the *disenchantment* of the world of Biblical religion. See Max Weber, "Science as a Vocation," in H. H. Gerth and C. Wright Mills, *From Max Weber: Essays in Sociology* (New York: Oxford University Press, 1945), p. 139. On the biblical origins of the "disenchantment of the world," see also Peter Berger, *The Sacred Canopy: Elements of a Sociological Theory of Religion* (Garden City, NY, Doubleday, 1967), pp. 99, 116, 118.

4. Population figures for France vary from 5 million to 10 million. While the exact figure is not known, Islam is nevertheless France's second-largest religion. See Jim Hoagland, "Europe's Gray Future," *Washington Post,* May 2, 2004.

5. John Kelsay, *Islam and War: The Gulf War and Beyond* (Louisville: John Knox Press, 1993), p. 118.

6. Wolfgang, Schwanitz,, "Europa wird am Ende des Jahrhunderts islamisch sein," *Die Welt*, July 28, 2004, interview with Bernard Lewis; http://www.welt.de/data/2004/07/28/310913.html.

7. Bat Ye'or, "Eurabia: The Road to Munich," *National Review Online*, October 9, 2002.

8. Ibid.

9. Jamie Glazov, "Eurabia" (interview with Bat Ye'or), *Front Page Magazine*, September 21, 2004.

10. Ibid.

11. The Jews of Algeria had been granted French citizenship in 1870 by decree of Adolphe Cremieux, minister of justice. Their citizenship was revoked in World War II during the Vichy regime.

12. Albert Guérard, *France: A Modern History* (Ann Arbor: University of Michigan Press, 1959), p. 482; Richard and Joan Brace, *Ordeal in Algeria* (Princeton: Van Nostrand, 1960), p. 72.

13. William I. Brustein, *Roots of Hate: Antisemitism in Europe before the Holocaust* (New York: Cambridge University Press, 2003), p. 299.

14. David Fromkin, *A Peace to End All Peace: The Fall of the Ottoman Empire and the Creation of the Modern Middle East* (New York: Henry Holt, 1989), pp. 322–23.

15. Ibid., pp. 292–93.

16. Barbara Amiel, "Islamists Overplay their Hand, but London Salons Don't See It," *Daily Telegraph* (UK), December 17, 2001.

17. Editorial, "French Fried," *Wall Street Journal*, December 26, 2001.

18. See Tom Gross, "Prejudice and Abuse," *National Review Online*, January 10, 2002, http://www.nationalreview.com/comment/comment-gross011002.shtml .

19. David Wyman, *The Abandonment of the Jews: America and the Holocaust, 1941–1945* (New York: Pantheon Books, 1984), p. 105.

20. Samantha Power, *"A Problem from Hell": America and the Age of Genocide* (New York: Basic Books, 2002).

21. If anyone in London was in a position to know what was "respectable at London dinner tables," it was Petronella Wyatt, daughter of Tory Lord Wyatt of Weeford. The fallout from her affair with Boris Johnson, Conservative MP, editor of *The Spectator,* and married with four children, included Johnson's dismissal as Arts Minister in the Conservative Party's shadow cabinet and Wyatt aborting the child she was carrying. See the *Irish Examiner,* November 14, 2004, http://breaking.tcm.ie/2004/11/14/story175775.html.; *The Scotsman*, November 13, 2004, http://news.scotsman.com/latest.cfm?id=3756243.

22. Amiel, "Islamists Overplay Their Hand."

23. Hillel Halkin, "The Return of Antisemitism," *Wall Street Journal*, February 5, 2002.

24. Brustein, *Roots of Hate*, p. 348.

25. Helen Fein, *Accounting for Genocide: National Responses and Jewish Victimization during the Holocaust* (Chicago: University of Chicago Press, 1984), pp. 91–92. I am indebted to Brustein for this citation.

26. See, for example, Carol Rittner and John K. Roth, eds., *Pius XII and the Holocaust* (Leicester: Leicester University Press, 2002); James Carroll, *Constantine's Sword: The Church and the Jews, A History* (Boston:

Houghton Mifflin, 2001); Richard L. Rubenstein and John K. Roth, *Approaches to Auschwitz: The Holocaust and Its Legacy,* rev. ed. (Louisville, KY: Westminster/John Knox, 2003).

27. For an informed overview of European antisemitism before the Holocaust, see Brustein, *Roots of Hate.*

28. See Eugen Weber, *The Hollow Years:France in the 1930s* (New York: W. W. Norton, 1994), pp. 100–101.

29. Ibid., pp. 102–3. On Céline's antisemitism, see Nicholas Hewitt, "Memory and Chronicle: Louis-Ferdinand Céline and the D'un Chateau L'Autre Trilogy," in Charles Burdett, Claire Gorrara, Helmut Peitsch, eds., *European Memories of the Second World War* (New York: Bergahn Books, 1999), pp. 88–98.

30. For an important examination of the significance of the Gibson film by leading scholars of religion and theology, see J. Shawn Landres and Michael Berenbaum, eds., *After the Passion Is Gone: American Religious Consequences* (Walnut Creek, CA: AltaMira Press, 2004).

31. Jules Isaac, *Jésus et Israël* (Paris: Albin Michel, 1948).

32. ADL, "The Oberammergau Passion Play: The New Script for the 2000 Presentation," http://www.adl.org/Interfaith/Oberammergau/Intro.asp.

33. Michael Schmidt, *The New Reich: Violent Extremism in Unified Germany* (New York: Pantheon Books, 1993), p. 219 (italics added).

34. The most authoritative book on this subject is Deborah Lipstadt, *Denying the Holocaust: The Growing Assault on Truth and Memory* (New York: Free Press, 1993). On Holocaust denial in the Islamic world, see, for example, Fiamma Nirenstein, "How Suicide Bombers Are Made," *Commentary,* September 2001, vol. 112, no. 2.

35. David A. Harris, "Europe on Israel, 2000–2001: A Sampling of Words and Images," http://www.ajc.org/InTheMedia/PublicationsPrint.asp?did=474.

36. Halkin, "Return of Antisemitism."

37. The *Protocols* had originally been prepared by the Russian police and given to tsar Nicholas II to influence policy. Although personally antisemitic, the Tsar detected the fraud and refused to use it. See Leon Poliakov, "Elders of Zion, Protocols of the Learned," in *Encyclopaedia Judaica*, CD edition (Jerusalem: Judaica Multimedia, 1997).

38. The belief that the Holocaust was not only justified but was regarded as

an urgent moral necessity is discussed at length by Peter Haas, *The Nazi Ethic* (Philadelphia: Fortress Press, 1988). Fortress Press is the publishing house of the American Lutheran Church.

39. Louis P. Lochner, ed. and trans., *The Goebbels Diaries, 1942–1943* (Garden City, NY: Doubleday and Co., 1948), p. 377. The date of the entry is 13 May 1943. German text in Elke Fröhlich, *Die Tagebücher von Joseph Goebbels* (München: K. G. Saur, 1993), vol. 2, pt. 8, p. 287 (13 May 1943).

40. Referring to "Brooklyn-born Jewish settlers," Paulin told an interviewer from the Egyptian journal *Al-Ahram*, "They should be shot dead. I think they are Nazis, racists, I feel nothing but hatred for them." *Al-Ahram Weekly Online*, 4–10 April 2002, http://weekly.ahram.org.eg/2002/580/cu2.htm. On A. N. Wilson, see Wilson, "The Tragic Reality of Israel," *Evening Standard,* October 22, 2001.

41. John Vinocur, "Did Chirac Say That?" *International Herald Tribune*, July 23, 2003.

42. Cited by Lisbeth Lindeborg, "Osama's Library," *Dagens Nyheter*, Stockholm, Sweden, October 25, 2001, reprinted in *World Press Review*, January 2002 (vol. 49, no. 1).

43. The number of death certificates suggests a real number three times higher.

44. Thomas Fuller, "Europe Poll Calls Israel a Big Threat to World Peace," *International Herald Tribune,* October 31, 2003; http://www.iht.com/articles/115858.html .

45. Dalia Dassa Kaye, "Is Israel Really the Biggest Threat to Peace?" *International Herald Tribune*, November 8, 2003; http://www.cfr.org/pub6515/dalia_dassa_kaye/is_israel_really_the_biggest_threat_to_peace.php .

46. James Carroll, *Constantine's Sword,* p. 219.

47. Christian Gerlach, *Als die Zeugen schweigen: Bekennende Kirche und die Juden* (Berlin: Institut für Kirche und Judentum, 1987), p. 282.

48. Robert Eriksen and Susannah Heschel, Introduction, Eriksen and Heschel, eds., *German Churches and the Holocaust: Betrayal* (Minneapolis: Fortress Press, 1999), p. 19.

49. For a succinct overview of Holocaust denial, see Manfred Gerstenfeld, "Denial of the Holocaust and Immoral Equivalence: An Interview with Deborah Lipstadt," Jerusalem Center for Public Affairs, Post Holocaust

and Antisemitism, No. 11, August 1, 2003 / 3 Av 5763; http://www.jcpa. org/phas/phas-11.htm . See also Deborah Lipstadt, *Denying the Holocaust: The Growing Assault on Truth and Memory* (New York: Penguin Books, 1994) and Richard J. Evans, *Lying about Hitler: History, Holocaust, and the David Irving Trial* (New York: Basic Books, 2001).

50. See Nirenstein, "How Suicide Bombers Are Made."

51. This statement was reported to have been made by a member of the highly politicized Columbia University Middle Eastern Studies Department. See Uriel Heilman, "Non-Academic Debate," *Jerusalem Post*, December 23, 2004, http://www.jpost.com/servlet/Satellite?pagename=JPost/JPArticle/ ShowFull&cid=1103776317627&p=1074657885918 .

52. See Halkin, "Return of Antisemitism."

53. See Mark Strauss, "Antiglobalism's Jewish Problem," *Foreign Policy*, November/December 2003, http://yaleglobal.yale.edu/article. print?id=2791, and Joshua Kurlantzick, "The Left and the Islamists," *Commentary*, December 2004.

54. For an account of the devastating consequences of globalization on undercapitalized small farmers in Central America, see Celia W. Dugger, "Supermarket Giants Crush Central American Small Farmers, *New York Times*, December 28, 2004, http://www.nytimes.com/2004/12/28/ international/americas/28guatemala.html?hp&ex=1104296400&en=617 bafd4c8cbf3e0&ei=5094&partner=homepage.

3

Antisemitism in France and Antisemitism of France

Michael Berenbaum

There has been much discussion of antisemitism in France and reportage of individual incidents. Many have recalled the historic antisemitism in France. After all, it was slightly before the dawn of the twentieth century that the Dreyfus trial exposed the imbalance between the aspirations of France for liberty, equality, and fraternity and the actual achievements of France, when a French captain, the first Jew to serve on the General Staff, was charged with treason. Even after the falseness of the accusations were exposed, he was only offered a pardon—not an exoneration—while in the streets of Paris, French citizens were chanting death to the Jews. Many have also recalled the clash between the French myth of *Resistance* and the reality of the close collaboration between Vichy France and Nazi Germany and the role of the French police in the deportation of Jews under German occupation. Jews were better off under fascist Italian occupation in southern France than they were under the Vichy regime.

Still I think some clarity is sorely needed on the current situation in France.

- There is a direct correlation between the situation in Israel and attacks on Jews in France; the more intense the violence in the Middle East, the more vehement the attack on the Jews;

- The assaults against the Jews are related to the significant demographic changes in France; namely the emergence of a significant Islamic underclass minority that may be one-tenth of the French population, and France is doing little—precious little—to address the root of the problem;

- France only began to seriously react to the Jewish situation when the disquiet in the Muslim neighborhoods spread to the general population of France;

- The more assimilated the Islamic population is in France, the more accepting it is of French norms, which includes the full participation of Jews within French society;

- As the government was slow to perceive the nature of the danger, no other segment of French society came forward to recognize the pattern of assault on the Jews; there was virtual silence from political leadership, the media, the Church, the opinion makers, and even the Jewish community;

- The most vulnerable Jews have been the least affluent, those who immigrated from Islamic societies and those who live alongside Muslims;

- There are three elements in the Islamic community living in France: the assimilationists, the separatists, and those in-between. The separatists are the most numerous and the least exposed to French culture and French norms. They are nourished directly by extremist elements in Islamic culture, by Osama bin Laden, by the situation in Iraq and in Palestine/Irsael;

- The French government, French elite, and public opinion comfortably distinguish between Jews in France who they warmly welcome as fellow citizens and whose presence in French society and French culture is venerated, and the policies of the State of Israel, which are abhorred;

- The vehemence of the attacks against Israel must raise the question that caused Richard Bernstein to ask in the *New York Times* ("Ugly Rumor or an Ugly Truth," August 4, 2002) "Does the ferocious moral condemnation of Israel mark a recrudescence of that most ugly of Western diseases, antisemitism? Or is it a legitimate, if crude, criticism of a nation's policies? Where does one draw the line? How does one judge?"

From Jerusalem to Paris

The number of incidents against Jews in France from 2000 through 2003 is under dispute. Estimates vary widely. French journalist Michel

Gurfinkiel writing in *Commentary* reported that CRIF, the umbrella organization of the French Jewish community, recorded 500 antisemitic incidents since October 2000. David Suissa, editor of *Olam,* used a figure of 400 to 800. Both numbers are unacceptable, but still there is a wide difference between 400 and 800.

Yet, there are no differences as to the timing of the incidents. They occurred with much greater intensity in three periods: October 2000, just after the start of Intifada II; post September 11, 2001, after the bombing of the World Trade Center; and in April 2002, following the bombing of Passover and the massive Israeli response to an intolerable bombings of its civilians. There can be no doubt about the correlation, but there can be considerable doubt as to whether the spur to violence comes directly from the Middle East or whether the intensity of French condemnation of Israel coupled with the conspiracy theories prevalent in France that blamed the 9/11 attack on the CIA, which led to a best-selling book that has been published in its English edition by the publishing arm of *The Nation,* is seen as license of Muslims in France for attacks against the Jews. They do not differentiate as easily as their French counterparts between French Jews and Israel.

This correlation is painful to Jews who for years held the comfortable belief that Israel was the answer to antisemitism. Jews learned in the aftermath of the Yom Kippur War and the oil embargo crisis that followed, and again in recent months, that Israel can also fuel the flames of antisemitism.

But who said the Jewish situation in our time—or anytime—is simple, and being Jewish at this moment in time is anything but comfortable.

Demographics

Mark Twain once said, "There is truth, lies, and statistics."

The statistics are simple, the truth more complex.

There are 600,000 French Jews constituting 1 percent of the population; there are at least 6,000,000 Muslims living in France, constituting 10 percent of the population.

Six hundred thousand Jews living in France makes France the fourth-largest Jewish community in the world. With size also comes capacity—schools and synagogues, Jewish culture and creativity, books and museums, music and art. One can see Jewish neighborhoods and

Jewish shops, Jewish schools and the emergence of Jewish centers. The French Jewish community consists of those long native to France and of immigrants from French colonies in North Africa who left these colonies with the decline and collapse of French colonialism and their descendants. They tend to be more traditional, perhaps more assertive, and certainly more intensely linked to Israel, but in recent years they have blended well with the French Jewish establishment and have contributed to the vitality of French Jewry, most especially as compared with its staid counterpart in Great Britain.

There may also be one-third as many French men and women of recent Jewish origin who have Jewish relatives and who take a not insignificant interest in Jewish affairs.

French Jews are Jews but also very deeply French, participating in French society and enjoying the collapse or weakening of barriers that restrained their advancement. They are proud of their dynamic community and mindful of their achievements in French society. Jacques Chirac, France's former president and the former mayor of Paris, loves these Jews as fellow citizens and admires them as successfully integrated Frenchmen (and women); his views on Israel are another matter.

The Islamic community is rather different. Demographic information seems to indicate it is far more numerous than formal census figures reveal, and it is growing rapidly. It may have doubled within the past decade.

There is a long-established Islamic minority in France, who, like the Jews, have assimilated and adopted the values and attitudes of their fellow countrymen. On the whole they get along well with the Jews and can comfortably differentiate between French Jews and the policies of the State of Israel.

Far more numerous—and far less French—are the recent arrivals who constitute an underclass and tend to want to maintain themselves as a separate community. They share many of the anti-Western, anti-Jewish attitudes current in the Middle East and are agitated by the suffering of their brethren under the policies of Israel. They despise the state of Israel whether led by Ehud Barak, Shimon Peres, Benjamin Netanyahu, Ariel Sharon, or Ehud Olmert.

France has been very slow to recognize the permanence of this "non-French" population, and government leaders all too comfortably maintain antisemitism is not of France even while it occurs within

France. Since these people are "non-French" even as they live in France, the leaders of France are not lying when they make these exonerating claims—merely misleading.

What happens to this separatist underclass is neither in the control of the Jewish community, nor is it likely outside political or moral pressure from the United States or the American Jewish community will have a large impact on the development of French policy. It has now caught the attention of French leadership because the discontent exploded in many different French cities. But Europe's efforts have been clumsy at best. (As an aside, the problem of Europe's nonintegrated immigrants should give pause to those who imagine that a guest worker program will solve the immigration problem in the United States.)

The attitude toward the other, the transformation of more or less homogeneous European societies into heterogeneous, multicultural, multinational, multireligious societies is a large—very large—question in contemporary Europe. The European Union, the Euro and the free exchange of populations coupled with the atmosphere created by globalism are dramatically reshaping France and all of Europe. These changes will loom large in the twenty-first century. Suffice it to say that the separatist Islamic community is of great concern to the future of the French Jewish community. Their participation in French society and the assimilation of values and moderation that follows are important, and things do not bode well at this time.

Again, the changes in the Middle East will directly impact these developments. When tension is high and France condemns Israel, and the media piles on, these statements are perceived as license to attack. The least prosperous, the least influential, and the least assimilated French Jews live adjacent to these separatist communities and hence their vulnerability took a long time to be recognized.

Antisemitism Is Antithetical to France

Really?

There is a great distance between aspiration and achievement. The government has not paid a great deal of attention to the underclass Islamic population. It has not paid attention to violence in their neighborhoods, as it does not differentiate between ordinary crimes and hate crimes. It was slow to perceive the problem and responded only belatedly and with some outside pressure to attacks against Jews.

Anyone visiting any Jewish institution in France knows there is a manifest presence of French police to guard these institutions, blockades to prevent car bombs or ramming of the institution, searches upon entry and the presence of uniformed officers outside. So the French formally recognize the possibility of attack against their Jews and have been responsive to security concerns, at a level far more intense than American counterparts.

But one must also pay attention in the aftermath of an attack.

In the United States after an attack against any synagogue or even the painting of a swastika, there is a virtual ritual. The mayor of the local city arrives to condemn the attack. The police pledge to devote all the resources necessary to catch the perpetrators. Local ministers and priest arrive to condemn the attack. They—and their congregants—participate in the cleanup; newspaper editorials are written and the message is communicated clearly and directly that such acts are heinous; they have no place in our communities. So even in the breech—specially in the breech—the values to which the community aspires, the norms of civility and mutual acceptance are reaffirmed. The attack is thus transformed into a defeat of hatred.

In the absence of recognition by government, other segments of society must step forward. In France they did not.

The Jewish community may have been reticent to go public for fear that such publicity would provoke more attacks rather than intensify their condemnation.

The American model has proved successful internationally. Notice how quickly Pope John Paul II responded to the desecration of the Jewish cemetery in Rome by writing to the chief rabbi and publicly condemning the desecration. The pope's statement speaks volumes. In Warsaw, when the Nozick synagogue was burned, the damage was shown to the community and a service was held featuring church and government leaders, a rabbi, and a priest inside the synagogue. There, as elsewhere, the model works, but not without a willingness to go public and a recognition of the deliberate attempt to divide by isolating and stigmatizing and hence the need to unite by joining together and reaffirming communal solidarity. Such was the behavior of President George W. Bush in visiting a mosque after September 11 and such was the behavior of priests, ministers, and rabbis in protecting mosques from desecration and visiting those damaged in the aftermath of the attack.

If you need two images to cement this idea in your mind, consider this:

- A French rally of 120,000 protesting antisemitism barely attracted a politician;

- Picture the cartoon published in *Le Monde* with a policeman standing in front of six damaged synagogues and asking his superior: "How many do we need in order to start mentioning antisemitism?"

Israel and the French

The French have been anti-Israel—vehemently so, vigorously so!

I do not read the French papers daily, so I am relying less on what I know and more upon the myriad of e-mail summaries of anti-Israel press clippings that I routinely receive. One cartoon from *Le Monde* frightened me to my core. It made me feel that the cartoonist and I are not denizens of a common universe, that one of the two of us is mad.

Naturally, the cartoon invoked an image of the Holocaust. On one side was a picture of Jenin and on the other an image of the Warsaw Ghetto and the caption read: "History Repeats Itself."

Written at the height of the false allegations of a massacre at Jenin, let me grant the cartoonist the right to accept what we now know is false, that some five hundred Palestinians were murdered at Jenin.

Still!

Between July 23, 1942 and September 12, 265,000 Jews were transported from Warsaw to Treblinka, where they were gassed on arrival as part of the systematic murder of European Jewry. When the remaining population rose in resistance, German statistics reveal the dimension of the mismatch. In the end, the entire ghetto was destroyed, burned building-by-building, block-by-block.

I am certain the cartoonist had access to the same photographs I saw on CNN showing the area of confrontation, the site of the alleged massacre. The comparisons are false. They are odious. One wonders how any journal, yet alone one as prestigious as *Le Monde,* could publish such trash. Yet its publication reveals a desire to equate what is happening in the Israeli/Palestinian conflict with the German assault against the Jews.

One can speculate as to the reasons why. Perhaps it alleviates guilt for what was done by the Jews. Richard L. Rubenstein argues that the equation of Israel with the Nazis psychologically purges Europe of its feeling of responsibility toward the Jews. Perhaps it is moral comeuppance, most especially after the collapse of the comfortable French myths regarding the Jews of the Charles de Gaulle era. Perhaps it is antisemitism. Above all, it is false and deliberately misleading. Perhaps the French do not know how to deal with an empowered Jewish people, with the ability to defend itself and not just suffer and plead.

As to all comparisons to the Holocaust, let us be clear.

Israel has the power and the opportunity to annihilate the Palestinians. It also has the provocation. It has *not* annihilated the Palestinians.

In fact, it has resorted to hand-to-hand combat in order to avoid the collateral loss of civilian life resulting from aerial bombardment. Major German resources were dedicated to the annihilation of the Jews, even at the cost of resources needed to fight the world war and provide food and labor for the German population and the war effort. No one can seriously offer a comparison.

There is no significant evidence of an increase of antisemitism in the United States—the experience of the college campuses notwithstanding. The support that George W. Bush offered Israel has robbed even those few who thought this an opportunity to attack Jews of the fuel to ignite the flame. It has starved even the critics of Israel of the oxygen they need to gain attention for their attacks.

In France, the vehemence of anti-Israel opposition from every segment of the society—the government and the press included—is interpreted as license. It is fuel to the flames of hatred.

Ironically, many French Jews are now contemplating aliyah. And Jews are rethinking their relationship with France, reassessing their comfort level. Some perspective is required: Only one Jew has been killed in the recent attacks—a French Jewish student. And Israel is tragically now the most dangerous place for Jews to live as Jews.

4

"Golem versus Muslim": Anti-Americanism and Antisemitism Reunited

Nicolas Weill

To reflect on the Jew in the late 1940s, as Jean-Paul Sartre famously said, one must consider the French Jew *en situation*. The situation of the French Jew today is that he is faced with the consequences of an antisemitism whose main features since 1999 are outlined in my previous text. Those features mark a clear distinction between this era and the former ones. I now wish to develop the following thesis: If we are to admit, as any earnest study of the subject ought to, that the Jew of the antisemite has nothing to do with the actual attitude of the real Jews (and even of the Jewish state), but that it acts only as a pretence, then we need to focus on the metamorphosis undergone by the depiction of the Jew held by the antisemite himself. What strikes us at once is that this figure has been generalized to such an extent that the burden the Jews have to bear is not only the burden of Israel but also that of "imperial America."

Since it seems impossible to grasp the virulence of French anti-semitism today through the sole notion of "anti-Zionism," even if it were to be defined by what the sociologist Pierre-André Taguieff calls "absolute anti-Zionism," we must discuss the amalgam between anti-Americanism and antisemitism. I will illustrate my point by borrowing quotations collected in books well known in the history of antisemitism and by exploring some themes concerning such an issue made popular in France by events such as September 11 and the war in Iraq. Following this line, I intend to stay on the tracks opened by Philippe Roger's major work, *The American Foe* (Seuil, 2002).[1]

Focusing on this amalgam, I think we may be spared the debate on whether antisemitism in France is "new." We shall nonetheless observe

that the depiction of the Jew has undergone certain changes. Since the
United States became the closest ally of the State of Israel after 1967, the
growing amalgam between the Jews and America has followed. Actually, this equation between Jew and America does revive a long French
tradition. In his *Memoirs* the recently deceased anti-Zionist Jewish
orientalist Maxime Rodinson deplored the fact that since World War
II, and especially since 1967, the Jew had shifted from a revolutionary figure to that of a bourgeois and reactionary. Except in Eastern
European countries where the Judeo-Bolshevik myth still prevails, the
negative image of the Jew has been more and more linked to so-called
American imperialism.[2]

Even though it was present earlier, the assimilation of the Jew into
America flourished, especially in the late nineties. For example, in
his scandalous lampoon the *Political Myths of the Israeli State* (1996),
Roger Garaudy, a former Marxist philosopher now converted to radical Islam, laid great stress on the "alliance" concluded between the
United States and Israel in 1967 and criticized, in the media, what he
calls the "Zionist lobby."[3] More recently Thierry Meyssan,[4] a popular
activist haunted by conspiracy theory and author of the best-selling
Fearful Imposture, in which he states that September 11 was the result
of a conspiracy planned by the military-industrial lobby and that there
had been no plane crash on the Pentagon, indirectly granted some cre-
dence to the widespread allegation in the Arab world that Jews had
been informed of the attack beforehand, etc.

At the present time, the figure of the Jew allied with the Americans, which emerged from the "neoconservatives" or the slogan "Bush-
Sharon," is a cheap legacy from a thought molded by some progressive
intellectual groups. These groups allowed all sorts of blunders, or even
provoked them. While anti-Americanism shifted after 1945 from
right-wing to left-wing extremism in France, the collective accusation
against Jews for the sins of Israel has, along with this shift, grown in
left-wing circles. Nowadays in France the "reprobation"—the rejection of Israel, to quote the famous formula of the philosopher Alain
Finkielkraut—goes together with that of the United States. Moreover,
since the beginning of the 1990s, during the Gulf War in 1991, the
extreme right had renounced its Atlantism, or sympathy toward the
United States stemming from the period of the Cold War, and downplayed its fierce anti-Americanism inherited from the 1930s. The Jewish condition now has to face this mutation. Of course, every sign of

hostility toward America cannot be reduced systematically to antisemitism. For instance, some of the neorepublicanists among French intellectuals can be very critical towards U.S. politics and at the same time
defend Jews against antisemitism.

Before investigating the sources common to both "Judeophobia"
and "Americanophobia" and the connections between them, I think it
useful to introduce a concept coined by the historian Shulamit Volkov
in her description of Germany at the turn of the twentieth century.[5]
In Wilhelmian Germany, according to Volkov, antisemitism tended to
become a "cultural code." Admitting one's antisemitism was perceived
as the adherence to a cultural identity. It meant committing oneself to
a party, within a particular frame of thought, and acknowledging one's
preference for specific norms, whether social, moral, or political. The
sign "Jew" became a sort of transition object likely to express all sorts
of earthly wretchedness: working-class misery, peasant misery facing
the havoc of industrial modernity, national misery, and so on.

Are we now witnessing in France a reinstitution of antisemitism
as a "cultural code" in the same ways as in the Germany of Wilhelm
II? Even though the answer must be qualified, the context can be
more easily understood by the radicalization of anti-Zionism. Still,
the direct expression of antisemitism generally remains excluded
from public debate, and it is different from what went on during the
1930s and worth mentioning. Unfortunately, it seems that putting a
kind of taboo on the expression of antisemitism, as it has been generally the case in the Western world since World War II, had paradoxically enough also contributed to strengthening it and to making it
more pervasive Of course, it is not a reason why one should campaign to abolish such an exclusion of antisemitism from the public
sphere. For example, that the Jew figure is once again universalized as
a symbol for every kind of disarray can be seen in the symbolic part
he plays in the theoretical construction of some essayists from the
left expressing the disarray they attribute to globalization, to "turbo
capitalism" (Edward Luttwak), or even to the shattering of all alternative systems since 1989 and the fall of communism. In this process of
universalization, the confluence of two streams running along parallel (though occasionally converging) lines, anti-Americanism and
antisemitism, plays a decisive part, even if it exceeds the intentions of
some of the above-mentioned authors.

Golem and Muslims

A symptom of this transformation, or better, of this resurgence, may be sensed in the latest book by the radical thinkers among the antiglobalization protesters, Toni Negri and Michael Hardt.[6] While these authors are not antisemitic, their views are a paradigmatic example of the disastrous consequences of the essentialization and universalization of the figure of the enemy (in this case "empire" as opposed to "multitudes"). We may, for example, wonder in this context what was it that prompted Hardt and Negri to make use of a myth borrowed from Jewish mysticism in order to define the enemy figure. I raise this question neither out of suspicion nor in the hope of aggravating the case against antiglobalization by making it responsible for the present situation, but because I am convinced that the spreading universalization can be traced not only to the preaching of imams from the Parisian suburbs or of Holocaust deniers, but the explanation lies also in unanticipated effects of theories emanating from people of eventual goodwill.

Let us then examine what those two authors have to say in order to illustrate a section suggestively entitled "Simplicissimus," in which they assert that the "American exception now grants its possibility and its legitimacy to the global exception state, that is to the limitation of legal guarantees and liberties in time of crisis": They state that "the Golem has now become an icon of endless war and of blind destruction, a symbol for the monstrosity of war." The blindness of the Golem is even set up as an image of the blindness of society and men: "Its tale echoes the well-known warnings against the dangers of modern society where technology has grown out of control, but the Golem is much more than a parable for men's loss of control over the world and the domination of machinery. It shows the blindness of war and violence.... Rabbi Loew's determination in claiming revenge against the persecutors of the Jews is such that he shuns the Messiah and the prophet Elijah when they appear before him." This intertwining of themes borrowed from the Jewish mystic as well as from the commonplace reprobation of America (mechanization, imperialism) knits a bizarre semantics opposing, in weird Christianizing undertones, the figure of imperial Golem, which refers to the universe of Jewish history, to the "redeeming power of love," a clear allusion to Christianity. As if the true disciples of Saint Paul would have been the new radicals or the antiglobalization protesters.

In the mental landscape of the new philosophical radicalities, which try to reanimate the heritage of the revolutionary potential of the defunct Marxism, we may oppose as countertype of the Golem another figure of oppression that appears in the works of the Italian philosopher Giorgio Agamben, known as the tireless denouncer of the lawless zone of Guantanamo, which, he says, bears proof of a certain unity between liberal democracy and fascism: that is the figure of the "Muslim" as the "*ultime biopolitique isolable dans le continuum biologique.*"[7] For Agamben as for Negri and Hardt, the United States follows a policy molded on the concepts coined by Carl Schmitt (whose sympathies for the Nazi regime recall those of Heidegger), namely, a policy based on exception and the state of urgency causing illegitimate international order, marked by nonapplication of the law.

Although Agamben himself does not assimilate the "Muslim" figure as he describes it in *Remnants of Auschwitz* (1998) with actual Muslims, and if he then is not to be held responsible for such instrumentalization, the assimilation has indeed been made by some Arab intellectuals who indulge in the interpretation of occidental history as a history of extermination,[8] a history whose real victim isn't the Jew anymore, but the Muslim. This delirious reversal denies the Jews the privileged status they are supposed to claim of the absolute victim, and compels them to yield the genocide to another wretched of the earth, the Muslim.

The next step in this reversal of the genocide is the metamorphosis of the victim into the tormentor, which to me seems to underlie all verbal manifestations of contemporary antisemitism. And the last straw is the competition of victims, or even the accusation now sometimes held against Jews in France, as in some Afro-American extremist groups in the U.S., of having benefited from the slave trade (thus from another genocide). I will simply observe that a sort of symbolic struggle between the Golem and the Muslim is being staged by a certain radical and Third Worldist stream, and has become quite fashionable and influential among students and younger generations. This apocalyptic struggle gives the discourse on Jews and Israel a new dimension, and the history of anti-Americanism lends a new meaning to the reprobation of Jews, who are thus deprived of their supposedly enviable status of victim for the benefit of the Palestinian.

Anti-Americanism, Antisemitism: The Past of a Confluent

At this point, it may be useful to go back to the common sources of French anti-Americanism and antisemitism. I will first mention briefly their history and I will then try to see what has been preserved of this past, although it may imply a shift from the right to the left. Once again, it must be stressed that when I speak of the amalgam between antisemitism and anti-Americanism, I do not mean that one cannot be without the other, but that those two phobias meet sometimes in a common refusal of modernity, of industrialization, in a fear, with many sexual connotations of imposing and glamorous women, of the razzle-dazzle and the cult of appearances embodied by Hollywood. The specialists of anti-Americanism usually date back to the 1920s and '30s, the actual amalgam of antisemitic and anti-American discourse,[9] which is to be found among certain writers and scholars, such as the founder of French political science André Siegfried or the now quite forgotten academician Georges Duhamel. Siegfried was indeed the one who spread the thesis of Jewish influence on the other side of the Atlantic, in his book *America Today*,[10] which was to influence generations of French students up to the 1950s, as Philippe Roger points out. But the origins of the confluence of the two themes can be traced back earlier.

At this point we may produce the following hypothesis, along with the German Anglicist of Hamburg University, Dietrich Schwanitz,[11] that the ancient origin of the amalgam could go back to the hostility aroused by English Puritanism, which was represented in Shakespeare's *Merchant of Venice*. Schwanitz believes, for example, that it is the Puritan, hidden beneath the features of Shylock, who is being criticized. The respect shown by the Puritans for the Old Testament, the tale associating them with the ten lost tribes of Israel, the readmission of Jews into England by Cromwell after Manasse ben Israel's diplomatic entreaties, all this is said to have contributed since the seventeenth century to establish a link between Protestant messianism and Judaism. This constellation may have influenced till today many of the current comments on the union between Southern Baptists and the Israeli state and sometimes of hostile perceptions. Together with the Puritans themselves, this connection migrated to the New World, but it also reenacted the Cromwellian primitive scene in the minds and representations of their opponents.[12]

The word "Americanization" was first introduced by Baudelaire (*Fusées*, feuillet 22, 1861) to describe a world agonizing under the onslaught of modernity that brings humanity backward to a repetitive and mechanic animality. The antimodern association of Americanization, apocalypse, and the reign of money will henceforth remain one of the main ingredients for the progressive association of anti-Americanism and antisemitism. If the turn of the 1920s and 1930s undoubtedly represents the era of crystallization of anti-Americanism into antisemitism, the preceding years cannot be reduced to a mere foreboding. As suggested by Philippe Roger,[13] an obscure French labor unionist, J. L. Chastenet, author of the suggestively titled *Oncle Shylock* (referring to the figure of Uncle Sam),[14] clearly finds his inspiration in one of the left-wing antisemitic lampooners of the nineteenth century, Toussenel, a disciple of Fourier's, who as early as 1845 had written *The Jews Kings of our Time*.[15] According to Toussenel, praised in Drumont's *La France juive*[16] as a pioneer of the antisemitism of the modern era, "Jerusalem has imposed a tribute on every State; the main profit of all the worker's production goes into the Jew's purse by the name of *national debt interest*." Anticapitalism and hostility toward financial "feudality" fidelities are soon to constitute the common point between the hatred for Jews and the hatred for America.

Edouard Drumont, whose sole ambition was to match Toussenel, devoted a few lines in his *France juive* to Americans, or should I say to American women. He classifies the American woman as the whorish and seductress Jewish female, hunting the fortune of the oldest French families, in a sort of inversion of Offenbach's *La Vie parisienne*, where it is the Brazilian merchant who is regularly being robbed by the Parisian whores. From America sprout Jewish creatures eager to skin the French aristocrats. "Paris is invaded by Americanism, almost as much as by Semitism," says Drumont. And he gibes at the "grand seigneur" who, in order to win some cute little Yankee, portrayed as "loud and spendthrift," sells his venerable château, which had been host to Louis XIV.[17] A detestation/fascination for the American female and for a female and Jewish America is found again in the character of Lola, the deceitful American girl supposedly fascinated by Jewish lovers, in Celine's *Voyage au bout de la nuit*, in a paroxysm of combined misogyny, anti-American, and anti-Jewish hatred.

But the amalgam of anti-Americanism and antisemitism will be strengthened by the problem of the nonsettlement of the debt contracted toward Washington during World War I. France's refusal to pay the debt, or at least its demand to merge it into German reparations, gave fuel to a great many speeches and lampoons whose motive, always the same, was soon to find its expression in the antisemitic myth of Shylock. According to the lampooners, France has already paid its pound of flesh with its 1.5 million dead, and did not owe anything more to the latecomers. The Marshall Plan undoubtedly revived this theme after the war, but in a form that expurgated its antisemitic dimension (for the time being at least).

One could hardly conclude this brief history without mentioning Celine. Because Celine not only is one of the greatest French writers of the twentieth century, whose influence is far more important than that of someone like Georges Duhamel, he was also the most violent and rabid antisemite. It would be unfair not noting that in the course of the decade preceding World War II, Celine was not the only one to mingle the hatred against America and the hatred against Jews. The bicephalous and monstrous "Golem" appears as early as 1931 in *La Grande peur des bien-pensants* [18] by the Christian and then monarchist novelist Georges Bernanos, who also wrote, after having given up his antisemitism and after World War II, *La France contre les robots*, which is sometimes described as one of the first explanations of political ecology (1945).[19] The United States is here hated for its "German" origins, as it was by Drumont, whose *La Grande peur* is actually a panegyric; it is the country of the Bad word as opposed to the evangelical Good word. Marcel Jouhandeau in his *Jewish Peril* (1936)[20] combines the two effects. As an explanation for the origin of his antisemitism, Jouhandeau mentions the visit of the Jew X. "On his returning from America, he triumphantly brings back with him the good news that France has been banished from the nations." We may observe following Philippe Roger and Tony Judt that in the late 1920s a continuous mass of reports on America overflows the French press. Paul Morand's *New York* is one of them, a book in which the diplomat insists on the common appearance and essence shared by Jews in Manhattan, Moscow, and France, and reactivates the theme of Jewish domination under the guise of a news report: "New York belongs to him [the Jew], whatever the 'one hundred per cent' Americans of Park Avenue may say. He holds the press, the film industry and the radio."[21]

Let's come back now to Celine. His anti-Jewish writings, never republished but widely circulated underground, represent the acme of the hatred against Jewish America. We shall not linger on the motives for Celine's antisemitism, whose virulence was such that he devoted three whole books to that topic. His unsuccessful love affairs, the fact that Hollywood turned down the screenplay of his *Voyage au bout de la nuit*, his contacts with Breton nationalism and in particular with the theoretician of the circular partly literary, partly political movement of the "bardic league" Taldir-Jaffrenou, the intrigues of the *Welt Dienst*, the laboratory for Nazi propaganda (whose contribution to the interconnection between the *Judenknechte*—"slaves of the Jews"—theme and the condemnation of "American plutocracy" personified by Roosevelt and his "Jewish ancestors" is better known since the discovery of Goebbels's diary): These are pretences for the rabid hatred towards Jews. The insistence on the Jewish theme was a means for Goebbels[22] to win over general opinion. All this has been put into light by various scholars, and particularly by Alice Kaplan. I will only add a few words concerning the intersection of antisemitism and the rejection of an America that, in the eyes of Dr. Destouches, was nothing less than mythical.

With Celine, our Judeo-American Golem, set off as a foil, reaches truly monstrous proportions. It was not with his lampoons (which were in fact real books) that Celine launched his attacks on "Jewish America." In fact, as early as the *Journey,* antisemitism looms up through an association: the "Negro-Judeo-Saxon music." But it is mainly in *Bagatelle pour un massacre*[23] that the Judeo-American myth reached its highest form. As we have seen with Drumont, the American female isn't spared, and it is once more through her that America becomes Jewish, while America spreads Jewishness all over the world thanks to Hollywood. "Between Hollywood, Paris, New York and Moscow," according to Celine, "a continuous propaganda circuit is established" and the artists "take part in the great colonization by the Jewish cinema." The Hollywood-Babylon theme is embodied by the image of the corrupting and producing Jew.[24] However, even in this aggravated form, in a filthy and scatological style, the heart of the matter isn't really different from Bernanos. For Celine, as well as for the author of *La Grande peur*, the Judeo-American Golem is represented by standardized modernity and progress. "The Jew holds all the governments, he commands all the standardization machinery, and he owns all the cables, all the currents, tomorrow all the robots." Here come the robots! Celine adds a typically Nazi touch, which has a great success in store: the reversal of the victim into the oppressor. Charlie Chaplin's persona is at the core of this mechanism of reversal of values, which had already appeared in *Mein Kampf*. It intimates that the Jews master the art of delusion and know how to appear as sympathetic characters in order to usurp the status of victims. Hence the obsession, among French antisemites, to exhibit the Jews' so-called "true nature," that of a predatory and repulsive animal: the *tenia* (the tapeworm). The comparison between the Jew and the tapeworm does in fact constitute a recurrent motto of anti-Jewish literature and, according to some psychoanalytic interpretations of the phenomenon, that stem perhaps from the anal fixation of the antisemite.[25] Actually, the image of the *tenia* is already quoted by Toussenel[26] as well as by Celine, and it has also been transmitted to the post-1945 world by Jean Genet: "I got up to shit at the rear of the plane, in the hope of getting rid of a three thousand years long tapeworm."[27]

With violence that the lampooners during the Occupation will barely be able to match, the Celinian rhetoric sets up the Judeo-American imagery as a foil for modernity in the good sense, that is, a modernity that allows for the clear distinction of popular culture and high culture.[28] Thus portrayed, modernity is opposed to a modernity that appears to be repetitive and unable to create, which blurs the distinction between art and kitsch and where the Jew's features remind those lent by Baudelaire to the Americanization of the world.

We shall now examine what became of the Golem in the following era, that is, after the Liberation.

"Crack-up within" the Golem:
An Anti-Americanism Temporarily Non-Antisemitic

After the war, anti-Americanism finds its main champion in Sartre, who is also known as the author of the *Réflexions sur la question juive* (1946).[29] While the Celinian influence can still be sensed among the right-wing extremists (soon to be neutralized by their Cold-War Atlantism), anti-American activism tilts over to the left wing. To put it bluntly: The contrast between our times and the postwar era, what we may consider as one of the novelties of the present time, consists in the reunion of anti-Americanism and antisemitism that had been set apart by Sartre. It is a reunion operated through the unlikely alliance of radical Islam and antiglobalization protest. It is highly meaningful that in the same year Sartre published *Antisemite and the Jew*, he published his famous play *La P...respectueuse* (1946). This play portrays for the first time the very French myth of "l'autre Amérique" (the other America). The good America is the one on the margins and is completly opposed to the white, conservative, WASP America, allegedly obsessed by the lynching of blacks.

It is an alternative that Sartre's followers, probably inspired by the virulence of his foreword to Frantz Fanon's *Les Damnés de la terre* (1961),[30] will fling themselves into. Jean Genet himself, supporting the Black Panther movement, granted it the same mythical dimension, as he was to do later on with the Palestinian "revolution" (unlike Sartre, who never failed to support Israel even during his Maoist period). This Palestinian revolution vested with a divinelike essence gives its opponents by comparison a diabolical aspect. "I did my best to understand how little this revolution resembled others and in some way I understood it," says the author of *Un captif amoureux*. Genet[31] here draws a parallel between Hitler and the heaps of dead bodies at Shatila, the scene of a refugee camp slaughter in Lebanon. The Palestinian as well as the Black Panther is even granted the mystical power of annihilating all lust in Genet.[32] With Genet the conflict opposing Jews and Palestinians is invested with a new eschatological gloss, in aesthetics of brutal and anguishing confrontation of good and evil.

Toward Rebirth of the "Golem"?

Although writers are most likely to bring it to its highest attention, the reconstitution of the frightful features of the Judeo-American Golem do not appear only among writers. It would also be interesting to observe how in the past ten years respectable sociologists and historians have exploited the recurrent theme of the New York intellectuals' right turn, as a kind of foreshadowing of the resurgence of the Judeo-American image currently assumed by the "neoconservative," or the alleged "Likudniks" of Washington, as they are sometimes described in France, whose supposed alliance with Protestant Baptists, modern avatar of the Cromwellian so-called association, is often set in front. In short, if the American Jews as they have been personified in France by Woody Allen (rather than Paul Wolfowitz or Robert Kagan) might have for a time won the sympathy of the French, especially the French liberal circles, this time seems now over. Because the conversion of a great many Jews to Zionism (with the end of communism and the reunion of former left-wingers to the old Jewish house) took place while public opinion, preceded by some of its writers, took a quite opposite direction. This hiatus between Jews and French public opinion may account for the present malaise. The violence concealed in the Judeo-American myth (the "Golem") has been preserved by the Sartrian and post-Sartrian anti-American violence. It might now recover the language of anti-Jewish hatred, if the antiglobalization protesters are not vigilant and if they carelessly set up radical Islam as the sacred icon of the revolutionary—as Genet did of the Fedayin in his *Captif Amoureux*. The success encountered at the European Social Meeting in November 2003 in the suburbs of Paris by the Islamic preacher Tariq Ramadan, who had publicly tackled a group he styled as "Jewish intellectuals," does not portend a very bright prospect.

Many signs seem to indicate this evolution, this association of the Jews with the right wing, on the side of the Bad America. For example, it is striking to note that Daniel Lindenberg, a historian from Paris VIII, the universitary stronghold of progressivism, where a kind of Third Worldist ideology as well as a fierce Palestinism is still culti-vated, entitled a whole chapter of his book published in October 2002: "When Jews Turn Right" (in English in the text). Without the least concern for collective stigmatization, he accuses Jewish intellectuals of a *"repli identitaire"* (withdrawal on identity). "The alliance of Jews with the forces of progress has been said to break off in America "and Lindenberg deplores it. "Are we now witnessing something similar in France?" he wonders.[33]

A new acme is reached once major philosophical works by Jewish writers are subject to radical ideological questionings directly related to geopolitical issues. It is very likely that the insistence on the origins of neoconservatism as espoused by the Jewish American philosopher Leo Strauss has much to do with this syndrome, which deeply modi-fies the image of Jews. In a fiercely ideologized interpretation, Strauss is sometimes reproached for his complacent attempt at dialogue with the Nazi philosopher Carl Schmitt. His studies on Maimonides are then scrutinized in quest of a proof of his elitism or his aristocratism. The German-born Strauss, whose works are slowly being translated in France and who has been rediscovered thanks to Aronian circles rep-resented by the journal *Commentaire*, is criticized for his famous work on *Persecution and the Art of Writing*. This text is said to bear undeni-able evidence for his support to the "right of lying" and deceiving the people (the allusion to the Iraq war and the debate over the massive destruction weapons is obvious).

Those in France as well as abroad who constantly refer to this short note dated 1952 usually forget to quote its conclusion, namely that Strauss believes the opposition between "exoterical" and "esoterical" discourse to be justified only for educational purposes in a democratic regime (and not in "tyrannical" regimes). But the thesis picturing Strauss as the "king of liars" takes a quite different dimension in France, where he is mainly and roughly known for his sympathy toward Zionism and his critique of the Enlightenment. In the portrait usually sketched of Strauss, his familiarity with Arabic philosophy and particularly with Al-Farabi is completely obliterated, as is the fact that his disciples were not only "neocons." The image of the philosopher inspiring the Washington "hawks" remains quite popular. The dominant discourse in France is that the United States is ruled by an organized sect, seated at the head of power, and influenced by a cunning philosopher whose political vision is prompted by the Schmittian distinction of friend and foe.[34]

Another Jewish philosopher who became popular in France in recent years and is now surrounded by general respect, Emmanuel Levinas, has also been attacked under the pretence that the texts collected in *Difficile Liberté*—a breviary for the young Jews of my generation—were responsible for the famous *"repli identitaire"* or "judeocentrism," which is now systematically ascribed to the Jews of France when they do not join in the chorus of public opinion or diplomacy. Levinas is condemned for having intimated, along with Hermann Cohen and Franz Rosenzweig, that Spinoza had been deservedly banished from the Jewish community. This seems unacceptable to those who, from Yirmiyahu Yovel to Edgar Morin, fancy in Spinoza an icon of Jewish modernity in the name of a sort of neo-Marranism, and the suggestion by both Strauss and Levinas that the author of the *Theologico-Political Treatise* is guilty of having fostered the Christian prejudice on Jews in order to gain popularity. This suggestion now ranks their works in the neoreactionary category, almost equivalent in France to "neoconservatism." In this exceedingly simplified polarity, whoever doesn't take sides with the progressive trends appears as a reactionary. In a recent interview with the journal (center–left wing) *Le Débat*[35] (according to which "there is now between those two nations [Israel and the United States] a messianism serving as a justification for every preemptive attack aimed at securing the sanctified State"), Jean Daniel, former chief editor of the weekly liberal *Nouvel Observateur* and whose latest book bears the suggestive title of *La Prison juive* (*The Jewish Prison*),[36] reproaches Levinas for having written in *Difficile Liberté* "that the thoughts and the creations of Jews in the world" sprang directly from a "Sacred History." He thus reproaches him for hanging on to a claim to "election" and shutting up Jews in "the goals of theological thought." We won't linger on the absurdity of this accusation, since we are well aware that such a claim to Jewish superiority is inconsistent with Levinas's reflections on alterity[37]. It is enough to point out how these insidious accusations can only disclose the malaise of this troubled era, when Israel is intellectually delegitimized because of its assimilation of wealth and power.

Conclusion

How come this rhetoric, whose themes endlessly repeat themselves, and whose core as we have shown was formed a long time ago, has now become unbearable for the Jews of France? How did Jews and Americans get trapped together in the representation of their union? It is certain that in the eyes of their adversaries it is America that surreptitiously gives anti-Zionism its universal dimension. The refusal of French intellectuals to interpret the Israel-Palestinian conflict other than on the mode of an eschatological struggle, where the fate of the planet is at stake and not as a local conflict, contributes to this process. In *Spectres de Marx* (ed. Galilée, 1993),[38] Jacques Derrida presented the Middle East, not unlike Genet (to whom he devoted part of *Glas*, by the way)[39] as the place or the figure for "the greatest symptomatic or metonymic concentration of what is still irreducible within the global conjuncture in which is now embedded the question "what of Marxism?" Derrida also writes that "the war for the appropriation of Jerusalem is the global war." Such formulas bestow a philosophical caution to a political mythology. Why such an amalgam? The answer comes precisely from the double reversal mentioned earlier on: that of the Jewish public opinion in favor of the support of Israel (that is definitively established in France in 1967, when the Jewish state is compelled to accept the United States as its new champion, after De Gaulle's defection, whose discourse reinstalled the public expression of antisemitism at the head of the government during a famous press conference on November 27, 1967, on "the elite people, self-confident, proud and dominating") and that of the progressive reversal of non-Jewish public opinion toward a certain hostility against Israel.

It is probably these that make it difficult for Jews to have access to public space or speech and submits them to a new oath *more judaic*, whose terms seem to radicalize: First requested to condemn "Sharon's policy," it is sometimes the very legitimacy of the Zionist enterprise that the Jew is expected to question if he wants to be given access to the public debate through the triumphant and uncritical reception made in France to the new Israeli historians (even though the best one of them, Benny Morris, came down in their regard, by designating Arafat as responsible for the failure of the peace process). Such is the invisible wall that renders the atmosphere intolerable for the Jews of France and makes them outcasts by depicting them again in the form of racist and potentially totalitarian white conservatism, the dark face of the modernity. All the more because the atmosphere thickens after two decades during which, via the Shoah testimony, the trials for crimes against humanity, but also through the public interest given by many French intellectuals to Jewish history and culture, which could induce them to think that the rise of Judeo-French union, more fertile even than the Judeo-German one (with all the reserve that may be made on its reality) was to be expected. The Jews of France lead a harsher life because of such letdowns, which at bottom could really carry a regression, if not a betrayal of the promises of emancipation. It is a fact that the road to a new symbiosis has not been taken or suddenly interrupted, which to quote the title of the famous book by Ahad Ha'am, brings anew the Jews of France *'al Parachat Drakhim*—at a crossroads.

Notes

1. *L'Ennemi américain. Généalogie de l'antiaméricanisme français*, Paris, Seuil, 2002.

2. *Peuple juif ou problème juif?* Paris, La Découverte/Poche, 1996.

3. *Les Mythes fondateurs de la politique israélienne*, Paris, La Vieille Taupe n°2, 1995.

4. *L'Effroyable imposture*, Paris, éditions Carnot, 2002.

5. "Antisemitism as a Cultural Code: Reflections on the History and Historiography of Antisemitism in Imperial Germany," Leo Baeck Institute, Year Book, XXIII (23), 1978.

6. *Multitude, War and Democracy in the Age of Empire*, New York, Penguin, 2004. We quote the French version of the text (and the translation is ours): *Multitude, Guerre et démocratie à l'âge de l'empire*, trs. from English (USA) by Nicolas Guilhot; Paris, La Découverte, 2004, pp. 23–25.

7. *Remnants of Auschwitz: The Witness and the Archive*, translated by Daniel Heller-Roazen, New York, Zone-Books, 2000.

8. See on this issue Goetz Nordbruch, *The Socio-Historical Background of Holocaust Denial in Arab Countries: Reaction to Roger Garaudy's* The Founding Myths of Israeli Politics, Jerusalem, SICSA, 2001.

9. Roger, *L'Ennemi américan,* and Tony Judt, *Past Imperfect: French Intellectuals, 1944–1956*, University of California Press, 1994.

10. *Les Etats-Unis d'aujourd'hui*, Paris, Armand Colin, 1927; see on this issue Roger, *L'Ennemi américan*, p. 398 sq.

11. *Das Shylock Syndrom oder Die Dramaturgie der Barbarei*, Diana Taschenbücher, 1998.

12. See also on this issue Michael Walzer, *The Revolution of the Saints: A Study in the Origins of Radical Politics*, Harvard University Press, 1965, and *Exodus and Revolution*, Basic Books, 1985.

13. Ibidem.

14. *L'Oncle Shylock ou l'impérialisme américain à la conquête du monde*, Paris, Flammarion, 1927.

15. Philippe Roger, *op. cit.*, p. 413. Alphonse Toussenel, *Les Juifs rois de l'époque. Histoire de la féodalité financière*, 1844.

16. *La France juive*, Paris, Marpon-Flamarion, 1886.

17. «L'Américanisme a envahi Paris presqu'autant que le sémitisme. [...] Certaines familles yankees, venues primitivement d'Allemagne et ayant laissé leur Juiverie dans la traversée de l'Atlantique, s'embarque un beau jour avec une petite fortune, deux ou trois cent mille francs, qu'elles dépensent bravement en un an avec un bruit étourdissant .[...] Le mariage a lieu... Voilà la petite yankee duchesse, marquise, comtesse. L'heure sonne où l'heureux époux juge qu'il serait temps de monnoyer quelques pépites de ces mines inépuisables, de se faire envoyer un peu

d'argent de ces maisons de banque ou de commerce. Hélas ! Les mines ont été inondées, la maison de banque est en faillite. Le père qui qui, souvent, n'avait pas même donné de trousseau, mais qui avait promis une rente énorme est devenu fou. Le réveil est dur pour quelques uns. Celui-ci prend son parti, vend son château où Louis XIV avait reçu l'hospitalité, envoie aux enchères les meubles anciens et jusqu'aux paravents de sa grand'-mère pour suffire aux caprices d'une enfant gâtée » , Edouard Drumont, *La France juive*, tome II, pp. 258–59. It is interesting enough to see in this fierce antisemitic book a kind of emergence of the myth of the Jewish American princess.

18. *La Grande peur des bien-pensants*, Paris, Le Livre de poche, 1998.

19. « Vous saurez ce que c'est qu'une certaine paix, concludes Bernanos at the end of *La Grande peur des bien-pensants*(…) celle qu'imagine peut-être, en croquant ses cacahuètes au sucre, quelque petit cireur de bottes yankee, un marmot à tête de rat, demi-saxon demi-juif, avec on ne sait quoi de l'ancêtre nègre au fond de sa moelle enragée, le futur roi de l'Acier, du Caoutchouc, du Pétrole, le Trusteur des Trusts le futur maître d'une planète standardisé, ce dieu que l'Univers attend, le dieu d'un univers sans Dieu », ibidem, pp. 367–68.

20. *Le Péril juif*, Paris, éditions Sorlot, 1936.

21. *New York*, Paris, Flammarion, 1930.

22. See on this issue Christian Barth, *Goebbels und die Juden*, Paderborn, Ferdinand Schöningh, 2003.

23. Paris, Denoël, 1937.

24. « Razzia tous les dimanches. La sélection française des petits tendrons de beauté se trouve particulièrement guettée par les grands chacals juifs de la Californie » (p.222). To conceive the level of violence reached by Celine in his antisemitic writings, let us quote quite exstensively some extracts stemmed from *Bagatelle*... where the anti-American sometimes roughly antimodernist thema crosses the antisemitic one: « propagande, or, publicité, presse d'Hollywood la juive à Moscou la youtre » ; « entre Hollywood, Paris, New York et Moscou un circuit de bourrage continu. Charlie Chaplin travaille aussi magnifiquement pour la cause […] c'est un grand pionnier de l'impérialisme juif » (p. 53) ; « le Juif a tout standardisé dans le domaine des arts majeurs » and further on « le Juif tient tous les gouvernements, il commande à toutes les machines à standardiser, il possède tous les cables, tous les courants, demain tous les robots » (p. 184) ; and about the circulation of artists between France and California: « [these actors] participent à la grande colonisation

mondiale par le cinéma juif…chacun apportant à Hollywood tour à tour sa petite trahison personnelle, ses petits renseignements intimes, ses petites félonies, infiniment anxieux de plaire encore aux Ben Mayer, Ben Zakor. » And about American women: « les Américaines yankees qu'on entend pousser de tels cris, créer de tels raffuts et universels hurlements (lynchage, pétitions, procès, etc.) dès qu'un nègre les encule (en public !) comment qu'elles se marient aux Juifs ! et à toute berzingue ! Et tant que ça peut ! Et plein les miches ! Les Juifs font le plein, comme épouseurs aux Etats-Unis. Le Juif est vicieux, le Juif est riche, le Juif bourre bien, le Juif 'négrite' bien plus que le nègre. Encore un flan très prodigieux que cette barrière des races aux U.S.A.! Une barrière de bites! Mais minute! Je vais, à mon tour, vous dire un peu l'avenir: Un jour les Juifs emmèneront les nègres, leurs frères, leurs troupes de choc sur les derniers 'centres' blancs, les réduiront tous ivrognes à l'esclavage. Hurlement dans le quartier 'blanc'… Les nègres en bringue, ils iront voir, il feront danser les blancs pour eux, la 'blanc-boula' » (p. 275).

25. See Bela Grunberger, Pierre Dessuant, *Narcissisme, christianime, antisémtisme*, Arles, Actes-Sud, 1997.

26. « [Le despotisme du coffre-fort] envahit la chaumière du pauvre comme le palais des princes ; tout aliment convient à sa voracité. Comme le mercure subtil qui s'insinue par sa pesanteur et sa fluidité à travers tous les pores de la gangue pour s'emparer des plus minimes parcelles de métal précieux qu'elle renferme ; comme le hideux ténia, dont les anneaux parasites suivent dans leur circonvolution tous les viscères du corps humain, ainsi le vampire mercantile fait courir ses suçoirs jusqu'aux ramifications extrêmes de l'organisme social pour en pomper toute la substance et en soutirer tous les sucs » *Les Juifs rois de l'époque*, quoted in *E.Drumont*, op. cit., Tome I, pp. 349–50.

27. « A partir de ce mot [« Sayonara »], je fus attentif à la manière dont s'enlevait par lambeaux de mon corps au risque de laisser nu et blanc la noire et certainement épaisse morale judéo-chrétienne. […] Je me levais pourtant afin d'aller chier à l'arrière de l'avion, espérant me libérer d'un ver solitaire long de trois mille ans » *Un Captif amoureux*, Paris, Gallimard, 1986 pp. 65–66. Genet also went as far as to write enigmatically: "Hitler est sauf d'avoir brûlé ou fait brûler des Juifs et d'avoir caressé un berger allemand," ibidem, p. 386. See on this issue by Eric Marty, *Bref Séjour à Jérusalem*, « l'Infini », Paris, Gallimard, 2003 ; and « Jean Genet, tabou » in *Que reste-t-il de nos tabous ? 15ème Forum Le Monde/Le Mans, octobre 2003*, directed by Nicolas Weill, Rennes, Presses Universitaires de Rennes, 2004, pp. 195–210. About Genet's antisemitism see also Eric Marty, *Bref séjour à Jérusalem*, Paris, Gallimard, 2003, and

Ivan Jablonka, *Les Vérités inavouables de Jean Genet,* Paris, Seuil, 2004, and for a counterargumentation, see René de Ceccaty, « Jean Genet antisémite ? sur une tenace rumeur », *Critique,* november 2006, N°714, Paris, Minuit, 2006, pp. 895–911.

28. See by Alice Kaplan and Philippe Roussin, "Celine, USA," *South Atlantic Quarterly* (spring 1994), vol 93, no 2.

29. Jean-Paul Sartre, *Antisemite and Jew: An Exploration of the Etiology of Hate,* with an introduction by Michael Walzer, Schocken Books, 1995. About the polemics and controversial aspects of Sartre's antisemitism and the Jew, see inter alia Pierre Birnbaum, « Réflexions peinées sur 'Réflexions sur la question juive' », *Les Cahiers du judaïsme,* automne 1998, n°3, pp. 87–106, and the English version of the text "Sorry Afterthoughts on Antisemite and Jew," *October,* n°87, hiver 1999, pp. 89–106.

30. *The Wretched Earth,* translated by Constance Farrington, New York, 1965.

31. See above note 27.

32. « Le seul trouble que j'éprouvais : que cette absence de désir correspondît avec la *'matérialisation'* de mes propres désirs amoureux, à moins, comme je l'ai dit, que cette *'réalité-là'* rendît vaine *'la réalité en moi'* des fantasmes. Ainsi en avait-il été des Panthères noires aux U.S.A. »

33. *Le Rappel à l'ordre: Enquête sur les nouveaux réactionnaires,* Paris, Editions Le Seuil, 2002.

34. To a more balanced view of this issue, see *Critique,* n°682, « Le philosophe et les 'faucons' », March 2004.

35. September-October, 2004, Gallimard.

36. Paris, Odile Jacob, 2004.

37. See also *La Prison juive,* op. cit., p. 114.

38. *Specters of Marx: The State of the Debt, the Work of Mourning, & the New International,* translated by Peggy Kamuf, London, Routledge 1994. Here the translation is ours.

39. *Glas,* translated by John P. Leavey Jr. and Richard Rand, Lincoln: University of Nebraska Press, 1986.

5

Eastern Europe:
Antisemitism in the Wake of Holocaust-Related Issues

Efraim Zuroff

No discussion of contemporary European antisemitism can avoid dealing with the Holocaust and its impact on Europe, from the bloody events of the Shoah to its present-day influence on European attitudes, policies, culture, and relations with Israel and the Jewish people. The subject is unavoidable, not only because of the enormous trauma wrought by that watershed event in the annals of Jewish history and of mankind, but also due to the interesting and surprising developments over the course of the past half century in how that event has been perceived in Europe and throughout the world.

For the past fifty years, and with particular intensity during the past three decades, the Jewish world has invested many millions of dollars in Holocaust commemoration and education.[1] The general assumption behind this enormous investment was that knowledge and understanding of that unique catastrophe and its historical context and lessons would constitute the best antidote possible to contemporary antisemitism, increase ethnic and religious tolerance, and help combat racism, xenophobia, and nationalist extremism.[2] After all, how could anyone but the most peripheral elements in society even consider being antisemitic after the Shoah? In that respect, the unwritten, never fully formulated, and openly admitted goal was to turn the Holocaust into the universal paradigm for the violation of human rights and the most widely acknowledged symbol of man's inhumanity to his fellow man, and World War II into the classic conflict between the forces of Good and Evil and thereby help ensure the security and physical future of the Jewish people throughout the Diaspora and in the state of Israel.

The extent to which this strategy has been successful, and that the Holocaust has indeed been turned into the universal symbol of barbaric cruelty par excellence and of unwarranted human suffering and has thoroughly permeated the European mind-set, can be illustrated by three random events that took place in three different European countries in the course of several days during the second week of October 2004.

The first is an initiative by the local council of the Scottish village of Dunscore, launched in early October 2004, to honor a Christian missionary named Jane Haining, who was born nearby and in 1944 was murdered in the gas chambers of Auschwitz as "a victim of the Holocaust." The idea that those seeking to honor a woman who devoted her life to influencing Jews to abandon their faith want her recognized as "a victim of the Holocust,"[3] clearly underscores the special resonance attributed to those victimized by the Nazis, and the pseudo-sanctification of those victims.

The second example relates to an honor bestowed by the Spanish government upon a soldier named Angel Salamanca, who was among the Spanish troops sent by Franco to fight with the Germans against the Soviet Union during World War II. Salamanca was honored at the October 12 parade to mark Spain's annual celebration of its armed forces, a step that aroused considerable controversy, and particularly angered leftist politicians, who rejected this gesture as an attempt to create a false equivalency between those who fought against fascism and those who fought alongside the Germans. Spanish defense minister Jose Bono claimed, however, that the initiation was motivated by a desire to achieve reconciliation and that the parade sought to honor "all Spaniards who fought for the principles they believed in."[4] This attempt to grant recognition to all the Spaniards who fought in World War II regardless of the side they took clearly emphasizes the enormous importance attached by Europeans to the events of World War II and the desire to achieve moral legitimacy for all those who served in that conflict.

The third incident took place on October 11, 2004, in France, where Bruno Golnisch, who is regarded as the second-ranking leader of the French extremist right-wing party, the National Front, expressed doubts as to the existence of gas chambers and hinted that he believed that the number of victims of the Shoah was less than the generally assumed figure (of 6 million).[5] The ongoing efforts by leaders of antisemitic elements such as the National Front to undermine the credibility of the commonly accepted narrative of the Holocaust are at least in part a reflection of the growing awareness of the importance of the Holocaust as a watershed event in European history and the effect of this recognition on the attitude of Europeans and others towards Jews and the state of Israel.

With the memory and awareness of the Holocaust an increasingly powerful factor in contemporary European life, and with Holocaust education increasingly regarded as a bulwark against antisemitism,[6] it is ironic that during the past fifteen years it has been Holocaust-related issues, more than any others, which have been the major catalyst for antisemitism in Eastern Europe.

Yet since this antisemitism, which has primarily focused on undermining the credibility and authenticity of the Jewish Holocaust narrative, has not resulted in widespread anti-Jewish violence similar to the attacks that reached such dangerous levels in Western Europe, it has hereto attracted minimal attention. But the underlying motivation for the animus against Jews and its impact on local societies throughout Eastern Europe are definitely worthy of scrutiny since they pose a serious potential danger and already are having a negative impact on Jewish life in these countries.

The best way to analyze this phenomenon is to examine the reactions in various countries to four of the six specific Holocaust-related issues, which have emerged as central questions in Eastern Europe in the wake of the fall of communism and the dismemberment of the Soviet Union. (While the fifth, and especially the sixth, issues are also relevant in this context, they are beyond the scope of this article and will be dealt with in future research.) Those events have produced the historical and political circumstances in which the newly independent and newly democratic regimes of Eastern Europe have been forced to confront their Holocaust pasts, which in most cases included extensive complicity by the local population in the murder of the Jews.[7] Thus, whereas all questions relating to the events of the Holocaust were previously determined by communist ideology and interests,[8] these questions were reopened in the late eighties and early nineties and for the first time these countries could acknowledge the truth and act upon it in a practical manner.

The specific Holocaust-related issues that had to be addressed by these governments were the following:

1. Acknowledgment of complicity by the local population in the murder of the Jews and an apology for those crimes

2. Commemoration of the victims

3. Prosecution of the perpetrators

4. Documentation of the crimes

5. Introduction of Holocaust education into the curriculum and the preparation of appropriate educational materials

6. Restitution of communal and individual property

Acknowledgment of Holocaust Crimes

Invariably, the first step that had to be taken in the process of facing the past was an acknowledgment of the crimes of the Holocaust and the participation of locals in the murder of the Jews. In many instances such an apology was made in the framework of a visit by the head of state to Israel, although there were also cases in which the local parliament passed such a resolution. Thus, for example, both Lithuanian prime minister Adolfas Slezevicius and President Algirdas Brazauskas formally apologized for Holocaust crimes during visits to Israel,[9] as did Latvian president Guntis Ulmanis,[10] Croatian president Stjepan Mesic,[11] and Polish president Lech Walesa.[12]

While these acknowledgments of guilt and apologies were considered in Jewish circles as a necessary first step toward reconciliation—and certainly a requirement of a state visit to Israel—such statements were often distinctly unpopular and severely criticized at home, where nationalist and other elements either denied the historical facts or believed that reciprocal apologies for crimes by Jewish communists should have been made by Israeli leaders. Thus, for example, both Slezevicius and Brazauskas were roundly criticized by a wide spectrum of Lithuanian public opinion for their apologies,[13] as was Polish president Lech Walesa for asking for forgiveness from the podium of the Israeli Knesset.[14] In Hungary, Prime Minister Gyula Horn was sued by the publisher of a local edition of *Mein Kampf,* who argued that by apologizing for Hungarian Holocaust crimes, the premier had violated his personal rights by suggesting that he was a member of a guilty nation.[15]

Particularly telling in this regard is the declaration condemning "the annihilation of the Jewish people during the years of the German occupation in Lithuania" passed by the Lithuanian Supreme Council on May 8, 1990. Although the declaration specifically stated that it was being issued "on behalf of the Lithuanian people," it attributes guilt for the crimes committed in Lithuania during the Holocaust to "Lithuanian citizens," a category clearly not restricted to those of Lithuanian nationality, which could even (by a twist of perverted logic) include Jews. Thus the Lithuanian parliament sought to differentiate between the ostensibly blameless "Lithuanian people" and the murderers who were "Lithuanian citizens," a distinction that is not supported by the historical record.[16]

Commemoration of the Victims

While this issue takes many different forms, the most important in our opinion is the decision to establish a special memorial day for the victims of the Holocaust. In fact, the growing number of countries that have taken this step, originally initiated by the state of Israel, which until 1979 was the only country to do so,[17] is another powerful indicator of the growing significance with which the Holocaust is regarded, especially in Europe. In this context, however, one of the key issues is the choice of the date for the memorial day, which often reflects local attitudes toward dealing with the Holocaust. Thus, for example, twelve countries, including Germany, have chosen January 27, the date of the liberation of the Auschwitz concentration camp, rather than a date linked to historic events in their own country, which could probably have added significantly to the impact of local observance. (Eleven countries have preferred to adopt a date linked to their own history.)[18]

One of the latest countries to choose January 27 has been Estonia, where the decision to observe a memorial day for the victims of the Holocaust aroused considerable controversy and was singularly unpopular. Typical of the local reactions to the decision was the following question posed to an official of the Simon Wiesenthal Center who had lobbied the government to choose a special day to commemorate the Holocaust:

> You're demanding that all the peoples of the world including Estonia introduce the Jewish Holocaust memorial day. I'm wondering when will the memorial day for [the] Estonian mass deportations of 1941 and 1949 be introduced in Israel. Do you think that the war sufferings of one nation should be put above others and the suffering of other nations are nothing to speak of?[19]

This sentiment was clearly expressed in a public opinion poll conducted by the popular Estonian daily *Eesti Paevaleht*, which asked Estonians whether they supported the establishment of a special memorial day for the victims of the Holocaust. Ninety-three percent of the respondents disapproved and only 7 percent approved.[20]

Also of note is the choice of January 27, which has no ostensible link whatsoever to the history of the Holocaust in Estonia. (No Estonian Jews were deported to Auschwitz.) In fact, Estonian officials rejected a suggestion by the Simon Wiesenthal Center that they choose either January 20, the date of the infamous Wannsee Conference in 1942, at which the implementation of the Final Solution was discussed and Estonia was declared *Judenrein* (free of Jews), or August 7, the date on which the 36th Estonian Security Battalion murdered Jews in Nowogrudok, Belarus.[21]

Another Eastern European country that chose a date for its Holocaust memorial day, which is of questionable value, is Lithuania. The date chosen in Vilnius, September 23, marks the day of the evacuation of the Vilnius (Vilna) ghetto,[22] which was primarily carried out by the Germans and was accompanied by the mass murder of the remaining Jewish inmates. More important, it is not linked to the extensive mass murders carried out throughout the country by Lithuanian vigilantes and security police during the initial half year of the German occupation. This (most probably intentional) decision to divert the focus of the Lithuanian observances of Holocaust memorial day facilitates the minimalization of Lithuanian participation in the crimes of the Holocaust, a tendency clearly reflected in government policy from the regaining of independence.[23]

Prosecution of Perpetrators/Nazi War Criminals

Of all the practical Holocaust-related issues that have faced Eastern European governments in the aftermath of the fall of communism, this has undoubtedly been the most problematic and on which the least has been achieved. Thus almost fifteen years after the breakup of the Soviet Union and the return of democracy to communist Eastern Europe, a total of three Nazi war criminals—Lithuanian Security Police commander Kazys Gimzauskas in Lithuania, Chelmno death camp operative Henryk Mania in Poland, and Jasenovac concentration camp commander Dinko Sakic in Croatia—have been convicted, with only the latter two actually having been punished for their crimes. These figures, more than anything, reflect a distinct lack of political will to deal with such cases, have proven to be extremely unpopular in these societies, and have aroused considerable antisemitic sentiment reflected in various ways.

Numerous examples can be adduced to illustrate the abysmal failure to prosecute Holocaust perpetrators. In fact, with the exception of Poland, there has not been a single country that has initiated an investigation of such a case upon its own initiative. To the extent that any such cases were ever dealt with, it was invariably instances where the suspects were investigated and/or prosecuted elsewhere, primarily in the United States, or were located by groups such as the Simon Wiesenthal Center which lobbied for their investigation, a demand usually supported by the United States and Israel. Even worse, several of the countries, such as Lithuania, Latvia, and Romania, granted pardons to Holocaust perpetrators convicted by the Soviets or communists, even though individuals who had participated in genocide were not eligible for such rehabilitations.[24]

This problem had been particularly acute in the former Soviet republics of Lithuania, Latvia, and Estonia, where local participation in the crimes of the Holocaust was particularly extensive, and contributed to the high rates of Jewish victimology in all three countries. Yet, despite the existence of numerous unprosecuted Nazi war criminals in the Baltic countries, as well as others living overseas, practically no concrete results have been achieved on this issue.[25]

This failure is most evident in Lithuania, which had the largest pre–World War II Jewish community in the Baltics, and in which over 210,000 Jews were murdered during the Holocaust, many by Lithuanians. Among those actively involved in these crimes were twelve individuals who had escaped to the United States shortly after World War II and against whom the United States had taken legal action for concealing their wartime activities, at least eleven of whom returned to Lithuania once it obtained independence. Among the returnees were several prominent figures in the World War II Lithuanian Security Police (Saugumas), such as Vilnius district commander Aleksandras Lileikis and his deputy Kazys Gimzauskas. Although both arrived in Vilnius (Gimzauskas in 1993; Lileikis in June 1996) in relatively good health, they were indicted only after they were no longer medically fit to stand trial (Gimzauskas on November 20, 1997; Lileikis on February 6, 1998). Neither was forced to appear in court (Lileikis did so voluntarily once for ten minutes on November 5, 1998, and briefly followed one session by video hookup on June 23, 2000), nor were they ever punished for their crimes. Liliekis died on September 26, 2000, before his trial was completed, whereas by the time Gimzauskas was convicted, on January 14, 2001, he was ruled unfit for punishment. Neither sat even one minute in jail despite the important roles they played in the mass murder of the Jews of Vilnius.[26]

The cases of these Nazi war criminals served as focal points of opposition by various segments of Lithuanian society to the prosecution of local Nazi collaborators, and especially to the exposure of the critical and extensive role played by Lithuanians in Holocaust crimes. In fact, any initiative to bring Holocaust perpetrators to justice in Lithuania invariably led to a variety of negative reactions, some of which included elements of violence. Thus, for example, in response to the launching in Lithuania of the Simon Wiesenthal Center's "Operation: Last Chance" project, which offers financial rewards for information that will facilitate the prosecution and punishment of Nazi war criminals, a member of the Taurage city council burned an Israeli flag in the center of town and drove around the town playing Nazi marches on a loudspeaker.[27]

Additional efforts to facilitate the prosecution of local Nazi criminals spawned numerous antisemitic reactions, particularly in local Internet forums and especially on www.delfi.lt, and who knows how many instances of vandalization of Jewish memorials and cemeteries.[28] I also believe they had an important impact on the decision of the Lithuanian government to seek the extradition from Israel of two Lithuanian Jews alleged to have committed crimes against Lithuanians in the service of the KGB.[29] In fact, Israel refused a Lithuanian request for judicial assistance in at least one of these cases, on the grounds that since approximately two dozen Lithuanians of equivalent or higher rank who served in the same unit as the suspect were never investigated, let alone prosecuted, the decision to investigate him stemmed from antisemitism and could therefore be legally rejected.[30] This fact was highlighted by nationalist elements whenever Jewish groups lobbied for the prosecution of Lithuanians for Holocaust crimes.[31]

Another country that has done very little to prosecute its own Nazi war criminals has been Estonia. The Estonian authorities have hereto never initiated a single investigation of a local Holocaust perpetrator, and the case of an Estonian suspect who returned to the country after being prosecuted in the United States, for example, has dragged on with no results. In July 2002 the Wiesenthal Center submitted the names of sixteen members of the 36th Estonian Police Battalion, who were decorated in December 1942 for their service with the Nazis, to the Estonian Security Police Board as possible suspects in the murder of the Jews of Nowogrudok, Belarus, on August 7, 1942, which was carried out by members of this unit (among others). The Security Police Board announced approximately two weeks later that there was no evidence to link the unit to the murder of the Jews of Nowogrudok, despite the fact that its participation in this crime was established by the Estonian International Commission for the Investigation of Crimes Against Humanity and confirmed by survivor witnesses. The fact that the Estonian Security Police Board did not even bother to mention their investigation of this case in responding to the Wiesenthal Center annual questionnaire on Nazi war crimes investigations is perhaps the best indication of the total lack of political will in Tallinn to prosecute Holocaust perpetrators.[32]

The situation in this regard is even worse in countries like the Ukraine, Romania, and Belarus, which since achieving independence or returning to democracy have not initiated a single investigation, let alone prosecution, of a local Nazi war criminal. Cases of crimes committed by their nationals or on their territory that have been prosecuted elsewhere have never elicited any interest or response by these countries.[33]

Documentation of Holocaust Crimes

The sins of omission and commission in this regard take various forms, among them the relativization of Holocaust crimes, the attempts to equate communist crimes to those of the Shoah, the minimalization of the participation of the local population in the mass murder of the Jews, the exaggeration of the help provided to Jews by local residents, and last, but certainly not least, outright Holocaust denial and even the attribution of Shoah crimes to the victims themselves.

One of the most prevalent tendencies in postcommunist Eastern Europe has been the attempt to create a false symmetry between Nazi and communist crimes, and the erroneous classification of the latter as genocide. This can clearly be seen, for example, in the Baltics,

where all three post-Soviet republics established historical commissions of inquiry to investigate the German and Soviet occupations of
their country. Despite protests from various quarters,[34] each country
insisted upon the establishment of a single commission to investigate
both the German and communist occupations, thereby strengthening
their contention of the equivalency of the tragedies.[35]

The theory of the "double genocide" or the symmetry between
Nazi and communist crimes was particularly strong in Lithuania,
where it achieved prominence in the wake of the revelations by the
Simon Wiesenthal Center in 1991 that the Lithuanian government
had granted rehabilitations to numerous Lithuanian Nazi collaborators.[36] Part of the response to these accusations was to emphasize the
role of Jewish communists in Soviet crimes committed in Lithuania
as a counterbalance and/or as justification for the participation of
Lithuanians in Holocaust crimes, a tendency that continues to remain
strong in Lithuania.[37] Along the same lines, in the wake of the apology for the crimes of the proffered by President Brazauskas in Israel,
numerous Lithuanians countered by pointing to Jewish participation
in communist crimes, asking "Who will apologize to the Lithuanian
nation?"[38] Typical of these comments was the article by popular writer
Jonas Avzyius, who wrote that:

> His Excellency obediently apologized for Lithuanian criminals, who
> murdered Jews during the Nazi occupation. But there was not the
> slightest hint that the President of Israel should do something simi-
> lar, condemning his Jewish countrymen, who worked in repressive
> institutions in Lithuania occupied by the Soviets and sent thousands
> of Lithuanians to concentration camps.[39]

Another example of the effort to present communist crimes as the
equivalent of those of the Holocaust can be seen at the very highest
level in Latvia. Thus in January 2004, at a conference sponsored by
the Task Force for International Cooperation on Holocaust Education
Remembrance and Research, Latvian president Vaira Vike-Freiberga
emphasized two major points: that communist crimes were just as ter-
rible as those of the Holocaust, and that the measures taken by the
communists in Latvia constituted genocide. Despite the relevance of
the Holocaust in this context, the Latvian president only mentioned it
once in passing, with nary a word about Latvian complicity in Shoah
crimes.[40] When an official of the Simon Wiesenthal Center explained

in an op-ed that the president's presentation did not reflect the historical events accurately,[41] there were calls for his murder as well as various
antisemitic comments on a prominent Latvian news website.[42]

Three additional tendencies prevalent in Eastern Europe, which
are to confront the participation of local residents in
Holocaust, are: the attribution of Holocaust crimes
entirely to German and Austrian Nazis (as opposed to locals); the exaggeration of the number of, and scope of, the assistance provided by
local, righteous Gentiles, and the attempts to claim that the only local
participants in Holocaust crimes were criminals and/or totally peripheral elements of society. Instances of each tendency may be found in
practically every postcommunist society. Thus, for example, various
Polish historians refused to accept the findings regarding the responsibility of Poles for the murder of the Jews of Jedwabne as described by
historian Jan Gross in his book *Neighbors*. In Lithuania, local officials
opposed the inclusion of the phrase "and their local accomplices" on
a memorial monument at Ponar (Paneriai), site of the mass murder of
the Jews of Vilnius, which attributed the killings to the Nazis. The Hungarian government planned in 1998 to rebuild the Hungarian pavilion
at Auschwitz in such a manner that the blame for the annihilation of
the Jews was almost exclusively placed upon the Germans.[43] In Estonia, the local media invested much effort to disprove the findings of
the international commission of historians which established that the
36th Battalion of the Estonian Security Police actively participated in
the murder of the Jews of Nowogrudok, Belarus.[44]

In Lithuania, the number of righteous Gentiles and the scope
of their assistance has been often exaggerated and presented as a
counterbalance to the deeds of the local perpetrators, to the extent
that they are acknowledged.[45] The latter are often portrayed as being
on the fringe of Lithuanian society, such as in the speech made by
Lithuanian prime minister Gediminas Vagnorius at the dedication
of a memorial monument at Ponar where he referred to the killers as
"a group of criminals."[46] In Latvia, the role of the Arajs Kommando
has been emphasized to the virtual exclusion of any other Latvians,
despite the involvement of many others in the killing of Jews.[47] In
Hungary, the tendency has been to focus solely on the Arrow Cross,
ignoring the role played by the Hungarian gendarmerie and others
throughout the entire country, whereas in Romania the blame is often
cast solely upon the Iron Guard, despite the fact that the Romanian

government bears most of the responsibility for the murder of the Jews.[48]

Finally, there are the cases of outright Holocaust denial and those in which the Jews themselves are blamed for the Holocaust. Thus, for example, Slovak deputy minister of culture Stanislavs Panis claimed in 1992 that it was "technically impossible" for the Nazis to murder 6 million Jews in camps and that Auschwitz was an "invention" of the Jews to extort compensation from Germany. Romanian presidential candidate Corneliu Vadim Tudor of the Greater Romania Party (PRM) described the Holocaust in 1994 as "a Zionist scheme aimed at squeezing out from Germany about 100 billion Deutsch marks and to terrorize for more than 40 years, all those who do not acquiesce to the Jewish yoke." (He has since changed his mind.) In Poland, neofascist political leader Boleslaw Tejkowski claimed that the Shoah was actually a Jewish conspiracy to enable Jews to hide their children in monasteries during World War II in order for them to be baptized and thereby take over the Church from within. In fact, according to Tejkowski and the Romanian Radu Theodoru, Pope John Paul II was actually a Jew.[49]

Perhaps the most fitting conclusion for an article on this topic is to cite several examples in which the Jews themselves are blamed for the Holocaust. Such arguments, as illogical as they are, have appeared in several East European countries. Thus, for example, right-wing elements in Slovakia claimed in 1997 that the Holocaust is the price the Jews have to pay for crucifying Jesus. According to Hungarian right-wing extremist Aron Monis, it was "Jewish world power" that produced Hitler, who was actually a Zionist agent. In Romania, Theodoru argued that Hitler had been a puppet in Jewish hands[50] and Professor Ion Coja claimed that during the infamous Bucharest pogrom of January 1941, Jews disguised as Iron Guard Legionnaires murdered Romanians whom they dressed up as Jews.[51] In Croatia, President Franjo Tudjman wrote in his book *The Wastelands of Historical Reality* that the number of Jewish victims of the Holocaust was grossly exaggerated and that Jewish inmates ran the Jasenovac concentration camp and controlled its liquidation apparatus. According to Tudjman, "The Jew remains a Jew, even in the Jasenovac camp....Selfishness, craftiness, unreliability, stinginess, deceit, are their main characteristics."[52]

The material presented in this article is only a small sample of the numerous cases in which attempts are being made throughout Eastern Europe to distort and negate the history of the Holocaust. Although it

is true that so
peripheral politica
reflect (and influence) man
is important to heed the warning oꞁ
dolph Braham, who survived the Holocaust iꞁ
to follow the political developments in that country.

> While the number of populist champions of antisemitism, ꞁe
> that of the Hungarian neo-Nazis actually denying the Holocaust,
> is relatively small, the camp of those distorting and denigrating the
> catastrophe of the Jews is fairly large, and judging by recent devel-
> opments, growing. Wielding political power and influence, mem-
> bers of this camp represent a potentially greater danger not only to
> the integrity of the historical record of the Holocaust, but also, and
> above all, to the newly established democratic system. For unlike the
> Holocaust deniers—the fringe groups of "historical charlatans"… the
> history cleansers who denigrate and distort the Holocaust are often
> "respectable" public figures—intellectuals, members of parliament,
> influential governmental and party figures, and high-ranking army
> officers."[53]

These developments, which have hereto attracted relatively little attention, clearly constitute a potential danger, which should be fully clarified and addressed before the negation of Jewish history escalates into physical attacks on living Jews.

Notes

* This article is based on a lecture delivered at a conference on Antisemitism and the Contemporary Jewish Condition, sponsored by the Sigi Ziering Institute of the University of Judaism, October 17–19, 2004.

1. During the past two decades alone, three multimillion-dollar Holocaust museums, or museums with a major Holocaust component, have been constructed: in Los Angeles (Simon Wiesenthal Center—1993), Washington (United States Holocaust Memorial Museum—1993), and New York City (Museum of Jewish Heritage–1997), besides dozens of smaller museums throughout the world. See, for example, Edward Linenthal, *Preserving Memory: The Struggle to Create America's Holocaust Museum*, New York: Columbia University Press, 1995; James E. Young,

The Texture of Memory: Holocaust Memorials and Meaning, New Haven: Yale University Press, 1993.

2. One of the most important expressions of this approach has been the activities of the Task Force for International Cooperation on Holocaust Education Remembrance and Research (hereafter TFICHERR) established by Swedish prime minister Goran Persson in 1998. See his remarks in a Stockholm meeting on the Holocaust; *Summary from the Meeting of 7 May 1998 in Stockholm*, Stockholm, n.d., pp. 4–9. For a dissenting view on the effectiveness of Holocaust education in combating antisemitism, see Peter Novick, *The Holocaust in American Life*, Boston and New York: Houghton Mifflin, 1999, pp. 239–63.

3. John Innes, "Villagers Plan to Honor Scot Victim of Holocaust," *The Scotsman*, October 14, 2004.

4. Renwick McLean, "Spain Reopens Old Wound," *International Herald Tribune*, October 13, 1944, p. 1.

5. "Bachir ba-Yamin ha-tzorfati: Mutar Lehitvakeiach al Mispar ha-Nispim ba-Shoa," Haaretz, October 13, 2004.

6. Whereas the TFICHERR was originally established in 1998 by Sweden, the United States, and the United Kingdom, it presently has eighteen members (fifteen from Europe), with at least four additional European countries candidates for membership. See "Fact Sheet," www.taskforce. ushmm.org

7. See, for example, Efraim Zuroff, "The Memory of Murder and the Murder of Memory," in Emanuelis Zingeris (ed.), *Atminties Dienos: The Days of Memory*, Vilnius: baltos lankos, 1993 (hereafter Zuroff: Memory), pp. 391–405.

8. Soviet memorials, for example, were notorious for hiding the Jewish identity of the victims of Nazism who were described as "Soviet citizens" or "victims of fascism," while the national identity of local participants was masked by references to "bourgeois nationalists" or "Hitlerite fascists." See ibid., p. 396, and William Korey, *The Soviet Cage: Antisemitism in Russia*, New York: Viking Press, 1973, pp. 83–98.

9. Vygantas Vareikis, "Double Genocide and the Holocaust Gulag: Rhetoric in Lithuania" (hereafter Vareikis), and Dov Levin "New Forms of Antisemitism in the New Established Lithuania" (hereafter Levin) in Jews and Antisemitism in the Public Discourse of the Post-Communist European Countries, a conference held on October 24–26, 2000, at the Vidal Sassoon International Center for the Study of Antisemitism, Hebrew University of Jerusalem.

10. Efraim Zuroff, "Latvia's Holocaust Role," *Jerusalem Post*, February 18, 1998, p. 10.

11. Efraim Zuroff, "Visiting President Mesic Courageously Tackles His Country's Past," *Jerusalem Post*, October 31, 2001, p. 4. Marinko Culic, "Mesic's Apology to Jews," November 5, 2001, www.aimpress.ch

12. Michael Shafir, "Between Denial and 'Comparative Trivialization': Holocaust Negationism in Post-Communist East Central Europe" (hereafter Shafir), *Analysis of Current Trends in Antisemitism*, no. 19, (2002), p. 28.

13. See note no. 9.

14. See note no. 12.

15. Ibid., p. 40.

16. "Declaration of the Supreme Council of the Republic of Lithuania Concerning the Genocide of the Jewish Nation in Lithuania During the Period of the Nazi Occupation," May 8, 1990. For an analysis of the wording of the declaration see Zuroff: Memory, pp. 397–98.

17. Michael Berenbaum, "On the Politics of the Public Commemoration of the Holocaust," *Shoah*, (fall-winter 1982): pp. 6–37.

18. Amiram Barkat, "Many Western Countries Also Mark Holocaust Day," Haaretz, April 19, 2004.

19. "Dr. Efraim Zuroff Online: Answers in English," *Eesti Paevaleht*, August 8, 2002, p. 6.

20. "Kas Eesti peab sisse holokausti paeva? (Does Estonia Need to Impose a Holocaust Memorial Day?)," *Eesti Paevaleht*, August 7, 2002; Internet Poll on Marking the Holocaust Day, "Estonian Media Summary," U.S. Embassy, Tallinn, Estonia, August 7, 2002.

21. Efraim Zuroff, "Holokausti Paev Eestis oleks suur samm desi (Holocaust memorial day in Estonia Would Be a Big Step Forward)," *Eesti Paevaleht*, August 7, 2002, p. 9.

22. See for example coverage of Holocaust remembrance day 2001 in Lithuania, *Lithuanian Review*, September 24, 2004, p. 1; Rachel Eisenberg, "Rivlin Marks 60th anniversary of Vilna Ghetto's Destruction," *Jerusalem Post*, September 24, 2003, p. 4.

23. Zuroff: Memory, pp. 391–405.

24. See Efraim Zuroff, "Worldwide Investigation and Prosecution of Nazi War Criminals: An Annual Status Report," for the period from January 1, 2001, until March 31, 2004 (three reports) published annually by the Simon Wiesenthal Center, Israel Office.

25. Efraim Zuroff, "The Failure to Prosecute Nazi War Criminals in Lithuania, Latvia and Estonia, 1991–1998," *Antisemitism Research,* vol. II, no. 1 (summer 1998): pp. 5–10.

26. See, for example, Michael MacQueen, "The Office of Special Investigations and the Case of Aleksandras Lileikis," a lecture delivered at the "Holocaust in Lithuania in the Focus of Modern History, Education, and Justice," conference conducted in Vilnius on September 23–25, 2002; Liudas Truska, "Contemporary attitudes toward the Holocaust in Lithuania," *Jews in Eastern Europe*, vol. 2, no. 45 (fall 2001): p. 24; Efraim Zuroff, "Can Lithuania Face Its Holocaust Past; Reflections of a Concerned Litvak," Gachelet, March 2002, pp. 75-76.

27. See for example "Laiko zenklai (Signs of the Times)," *Lietuvos Rytas*, June 21, 1996, p. 4; "E. Zuroffas pasigenda normalaus naciu nusikalteliu teismo proceso (E. Zuroff Finds a Lack of Normal Trials of Nazi Criminals)," Baltic News Service, July 13, 2002 and comments on www.delfi.lt; Geoffrey Vasiliauskas, "No One Rules the World," *Laisvas Laikrastis*, March 16, 2004 (hereafter Vasiliauskas), pp. 1–8.

28. "Taurageje surengta antisemitine akcija (An Antisemitic Incident Was Organized in Taurage)," *Lietuvos Rytas,* July 29, 2002, p.2. "Lithuanian Politician Burns Israeli Flag, Plays Nazi Songs," Agence France Press, June 29, 2002.

    Among the Jewish sites vandalized during the period since Lithuania obtained its independence were several Holocaust memorial monuments, particularly in smaller communities. See for example "The Baltic States" in Dina Porat (chief editor), *Antisemitism Worldwide, 1994*, Tel-Aviv: The World Jewish Congress and the Anti-Defamation League, 1995, p. 129.

29. Mel Huang, "History Greets the New Year on the Baltic," *Central Europe Review,* vol. 2, no. 1 (January 10, 2000). The individuals in question are Nachman Dushanski and Semyon Berkov.

30. Letter of Irit Kahan, director of the Department of International Affairs of the Israeli Ministry of Justice, to Lithuanian prosecutor-general Kazys Pednycia, February 2, 2000, Archives of the Israel Office of the Simon Wiesenthal Center (hereafter SWCIA), Lithuania, file no. 28.

31. Vasiliauskas relates that following a visit to Lithuania by this author, who had submitted particularly damning testimony, obtained in the

framework of "Operation: Last Chance" (which featured special ads calling upon individuals to volunteer information regarding the identity of local Nazi perpetrators), regarding the participation of Lithuanians in the murder of Jews in the town of Rokiskis to the Lithuanian Special Prosecutor for genocide crimes, the Lithuanian Center for the Study of Genocide and Resistance sponsored special radio advertisements calling for people with information on communist crimes in the Rokiskis area during and after World War II to come forward. Vasiliauskas, p. 4.

32. Efraim Zuroff, "Worldwide Investigation and Prosecution of Nazi War Criminals: An Annual Status Report," Simon Wiesenthal Center, June 2003, pp. 30–31.

33. See note no. 24.

34. See for example, "Lithuanian State Head Spurns Jewish Organization's Rebuke," Elta (Lithuanian News Agency), November 20, 1998; "E. Zurofas nerimsta (E. Zuroff Is Nervous)," Kauno Diena, November 20, 1998.

35. See for example the history of the Lithuanian International Commission for the Evaluation of the Crimes of the Nazi and Soviet Occupation Regimes, at www.komisija.lt.

36. Stephen Kinzer, "Lithuania Starts to Wipe Out Convictions for War Crimes," New York Times, September 5, 1991, p. 1.

37. Typical of the articles expressing this notion was a piece by Valentinas Ardziunas in Lietuvos Aidas (March 14, 1995), which was accompanied by two illustrations: a monument to the victims of the Holocaust in Alytus, and a chapel built to commemorate the murder of dozens of Lithuanians by the communists at Rainiai forest. Vareikis, pp. 4–6.

38. Ibid., pp. 6–8.

39. Jonas Avyzius, "Kam Prezidentas tikras tevas? (Who Is the Person Whose Real Father Is the President?)," Respublika, March 25, 1995, quoted in ibid., p. 8.

40. Address by H. E. Vaira Vike-Preiburga, president of the Republic of Latvia at the International Forum Preventing Genocide: Threats and Responsibilities, Stockholm, January 26, 2004.

41. Efraim Zuroff, "Misleading Comparisons of 20th Century Tragedies," Baltic Times, February 19–25, 2004.

42. Among the comments on www.delfi.lv were the following:
1. "To the wall [to be shot] this person and finish[him off]." (February

20, 2004, 9:31).

2. Zuroff thinks that the only nation which suffered in world history are the zhids [derogatory term for Jews—EZ], All the other people are their butchers...Jews were always successful in trade and usury." (February 20, 2004, 9:33)

3. "It is written in the Bible that zhids are an experimental mistake. G-d himself wanted to annihilate them because the nation is wicked, without honor and virtue. All their history is war, killings, and treachery. We must state clearly: Zuroff and the zhid government in Israel are criminals." (February 20, 2004, 16:27).

43. Michael Shafir cites these examples to describe a phenomenon, which he calls "deflective negationism," which in this case relates to the attempts to attribute guilt for the crimes of the Holocaust solely to the Nazis. Shafir, pp. 24–37. In the case of the monument at Ponar, the term "and their helpers" appears in the inscriptions in Yiddish and Hebrew but not in Lithuanian or Russian, and the all-important adjective "local" does not appear anywhere. Efraim Zuroff, "Can Lithuania Face Its Past?" *Jerusalem Report*, August 1, 1991, p. 48.

44. The Estonian daily *Eesti Paevaleht* was so intent on discrediting the findings of the international commission regarding the participation of the Estonian 36th Battalion in the murders at Nowogrudok, that it featured an interview with Vassili Arula who served in the unit and denied its involvement, but whose testimony in this regard was of little relevance since he only joined the battalion long after the murders had taken place. Toomas Kummel, "Ainus elav tunnistaja kaitseb 36. eesti politseipataljoni (Only Living Witness Defends 36th Estonian Police Battalion)," *Eesti Paevaleht,* August 5, 2001.

45. The most obvious reflection of the Lithuanians' eagerness to uncover righteous Gentiles (as opposed to their reluctance to prosecute Nazi war criminals) is the large discrepancy between the numbers claimed by the Lithuanians (approximately 2,300 families as of late 2000) and the far smaller figure officially recognized by Yad Vashem, the Israel national remembrance authority (513 individuals). Thus, for example, Knesset speaker Reuven Rivlin on a visit to Lithuania on Holocaust memorial day there, refused to participate in a ceremony honoring thirty Lithuanians, whom Lithuanian sources claim helped save Jews during the Holocaust, since only twelve of them had been recognized by Yad Vashem. Rachel Eisenberg, "Rivlin Marks 60th Anniversary of Vilna Ghetto's Destruction," *Jerusalem Post*, September 24, 2003, p. 4. For mention of the symmetry Lithuanians seek to create between local perpetrators and rescuers, see Jonas Patrubavicius, "Blatant and Latent Asymmetry

of Lithuanian Antisemitism," *Laisvas Laikvastis,* April 13, 2004, p. 9. The figure on the righteous Gentiles recognized in Lithuania appears in Solomonas Atamukas, "The Hard Long Road toward the Truth: On the Sixtieth Anniversary of the Holocaust in Lithuania," *Lituanus,* vol. 47, no. 4 (winter 2001): p. 11. The figures for Yad Vashem are correct as of January 1, 2004, and were supplied by that institution. "Righteous among the Nations—per Country & Ethic Origin," January 1, 2004, Yad Vashem Department for the Righteous among the Nations.

46. "Address by Gediminas Vagnorius, Prime Minister of the Republic of Lithuania on 20 June 1991 At Dedication Ceremony Of The Memorial At Ponar," SWCIA, Lithuanian criminals, file no. 3.

47. Andrew Ezergailis, "Sonderkommando Arajs," lecture at 9th International Conference on Baltic Studies in Scandinavia, June 3–4, 1987; idem., *The Holocaust in Latvia, 1941–1944,* Riga and Washington D.C.: The Historical Institute of Latvia in association with The United States Holocaust Memorial Museum, 1996.

48. Shafir describes this phenomenon as another example of "deflective negationism," with the primary guilt being attributed to fringe elements. Shafir, p. 37.

49. Ibid., pp. 14–15.

50. Ibid., pp. 42–43.

51. Professor Coja wrote an article with this spurious accusation as recently as January 2004 after his political patron Tudor had already apologized for his previous Holocaust denial and antisemitic comments. Ion Coja, "De ce n-au luat romanii Premiul Nobel pentru Pace in 1994 (Why the Romanians Did Not Win the Nobel Prize in 1994)," *Romania Mare,* January 21, 2004.

52. Thomas O'Dwyer, "Where's the Croat Havel?" *Jerusalem Post,* August 7, 1997; "Nazi-Hunter Slams Croatian Links," *Jewish Chronicle,* September 12, 1997.

53. Quoted in Shafir, p. 11.

Section II
Antisemitism in Islam

The reader may have noticed that we have used an untraditional spelling of the word antisemitism throughout this work—except when the author is citing a published work. Instead of spelling antisemitism with a hyphen and a capital S (anti-Semitism) or with a hyphen and a capital A and a capital S (Anti-Semitism) we have consistently and deliberately spelled it as one word: antisemitism.

Two important considerations are involved in this decision. The first is that there is no such word as "Semitism," and antisemitism specifically means hatred of and prejudice toward Jews. The second is to eliminate the simple twist of a phrase. We often hear the argument that Arabs can't be anti-Semites, because they are Semites. The specificity of the word antisemitism insists that one deal with the anti-Jewish nature of the hatred.

The process of importing discredited antisemitic myths into the Arab and Islamic world has intensified in recent years. One can cite thousands of examples, but a few will illustrate a general pattern. A random review of websites devoted to monitoring antisemitism in the Arab press on the eve 2005 revealed that:

- On July 15, 2001, the Egyptian opposition newspaper *Al Arabi* reprinted a photo montage of Israeli foreign minister Shimon Peres as a Nazi with the caption "The return of the Nazi pollutes Egypt's air." The photo coincided with Peres's visit to Cairo to meet with Egyptian leadership. *Al Arabi* first printed the photo on April 29 during another Peres visit to Cairo. Peres is Israel's leading dove. Prior to Intifada II, and perhaps even now, Peres envisioned a new Middle East.

- Drawing on references to the infamous forgery *Protocols of the Elders of Zion*, a June 23, 2001, article in Egypt's leading daily newspaper accused the Jewish people of attempting to "destroy the world's religions."

- A recent television show depicts Israeli leader Ariel Sharon as a vampire who craves the blood of Arab children. He is portrayed as leading a massacre, personally overseeing the tossing of Arab children into the bonfire and reporting to former prime minister Menachem Begin that he has fulfilled his twentieth birthday wish by providing the blood of twenty Arab children.

- A demonstration of Muslims at the International Conference on Racism, in Durban, South Africa, chanted "Hitler should have finished the job."

- At the same international conference, NGOs called for the reinstatement of the repudiated United Nations resolution "Zionism is Racism."

- The claim that four thousand Jews were warned in advance about the World Trade Center bombing is accepted unquestionably by broad segments of the Arab world, especially among the elite. In Arab societies antisemitism is a mainstream and not fringe phenomena as it is in the United States.

- Suha Arafat, wife of the then Palestinian leader, greeted First Lady Hillary Clinton on a November 12, 1999, visit with the following statement: "Our people have been subjected to the daily intensive use of poisonous gas by the Israeli forces, which have led to an increase in cancer cases among women and children." The charge of gassing has no basis in fact, but the fact it could be uttered by the wife of Chairman Arafat to the wife of the president of the United States means the charge, however demonstrably false, has widespread currency in the Arab world.

- The editor-in-chief of the Palestinian Authority daily, *Al-Hayat Al-Jadida*, Hafez Bargutti, says American columnists who support Israel are "infected with moral AIDS" and should be "tried in an international court, for they are considered inciters who have committed crimes against humanity."

- A sermon by Sheik Ibrahim Madhi in the Sheik 'Ijlin Mosque in Gaza said: "The greatest enemies of the Islamic nation are the

Jews, may Allah fight them.... All spears should be directed at the Jews, at the enemies of Allah, the nation that was cursed in Allah's book. Allah has described them as apes and pigs, the calf-worshipers, idol-worshipers...."

- A website registered to Qatar's Ministry of Endowments and Religious Affairs published reports "containing accusations of "Zionists of plotting and executing the September 11 attacks on the United States," the "Zionist-controlled media," "the Zionist-controlled FBI," and the "alleged mass-slaughter of Jews during WWII."

- The Saudi Arabian daily *Al-Watan* published a two-part article on the "The Superiority of Jews in the World," a study conducted by the American-European Center for Security and International Studies. Written by Abdallah Aal Malhi, the article contended "At the end of the last century, (nineteenth) the Jewish organizations consolidated a hellish plan to take over the world by sparking revolutions or taking control of the keys to governments in various countries, first and foremost the U.S. and Russia." Jews act by means of their control of the media, politics, and the economy in order to weaken the non-Jewish groups and bring about their disintegration, in order to secure their goals."... Jews have infiltrated "and control the top positions in the American administration. This control aroused astonishment in the days of the Clinton administration...: Secretary of State Madeleine Albright, FBI chief George Tenet, Defense Secretary William Cohen, Clinton's national security advisor Sandy Berger—all Jews. Through this infiltration of the various American administrations, and through controlling the media and money, the Jews impose their agenda on the other peoples, and the Jewish sense of superiority, whose aim is to recruit the peoples and their resources for the good of Jewish interests and their racist state Israel, remain unchanged." (For the record, Albright discovered that her grandparents were Jewish and murdered in the Holocaust only when she served as secretary of state. George Tenet is not and has never been a Jew. William Cohen was born to a Jewish father and a non-Jewish mother. He renounced any Jewish affiliation when his family rabbi insisted on conversion prior to his bar-mitzvah. Only Sandy Berger is a practicing, identified Jew.)

- During the second half of Ramadan, a number of television stations, including Egyptian stations, screened the thirty-part series *Horseman without a Horse,* starring the well-known Egyptian actor Muhammad Subhi and a cast of four hundred others from Egypt, Syria, and France. The series, whose budget ran 6 to 8 million Egyptian pounds, was produced by Arab Radio and Television (ART), established in 1993, which broadcasts to the Middle East, North America, Latin America, Australia, and Africa. The series was based on the *Protocols of the Elders of Zion,* contending that they are the central line that still—to this very day—dominates Israel's "policy, political aspirations, and racism..."

- Palestinian leaders have argued that Jews have no connection to Jerusalem, no historic link with the land of Israel, which they clearly call Palestine.

- A Report by the Middle East Media Research Institute reveals that Syrian textbooks for grades 4 to 11 are replete with antisemitism, Holocaust denial, demonization of Israel, and an open call to exterminate Jews from the earth.

- A similar study of Palestinian textbooks concludes that antisemitic stereotypes portraying the Jews still exist and the present-day conflict is tied to ancient religious disputes and enmity.

- A recent report by by Dr. Husniya Hassan Moussa, lecturer at the National Research Center, in a government-sponsored Egyptian scientific journal, maintains that Jewish tourists infected with AIDS are traveling around Asian and African countries with the aim of spreading the disease, and Israel continues to use germ warfare to destroy the Palestinian people on its occupied land, while it challenges the international community."

In the years since this random survey, Iranian president Mahmoud Ahmadinejad has repeatedly denied the Holocaust, even hosting a conference to "reevaluate" the Holocaust, and has threatened the extinction of Israel. In the aftermath of the publication of a Danish cartoon, which portrayed Muhammad disrespectfully, press throughout the Arab world displayed antisemitic and anti-Jewish cartoons without any display of sensitivity—to put it mildly—toward the sensibilities of Jews, or Christians, for that matter. Each of the authors takes it as a given that Islamic antisemitism is a genuine and intensifying problem.

The first two essays in this section deal with the sources for anti-semitism in classical Islam. Both are by historians of religion—one a Christian and the other a Jew—who use the tools of their profession, including the sociology of religion, to understand not only whether there are such sources but how extensive and how deep they are.

John Kelsay argues that the sources for antisemitism in classical Islam are strong, but they can be marginalized. Jews, as he and Reuven Firestone discern, are far less central to the Muslim narrative than the Christian one. Implicit in their argument is what Michael Berenbaum makes explicit, that if Christianity could build on other segments of Christian tradition to rebuild its relationship with the Jews, the task will be easier with Islam. Because Muhammad turned north from Mecca to Medina, where Jews were present in substantial numbers, and not southeast to Najran, where Christians were present, and because Jews, contrary to his expectations, rejected his teachings, his disappointment was expressed in antagonism, which while deep and explicit is certainly not on a par with Christian Scripture, where Jews were portrayed as deicide—the killers of Jesus—and the deniers of his mission.

Muslims believe they are the legitimate superintendent of Jews, Christians and other protected people. They seek a territorial zone for the security and practice of Islam, one that is not threatened by unbe-lief. It is the empowerment of Jews, their sovereignty—not their pres-ence—in land that was formally Islamic that is the affront to Islam.

Still, classical Islam could distinguish between what certain Jews who were contemporaries of the Prophet did and the behavior of all Jews, at all times, everywhere.

Reuven Firestone's essay mixes personal observations from his life as a rabbi married to a rabbi and an observant Jew living in Cairo, Egypt, where he witnessed firsthand dimension of Islamic antisemi-tism among the elite of Egyptian society as well as among the ordinary people he encountered while on fellowship there in the spring of 2006. But anecdotal impressions are not the core of his essay. Rather Fires-tone focuses on the problem of chosenness as a feature of monotheism. For Firestone as for Kelsay, the tension between Islam and Judaism is a historic result of Muhammad's move from Mecca to Medina and of the tensions inherent as a new religion seeks its place in society and faces stiff condemnation from the established religions. For Muhammad, the primary opponents were Arab idolaters, not Jews, but his disap-pointment toward the Jews, reminiscent of Martin Luther, was keen.

Sometimes in classical Islam, Christians and Jews are lumped together as people of the book; more often Jews are singled out by being particularly disloyal to God, which was manifested in their obstinate refusal to accept the prophecy of Muhammad. Firestone poses the two central questions of our time.

- What activates latent Scriptural antisemitism into an operational state?

- What proactive strategies can be undertaken to keep such anti-semitism latent?

He cautions that Islam is no different in this regard from other religions and the collective goal of our age is to move Islam—and other religions—away from validating and justifying fear and hatred of the other and toward a greater compatibility and amity. Unlike Protestant-ism with its emphasis on *solo scriptura*, in Judaism, Catholicism, and Islam, Scripture does not operate alone; it is a formative part of an interpretive tradition, which allows for diverse emphases reflective of the tradition and the needs of the time.

Firestone Essay Forms a Segue

A denizen of many worlds, Mehnaz Afridi also begins with her own situation as a Pakistani woman who has lived in Europe, the Middle East—including Israel—and now in the United States as well as in her native land and who has studied Judaism and Islam in a secular American university. She urges the practice of self-criticism, which she describes as "listening to how others understand their own Scripture, the right to ask embarrassing questions and to quote from one's own sacred text even if one is embarrassed." Like Firestone, she too argues against the religious tendency in many faiths to rely on Scripture alone without regard to the interpretive tradition that is central to both Islam and Judaism. "It is always useful to take an example of …hyperbolic interpretation and put in a new reading or even a context that allows for the interpreter to seek justice."

The problem of Islam today is that it has somehow been silenced by its literalism, dare one say a fundamentalist reading by its leading cler-ics for "concepts such as Jihad, conversion, killing the infidel, suicides, beheadings, and the negligence of allowing others to enter into the fore to complexity and reinterpret the Islamic intellectual philosophy that is the important aspect of being Muslim." As a voice of moderation she wants to portray and see Islam practiced as a "diverse, rich, just and peaceful faith and Muslims characterized as people of faith who are not steeped in violence.

Michael Berenbaum contrasts the improving conditions of Roman Catholic–Jewish relations with the deteriorating conditions of Muslim-Jewish relations. Over the past half century, Roman Catholicism recognized the problem of antisemitism, employed the tools of religion to stress one aspect of tradition and to deemphasize another, institutionalized those changes in liturgy, education, teaching, preaching, and textbooks and endorsed measures of moderation and cooperation. This has led to a period of the flourishing of Jewish-Catholic relations. Was Islam willing and were Muslims cooperative, similar strategies could be employed. In the interim it would be wise for the West to study Islam, much in the ways that Jews studied Christianity and Christians Judaism, which facilitated conversation and dialogue when the opportunity was forthcoming. Moderate Muslims must be cultivated, understanding well that such cultivation diminishes their credibility within the Muslim world. Above all, patience is required, for the situation is not hopeful. And yet, if one looked at Jewish-Christian relations sixty-five years ago, amidst the destruction, there would have been much less grounds for optimism.

6

Antisemitism in Classical Islamic Sources
John Kelsay

Introduction

I think everyone can agree that recent developments give cause for
concern with respect to antisemitism in Islamic communities. Other
essays in this volume provide details of this phenomenon; at least one
other essay deals with the proximate causes of Muslim antisemitism.

My task stems from the way contemporary expressions of antisemitism cite sources from classical Islam. Specifically, the warrant for
this essay follows from the fact that these expressions refer to the foundational narrative of Muhammad and the reception of the Qur'an, to
themes in Islamic theology, and to political-legal (that is, Shari'a) precedents developed during the period of Islamic empire, and thus associated with Islamic civilization. In brief, I am to take up the questions:

1. Is there material for antisemitism in classical Islamic sources?

   and

2. How strong and/or deep is this material?

The answers are: (1) Yes, there is such material; and (2) it is substantial and strong. There are ways to approach this material that miti-
gate or marginalize it. Some of the best examples of this, in our current
context, come from Muslim scholars working in the United States.
There can be no doubt of the multitude and strength of antisemitic
sources in classical Islam, however. And one should be straightforward
about this.

In discussing the relevance of classical materials to antisemitism
among contemporary Muslims, I should like to keep in mind two

themes developed by the great sociologist and student of religion, Max Weber. In one of the best, though unfortunately least often read of his programmatic essays, Weber writes, first, about the peculiar contribution of religion in human affairs.[1] He argues that, whatever else religions may be, they are first and foremost responses to what might be called the "problem of order." Religions supply their adherents with an image of the world, especially the world of social-political relations, in which they behold a pattern of ordered relationships. For a community of believers, this pattern is associated with legitimacy. Conformity with it is a goal of religious activity. And those times when the pattern holds are times when one knows that all is right with the world.

At the same time, Weber writes (secondly) about the phenomenon of change in religious traditions. "Neither religions nor human beings are open books," he observes.[2] When it comes to religion, we find historical rather than logical or psychological constructions. Believers innovate, and call this "tradition"; religious communities construe their rituals and texts in ways that defy logic, and embrace this as "faithfulness." This means, as Weber put it, that in the realm of religion, consistency is the exception rather than the rule. For our discussion, it means we must deal forthrightly with a deeply entrenched notion of legitimate order by which Muslims believe they are the legitimate superintendents of Jews, Christians, and other "protected" peoples, while at the same time respecting the fact that Islam is a living tradition, in which human responsibility may be and is sometimes construed, in contemporary settings, as a process of arguing about whether or not superintendency holds good in modern societies.

Islam's Foundational Narrative

The story of Muhammad, and with it, of the revelation of the Qur'an, provides the first set of materials to be considered. We may summarize by saying that this is the story of the struggle for *al-islam*, "the submission to the will of God" in seventh-century Arabia. The main lines of the struggle are between the *umma* or community gathered around the Qur'an and the Prophet, and the Arab idolaters (*al-mushrikun*) and hypocrites (*al-munafiqun.*) The goal of the struggle is the creation of a territorial base or a zone of security for the practice of Islam. As David Little once put it, the foundational narrative of Islam indicates great concern over the threat of unbelief.[3] Muhammad and his community struggle to deal with this threat.

Where do Jews come into the story? They are not on center stage. They do play an important supporting role, however. For the story of Muhammad casts the Jews, first, as potential or even presumptive allies in the struggle with unbelief. In the end, however, it paints them as betrayers, who attempt to discredit the Prophet and assist his enemies.

These two motifs roughly correspond with the two great periods in the Prophet's ministry. From 610–622, Muhammad works in Mecca. His followers are subjected to verbal, economic, and physical harassment. They draw comfort from the fact that they are part of a long story, in which Jews and Christians—or more properly, the "people of Israel" and the "people of the messiah"—struggled as well. This identification with prior communities is effected by the Qur'an, the Prophet's preaching, and perhaps most of all, by the practice of *salat* or right worship. In Mecca, we are told that the *umma* of Muhammad prayed facing the Ka'ba, that great ancestral shrine which Muhammad and the Qur'an depict as the work of Abraham and Ishmael. At the same time, they faced toward *al-quds*, Jerusalem, the city of the prior communities. In other words, *salat* involved ritual prayer during which the followers of Muhammad faced both the Ka'ba and Jerusalem, reinforcing the notion (to which I will return) that the story of Muhammad constitutes an Arabic-speaking chapter in the universal story of God's dealings with the world.[4]

In 622, the second period begins. Here, the Prophet moves to Medina. His main concern is with the security of Islam vis-à-vis the unbelievers of Mecca. Internal threats, meaning threats from those non-Muslims living in Medina, must be controlled as well. And this latter is accomplished by the so-called "Medinan Constitution."[5] The point of this document is to show that Muhammad established an alliance with the non-Muslim tribes of Medina. Notably, these included three tribes identified with the practice of Judaism.

We do not have much information regarding the practice of these Jews. Nor do we know many of the facts regarding their relations with Muhammad's followers. If we take the Qur'an as reflecting historical reality on this point, we would say the Jewish tribes had a rabbinate, recited Torah, and elaborated on the Torah portions in the tradition of Midrash. Again, if we take the Qur'an as historical, we'd say that members of the Jewish tribes interacted with followers of Muhammad. Hearing Muhammad's version of the stories of Joseph, Moses, and Abraham, these Jews said, in effect: "Not bad, but not completely right. Come hear the reliable version from our rabbis." The rabbis in turn taught that Muhammad was not learned; a man of zeal but little substance, certainly not the equal of Moses or Abraham.[6]

Tension grows from such homely roots. Then, too, from the Muslim side of the story, the Jewish tribes violated the "constitution." They gave shelter to spies from Mecca, and sent information to the Meccans. They undermined Muhammad's diplomatic and military initiatives. The story is one of escalating tension, which we can follow through Qur'an 2–10, especially 2 and 9, as well as in the biographer's reports of events in Medina.[7]

With respect to the former, Qur'an 2 (*surat al-baqara*) treats the people of Israel as perpetually resisting the plan of God. They are ingrates, hypocrites, who receive God's gifts but will not follow God's guidance. Moses delivers God's commands; the people put off obedience, preferring to dispute meaningless questions. The events of salvation history render the Jews blameworthy: "Say unto them: Evil is that which your belief enjoins upon you, if indeed you are believers!"[8]

This vigorous denunciation is reiterated throughout those portions of the Qur'an revealed in Medina. In Qur'an 2, the focus is on salvation history. Interestingly, this *sura* also contains verses that establish the *umma* of Muhammad as an independent entity. Thus, we have the verses on the direction of prayer. The most likely gloss is that, once Muhammad moved to Medina and it was no longer possible simultaneously to face the Ka`ba and *al-quds*, the tension between the notion of Muhammad's struggle as "an Arabic-speaking chapter in the universal history of God" and as "a new and decisive chapter, with universal import" came to the fore. In Medina, it seems the Muslims first prayed toward Jerusalem, out of solidarity with their forebears and, they thought, coreligionists. But this meant turning *away* from the Ka`ba.[9]

Remembering that the Ka`ba was described as the work of Abraham, it is hardly strange to find *surat al-baqara* reminding us of this, in conjunction with its authorization of prayer facing the Ka`ba. That shrine, we are told, is the oldest in the world. It is in Muhammad's heart. One who faces it, imitates Abraham. And Abraham, in the Qur'anic view, was neither a Jew nor a Christian, but rather *hanif*—an "unaffiliated monotheist," which in some contexts indicates one who follows the natural religion. As we shall see, this natural religion is *al-islam*, "the submission," albeit with a "small i." "Small "i," because the *umma* of Muhammad, as others, has particular disciplines. God gives all communities particular times for worship and fasting, and these do not possess the same universality as the basic tenets concerning God, moral responsibility, and divine judgment. In *surat al-baqara*, the Muslims are freed from the fasting practices of the Jews. The Jews have their times, now the Muslims will have Ramadan. Similarly, Friday (*yawm al-jum`a*) will be the weekly day of prayer. One response to Jewish rejection of Muhammad is thus a kind of Muslim declaration of independence.

Conflict did not stop there, however. As Qur'an commentaries tell us, chapters 2–10 may be read as the record of Muhammad's struggle to build the new *umma* or people of God. Most of the material in these portions of the Qur'an focuses on Arab idolaters. Some focuses on hypocrites or "slackers" with the Muslim community. Other material focuses on the people of Israel or the people of the messiah. In *surat al-tawba* (chapter 9), we read the famous verses of the sword that command fighting against these peoples of the Book, on the grounds of their treachery. These so-called believers broke their treaty with you, the verses say. So fight them until God's justice is established. If they repent or pay tribute, give them peace. But know that they are not to be trusted.[10]

These are much-discussed verses. Let us tie them to the stories of Muhammad and the Jews of Medina. In successive periods, roughly between 624 and 627, the Jewish tribes were accused of various levels of treachery. In 624, Banu Qaynuqa was banished from Medina. In 625, Banu Nadir suffered a similar fate. Finally, in 627 Banu Qurayza saw its men killed and its women and children enslaved.[11]

The stories are very clear. From the Muslim point of view, these punishments were administered for the sake of security. Jews broke treaties meant to establish that. Indeed, one could go further, and describe the treaties as mutual security pacts. Thus the tribes not only undermined Muslim security. They refused the offer of protection for themselves. Thus, they were ingrates, rejecting the offer of God and God's Prophet to bring them under the umbrella of Islam which, as we shall see, is the natural religion of God.

As in many cases in the history of religions, stories with a negative moral may be read in diverse ways. Thus, Muslims *can and do* read these stories of Muhammad's dealings with the Jewish tribes at Medina as an account of what some Jews did in relation to Muhammad, without thereby making any grand point about Islamic-Judaic relations. Others read the stories as a reason for suspicion, viz., that Jews always tend or have the potential to act treacherously. Many have seen these stories as reinforcing the need for strict security, by in effect establishing patterns of superintendency, with Muslims protected by the establishment of Islamic hegemony. And this, it should be noted, is also seen as a gift to Jews, who, left to their own devices would engage in fighting and backbiting wherever they might go.

This set of stories thus serves as a kind of "stock" or "deposit" of tales that come to the fore in connection with certain historical experiences. Their power is reinforced when we put them in the context of Muslim theology, by which Islam is the natural religion of humanity.

Islamic Theology

To this point, my presentation is nothing unusual. The encounters between Muhammad and Jewish tribes, the denunciation of the people of Israel (and, more specifically, of the Jews of Medina) in the Qur'an— this is familiar material.

We do not yet have a theological context, however. And this is important, if we are to grasp the fullness of the view of Jews and Judaism presented in classical Islamic sources. Many of the scholarly or semischolarly discussions of this topic note the stock of negative stories and texts in the early period. They then go directly to the experiences of Jews under Islamic rule, that is, in the context of the Islamic polities associated with Umayyad, Abbasid, and other dynastic rulers. In terms of my account, such discussions move quickly from the foundational narrative of Islam to an account of Islam as a world civilization. In the latter setting, Jews lived as *ahl al-dhimma*, which is usually connected with Muslim "toleration" of the "peoples of the book."[12] From this point, the usual analyses move to argue that the relation of "toleration" is one in which Jews are in fact dominated by Muslims, since the political arrangements of classical Islam presupposed Islamic hegemony. Such is the emphasis, for example, of various works by Bat Ye'or, or even of the more nuanced account of Mark Cohen.[13]

As suggested, such accounts miss a step. The theological dimension of Islam, in which *al-islam*, "the submission" to the will or guidance of God, is crucial to an understanding of classical Islamic sources. For this dimension sets the tone or provides the angle of vision by which Islam views Judaism. As I shall argue, this angle of vision is one by which the *umma* or community of Islam sees itself as the "superintendent" of the people of Israel. The Muslim community is charged to protect its Jewish comrades, setting boundaries around them for their own good, and for the good of humanity as a whole. In stressing this way of looking at the matter, I am following the literal meaning of *ahl al-dhimma*, viz., the people of protection or the people under protection. One may speak of the arrangements associated with this terminology in terms of tolerance or toleration. "Protected" serves better, however, as a way of signaling the kind of "beneficent paternalism" envisioned by normative Islamic thinking.

Such thinking begins, for our purposes, with the notion that Islam is the "natural" religion of humanity. To speak in this way is to suggest that submission to divine guidance is the rightful condition of humanity, or is the condition which accords with the purpose for which humanity was created. At Qur'an 7:172–73, we read of a primordial covenant, in which all humanity stands before God. God challenges each and every one: "Bear witness. Am I your Lord?" To which the text has each one answer: "Yes, truly, you are our Lord!"

As this impressive passage proceeds, the reader is told that this exchange occurred so that, on the Day of Judgment, no human being will be able to say "I did not know of my responsibilities to God." As the Qur'an has it, all human beings do know, or at least, they have the capacity to know, the first principles of religion. It is this text that gives the sense to the report in which the Prophet Muhammad says: "Every child is born a Muslim. It is the child's parents who make him or her into a Jew, Christian, or Zoroastrian."[14]

Every child is born a Muslim....*al-islam*, submission, is the natural state of humankind. This judgment is critical to the Islamic view of salvation history. The record of human beings is the record of submission, or better, of the long struggle between *al-islam* and *al-jahiliyya* (heedlessness). In various passages, the Qur'an challenges its hearers to reflect on God's signs, and thus to become aware of their duties.[15] Human beings have the capacity of thought. Utilization of this capacity leads to an understanding of the dependence of humanity upon a powerful Other, to whom gratitude is owed.

In this connection, the Qur'an's retelling of the story of Abraham is instructive. As various passages have it, Abraham is a seeker, meditating on the world around him.[16] He knows he did not come into the world by his own power. His growth and eventual departure from the world are similarly outside of Abraham's control. Seeking the source from which he came, and to which he will return, Abraham turns to the evening star, to the moon, and the sun. As he comes to understand, all these wax and wane in their power to affect human existence. Gradually, light dawns, and Abraham sees that the Power he seeks must be unlike all others in its eternity, constancy, and lack of dependence. This Power is *al-lah*, "the god," the unique Source from which all things come, and to which all things must return.

These are the familiar strains of natural theology. For our purposes, the important point is that Abraham stands as an example of true or natural humanity. Each member of the human race has the power of reflection, and thus the capacity to comprehend the first principles of religion. And similarly, each one has the ability to comprehend and follow the religious path trod by Abraham: awareness or "remembrance" (*al-dhikr*) of God, acknowledgment of one's duty to do that which is right, and thus to prepare for divine judgment. The natural religion of humanity is a matter of the interplay of these three themes: God, moral responsibility, and divine judgment. These are common to all people, in all places and times. They are the themes presented in the proclamation of all the prophets.

Now, why the need for prophets? As Islamic tradition has it, these come to foster remembrance of God. Prophets repeat the threefold message of *al-islam* to particular groups of people in particular times and places. In particular, the various prophets proclaim the themes of God, moral responsibility and divine judgment in the languages of particular groups of people. Every nation has its prophet; some have more than one. The peculiar prophetic gift is eloquence, so that prophets remind people of their natural or rightful state through the use of powerful images, crafted in the language of a particular time and place.

Among the prophets, three stand out: Moses, Jesus, and Muhammad. Each brings a book and founds a community that is charged to carry on the prophetic mission. The structure of comparison is perfectly symmetrical, and one must say it rightly. Moses brings the Torah to the Banu Isra`il, the "tribe of Israel." Jesus brings the Gospel to the people of the Messiah. And, in the latter days, Muhammad brings the Qur'an to the Arabs. Each preaches the threefold message of submission; each community accepts the prophetic discipline, in the sense of carrying out specific ritual as well as moral directives; and each in its common life bears witness to the natural religion, calling humanity back to its true nature.

Thus far, all is harmonious. There is no conflict between human beings, who have been divided into diverse communities of language so that, as the Qur'an has it, they "may acknowledge one another."

And yet, the precise formulations utilized above should signal the potential of conflict. Moses brings the Torah to the Banu Isra'il—not to the Jews. Jesus brings the Gospel to the people of the Messiah—not to the Christians. As one reads classical Islamic sources, the reason for this is clear. Moses, and with him, the Torah, did not proclaim or "found" a religion called Judaism. The set of practices associated with that term is a later invention. Moses preached *al-islam*; the submission suggested by that term is also the religion of the Torah. Judaism is something different. It is an admixture of the true and the false, developed as the community altered or misinterpreted the Torah, over time. The Jewish tribes of Muhammad's day and the Jews encountering the *umma* of Muhammad in later times practice a partly true, partly false religion. They certainly have the potential to acknowledge *al-islam*; perhaps this potential is even stronger among them than among ordinary human beings. Ironically, however, this makes Jews all the more resistant to those who point out their error.[17]

Similarly with Christians. Members of both communities think they are special, and according to Islamic sources, they are so. In both cases, however, error has crept in. Jews are those who either suppress or misconstrue verses of the Torah which proclaim the coming of the Arab Prophet. Christians similarly deny the connection between the Gospel and the appearance of Muhammad. Both communities need correction, discipline, and protection. Both need supervision or, as I would put it, Jews and Christians need a superintendent. Filling this need is the task of the *umma* of Muhammad. Thus, Qur'an 2: 139–141:

> Say [to the Jews and Christians], "How can you argue with us [Muslims] about God when he is our Lord and your Lord?
> Our deeds belong to us, and yours to you.
> We devote ourselves entirely to Him.
> Or are you saying that Abraham, Ishmael, Isaac, Jacob, and the Tribes were Jews or Christians?"
> Ask them, "Who knows better: you or God?

Who could be more wicked than those who hide a testimony from God?
God is not unmindful of what you do."
That community passed away: what they earned belongs to them, and
     what you earn belongs to you.
You will not be answerable for their deeds.

Or again, at 6:161–65:

Say, "My Lord has guided me to a straight path
An upright religion,
The faith of Abraham, a man of pure faith.
He was not a polytheist."
Say, "My prayers and sacrifice, my life and death are all for God,
Lord of the Worlds;
He has no associates.
This is what I am commanded, and I am the first to devote myself to
     Him."
Say, "Should I seek a Lord other than God, the Lord of all things?"
Each soul is responsible for its own actions;
No soul will be the burden of another.
You will all return to your Lord in the end, and He will tell you the
     truth about your differences.
It is He who made you successors on the earth
And raises some of you above others in rank,
To test you through what He gives you.
Your Lord is swift in punishment,
Yet He is the most forgiving, the most merciful.

Islam as Civlization

One way to read the struggle of Muhammad with the Jewish tribes
describes the evolution of Muhammad from the status of a Prophet
who speaks Arabic, to that of an end-time messenger presenting the
final revelation of God's word to humanity. Or again, one can focus
on the Qur'an as its claims develop from the notion that this is "an
Arabic lecture" to the "decisive criterion" by which people may settle
questions of religious truth. Still again, one can think of the companions
of Muhammad moving from the status of a force among the Arabs,
to a community with a universal mission of commanding right and
forbidding wrong, as in Qur'an 3:102–10:

You who believe, be mindful of God, as is his due,

And make sure you devote yourselves to Him, to your dying
    moment.

Hold fast to God's rope all together;

Do not split into factions.

Remember God's favor to you;

You were enemies and then He brought your hearts together and you
    became brothers by His grace;

You were about to fall into a pit of Fire and He saved you from it—

In this way God makes His revelations clear to you so that you may be
    rightly guided.

Be a community that calls for what is good, urges what is right, and
    forbids what is wrong: those are the successful ones...

You are the best community singled out for people:

You order what is right, forbid what is wrong, and you believe in
    God.

If the people of the book had also believed, it would have been better
    for them.

For although some of them believe, most of them are lawbreakers...

Such readings lead rather naturally to a discussion of Islam as a
civilization, and more specifically to the political-legal precedents
regarding the status of Jews and other non-Muslims in the imperial
Islamic states established following the death of the Prophet in 632.
Within a generation, the *umma* of Muhammad swept out of the Ara-
bian Peninsula and conquered most of the Middle East. Eventually,
Islam would be the established religion of a vast realm, stretching from
North Africa to China and (moving in another direction) from South/
Central Europe through the Indian subcontinent.

Historians debate the reasons for the original push out of Arabia.[18]
What we know, and what is germane to the task of this essay, is how
the Muslims spoke about this, after the fact. The majority saw the conquests as wars of "opening," in which military and diplomatic action
leading to the establishment of Islamic government was an aspect of
the mission of the *umma* or of "making God's cause succeed."[19] Specifically, the establishment of Islamic government "opened" the conquered
territories to the preaching of Islam, and at the same time conferred
the benefits of Islamic rule upon the conquered peoples.

This is the sense with which one must approach some of the more
famous categories by which Muslim religious authorities spoke about

religious and political realities. For example, they divided the world into *dar al-islam* and *dar al-harb*, the abode of submission and the abode of war. As many put it, the first indicates the territory in which Islam is the established religion. The second indicates the territory not yet under Islamic government, and which thus becomes the object of war.

This is accurate enough, provided one allows for consideration of *ahkam al-jihad*, the Muslim rules of engagement for war or the Islamic version of the just war tradition. Yet such a characterization misses what must be, for Islam, the heart of the matter. Recalling what has been said above, we may depict the reasoning behind such judgments as follows: the expansion of *dar al-islam* is a blessing to humanity. *Dar al-harb* is so named, not only because it is, under specified conditions, the object of Muslim military action. It is also the abode of war because its inhabitants, lacking proper guidance, fight with one another. In bringing these people under the umbrella of Islam, Muslims are doing them a favor. The establishment of Islamic governance provides the best chance for human beings to live together in peace and justice.

The appropriate sense attached to the political categories of classical Islam is thus one whereby we understand Muslims as engaged in a civilizing mission. If one likes, Muslim intentionality is consistent with the kind of attitude described above as a beneficent paternalism. The Muslim calling is to establish order in the world, consistent with the natural religion of humanity. Like the prophets, Muslims are to call humanity to acknowledge God as Lord, reminding people of the primordial covenant between God and human beings—each and every one of them.

It is this civilizing motif that gives the sense to the *dhimmi* system so forcefully explored by Bat Ye'or.[20] Jews, Christians, and others are thereby placed under the "protection" of Islam. This must be the case, since these communities have, over time, proven that they are not faithful to the natural religion proclaimed by the prophets and set forth in the holy books. These communities are protected from the full consequences of their error through the requirement that they live under Muslim rule. In turn, the world is protected from Jewish and Christian errors, because Islamic government delimits the spread of these religions. Ultimately, Islamic governance seeks to bring Jews and Christians into the *umma*. And, from the Muslim point of view, this is not so much a matter of destruction as of restoration. It does involve restriction, however, as a kind of discipline "for their own good," ranging from relatively minor inconveniences to outright discrimination and persecution. In this regard, one might think of the protected peoples as experiencing a range of disabilities, from benign neglect to discrimination—for example, paying special taxes, and wearing special clothes— to persecution. As a hypothesis, at this point, one might suppose that the more severe instances of disability correlate, as reactions on the part of an angered majority, to instances where Muslim rulers appointed Jews to government offices, in direct violation of the letter and spirit of *ahl al-dhimma*.

Where Muslim-Jewish relations stand along this spectrum, at any given point in time, depends on a variety of circumstances. What is consistent in the standard imperial model of Muslim government, is the notion that Muslims are the overseers or superintendents of Jews and others.

A Brief Conclusion

Let me return to the proposals of Max Weber, cited at the outset of this essay. I began with his proposal that religions address the problem of order. I think it is evident that, when we consider the depiction of Jews in classical Islamic sources, we are dealing with deeply entrenched patterns of thought, feeling, and action. This is important in our current circumstances, where people like Osama bin Ladin can be interpreted as suggesting that the world is out of joint, and needs to be put right. With respect to Jews, this means there ought not to be a state of Israel. The land belongs to Muslims, or as Osama bin Ladin and other jihadists have said, the land was given to Muslims as a trust, and will remain in that category until the Day of Judgment. The *Charter* of Hamas provides one way of putting this when it judges that "no Arab state...no King or leader...no organization, Palestinian or Arab has such authority" that it may negotiate away any portion of the land of Palestine.[21] Those who would behave in ways counter to this judgment fail to honor God's trust, and in doing so, *harm humanity*.

Now, Weber also suggests the possibility that religious notions of order can change. Religious communities and their traditions take surprising turns. Thus, in the United States, we actually have Muslim groups which claim that the *U.S.* is *dar al-islam*, because it is the place where Islam may be practiced in freedom. As well, we have scholars who argue that the political-legal context of the United States provides an opportunity to disentangle Islam from patterns of empire, and thus to recover something that was lost when the majority of Muslims accepted political and military expansion as a means of "making God's cause succeed."[22]

There is more to be said about the relationship between order and change in Islam. For now, though, the point of this essay has been to describe antisemitism in classical Islamic sources. I think it is clear that there are strong and deep notions of a pattern of order in these sources, in which Muslims are to rule over Jews and others. Equally important in these sources is the notion that Muslim rule is for the good of Jews and others, because, as the Qur'an has it, Muhammad and his followers walk in the way of Abraham, the natural monotheist, whose practice of submission is consonant with the will of God.

To make progress in understanding antisemitism in Islamic sources, we must deal with this line of thought.

Notes

1.   "The Social Psychology of the World's Religions," in *From Max Weber*, translated and edited by H. H. Gerth and C. Wright Mills (New York: Oxford University Press, 1946), pp. 267–301.

2.   Ibid., at p. 291.

3.   See David Little, John Kelsay, and Abdulaziz Sachedina, *Human Rights and the Conflict of Cultures* (Columbia, SC: University of South Carolina Press, 1988).

4.   See the traditions related by Ibn Kathir, *Tafsir* (New York: Darussalam Publishers, 2000), vol. 1, 42ff, commenting on Qur'an 2, 142ff.

5.   For the text, see the biography by Ibn Ishaq (d. 775), as translated by A. Guillaume, *The Life of Muhammad* (Oxford: Oxford University Press, 1955), pp. 231–33.

6.   Ibid., pp. 239–70.

7.   Ibid., passim, and also the account of al-Tabari (d. 935) in *The History of al-Tabari*, 39 vols., with various translators (Albany, NY: State University of New York Press, 1997), especially VII, pp. 94–104, 156–60, and VIII, pp. 27–41.

8. Qur'an 2:93

9. Qur'an 2:142–52, and Ibn Kathir, op cit.

10. 9: 5 deals with polytheists; 9: 29ff. with Jews and Christians.

11. See al-Tabari, op cit; also W. M. Watt, *Muhammad: Prophet and Statesman* (Oxford: Clarendon Press, 1961), especially pp. 112–75.

12. I shall return to this below, where I argue the importance of a more literal translation, that is, "people of or under protection." Along with Christians, Jews are usually taken as the primary referent for the category of "peoples of the book." It should be noted, however, that the Qur'an speaks also of "Sabeans" (usually understood to indicate Zoroastrians, and that during the period of empire, other groups—for example, Hindus or as Muslim accounts had it, "Brahmins"—should also be counted as peoples of the Book, and thus eligible for Muslim protection. See G. Vajda, "Ahl al-Kitab" in *Encyclopedia of Islam*, 2nd ed., edited by C. Bosworth, et al (Leiden: E. J. Brill, 1960), I: 264; also, Claude Cahen, "Ahl al-dhimma," in idem, II: 227."

13. Bat Ye'or's various works include *The Dhimmi: Jews and Christians Under Islam*, trans. David Maisel (Madison, NJ: Fairleigh Dickinson University Press, 1985); *The Decline of Eastern Christianity under Islam: From Jihad to Dhimmitude* (Madison, NJ: Fairleigh Dickinson University Press, 1996); *Islam and Dhimmitude: Where Civilizations Collide*, trans. Miriam Kochan and David Littman (Madison, NJ: Fairleigh Dickinson University Press, 2001); and *Eurabia: The Euro-Arab Axis* (Madison, NJ: Fairleigh Dickinson University Press, 2005). In the same vein, one might cite Andrew Bostom, *The Legacy of Jihad: Islamic Holy War and the Fate of Non-Muslims* (Amherst, NY: Prometheus Books, 2005). The typical scholarly criticism of these works is that they are incomplete or lacking in nuance. This certainly seems accurate, and Cohen's comparative work, *Under Crescent & Cross: The Jews in the Middle Ages* (Princeton, NJ: Princeton University Press, 1994) provides a partial correction. In my view, however, a more important problem in such accounts is the lack of a solid account of the religious or theological perspective that informs the classical Islamic political order, and in relation to which the institutions associated with *ahl al-dhimma* make sense. For a fuller account of this matter, see my forthcoming volume, currently entitled *Islam and the Political Future: The New Jihad and the Crisis of Shari`a Reasoning*.

14. Cf. *Sahih Muslim* (one of the standard collections of reports or *ahadith* concerning the prophetic example, or *sunna*). In the English trans. by Abdulhamid Siddiqi (Delhi: Adam Publishers and Distributors), this is

report 2658, which is reported in several versions; cf. vol. 4a: 216

15. Qur'an 56:62; 59:21; 7:176, among others.

16. Qur'an 6:74–83; 26:51ff., among others.

17. Cf. especially Qur'an 2.

18. See especially Fred McGraw Donner, *The Early Islamic Conquests* (Princeton, NJ: Princeton University Press, 1981).

19. Qur'an 8:39.

20. Op cit.

21. The *Charter* is translated by M. Maqdsi (Dallas: Islamic Association for Palestine, 1990); the passage cited, which is article 11, is at p. 17 of this version.

22. The former claim, which appears to resonate in certain Shi`i, particularly Isma`ili, groups, rests on a saying attributed to Ja`far al-Sadiq (d. 765) , recognized as the sixth imam or designated leader by all Shi`i groups:

    [An inquirer asked] "I enter the lands of unbelievers and some of our people say that if I die I will die one of them." Al-Sadiq asked: "Hamad, when you are there [in the land of unbelievers] do you mention our message and invite to it?" I said: "Yes." He [al-Sadiq] said: "When you are in these cities, the cities of Islam, do you mention our message and invite to it?" I said: "No." He [al-Sadiq] said: "If you die you will be resurrected a nation unto yourself your light between your hands." As per Khaled Abou El Fadl, "Legal Debates on Muslim Minorities: Between Rejection and Accomodation," in *Journal of Religious Ethics* 22/1 (Spring, 1994): 127–62. In general, Abou El Fadl concludes, Shi`i jurists (and with them, those associated with the Mu`tazilites) are particularly associated with lines of thought which suggest that the duty of Muslims is "to seek a place where they can perfect their religion—regardless of any formal classification of territory." (142) Those groups suggesting that the United States is such a land emphasize the way that freedom of religion allows genuine practice, including missionary activity, in ways not allowed in certain historically and legally Muslim states. While the historic and contemporary evidence suggest that Shi`i scholars took this line more often than others, there is no reason why one ought not interpret some Sunni judgments as consistent with it. For example, see the opinion of Rashid Rida (d. 1935) in response to questions about the obligations of Bosnian Muslims living under the hegemony of Austria: "The essential point is that, as demanded by their religion, Muslims must establish justice and do good, and if they are unable to do so in [certain] countries, then they should migrate." (also in Abou El Fadl, 152).

With respect to scholars arguing that the early expansion involved a loss to Islam, cf. Abdulaziz Sachedina, "The Development of *Jihad* in Islamic Revelation and History," in James Turner Johnson and John Kelsay, eds., *Cross, Crescent, and Sword* (Westport, CT: Greenwood Press, 1990), pp. 35–50. More generally, see the following works by Muslim scholars working in the United States, who argue in various ways that the political-legal precedents associated with classical Islam no longer fit with contemporary political conditions, and thus may, or in some cases, must be reconsidered: Abdulaziz Sachedina, *The Islamic Roots of Democratic Pluralism* (New York: Oxford University Press, 2001); Khaled Abou El Fadl, *Rebellion and Violence in Islamic Law* (Cambridge: Cambridge University Press, 2001); Abdullahi an-Na`im, "Project on the Future of Shari`a," at http://www.law.emory.edu/cms/site/index.php?id=2148/

7

Contextualizing Antisemitism in Islam: Chosenness, Choosing, and the Emergence of New Religion

Reuven Firestone

I am writing this paper in Cairo near the end of a sabbatical experience with a family in Egypt, and as such I ask a certain indulgence for framing my discussion in the form of anecdotal observations about my family's experience here. My wife and I met as Talmud study partners in rabbinical school, and my children have attended Jewish day schools all their lives before coming to Egypt. We lived for some years in Israel, where our children attended Israeli public schools in the Jewish, as opposed to Arab, education system.[1] We are "observant" Jews, meaning we observe Jewish religious traditions that require certain particularistic behaviors that have tended to surprise (and occasionally delight) our Egyptian friends. While in Egypt, our children attended an English language school that was attended primarily by Egyptian students (about 70 percent according to the school's account). Many of their friends are thus Egyptian, both Muslim and Christian. While we are living in an area of Cairo that is home to many U.S. and European expatriates, I speak Arabic, and both my wife and I have been involved in intensive Arabic language programs that encouraged and enabled us to engage with Egyptians of all social and economic classes.

We also are friends with Muslim Palestinian Arabs, whom we visited this year as well, both within the "Green Line" that defines the official borders of the state of Israel, and also in an area contingent to Jerusalem but officially associated with the territories governed by the Palestinian Authority. Most of our time has been spent within Egypt, however, so my anecdotal observations will be restricted primarily to this country.

I can confirm from my family's experience that anti-Jewish as well as anti-Zionist anxieties and prejudice are an integral part of the Egyptian cultural milieu. This observation applies to Egyptian Christians as well as Muslims, and in fact some of the most antisemitic sentiments we have experienced have originated among Egyptian Christians. There is no need to belabor the point, since most observers, including most Egyptians I have asked point-blank, would confirm that Egyptian culture is steeped in a kind of anti-Zionist and anti-Jewish resentment. Many would even use the term antisemitism without hesitation, though it is a loaded term here.

One example of this observation may be found in the manner in which our two boys were welcomed by their school, which had not previously had any students who identified themselves as Jews. After receiving our enrollment application, the headmaster (who is Arab but not originally Egyptian) approached the high school student leadership cadre in a private meeting, described our boys' religious identity, and asked the leaders' advice about how to welcome them to the school community. Although not everyone in the leadership group agreed, they strongly recommended as a group that our children not identify themselves as Jews until after they had established strong friendships, and that they only share that information with their close friends. When the headmaster informed us of this recommendation, we were initially shocked at the clear acknowledgment that our children might suffer social ostracism or worse, but then relieved that both the professional staff and the student leaders themselves were aware of the possibility and were committed to minimizing it and ensuring the boys a positive experience. Later, we learned that some among the administration were anxious enough about our children's experience as Jews that they considered denying our application for enrollment. As it turned out, however, our children were never personally attacked or humiliated, either physically or emotionally, though they often expressed to us in our dinnertime family conversations the discomfort they felt in their role as Jews in what we came to call the "Egyptian narrative" with regard to Jews, Judaism, and Israel.

The Issue of Narrative

It became clear to us early on that we were living in a world in which many of our basic assumptions about history and current affairs were not shared by the local population. A classic expression of this conflicting narrative was made manifest during our family visit to the October War Panorama Museum, where we joined Egyptian families and school groups to view the Egyptian "victory" against the "Israeli aggression" in the "October War" of 1973. Having lived in Jewish America and Israel, the narrative we were accustomed to would have termed the war to have been an Israeli victory (or at least successful defense) of a scurrilous Egyptian attack against Israel on the most sacred day of the Jewish religious calendar year in the "Yom Kippur War." While the October War Panorama Museum epitomized for us what we considered to be a manipulation of data based on a narrow and inaccurate historical analysis, it also caused us to reevaluate some of our own previously unexamined assumptions about the heroes and villains of history.

Another example of the lack of shared narrative was our observation of Egyptian reactions to the Muhammad caricatures published by the Danish newspaper *Jyllands-Posten* in the fall of 2005 (these caricatures portrayed the Muslim prophet in ways that were considered insulting to the point of blasphemy in many Islamic quarters). It was clear to us that the foundational assumptions about free speech and respect for religious symbols were fundamentally different in most of Egypt than in the world out of which we had come. This led to family discussions about the sometimes vitriolic language referencing Islam and Muslim believers by Westerners and even among our friends back home in the U.S., and we concluded that such public language certainly would not have been culturally acceptable in contemporary America had it been applied to Jews or Blacks.

A month or so after the excitement over the caricatures had subsided, we went to the American University in Cairo where we met up with a group for a university sponsored tour of a Cairo historical site. In the middle of one of the most public spaces at AUC, we saw a large cartoon blown up to a very large poster size and placed prominently in the middle of the area where most students, faculty, and administrators would pass. On the billboard was depicted a characterized portrait of a conductor leading an orchestra. Each of the musicians represented a nation, and they were perspiring and expending great energy in their efforts to follow the lead of the conductor. One of the nations, however, was entirely out of tune with everyone else and causing a screeching, unpleasant sound. It was, in essence, playing its own tune, while all the others were obeying the commands of the conductor. That errant nation was Palestine and was represented by Hamas. The conductor was a caricature of an Orthodox Jew. We found this very upsetting, since it played entirely into the antisemitic canard of Jews in control of the world, and very puzzling since the billboard appeared so soon after the caricatures controversy and remained in the public space for a full week. Within the context of Egypt in 2006, only weeks after violent and deathly riots in many parts of the Muslim world over the slandering of Islam, no one, it seems, even in this American university, found the antisemitic caricature problematic enough to remove it.

Based on our personal experience in 2006, we found that anti-Israel attitudes are a powerful and obvious factor in Egyptian society. Antisemitism, although less forthright and bold, is clearly a significant factor as well. Given our contacts and discussions with citizens of other Arab countries and our awareness of the Arab press, we would not feel uncomfortable in extrapolating from our own experience to presume a similar level of anti-Israel and antisemitic attitudes in other Arab Muslim countries. The reasons for the significant level of antisemitism in the Muslim world are complex and are in need of examination and research. Most researches in this area employ methodologies of history, sociology, and political science. In the following, I attempt to contextualize the antisemitism that appears in contemporary Islam through theory and observation in the study of religion, with special consideration for some traits and processes that seem to have become inherent among expressions of monotheism.

The Problem of "Chosenness" as a Feature of Monotheism

Cultures and societies tend to have their scapegoats, and the act of blaming others for one's own failures may be as long as human history (Girard). While this may be unacceptable from current perspectives of a universal human ethic, it has been the way of the world, and also the way of religion, for a very long time, and is perhaps particularly pronounced among those religions that consider themselves monotheist.[2] I will suggest why I believe this to be the case, and why this is even more so among those religious systems that believe they have a mission to bring the religion of truth to all of humanity.

One commonality among scriptural monotheisms is the presumption that God has communicated directly to a particular group. That communication is commonly known as revelation, the revealed will of God, and although the nature of revelation is different among the three primary scriptural religions of Judaism, Christianity, and Islam, the phenomenon of direct communication from God to a particular group through the medium of the revealed word is common to all of them. In the revelation known to Jews as the Hebrew Bible,[3] the revelation is conveyed through human witness of God giving the rules for right conduct, both ritual and ethical, at Mount Sinai. The revelation is conveyed in words, some of them written by the "finger of God" (Ex. 31:18, Deut. 9:10). If that people is in possession of the divine will, then it has access to a truth that transcends the mundane wisdom of humanity. God promises happiness and success to those within the designated group who respond positively to the divine will, and unhappiness and failure to those within it who do not (Deut. 11:26–28, 30:19–20).

Although Judaism has experienced periods of interest in mission, including interest in conversion, it has been far less interested, for both theological and historical reasons, in propagating the faith than has Christianity or Islam. Its concern has been directed more toward preserving its own unique religious identity than in promoting it among others. The early reason for this seems simple enough. Judaism emerged in its early, biblical form, with a unique vision of divinity in the form of monotheism. The "God of Israel" had been conceived in the earliest periods largely as a tribal God parallel to the tribal Gods[4] of neighboring peoples, but during the period characterized in the Hebrew Bible as the period of the great classical prophets (roughly eighth to the sixth centuries, BCE), there emerged among the Israelites the conviction that the God of Israel is also the God of the entire universe of their existence (Smith, 2001). It was not merely more powerful than the other Gods (Ex. 12:12), but actually the *only* God (Deut. 4:35, 39; 1 Kings 8:60; Isaiah 23:10, 45:5, 6, 18, 21).

Israel[5] was not the only community to have developed this view (Athanassiadi and Frede, Hawting), and may not have been the first. Other monotheisms or proto-monotheisms, such as that of the Egyptian pharaoh, Akhenaton, may have existed for a limited time (Redford, 11–26, Horning, 87–94), but they could not be sustained. Israel was the only community that successfully held on to this view in the ancient Near East, and as such it was constantly on the defensive in a world in which there were many enticements to engage in worship of foreign Gods (Numbers 25:1–9; 2 Kings 23:4–15).

The idiomatic expression of infidelity to the God of Israel in the Hebrew Bible is straying after or worshiping "other Gods" (Ex. 20:2, 23:13, Deut. 5:6, 6:14, 11:16, Jer. 1:16, 7:6, etc.), but what is more likely is that the Israelite community at this time was not completely convinced that the old, premonotheistic Israelite religious practices of its earliest days were totally false or inefficacious (Niehr, 51). A partial menu of what was available can be seen in 2 Kings 23:4–15. This is the story of King Josiah's reforms, and it lists many of the old practices by applauding Josiah's destruction of the means to engage in what appears to be the extremely popular and varied modes of polytheistic worship practiced in one fashion or another by Israel. He destroyed the objects made for Ba'al and Asherah and the "Host of heaven," he suppressed the idolatrous priests who made offerings to Ba'al and the sun and moon and constellations throughout Judah, tore down the cubicles of the male religious prostitutes within the Temple itself, destroyed many altars and shrines, including the Tofeth in *Gey Ben-Hinnom* where people burned their sons or daughters to Molekh,[6] got rid of the horses dedicated to the sun and burned the chariots of the sun, defiled shrines built for the Goddess Ashtoret and the God Chemosh on the Mount of the Destroyer, and shattered the sacred pillars and posts.

According to the direction of most current biblical scholarship, these were not foreign deities, the Gods of the hated "Canaanites," but were actually Gods *traditionally* worshiped by Israel (Smith, 2001). Lemche has shown that "Canaan" refers more to a geographical area than a people, a land in which lived a variety of peoples we know from biblical texts as Hittites, Girgashites, Emorites, Perizites, Hivites, etc., often lumped together in the Hebrew Bible (and Egyptian and Mesopotamian texts) as Canaanites (Lemche, 25–62). The Israelites lived there, too.

Israel, it now appears, emerged out of Canaan. To put it bluntly, Israelites *were* Canaanites, but they were one group of Canaanites that was experimenting with or were "growing" an innovative religious idea, and the Bible itself witnesses the bumpy road to monotheism.

In the system represented by the Hebrew Bible, responsibility to follow the revealed will of God found in the Torah is not universal. It is directed to Israel. It may seem strange to moderns that a religion espousing a concept of a universal God would appear to be unconcerned about the religious welfare of those situated outside of the receiving group. But in the ancient Near East out of which Israelite monotheism emerged, religion was by definition distinctively ethnic. Each ethnic or national group had its own God or pantheon of Gods, which had a unique relationship with its ethnic community. Thus, the normal tensions that arose between ethnic or national communities were often mirrored by tension between their Gods (Firestone, 2004). There was no concept of conversion in this world because religion was equal or exactly parallel with ethnicity and kinship. One could no more convert to another religion than one could become a different person.

On the other hand, intermarriage between peoples representing different religions may not have been a theological problem within the ancient polytheistic communities. If one traveled across national boundaries, one would pass from place to place but often find very similar Gods. Those Gods might have had different names but they were easily recognizable by strangers because they occupied a similar or identical place on what one might call "the food chain" of divinity. This was not the case with Israel, however, which had only one God, a "zealous God" (Ex. 20:4, 34:14; Deut. 4:24, 5:8, 15), who countenanced no confusion or association with other deities. Intermarriage, therefore, was always a threat to the unity and survival of the small community of Israel. Even those among whom Israel was permitted to intermarry, such as the Egyptians and Ammonites, could only intermarry with Israel after three generations of assimilation into the Israelite cultural and religious system (Deut. 23:8–9).

Israel was only one small religious-ethnic people among the many peoples and religions of the ancient world. According to the sentiment expressed repeatedly in the Hebrew Bible, Israelite religious leaders felt beleaguered by the theological insistence on monotheism in a world of multiple deities. Some neighboring religious systems, for example, had enticing ritual practices such as sacred prostitution, most likely human sympathetic acts of public coitus in order to stimulate the Gods to do the same and thus provide fertility to their people's pastoral or agricultural economies (1 Kings 14:24, Hosea 4:12–19, Ezek. 23:5–10). As Deuteronomy articulates the relationship,

> [Many nations] will turn your children away from Me to worship other gods…For you are a people consecrated to the Lord your God: of all the peoples of the earth the Lord your God chose you to be His treasured people. It is not because you are the most numerous of peoples that the Lord set His heart on you and chose you—indeed, you are

the smallest of peoples; but it was because the Lord favored you and kept the oath He made to your ancestors that the Lord freed you with a mighty hand and rescued you from the house of bondage, from the power of Pharaoh king of Egypt. Know, therefore, that only the Lord your God is God, the steadfast God who keeps His covenant conscientiously to the thousandth generation of those who love Him and keep His commandments, but who instantly requites with destruction those who reject Him....Therefore, observe conscientiously the Instruction—the laws and the rules—with which I charge you today. (Deut. 7:6–11, New Jewish Publication Society Translation).

"A people consecrated to the Lord..." is often translated from the Hebrew as "a holy people" (`am qadosh*), and the root meaning of *qadosh* is to separate, put aside, or consider unique. In the religious context of the ancient Near East, Israel was indeed unique and needed to remain separate in order to survive under the overwhelming pressure toward religious assimilation. The concept of "chosenness" was a natural strategy that evolved out of the need to maintain a unique religious-ethnic identity in an extremely taxing and difficult religious-ethnic environment.

This does not mean that ancient Israelites felt smug about their chosenness, or even that they had a consistent definition for it. There seems to have been disagreement over the meaning and responsibility associated with chosenness among biblical references to it. Some seem to relate to it as a unique privilege and benefit (Gen. 12:1–3; Ex. 19:1–6; Deut. 14:2). Others note the Israelites earned it through their merit (Gen. 22:15–18; Ex. 24:3–8). Still others consider the status to be one requiring great responsibility and extraordinary behavior (Amos 3:2), and others suggest that "chosenness" is only a relative term, for God has chosen other peoples as well as Israel (Isaiah 19:24; Amos 9:7).

It is likely all ethnic religions considered themselves unique at some level because of their special relationship with their ethnic Gods. The natural tendency toward ethnocentrism was naturally expressed in such systems through religio-centrism as well. Conquering peoples often insisted local populations include worship of the Gods of the conquerors in local ritual. On the other hand, we have records of peoples in the ancient world making offerings to foreign Gods, especially when they were in foreign territories where their own Gods had little or no jurisdiction (Tripolitis). When the great Achaemenid Persian Empire conquered much of the ancient Near East, it united many national religions with their individual pantheons under the overarching rule of the Persian emperor, the king of kings, and the transcendent God of spirit, Ahura Mazda.

When the Greeks conquered Egypt under the Ptolemies, they simply merged their own polytheistic system into the similar systems already in place in Egypt and governed previously under the pharaohs. The Ptolemaic kings thus fancied themselves as pharaohs as well, with the result the Egyptian Osiris, for example, was merged into a synthetic Hellenistic Dionysis or Hades, and the Egyptian Thoth with the Greek Hermes. This process of religious syncretism, however, was not successful with the strident monotheism of Israel. One of the problems the Jews faced during the Greco-Roman period was that they were expected, like all foreign peoples, to make offerings to the Gods of the Greeks after the Greeks had taken political control of Judean territories. Because Israel simply refused to do so, a compromise was eventually reached that allowed the Jews to worship in their own unique manner and make donations to their temple in Jerusalem (Gager).

When the Roman Empire imposed its political will over the conquered peoples, it also imposed its religious system, requiring that subjugated peoples make offerings to the Roman Gods, including eventually, the figure of the emperor. The ethnic religions centered around local Gods and temples that had survived the Persian and Greek empires eventually lost their unique religious identities under the Romans. They finally succumbed to the imperial system and assimilated religiously. The Jews could not do likewise, but they were "grandfathered" under the previous Greek system and thus remained exempt. Another group of emerging monotheists, however, who, like Israel, refused to recognize the Roman God-king but was not grandfathered along with Israel, was brutally persecuted. Christian monotheism, like the monotheism of the Jews, could not compromise the exclusive relationship with its God.

This illustrates what became a phenomenon of monotheism: an absolute and uncompromising requirement of exclusive relationship between monotheists and their God. Polytheists were able to make the transition to the dominant religious system. Monotheists could not.

Of critical importance is the observation that the religious requirement of exclusive relationship was experienced also as a social truth. The community that suffered for its unique relationship also had an exclusive status in the eyes of God. By the emergence of Christianity (and in parallel, Rabbinic Judaism), the chosenness that had emerged largely as a survival mechanism in ancient Israel became deeply associated with monotheism in general.

Choosing Religion

Hellenism not only introduced its religious pantheon to the Middle East, it also introduced the philosophical idea that an intelligent person could examine the available schools of systematic thinking about the universe until one found a system that made the most sense. The concept that one could scope out the philosophical market until a sensible system could be found had a profound influence on religion as well. It introduced the possibility of an individual deciding which religion was most reasonable, which made most sense. This was quite revolutionary because one was no longer bound to one's religion merely by one's ethnicity. One could convert to another religion. One could also proselytize (Nock).

We have suggested above that the phenomenon of chosenness had developed historically both in relation to and as a defense against the old ethnic religious systems. But when new forms of monotheism such as Christianity emerged that transcended the old ethnic or national forms under the influence of Greek thinking, the idea of chosenness remained. In Christianity, chosenness is not associated with peoplehood as in the biblical system, but with faith. The new "chosen" people are those who have "chosen" Christ, but the language of election in the New Testament still conveys an ethnic feel because it is an interpretation and permutation of the older ethnic sense of chosenness.

So for you who have faith it has great worth; but for those who have no faith "the stone which the builders rejected has become the cornerstone," and also "a stone to trip over, a rock to stumble against."[7] They trip because they refuse to believe the world; this is the fate appointed for them. But you are a chosen race, a royal priesthood,[8] a dedicated nation, a people claimed by God for his own, to proclaim the glorious deeds of him who has called you out of darkness into his marvelous light. Once you were not a people at all; but now you are God's people. Once you were outside his mercy; but now you are outside no longer[9] (1 Peter 2:7–10).

The application of "chosenness" from ethnicity to faith community is also clear from the exegesis of the Pauline school. As in 1 Peter,

Romans 9:7–8 and Galatians 4:21–22 clearly make the switch in chosenness from Jews to Christians by subtle use of the symbols and paradigms established in earlier scripture.[10]

The Polemics of Emerging Religions

New religions represent a challenge to the religious status quo (Stark, 1987). Thus in our own generation, for example, newly emerging religions are denigrated as "sects" or "cults." Established religions feel threatened by the challenge to their dominance and typically attempt to prevent the entrance of competition into the "religious market." Those new religions that survive the efforts to destroy them emerge after successful struggle against establishment forces.

Because revelation among the scriptural religions is generally coterminous with their earliest history, it inevitably contains—and sanctifies—the record of that early struggle. Argument or polemic against establishment religions is, therefore, a core component of scripture within Judaism, Christianity, and Islam. It typically identifies and demonizes the enemy that had tried to prevent the success of the divine will.

Thus one finds a repeated trope in the Hebrew Bible of divine rage directed at all the ethnic communities and their religions that tempted Israel away from its exclusive relationship with the one great God (Numbers 25:1-9, Deut. 7:1–4, 12:29–30, Judges 2:11–13, 10:10–16, 1 Kings 16:31, Ezek. 23:5–10, Amos 5:25–27). God's anger is directed against Israel for succumbing to the temptation of idolatry, but it is also a polemic directed against the establishment religions of the day. The threat was not that the competition refused to join Israel in its worship of a monotheistic deity, because such an option was impossible under the ethnic religious system of the age. The threat was, rather, that Israel would backslide into its polytheistic origins. The closest competition was the most threatening.

As Christianity emerged and distinguished itself from biblical religion, emerging rabbinic Judaism, and the Roman religious systems, it engaged in heated polemics with the religious (and political) establishments that were trying to destroy it. The closest competition phenomenologically was early rabbinic Judaism represented in the New Testament by the Pharisees. Paganism represented by the Roman Empire and the Roman Empire itself were certainly no less of a threat, but they were virtually untouchable because of the empire's overwhelming power in the region. The polemics against Rome are thus veiled, but the polemics against the Jews who countered the claims of the early Christians are quite clear and harsh. Not only are those who have chosen Christ the new chosen people, those Jews/Pharisees who consider themselves Israel (i.e., chosen and with a unique relationship with God) are really hypocrites who do not practice the real religion (thus the need for a new and uncorrupted one) and are, therefore, to put it bluntly as is occasionally done in the New Testament, evil (Matt. 23, John 8).

Unlike during the period of emerging biblical Israelite religion, however, at the time when Christianity was emerging, conversion *was* an option, and the very stubbornness of most Jews who refused to accept the messiahship of Christ became a major sticking point and a thorn in the side of the mission of the early Church. A classical, if radical, example is the anti-Jewish polemic of John Chrysostom, who complained that Greco-Romans interested in monotheism would attend his church but not fully commit, as it was also their habit to attend the synagogue (Gager, 118–120; Simon, 217–22). The overwhelming majority of Jews, who knew something about God and religion, rejected the religion of emerging Christianity. They represented established religion, and as in the biblical model, established religion was vehemently rejected by the new emerging religious movement of Christianity. That rejection was canonized in Christian Scripture. But the ancient and biblical origins of Israel were also difficult to compete with, so the Church claimed that it was the "true" Israel, *verus israel*.

In the world of Christian polemics, there is a presumption that there can be only one chosen. If one is chosen, the other(s) is rejected. This was not the position of the Hebrew Bible, which as noted above, was engaged in a different kind of polemic with its neighboring religious competition. We have observed how at least one strand of thinking about chosenness in the Hebrew Bible refrains from making any exclusive claims about it.

> In that day, Israel shall be a third partner with Egypt and Assyria as a blessing on earth; for the Lord of Hosts will bless them, saying "Blessed be My people Egypt, My handiwork Assyria, and My very own Israel" (Isaiah 19:24–25).

> To Me, O Israelites, you are just like the Ethiopians. True, I brought Israel up from the land of Egypt, but also the Philistines from Caphtor and the Arameans from Kir (Amos 9:7).

The difference may reflect another difference in the context of the early Christian world. Once the possibility of conversion became a reality, it created a pressure to engage in conversionary mission. If conversion was not a conceptual possibility as in the period of the Hebrew Bible, those who do not become part of the system cannot be blamed for it. But when conversion is possible, a certain weight passes onto the new religion to engage in a program for its propagation, and onto the nonbeliever to acknowledge the truth of the new religion. Refusal to recognize the truth not only represents stubbornness, it also damages its program and mission. Given that the New Testament is the earliest record of relations between the followers of Jesus and those who refused to follow, it should be no surprise it contains polemic. That is to say, the anti-Judaism of the New Testament is a natural, even if undesirable, aspect of the birth process of an emerging religion. The vituperative language and abusive and slanderous rhetoric in such texts as Matthew 23 and John 8 are arguably no more repulsive than the calls in the Hebrew Bible for the total destruction of the Canaanites who would tempt Israel from its monotheism. There is, however, one very significant difference between the two situations. Canaanites no longer exist and can thus serve as a symbolic scapegoat, victimized and vilified within the religious system without damaging the reputation or the physical existence of a living community.[11] This is, of course, not the case with Jews.

There is thus a latent anti-Judaism or antisemitism in the New Testament that, because of scripture's unique status as the word of God, can never be excised. Anti-Judaism was not uncommon in pagan Roman writings long before the canonization of the New Testament, but these never achieved the sublime status of scripture and therefore never had the same influence (Gager). Unlike human writing, the divine word cannot be erased by human authority. Antisemitism, therefore, will always exist, at least in its latency, in the most authoritative source that exists for the largest population of religious people in the world. The question is: How is latent antisemitism activated? We have observed in the last century how Christian, New Testament-based antisemitism has been activated (or simply remained active) in some contexts, while deactivated in others. One now classic example of activation is the role of Christian antisemitism in the secularist fascist racism of Nazi Germany (and areas influenced by its ideology), and that of deactivation in the abrupt turnaround of the Catholic Church with Vatican II. Exactly what psychological, social, political, and economic factors were instrumental in both still need examination, and why some groups or individuals went one way or the other in response to the authorities in each case is also a topic for further study.

Cultural Continuity for Successful Religion

When new religions emerge, those that are most successful manage to distinguish themselves from established religions at the same time they incorporate into their systems some of the more successful authenticating traits of those establishment religions. That is to say, successful emerging religions maintain a cultural continuity with prior religions that avoids making them appear so alien that they seem deviant to the potential pool of religious consumers (Stark, 1987). The sacrificial mode of worship within biblical monotheism, for example, maintains a powerful cultural continuity with the surrounding establishment polytheistic systems. The method of worship was virtually the same; it was the theology that changed. And when Christianity emerged it incorporated key aspects of both biblical religion and Greco-Roman paganism within it, thereby providing a level of comfort and recognizability through cultural continuity. Chosenness, understood in general as the unique relationship between the monotheistic God and God's chosen community, is an example of cultural continuity between new and established monotheisms. As new forms and communities of monotheism emerged through the past two millennia, all considered themselves the most chosen or truly chosen of God. Chosenness has thus become a sine qua non of monotheism.[12]

Once conversion became a possibility, a market of competing religions naturally developed in the Mediterranean and its environs through the growth of sectarianism and new religions. Proselytizing became a religious act and polemic a tool, with physical and spiritual rewards and compensators proffered to those who would join up (Stark and Bainbridge). It became standard procedure to claim that only those within the chosen (or those who had chosen correctly) would achieve everlasting life in the world to come, for example, all others either ending their existence with the their own mortality or worse, suffering damnation for their stubbornness. With the possibility of conversion and the increase in mission, the stakes were thus raised considerably. Martyrdom guaranteed immortal life in a world to come, and "holy war" on behalf of God's community (which could be conceived of as violence engaged even on behalf of the souls of those who would resist the growth of God's community), became operative.

Jews and Christians both engaged in martyrdom during the first two centuries of the common era (Boyarin). Jews engaged in a kind of holy war as well, though for political freedom against Rome rather than for the souls of Gentiles. Christians would wait some centuries before they would develop a different holy war phenomenon in a later, Christian context (Thompson, 1988: 24–26; Abdel Haleem, Ramsbortham, Risaluddin and Wicker: 32–37; Firestone, 2007). After Christianity dominated the Mediterranean religious market by the fourth century and then was established as a virtual Christian monopoly in the now Christianized Roman Empire, it became an increasingly totalitarian religion (Boyarin). Jews remained "grandfathered" into the religious scene as they had under the older Greco-Roman system, but now with many difficult restrictions and much discomfort. They nevertheless survived as distinct religious-ethnic communities throughout the Byzantine Empire and beyond into Persia, Arabia, and elsewhere.

The Emergence of Islam

By the time Islam began to emerge in the seventh century, chosenness and mission had become a major part of the religious repertoire of monotheisms. The Qur'an assures the emerging community of believers who followed Muhammad, "You are the best community that has been brought forth for humanity, commanding the reputable and forbidding the disreputable, and believing in God. If the People of the Book had believed it would have been better for them. Some of them are believers, but most are degenerate" (Qur'an 3:110). In Q. 5:3b, God proclaims, "This day I have perfected your religion for you, completed My favor upon you, and have chosen for you Islam as your religion" (see also Q. 24:55, 3:65–67).

Jews and Christians were well-ensconced in Arabia by the emergence of Islam, along with believers in the indigenous pre-Islamic Arabian religions. All fit the role of "establishment religions" in the Arabian model and were all less than interested in allowing a new religion to come onto the local market.

For establishment religions that are threatened by the emergence of new religious movements, motivation for thwarting the competition may derive from deep spiritual antipathy, or may simply be politics as usual, such as eliminating the growth of institutional competition that would deflect resources away from itself. But from the perspective expressed through the scriptural record representing the earliest testimony of newly emerging religions, it is clear such rejection is felt deeply, painfully, and existentially. When one is in the presence of priests, prophets, messiahs, or other inspired religious leaders of new religions who can communicate directly with God and who personally receive God's approval and blessing, public rejection by establishment religious authority is worse than appalling. It is an abomination. In the Arabian context, therefore, and for the same basic reasons the Hebrew Bible condemns the establishment polytheisms of its day and the New Testament condemns the establishment religions of its own, the Qur'an condemns the establishment religious systems of Arabia, those being indigenous Arabian polytheisms, Judaism, Christianity, and hints of competing Arabian monotheisms (Eickelman, Rubin, Landau-Tasseron). Much of the Qur'an is articulated in an environment that is polemical toward those establishment religions (Q. 2:75–81, 109–13, 4:48–52, 116–21, 5:12–14, 5:59–66 10:15–16, 34–39).

The greatest and most threatening establishment religion for the Qur'an is indigenous Arabian idolatry. Modern readers of the Qur'an tend not to resonate with the invective against polytheism, so they often miss this important fact. Western readers tend, rather, to be much more tuned in to the vigorous polemic directed against Judaism and Christianity. It is quite true that the Qur'an contains verses that are welcoming of Judaism and Christianity as well (Q. 2:62, 5:69), and verses that are markedly tolerant of other religions in general (Q. 2:256–7, 5:48, 10:99, 18:29, 42:15, 88:21–26, 109:1–6). But one cannot help but notice an overwhelming discourse of argument and polemic in the Qur'an toward all establishment religions, quite in parallel to such discourse in the Hebrew Bible and the New Testament.

After Arabian polytheists, the next most condemned religious opposition is Jews, and the third, Christians (Q. 2:120, 113, 135, 5:18, 51, 9:30).[13] This hierarchy appears not to reflect theological, ethnic, or cultural difference, though the Qur'an's opposition to polytheism is often reflected in theological terminology. Underlying the polemic and the hierarchy of resentment, rather, seems to be the level of existential threat each religious establishment represented for the nascent community of believers following the leadership of Muhammad. Given the particular history of the early Muslim movement, indigenous Arab polytheists were the most threatening to its success. For reasons examined below, Jews represented a lesser but still dangerous level of threat, and Christians the least. The specific arguments against these religious establishments have been examined elsewhere and are not of concern here (Waardenburg). We are interested at this point, rather, in understanding why greater invective against Jews in the Qur'an represents their greater threat to the nascent Muslim community than Christians (Q. 5:82).

It might seem surprising that Jews were considered more threatening than Christians. After all, the mightiest world power at the time of emerging Islam was the Christianized Roman Empire, known today as the Byzantine Empire, while Jews were dispersed throughout the Mediterranean world and the Middle East with no political control of any land and with no standing armies.

The power of empires, however, had little meaning for politics within the Hijaz, the area of Arabia out of which Islam emerged. Empires had never managed to control Arabia, which remained always outside their reach. Great powers had proxies and parties that represented their interests when it suited these groups within certain regions, but we have no evidence these were operative in the Hijaz during the period of emerging Islam.

It would seem logical, then, to assume the Jews living within Arabia and outside the influence of the empires were more powerful than the Christians in Arabia, but there does not seem to be evidence of this, either. What does appear clear, however, is during the century or two prior to the emergence of Islam, Jews had become influential or even occasionally dominant religiously, politically, and/or economically in particular areas of Arabia, while Christians became dominant in others. Neither community seems to have been organized in Mecca during the period of the emergence of Islam, probably because Mecca was an important religious center for pre-Islamic Arabian polytheisms. Jews and Christians would not have felt particularly comfortable living there. The first and most dangerous threat to emerging Islam, therefore, came from the polytheistic religious establishments of Mecca.

Although virtually nonexistent in Mecca, Jews had a powerful presence in Medina, a town (or more accurately, cluster of agricultural villages) about 360 kilometers (200 miles) due north of Muhammad's native town. Likewise, Christians were the dominant force in

Najran, about double the distance from Mecca in the other direction (southeast). Medina is in the Hijaz, while Najran is near the border between today's Yemen and Saudi Arabia in a region today known as `Asir. When Muhammad and his community were expelled from Mecca, they found refuge in Medina, the nearby area in which Jews were highly influential and relatively powerful. We have no record of any organized Christian community in Medina. It was in Medina that Muhammad encountered threatening resistance from a sophisticated, organized monotheistic community, and this community was Jewish (Lecker, Firestone, 1997, Wensinck).

When Muhammad preached against the polytheism of Mecca in his hometown, it appears clear from the sources that he was aware he would be opposed by those interests representing Arabian polytheism. But when he fled to Medina, he seems to have expected a welcome by the monotheists he knew lived there. After all, the Jews knew about prophecy and prophets, and they had a reputation for being an ancient and wise community with a special relationship to the one great monotheistic God.[14] Because Jews had a great history of prophets like Muhammad, one could easily expect that they would recognize him and welcome him. But Muhammad was profoundly disappointed, and not merely because he was not recognized as a prophet by the Jews of Medina. He was also vigorously opposed, a normal if unpleasant reality that all emerging religions face from establishment religions. This unexpected rejection seems to have been particularly painful. The Qur'an very clearly articulates the shock, disappointment, and anger that Muhammad must have felt at the betrayal of recognized monotheists. Sometimes the anger is directed metaphorically toward the ancient Israelites (Q.2:40–96, 211, 3:181–88, 4:46–47), sometimes directly to Jews contemporary to Muhammad (2:146, 159, 3:78–79, 5:41–44, 64, 62:6–8), and sometimes the two are conflated (4:153–61, 59:2–4).

In the Qur'an, Christians are sometimes included with Jews in the category of those who are disloyal to the true divine dispatch of the Arabian prophet. Sometimes they are listed specifically as Christians, and sometimes the two are lumped together as "People of the Book," referencing communities who were given previous Scripture by the same God who sent Muhammad.[15] But more often, the Jews are singled out as being particularly disloyal to God and deceiving the larger community in their obstinate refusal to accept the prophethood of Muhammad.

Had Muhammad turned south to Najran rather than north to Medina, the balance of polemic would have turned decidedly against Christians and Christianity, because in Najran it would have been the Christian community that would have inevitably opposed the claims of a new prophet. When the Muslims eventually did encounter organized Christian communities, they met vigorous opposition. In fact, the most enduring foe that the Muslim empires ever encountered historically was the Christian Byzantine Empire.

Activating Antisemitism

Because of the typically active and vigorous opposition to new religious movements by establishment religions and other power institutions, most emerging religions fail to survive. Those that do survive naturally incorporate a powerful antagonism to the establishments of their day, though this antagonism is often encouraged also by dissatisfaction with the way things were that provided impetus for the new movement in the first place (Saliba). It should not be surprising from this perspective, therefore, that a latent anti-Judaism or antisemitism is embedded in the Qur'an, as in the New Testament. Because Scripture is considered by communities of believers to be of divine origin, given by no less than God, they cannot countenance that any part of it be erased by human authority.

The question that remains, therefore, is what activates the latency of scriptural antisemitism into an operational state? This is an important question because the vital core scriptural authority of the New Testament and Qur'an that can and has been invoked to authorize and justify violence against Jews can never be eliminated from the consciousness of those who accept the divine origin of these scriptures. One can always point to certain scriptural texts to justify antisemitism. Antisemitism, therefore, will always remain potential. What makes it actual?

A closely related question is what makes activated antisemitism subside and revert to its latency? What influences scriptural interpreters to pass over verses that condemn Jews or Judaism and concentrate, rather, on other verses of divine writ? These are big questions and deserve consideration as topics for research.

Despite the fact that the processes influencing the activation or deactivation of antisemitic exegesis have not yet become an object of significant study, the scriptural basis and support for Christian antisemitism has been an object of intense scrutiny since the document known as *Nostra Aetate,* which resulted from Vatican II was published by the Catholic Church in 1965 (Gilbert, Gilman and Katz, Evans and Hagner). Similar and expanded study of these phenomena needs to be engaged in relation to Islam and in relation to religion in general. Antisemitism is one well-known case of religiously authorized hatred, but it is not unique. Antisemitism needs to be studied within the context of religiously sanctioned prejudice and scapegoating in general.

Conclusion

The Qur'an is not the only authoritative source in Islam that is relied on by religious leaders to justify calls for violence against Jews and Israel. The Hadith and the biographical literature chronicling the life of Muhammad are also regularly cited for this purpose. But the Qur'an is both the most authoritative and the best known among all Muslims, whereas there is disagreement among various expressions of Islam over the level of authority of other Islamic literatures.

The Qur'an is not monolithic in its view of Jews, Judaism and other religions in general. It appears less totalistic and absolutist, for example, regarding the salvation of those professing other religions, than the New Testament (the Hebrew Bible is hardly concerned with the issue of personal salvation as articulated in the later scriptures of Christianity and Islam). Take Q.2:62, for example: "Those who believe, and who are Jews, and Christians and Sabaeans—whoever believes in God and the Last Day and who works righteousness: they have their reward with their Lord, they shall not fear nor should they grieve" (see also 2:256, 5:48, 69, 10:94, 99, 16:93, 22:17, 42:15, 49:13). Various exegeses have been applied to the verses cited here, and their contextualization varies according to different readings, but they can and have been cited by Muslims and non-Muslims alike to demonstrate authoritative endorsement of religious tolerance and even pluralism in Islam (Sachedina, Ramadan).

Perhaps the most basic, egregious, and oft-repeated error with regard to scripture is to presume (or claim) that it is simple and straightforward. Divine scripture is, by definition, complex, and scriptural interpretation only deepens its complexity. Every reading of scripture includes interpretation, and scripture has existed in parallel with its interpretation for as long as we have had a scriptural record.

Despite the powerful and effective current activation of Islamic antisemitism authorized, in part, by readings (interpretations) of the Qur'an and amplified through the media in both the Muslim world and the West, Islam, like Judaism and Christianity, has a broad and complex array of interpretive vectors—a broad range of exegesis on virtually every topic that can be teased from and through the text. The antisemitism that currently infects much of the Muslim world finds support through the scriptural record of animosity toward the established religions that opposed Islam at its very genesis. It also finds support through the ways in which current events are played through traditional and paradigmatic narratives regarding the early community of believers and those who opposed them.

But Islam is not different in this regard from other religions that have institutionalized antipathy toward the other in various ways, often with horrendous historical results. The goal is to move Islam as well as other religions away from validating and justifying fear and hatred of the other, and toward a position of greater compatibility and amity. The interpretive tools and authoritative scriptural raw material for building more welcoming authentic religious attitudes are all in place. Rather than wait for however long it may take for a change in history that would naturally encourage such a positive development, what is needed today is to develop proactive strategies appropriate for the current historical context. It would also benefit us all to consider more carefully how political and policy decisions on all sides affect and/or activate those paradigmatic narratives that so powerfully influence the way we all react.

Notes

1. They attended both Jewish "religious" (*mamlakhti dati*) and "secular" (*mamlakhti*) schools.

2. I am not qualified to judge other religious or ethical systems such as the Hindu or Buddhist systems.

3. This is the preferred term, since the old Christian reference to the "Old" Testament carries the theological condemnation of that revelation as being outdated and no longer fully in force, while the "New" Testament reflect God's current will.

4. Standard English convention is to capitalize only designations for the monotheistic deity while referring to deities in polytheistic systems in lowercase. Because this is, at core, a historical/phenomenological rather than theological study, I prefer to refer to the deity or deities in the same manner.

5. In Jewish religious discourse, the word "Israel" refers to the Jewish people, which derived from Jacob, also known as Israel (Gen. 32:23–29). The official name of the modern nation-state is Medinat Yisrael, meaning the State of Israel or "Nation-state of the Jews."

6. This valley associated with the burning of children became associated in later times with hell or "gehenna" (*jahannum* in Arabic).

7. Cf. Psalms 118:22–23.

8. Cf. Ex. 19:6.

9. Cf. Ex. 19:5–6.

10. For a subtext to these exegeses, see Genesis 21:10–12.

11. This is not the forum for suggesting how to respond to the many complex problems that this reality presents for us. Much needs to be done in terms of interpretation and education.

12. Many more interesting aspects and details may be teased out of the notion of chosenness in religious systems, but they extend beyond the scope of this study. This author is in the process of preparing a book-length study of the phenomenon.

13. As in previous scriptures, the Qur'an also counters powers other than religious establishments that opposed the young emerging religious community, but we are not concerned with these categories of opposition.

14. This is evident from the Hadith, the genre of literature that purports to express the words and actions of Muhammad during his prophetic mission. Two of the most authoritative Hadith collections of Sunni Islam have been translated into English. On the great respect and wisdom accorded to the Jews in the pre-Islamic period by this authoritative Hadith, see Siddiqi, 1:181–82, 1:290, 4:1461, 1463; Khan 3:526, 9:46–61, 9:314–15.

15. The term "People of the Book" seems to have originated in the Qur'an. Sometimes it references both Jews and Christians as those who received prior Scripture (2:105, 109, 3:64, 5:68), but it may also refer specifically to Jews (2:101, 109, 145, 4:46–47, 153–55).

8

Antisemitism, and Contemporary Islam
Mehnaz M. Afridi

Bismillah irrahman nir rahim (The name of God the most merciful, and beneficial) Verily, God does not change men's condition unless they change their inner selves... (Surah: 12:11 Ar-rad).[1]

Memo by M. A. Muqtedar Khan at Adrian College after September 11th, 2001:

"To kill one innocent person is like killing all of humanity."

"Allah, through the Qur'an, tells Muslims to forgive injustices that Jews and Christians commit against Muslims."

"Let every Muslim know that there is no room in Islam for fanaticism, for hatred, racism, for terrorizing innocent people, for indiscriminate killing, even in a state of war."

"Islam is not about defeating Jews or conquering Jerusalem. It is about meaning, about virtue, about sacrifice and about duty. Above all it is the pursuit of moral perfection. Nothing can be further away from moral perfection than the war and slaughter of thousands of unsuspecting innocent people."[2]

I am a Muslim, a Muslim woman who is marked by the submission to God faithfully yet someone who does not claim a singular truth or possession to Islam which to me is as diverse as the many cultures that I have experienced throughout my life. The delight, honor, and anxiety stem from my personal experience of having lived in various places such as Europe, Pakistan, the Middle East, and now in the United States as a Muslim woman, but in the constant state of being *othered* within one's own community and in other's communities. Having lived within such an intermingling of so many cultures but still marked with a profound sense of identity, I also want to make clear that I do not possess all of the multiple qualities that classify the images of Muslims, nor can I represent all Muslims. I am simply one voice among the billion voices of Islam all over the world.

I want to make two vital points before I begin my attempt at a paper on "Antisemitism and Contemporary Islam." These personal nuances I hope will encompass and frame my talk today. I consider myself an optimist, and since most optimists exit with hope, let me then first begin with why I felt anxious about this presentation but also a joyful delight and hope for Jewish-Muslim relations.

Real dialogue, I believe, between traditions begins with the willingness of the participants, even if from a position of fear, helplessness, or disempowerment, to accept the vulnerability and "truths" that all of us believe in but, most important, how to create a new manner of imagining two traditions like Judaism and Islam that seem to be taut with mistrust, fear, and fragility where we can unhinge, break, and kill at a spoken word, attitude, name-calling or other deep misunderstanding. Therefore, to simply state that there is in fact antisemitism from various Muslim perspectives is to ignore the wider and dangerous misunderstandings from both the Jewish and Muslim perspective. I was/am anxious to speak as a Muslim about antisemitism because not only do I experience Muslim antisemitism, but also Jewish antisemitism all over the world as I seek out fellow Muslims and Jews to discuss my own work on contemporary Judaism and Islam. I begin with the sad assumption that there exists antisemitism everywhere in the world and within many Muslim communities globally on various levels, whether religious, political, economic, racial, or social.

So, where do *I* stand and how can I stand comfortably in front of an audience and tell a new story that you may already have heard for thousands of years? What can I shed light upon that may become a start of a fresh dialogue, but also a way of taking responsibility for antisemitism as a Muslim? And at the same time deconstructing the image that all Muslims are in fact antisemitic, anti-Jewish, and believe that the Jews are infidels? I am caught by the anguish of both communities and feel that as a Muslim I may be able to illuminate some theological and contemporary perspectives on antisemitism in a self-critique of Islam. It is important to note that not all Muslims are anti-Israel, but by openly accepting the state of Israel as a viable and independent state, there can be a relief and a small light of hope. My link with Israel as a young student at Hebrew University with a Pakistani passport clarified that both Palestinians and Israelis have deep theological and personal roots within Israel. I went to Israel to learn about Jews and the revelations of the Jewish tradition from the Jewish perspective and this was an important lesson that revealed to me that reading the Torah and the covenantal promise of the land of Israel left me in a position that I could in fact support the existence of Israel, and a land that Jews could finally call their own state after the horror of the Holocaust, but my experience was also influenced by the Palestinian poverty, border restrictions, mistrust of Palestinians, and the inequality of possessions, and this allowed me to see both sides as creating a gulf of mistrust, fear, and antagonism.

I will propose today as best as I can to see how antisemitism is interpreted from extreme interpretations of texts, and the political arena, and how Muslims can fall into a gruesome justification. Is this justification theological? Is it inherent in the politics of Israel and Palestine, in myths of Jewish conspiracies, in religious denunciations, in power dynamics within minor religious communities of Jews and Muslims? The list goes on, but permit me to stay within both the classical and modern periods of Islam. I felt that discussing classical Islam could perhaps shed some light on the discussion of the roots that Islam may be read by some as antisemitic and the interpretation from the Muslim literalist perspective and how both classical and contemporary Muslims have reconstructed and deconstructed such rooted beliefs today. My question though, is what type of Muslim/Jewish antisemitism are we experiencing today, and are we Jews and Muslims experiencing similar patterns or a different form? Or is this hatred impossible to undo? I am interested in these questions through an analysis of some of the commonly anti-Jewish verses of the Qur'an, and its interpretation, and why many Jews are seen as political allies of the West on the war on terror and believed to be behind the loss many innocent Muslim lives in Afghanistan, Iraq, and Palestine. Similarly, the rise of antisemitism in Europe, the United States, Israel, and many Muslim countries has consumed the lives of innocent Jews, and how Jews might see themselves mistrusting Muslims, a fear of the antisemitism, and the Qur'an as particularly violent to their own communities.

This is the paradox for me and deeply problematic, where I can feel the hardships and misgivings of being both Jewish and Muslim at the same time, and accept the revelations of these traditions as mine even if I were born Muslim and remain to be one. On a more positive note, I think that if we can flesh out the problems on both ends of these perceptions, then we may be able to have some meaningful dialogue and understanding. The practice of self-criticism, listening to how others understand their own scriptures, the right to ask embarrassing questions and to quote from one's own sacred text even if one is embarrassed, is to make our first step better to Muslim and Jewish relations in a world that has portrayed us as long-standing enemies, even though we have been pulled apart by the loss of innocent lives since the creation of the state of Israel on both Jewish and Muslim sides (not to ignore Christian and secular lives).

My second point on why I am delighted to be here is as important if not more: I need to be here, more Muslims need to be here, and more Muslims need to speak out against antisemitism, which I believe has been left up to an uncanny silence or the "extremists," who have stolen our own interpretation and blindfolded many Muslims even in America. This silence is one that left so many great Jewish post-Shoah writers to teach us that silence is itself the perpetrator of murder, genocide, war, and antisemitism, that has left an indelible mark of so much horror past, present, and future. Therefore as a Muslim I am happy and honored to be among some of the most distinguished scholars in the field of Judaism, and as a Muslim this moment is a positive indication that yes! Yes! Yes! There is hope and we must continue this type of discussion and dialogue.

I begin with a quote from Richard Rubenstein in his book *After Auschwitz*, which has resonated with me since I was an undergraduate student at Syracuse University. He writes:

> When we finish *The Plague*, we are aware of the fact that this solidarity is the deepest root of Camus's atheism. He refuses, as does Ivan Karamazov, to see man as inevitably and inescapably guilty before God. He accepts the tragedy, the inevitability, and the gratuitous absurdity of suffering, but he refuses to consent to its justice. He would rather live in the absurd, indifferent cosmos in which men suffer and die meaninglessly but still retain a measure of tragic integrity than see every last human event encased in a pitiless framework of meaning which deprives men of consolation that suffering, though inevitable, is not entirely merited or earned. (Rubenstein, *After Auschwitz*, p. 67)

This statement maintains that the suffering of human beings is inextricably linked with both atheism and religion, or the identifiable human being lies in an inevitable, vulnerable position with or even without God. Therefore, we humans regardless of faith and identity are vulnerable to death, suffering, and meaninglessness.

As Muslims we believe in a very important concept like our Jewish cousins that defines the oneness of God in the manner of Tawhid. Tawhid encapsulates God as the one, the only one, and God who is everywhere and anywhere. Muslims see this as the absolute oneness of God: the first principle, creator of all, eternally present in history and at each moment. This is the cornerstone of Islam but also within Judaism, which presupposes that human beings have to rely on themselves to recognize where and how God is, but one cannot fully grasp or know or hold God. As the Jews believe that "God is the creator of the universe, with which He made a covenant to sustain it. God appointed humanity to be stewards of nature (Gen. 2:15) and made a covenant, stands above nature as its steward but under God as its lord." Similarly, Camus's character in *The Plague* had taken in human suffering and realized that to justify death and give innocent suffering meaning was to accept injustice on innocence, yet the religious community, which Jews and Muslims rely upon, are not always justifiable. Perhaps what Camus fails to see is how it gives them meaning. I start with a problem of meaning and justice because Judaism has a profound tradition in undertaking these two moral precepts and similarly Islam, even in its understanding of death and suffering, has offered up a meaning that has to rely on a justice that human beings cannot come to on their own but through their reliance on God. I begin with the central commonality of Judaism and Islam as both submitting to the idea of the one God but also that individuals with the guidance of prophecy, context, compassion, and forgiveness may decide to proceed with their own life, as they will with the direction of God. Therefore, Muslims and Jews are not gods, but the carriers of the messages of God that live by example as Fackenheim has said:

> If he remains frozen in stark terror, he cannot observe the commandments at all. And, if he evades that terror, he may observe the commandments, but he has lost the divine commanding presence. Only by reenacting both the terror and joy can he participate in a life of commandments which lives before the sole Power and yet is human." (Fackenheim, p. 16)

Classical Period: Jews and Muhammad

It is a fact and not a myth that there are unfavorable verses toward Jews, Christians, and non-Muslims in the Qur'an, paradoxically there are positive and favorable verses in the acceptance of Jews, Christians, Sabeans, and others. It is important to know that the Qur'an can be interpreted like the Torah, and the Christian Bible without the knowledge of the wider body of legal and theological Islamic literature, commonly known as Tafsir, which is interpretation relying on several sources that recount the story of Muhammad; the first is the Hadith, then Sira or even the Sunna. Similarly, in the Jewish tradition one can rely on the Talmud, Mishnah, and Gemara for parallel understanding of Tafsir, which even Islamic scholars in the eighth century relied upon to make sense of revelation and inconsistent chronological order in the Qur'anic manuscript.

Verses in any tradition do not stand on their own without context, and the meanings of these verses after they are contextualized must be further read as much more nuanced and sophisticated than the literal meaning of any verse. Commentary is an essential tool not only of religious transformation but also of the transmission of tradition. To rely on verses that have no context historically that state that the Muslim must either conquer, kill, dictate, and convert any others is to be ignorant of the particular context. This is not an apology for the extremists who do in fact transform the literalism and command of submission to death, antisemitism, or even anti-Christian doctrine, it is however always useful to take an example of this type of hyperbolic interpretation and put in a new reading or even a context that allows for the interpreter to seek justice. Herein lies the paradox that one can read within Islam: How can a religion accept other faiths and reject them simultaneously? How can Muslims "justify" as Camus could not the reference to violence? Like the Jewish tradition, we find this type of violence with earlier groups in Deuteronomy and also in the most important story of the Akedah, where Abraham is asked to sacrifice his own son Isaac. Do Jews then interpret these narratives as literalists as well? In the Qur'an one may find the following example, which seems to paradoxically lend itself to extreme interpretations by some Muslims to see the Jew or others as enemies and a justification to mistrust them. Sadly, this type of justification has been carried out by too many Muslims today who do in fact literally believe in the Jew as an enemy and Israel as the deepest problem of the Muslim psyche and this is carried out in e-mail exchanges, interviews, on websites, videotapes between extremists such as Osama bin Laden, Al-Zawahiri, the Iraqi insurgents who justify beheadings, and the suicide attacks all over the world. Neither beheadings nor suicide attacks are permitted in Islam especially in the face of innocent murder and martyrdom. This horror must be condemned, and in the face of Islam, and cannot be justified through any case even when the Israeli military has used its might against Palestinians and the U.S. has killed innocent civilians in the time of war. Let me be clear: Antisemitism and anti-Americanism by Muslim extremists cannot be justified by actions committed against them, as the Qur'an and Muhammad have forbidden the loss of innocent lives at any cost.

Herein lies the problem of how Muslims see Jews and the West, and how the Qur'an lies in a vulnerable position with human interpretations that have a presupposed intent and rage against others. Let me share a few verses with you to try to explain what the Qur'an says, and in what connection, which is the paradox of me as a Muslim.

> Many people of Scripture would love to turn you back from your belief to unbelief because of their envy when the truth has been revealed to them. But be forgiving and pardon until God gives his command, (hatta ya'ti allah bi'amrihi) for God is able to do all things.[3]
>
> Sura 2:109

This verse was written when Muhammad encountered Jews in Medina and shows the growing Muslim polity. Then the next *suras* are important in the differences of opinion but acceptance of Jews, especially in this case.

> Because of their breaking covenant, we cursed them and hardened their hearts. They change words from their contexts and forget some of what they were taught. You will continue to uncover treachery from all but a few of them, but be forgiving and pardon, for God loves the kindly.[4]
>
> Sura 5:13

The first verse refers to the Children of Israel, but treachery here represents a transition from the Jews. So here we see a small example of both chronological but referent difference. The last verse, which is important in looking at Muslim–Jewish relations, is in Sura 29:46.

> Only argue nicely with the people of the book, except with the
> oppressors among them. Say: We believe in what has been revealed
> to us and revealed to you. Our God and your God is one, and it is
> Him to whom we surrender.[5]

Muhammad expected many Jewish communities of Medina to
accept the monotheistic revelation that he believed was the same as
Moses, but it had been transformed and changed through the people
and transmitted again through Jesus and Esau. These verses show how
interpreters can find a manner in which, if one were forced to rely only
on the sacred text, the commandments of restraints are much more
emphasized rather than war or the killing of others. However, the danger of antisemitism from a Muslim perspective can be exacerbated
within the period of classical Islam when Muhammad led battles for
defense against the Kafirs, which many translate as infidels or miscre-
ants. Tariq Ramadan has explained it in the following manner:

> Thus, one finds in the Qur'an verses that define Jews and Christians,
> even though they are among the "people of the book" as Kuffar (plu-
> ral of Kafir, most often translated as "infidels" or "miscreants"): they
> are certainly in a state of denial (Kafara), those who have said god
> was the Messiah the son of Mary: or again, "Those among the people
> of the Book and the polytheists who have denied (kafaru)." Accord-
> ing to the perspective of the majority of literalist scholars, this leaves
> no doubt as to their fate, especially since the Qur'an says explicitly
> "Religion in the sight of God is Islam" and again : "He who desires
> religion other than Islam will not find himself accepted and in the
> hereafter he will be among the losers." "Jews and Christians will not
> be pleased with you unless you follow their religion."[6]

Even though these verses seem to become monotonous in condemning non-Muslims, they call for a deeper analysis that Muslims
need to reconsider in their own interpretations, but also as a requirement for all Muslims. For Muslims it is ordained that they should not
deafen their ears or ignore their own interpretation since Allah has
called them to do so. As Ramadan goes on to point out, "Kafir is one
who is a denier with a veiled heart: this refers to those whose original
longing for the Transcendental had been stifled, veiled, shut off in their
hearts to the extent that they deny the present of the creator" (Ramadan, 206). Therefore, the translations that block our perspective con-

clude that most human beings do indeed believe in the creator and in Islam, which has two meanings, the first simply for those who submit to a Creator, which may include under this definition Hindus, Buddhists, etc., and the second meaning of Islam for those who accept the Qur'an as revelation and Muhammad as the last prophet, which is a meaning that most literalists have interpreted. One might see these as justifications for relieving the burden from Muslims, but this is where my anxiety of being a Muslim and Islam as the path to peace is no longer a domain where I can feel fully proud. As I move along in these different interpretations by some very recent Muslim scholars, however, the paradox of Islam today is that it has somehow been silenced by its literalism toward others like Jews and also been imaged as having a dominating clerical call for concepts such as jihad, conversion, killing the infidel, suicides, beheadings, and the negligence of allowing others to enter into the fore to complexity and reinterpret the Islamic intellectual philosophy that is the important aspect of being Muslim. The first call to submit was to God, and the second was to do moral good and protect one's belief in the creator. Camus would argue with me here that this type of theological dimension or reinterpretation may lead to more unjustifiable acts away from justice, however, what we can learn from some of these Qur'anic verses is that we humans are the interpreters and that perhaps Muslims are feeling the unjustifiable desperation through death but also the death of their own faith. As Amin Maalouf has written:

> Nor, as I have already had occasion to note, do I think religion can
> be entirely dissociated from the fate of its followers. But it does seem
> to me that the influence of religion on people is often exaggerated,
> while the influence of people on religion is neglected. [7]

Contemporary Antisemitism and Islam

I would like to note that there are many Muslims who have condemned suicide attacks, beheadings, what has been termed terrorism, and numerous statements have infiltrated the media in Europe, Asia, and the Middle East, but there are many Muslims who have been silenced by the international political scene all over the world and committing crimes against humanity by defending, justifying, or even accusing the victims for the alliances with the U.S., Israel, Iraq, Serbia, and India.

As a Muslim in America, there is a social contract that we sign with Americans as a country with regulations that allows for religious freedom but also for the freedom of speech. This allowance and democracy should and must become a vehicle for American Muslims to speak out against injustices, especially toward our Jewish cousins. This I believe is a lesson that we have to begin to learn. This should disturb Muslims deeply and question their own roles as representative Muslims here in America, and they should come out and condemn the horrific killings of innocents whether in Egypt, Israel, Palestine, Iraq, Sudan, Pakistan, and now in Indonesia. A cycle of violence has somersaulted into what now the majority of non-Muslims believe is the nature of all Muslim people, whether violent, apologetic, or polemic. This is appalling and embarrassing, but the deeper issue is that many Muslims do in fact feel that the Jewish world community of about 18 million is in alignment with the United States and has become the "Zionist" enemy who will want to oppress the Muslims. However, I would argue that today most Muslims do not hold contempt for Judaism, but instead for the actions of both the Israeli and American governments. Unfortunately, Jews have experienced this type of antisemitism and hatred in Europe for hundreds of years well before the Holocaust. Some had make claims on the culpability of some Catholics who condemned Jews for the death of Christ, others Nazism, some Fascism, and simply the horror to use Hannah Arendt's words "the banality of evil" that pours forth from all of us at various times within history.

Let me flesh out some e-mail exchanges that have galvanized the Internet and the Muslim perspective that has been a place of justification, jihad, and defense of Muslim extremists who have polarized the Muslim community in many ways that shattered the hope that non-Muslims could indeed see Islam as a diverse, rich, just, and peaceful faith and Muslims as human beings who are not steeped in violence but trying to struggle with the violence themselves.

As a Muslim, the anguish of reading the newspaper every day, watching suicide bombings, and simultaneously knowing that 70,000 Iraqi civilians have died, 1 million Sudanese displaced, thousands of Israelis and Palestinians have died, one can only feel that one's banner of faith is as guilty as humanity is for all of its crimes. However, I think it is useful to share some extremely violent e-mail exchanges that can draw out this type of extreme violence from groups of Muslims who feel justified in committing murder.

I want to share some of these postings that have been referenced in Gilles Kepel's most recent book *The War for Muslim Minds: Islam and The West*:

> In the name of Allah the Merciful, the Compassionate, Praise to be to Allah, who has said, "slay the infidels wherever ye find them, and seize them, beleaguer them. Blessings and praise upon the most noble of prophets, Muhammad, and upon his people. In this holy month [Ramadan], and in these past ten blessed days, we would like to congratulate, first, our people in Palestine, and then all Muslim Ummah. We delayed these congratulations deliberately, so that they would coincide with the two operations in Mombassa, Kenya, against Zionist interests, and so that our greeting would be more meaningful in the circumstances under which the Ummah is suffering by the fault of its enemies, the Crusaders and the Jews.[8]

Here we witness Osama and Zawihiri's call to prohibit Muslims from trying to live peacefully and deal with others with respect that would rather succumb to a victimhood of the many unfortunate circumstances that have befallen upon Muslims, but violence is not the answer and the silence is the perpetrator of such an extreme vision of terror.

The rise of antisemitism is a problem for Jews and Muslims; innocent victims are being terrorized because of the proclamations of both extreme Jewish and Muslim perspectives on each other's motive. How can such proclamations be accepted when Islam accepts Jews and Christians as valid sacred religions given through the same God, even at the time of Muhammad he sanctioned peace with Jews and Christians. And today, the contemporary situation has worsened due to religious alliances, memories of injustices, and economic inequalities.

Notes

1. Al-Qur'an, translated and explained by Muhammad Assad.

2. M. A. Muqtedar Khan, Memo to All Muslims, September 2001 (please see website, www.memotomuslims.com).

3. Al-Qur'an, trans. Mohammad Asad (Gibraltar: Dar Al-Andalus).

4. Al-Qur'an.

5. Ibid.

6. Tariq Ramadan, *Western Muslims and the Future of Islam* (Oxford: Oxford University Press, 2004), p. 205

7. Amin Mallouf, *In the Name of Identity: Violence and the Need to Belong* (New York: Arcade Publishing, 1996), p. 60.

8. Gilles Kepel, *The War for Muslim Minds: Islam and the West*, trans. Pascale Ghazaleh (Cambridge: Belknap Press of Harvard University Press, 2004), p. 70.

9

The Cross and the Crescent: Divergent Responses to Antisemitism in Contemporary Islam

Michael Berenbaum

As Bishop of Rome and Successor of the Apostle Peter, I assure the Jewish people that the Catholic Church, motivated by the Gospel law of truth and love and by no political considerations, is deeply saddened by the hatred, acts of persecution and displays of anti-Semitism directed against the Jews by Christians at any time and in any place. The Church rejects racism in any form as a denial of the image of the Creator inherent in every human being (cf. Gen. 1:26).

In this place of solemn remembrance, I fervently pray that our sorrow for the tragedy which the Jewish people suffered in the twentieth century will lead to a new relationship between Christians and Jews. Let us build a new future in which there will be no more anti-Jewish feeling among Christians or anti-Christian feeling among Jews, but rather the mutual respect required of those who adore the one Creator and Lord, and look to Abraham as our common father in faith (cf. *We Remember,* V).

Pope John Paul II at Yad Vashem

They [Israelis and Jews] try to kill all the principles of divine faiths with the same mentality of betraying Jesus Christ and torturing Him and in the same way that they tried to commit treachery against Prophet Muhammad.

Syrian president Bashar Al-Assad welcoming Pope John Paul II to Syria, May 5, 2001

153

These two papal events exemplify the two contrasting possibilities of interreligious life in the twenty-first century, the promises and the dangers.

First to the good news:

As part of his carefully orchestrated pilgrimage to the Holy Land early in the new millennia, Pope John Paul II completed a process of reconciliation set in motion more than a third of a century earlier by his predecessor Pope John XXIII at the Vatican Council.

Students of the Holocaust well understand that the destruction of the Jews was built on a foundation established by religious anti-semitism. Clearly religious antisemitism did not operate alone. It was intensified by political antisemitism and brought to its fulfillment by the unique Nazi contribution of racial antisemitism. At the beginning of his magisterial work *The Destruction of the European Jews,* Raul Hilberg put it succinctly: "The Church said: you have no right to live among us as Jews, therefore convert. Political leaders who followed said, "you have no right to live among us, therefore leave," and the Nazi who followed said: "you have no right to live!"[1] The result was "the Final Solution to the Jewish question"—systematic murder, which the Nazis called extermination.

Irving Greenberg has pointed out that there is a paradox relating to the Holocaust: "The innocent feel guilty, and the guilty feel inno-cent." Let us focus on the example of Pope John XXIII, whose efforts on behalf of the Jews were exemplary. More than fifteen years before he became pope, Monsignor Roncalli used his good offices as the apos-tolic delegate in Istanbul to gain vital information on the fate of the Jews, to rescue those Jews fleeing German occupation that he could, and to forward pleas to the Vatican on behalf of the Jews. As pope he was determined to ensure that the Holocaust would not recur. He met with Jules Isaac, a survivor of the Holocaust and the leading scholar of antisemitism, and set out to transform Christian teaching regarding the Jews by undertaking three vitally important reforms to insure that the foundations of Christian antisemitism were broken.

As pope, he convened Vatican Council II and initiated the pro-cess that led to the promulgation of *Nostra Aetate,* which dropped the charge of deicide, that Jews were responsible for the crucifixion of Jesus, and accorded fundamental respect to Judaism not only as the mother religion of Christianity, but as an ongoing religious faith. Even Church liturgy was changed for Good Friday to eliminate the mention of "perfidious Jews," and Scriptural readings were altered so as not to reinforce antisemitism and endow it with Scriptural sanctions.

Pope John XXIII understood that religious antisemitism was neither the most pernicious nor dangerous of the charges leveled against the Jews. Coupled with religious antagonism were social structures that reinforced the Jew as outsider and that imposed restrictions on Jewish participation in society and a in series of recurring myths regarding the Jews, accusations of the poisoning of wells during the Black Plague, the slaughter of young boys for Passover matzah, and to the myth of Jewish world domination contained in the forgery of *Protocols of the Elders of Zion*. The pope had witnessed the results of racial antisemitism. He had been engaged in the efforts to combat them.

The changes promulgated by Vatican II were, dare one say, revolutionary. The charge of deicide was eliminated. In common street language, Jews were no longer "Christ killers." The tradition of supersessionism, that Christianity had come to fulfill Judaism, to complete Judaism, and thus that there was no reason for the mother religion to continue, was deemphasized and not transmitted, and the religious rituals that had the potential to stir antisemitism were restrained and recast. The result was a dramatic change in Roman Catholic teaching and an equally dramatic improvement in Roman Catholic–Jewish relations, especially in the American Church. Civility was achieved and, more important, deeper mutual understanding.

The change in Roman Catholic teaching was a wonderful example of Jewish theologian Emil Fackenheim's axiom that where there is recognition of the Holocaust as rupture and *mending* takes place, the strength of the tradition is to be found.

And yet, the change brought about by Vatican II was not quite complete. Roman Catholicism had come to terms with 1,878 years of Jewish life, and Jewish existence in the Diaspora, but not with a form that Jewish life had taken since 1948, namely, the existence of a Jewish state of Israel.

Pope John XXIII died before the work of the Vatican Council was complete. He died well before the Vatican was ready to accord diplomatic recognition to Israel, and his successor Pope Paul VI took deliberate steps not to recognize Israel de facto or de jure, even entering the country not at a marked border crossing in order not to imply recognition when he visited Israel in 1964 as part of his pilgrimage to the Holy Land. He never once even mentioned the word Israel during his stay in that country.

Enter Pope John Paul II, who as a young man in Krakow grew up among Jews and as a Pole witnessed the Holocaust directly and at close hand. In the aftermath as a young parish priest, the future pope would not baptize Jewish children saved by Polish Christians during the Holocaust unless they were told of their religious heritage.

The battle against Christian antisemitism has been a significant focus of his papacy. Among the major efforts, he visited a synagogue in Rome and prayed with its rabbi and congregation, which was an unprecedented gesture by the bishop of Rome. Under his leadership, the Vatican granted diplomatic recognition to the state of Israel and exchanged ambassadors with the Jewish state. In 2000, Pope John Paul II visited Israel, arriving at its international airport, meeting with the president and prime minister, visiting the offices of the chief rabbinate and according them the very same honor he would accord the leaders of other faiths.

The pope then took the unprecedented step of visiting Yad Vashem, Israel's memorial to the Holocaust, and the Western Wall, inserting a prayer of apology in the Wall.

Of course, there are still problems outstanding in Jewish-Roman Catholic relations, such as the varied and contrasting assessments of the role of Pope Pius XII during the Holocaust, which have been the subject of many books in recent months. His canonization has been postponed because of the controversy associated with his papacy. So too, there has been controversy over the failure to open Vatican archives relating to the Shoah for independent scholarly review, the canonization of another Pope Leo IX, and the controversy surrounding the case of Edgardo Mortara, a young Jewish child who had been baptized by his family's maid without their knowledge and approval and who was kidnapped by Church officials and not returned to his parents despite their repeated protests. One can think of this as another Elian Gonzalez case, with religion taking the place of politics.

Still, when the history of the last third of the twentieth century is written, the mending in Catholic-Jewish relations and the unprecedented civility, harmony, and mutual respect of the relationship between these two ancient faiths will be one of its most significant—and most honorable—achievements. It is a model for where interreligious relations must go as the global universe takes shape in the twenty-first century.

The results have been impressive not only for Christianity but for Judaism as well. Israeli commentator Yossi Klein Halevi said:

A penitent Christianity enables Jews to stop blaming Jesus for the persecutions of the past and appreciate his role in transforming humanity. Obviously, those of us who now embrace Jesus as a long-lost brother relate to him in a particularly Jewish way. For Christians, Jesus is the sacrificial redeemer who took upon himself the sins of humanity; for Jews like me, Jesus is a prophetic figure through whom faith in the God of Israel was spread among nations.

Rabbis engaged in dialogue with Roman Catholics have also come a long way. In a recent statement called *Dabru Emet* [*Speak Truth*] signed by two hundred rabbis and Judaic scholars, they sought to find a positive theology of Christianity. "While Christian faith is not a viable religious choice for Jews... through Christianity, hundreds of millions of people have entered into relationship with the God."

Let us heed what was required to make these substantive changes and to initiate significant shifts in attitude.

The problem was recognized. Deeply and profoundly. Perhaps not every apology was made or every responsibility accepted, but if we look at the long record of the past four decades—and judge by deeds—then it is clear that the problem was recognized.

The tools of religion were employed. The Roman Catholic faith did not abandon its religious teaching. Through new scholarship and exegesis, through building on traditions that were ignored or under-represented such as Jesus the Jew, religious teaching was transformed and renewed and a new sense of mission achieved.

Change did not happen in isolation. The teaching about the Jews was one part of *Nostra Aetate,* which indeed charted the Roman Catholic Church's acceptance of the reality of Christian pluralism, its embrace of ecumenicism, and its embrace of other faiths. It was a response to modernity and to the ethics of interreligious civility that facilitated the Church's role in the modern world.

It was institutionalized. The changes were reflected in prayer and liturgy, in teaching and catechism. A generation ago they were revolutionary, now they are routine. Many devout Catholics and their priests do not remember a time when this was not the Church teaching.

So much for good news!

There is a tragic irony of contemporary interreligious life. As Christianity has sought to rework its outlook toward the Jews, rejected and discredited views of Christians—alien to Islam—have been imported into Islam, where they form the backbone of contemporary Islamic antisemitism.

A bit of history is in order: Robert Wistrich, an Israel historian of antisemitism, commented that it is difficult to generalize regarding the long history of Islamic-Jewish relations, which differed in times and in places. "The Jewish condition in the age of Mohammad and the early Muslim conquests, in the relatively flourishing period until 1200, in the later Middle Ages, under the Ottoman ascendancy, during the period of Western colonialism and in the later twentieth century has, after all, been far from uniform."[2]

The teachings of Islam toward the Jews are complex. The Hebrew Bible and the Christian Bible are regarded as authentic revelations of God but superseded by the Qur'an, the direct revelation of God to the Prophet Muhammad. There are negative images of Jews found in the Qur'an just as there are negative images of Jews and Judaism in the Christian Bible. If the latter reflect the tension between those Jews who accepted Jesus as their teacher and those who did not and the subsequent breaking away of Christianity from Judaism, the statements of the Qur'an reflect the resistance that Muhammad encountered from Jews. Thus, the Qur'an speaks of Jews being laden with God's anger because they had disbelieved the signs of God and slain the Prophet unrightfully. "The unbelievers of the children of Israel were cursed by David and Jesus."[3] Jews were accused of falsehood, of distortion, of being the "corrupters of Scripture."[4]

Certainly, these verses—and the attitudes they reflect—pose problems for the believer and opportunities for extremists to invoke the authority of tradition against the Jews—then as now. Yet, in practice over centuries Jews were treated as dhimmis (protected people), a more honorable category than pagans, and were permitted to practice their religion and to have their own communal organizations.

Because Jews were *not* the only dissident religion within the Islamic world, and because they never were quite as prominent in the drama of Muhammad's career as they were in the life and death of Jesus as told by the later Gospels, they never played the same central role in Islamic teaching until contemporary times.

To exacerbate tensions and to reinforce antagonisms one can return to Scripture and reemphasize certain core teachings, often to the exclusion of other contrasting teachings.

The converse is also true; to diminish tension and strengthen a sense of mutual understanding one can use the interpretive tradition inherent in each of the three monotheistic faiths to ameliorate difficulties and provide a basis for mutual understanding and pluralism.

As Reuven Firestone, the distinguished Jewish scholar of Islam has written: "Exegesis is powerful. Where there is a will, there is often a way to locate the right sacred texts and then find a way to read them so that they can be understood to support a broad array of beliefs and behaviors."

Recent Christian exegesis has recast the narrative of the crucifixion just as later New Testament Gospels recast the earliest narrative to reflect sociopolitical changes and perhaps also initiate them. Jewish exegesis in Talmudic time muted the militancy of biblical teaching just as Jewish exegesis in contemporary times struggles with the transformation in contemporary Jewish life. Fundamentalist Jewish extremists returned to that militancy while more moderate but equally fundamentalist factions embrace a more moderate exegesis.

The issue is not, as many commentators have it, a question of fundamentalism, but of religious extremism and a political agenda. One can accept religious texts literally and believe them wholeheartedly without embracing the urgency of the political agenda and the imminent realization of the religious view that extremists urge.

Historically, in the Islamic world, Jews were subject to certain forms of discrimination. They could not bear arms, they could not ride horses, and they were forced to wear distinctive clothing—at least in theory. Wistrich affirms that the position of *dhimmi,* however far from the standards of contemporary Western practice, was certainly far better than anything that existed in premodern Christendom. Jews could own land, practice crafts and trades, and participate fully in the economy. There were few stigmas associated with the Jews and few instances of expulsion. In fact, some Jewish communities enjoyed an uninterrupted presence within Islamic lands since the time of the Prophet Mohammad.

Indeed, Jews *were* not discriminated against as Jews. The position of *dhimmi* is a status they shared with Christians and Zoroastrians. And consequently, while for the most part in Christian Europe, Jews were the only outsiders—the one dissident voice—in Christian Europe they were one of several outsider groups within Islam and their situation was significantly less precarious.

A word about the period of the Jewish flourishing under Islam: From the time of Saadia Gaon (882 CE) to Maimonides, who died in 1204, medieval Jewry thrived in a receptive Islamic environment. From biblical commentaries to Jewish philosophy, from the liturgy used in the synagogue even today to Jewish law, the creations of these Jews living in Islamic lands have become the standards for Jewish life and essential to Jewish scholarship. And Muslim and Jews together preserved the genius of Greek civilization. The teaching of this period of flourishing does not merely speak of the past. It is an essential part of contemporary Jewry. Every rabbi is trained in these works. All Jewish prayerbooks—Orthodox, Conservative, Reform, Hasidic, Renewal, and Reconstructionist—contain these poems. One cannot conceive of Judaism from the ninth century onward without these contributions.

Historians have noted that some of the worst aspects of Christian stigmatization of the Jews were imported into Islamic society. Bernard Lewis, Princeton University historian of Islam, has demonstrated that the blood libel—the charge that Jews would slaughter a young Christian boy to prepare matzot for Passover, was first introduced in Islam by Greek Christians. By 1840 it gained currency, and Jews were subject to blood libels in several countries from Lebanon to Libya. The most tragic occurrence happened in Baghdad. These accusations were not supported by the Ottoman state. Nevertheless, they gained currency and were repeated by prominent Arab leaders, especially in recent times.

For example, in the 1970s, King Faisal of Saudia Arabia said: "Jews have a certain day on which they mix the blood of non-Jews into their bread. It happened two years ago, while I was in Paris on a visit, the police discovered five murdered children. Their blood had been drained and it turned out they had murdered them order to take their blood and mix it with the bread that they eat on that day."

Former Syrian defense minister Mustafa Tlas wrote a work entitled the *Matzah of Zion*, which accepts as fact the blood libel and interprets Jewish history accordingly. His misstatements of history did not hamper his ascent to the highest level of Syrian leadership or his acceptance at home and abroad.

Clearly with the onset of Zionism and significant Jewish settlement in Palestine, relations between Jews and Muslims, Judaism and Islam were politicized. The challenge to Islam was political—but not only political—it was religious as well, perhaps even at its core.

Islam had accepted Jews as *dhimmis,* but not the emergence of an independent Jewish political entity in what was considered by Islam *Dar-al-Islam*, Islamic lands, and not in *Dar-al-Harb*, the world of war, the term that is used to refer to the non-Islamic world. Islam was not prepared to accept a non-Islamic state on Islamic land. The religious expectation of classical Islam was the creation of a universal state [much like the universal Church in Roman Catholicism] and the problem was to adjust to the failure of that universal state much like the Roman Catholic Church had to adjust to the lack of being a universal Church.[5]

Thus, the existence of Israel continues to pose a theological as well as a political problem. It seems to negate the promise of Islam[6] and it arose precisely as the world of Islam was emerging from Christian domination under colonialism. It is fair to say that Israel receives not only the antagonism of its own presence, but also the hatred once directed—or even once not fully directed—at Western colonialism. Israel is perceived as a continuation of that very Western colonialism.

This is not the occasion to rehearse a list of political grievances or lost political opportunities but to explore the recurrence of antisemitic themes within contemporary Islam, to reiterate that whatever the political grievances or the political climate, the prevalence of antisemitic themes and the resurgence of discredited myth obscures the genuine problems and only makes a political settlement all the more difficult if not near impossible. Adjustments have to be made in religious teachings in order to make it possible for political leaders to negotiate. The Muslim assassins of Egyptian president Anwar Sadat felt that he had betrayed Islam by making peace with Israel. The Jewish assassin of Israeli prime minister Yitzhak Rabin also responded to strident religious teachings.

The process of importing discredited antisemitism has intensified in recent years. One can cite thousands of examples, but a few will illustrate a general pattern. A random review of websites devoted to monitoring antisemitism in the Arab press reveals that.

It is clear antisemitism is a widespread phenomenon, enjoying mainstream support of the elite, reflected in the press and the government as well as the mosques and the Arab streets. Explanations vary, but they are also quite familiar. Some have described it as a deflection onto others of the failure of Arab societies to enjoy the progress and prosperity of the West. Others have seen it as the glue that imposes unity and silences dissent, the very means by which authoritarian regimes maintain their hold on power.

It is important to stress that these are not the only manifestations of Islamic-Jewish relations. The American experience even today provides one vivid example of mutual cooperation and strong Jewish-Islam cooperation. Jews and Muslims are both prohibited from eating pork products. In both religions the slaughtering of the animal is a religious act and in practice American Muslims have long been an integral part of the kosher meat business. In recent years, several campuses—Cal State, UCLA, and Mount Holyoke among them—have joint dining facilities for observant Muslim and Jewish students. In many areas meats are slaughtered by a Jewish ritual slaughterer but also blessed by the appropriate Muslim religious figure. To accept the religious integrity for *halal* of Jewish *Kashrut* preparations, Islamic clerics must accept the legitimacy of Jews as "people of the Book," and thus their essential monotheistic honor. In the aftermath of the September 11 atrocities, Jews have reached out to Muslims, rabbis to imams, in the manner that characterizes interreligious concord in the United States. And the actions of Jewish defense leaders of allegedly plotting to blow up a mosque have been roundly condemned.

Still, the dominant voices within the Islamic world are bringing to prominence antisemitism that has long been discredited in the Western world. Religious exegesis and has joined with political exigencies and the results are explosive and getting worse.

What Can Be Done?

Permit me a personal aside. When I was an undergraduate I took a course on the racial divide in the United States. This was during the height of the civil rights revolution and just after the Kerner Commission had issued its report to the president describing growing racial divisions in the United States. For the final examination the professor asked us to delineate a series of programs that might heal the racial divide. In frenzy, I wrote six exam booklets because I thought I had so much to say, and then in a moment of lucidity wrote in large letters on the first page of the seventh exam booklet OR TIME, PERHAPS?

- **Recognize the problem**. There is a world of difference between political grievances, political struggles, and antisemitism. The inability to differentiate between the two only exacerbates the political and the problem.

- **Condemn antisemitism in all of its manifestations and quarantine it**. The basic requirements of a pluralistic global universe and the key values embedded in American traditions are civility, tolerance, and mutual acceptance. They form the fiber of American democracy and are the values that have allowed the United States to flourish and religious life within the United States to deepen. They are the source not of our religious weakness but of our religious strength. Intellectuals and political leaders, writers and artists, kings and princes, journalists and titans of business must all know that the antisemitism that is an accepted part of their society is disrespected here, discredited here, unacceptable here—and perhaps at some time there.

- **Study Islam**. By understanding the religious tradition one can find appropriate ways to dialogue that respect into the integrity of a religious faith and yet provide means for it to engage the other. Be mindful of nuances and also of diverse interpretations.

- **Patience!** It takes a long time for religious traditions to change, to accommodate a new reality. As Firestone has written: "The discourse of modernity did not enter Islam as it did Christianity and Judaism. Islam had its reformist movements during the first part of the last century, to be sure, but they have become largely discredited because of their close association with the West and the activities of first colonialism and then imperialism. Muslims may choose to ignore or moderate the militant nature of classical Islam and its binary division of the world, but this takes some effort and must be a conscious act." Democracies by their very nature invite discourse and push toward compromise. Authoritarian regimes act from a very different set of norms. The combination of religious authority and political power and the absence of the requirements of pluralism mean that this problem will be with us for a long time.

- **Cultivate Western Muslims.** They are denizens of two worlds, the Muslim world and the modern world. There has been much discussion of antisemitism in France and reportage of individual incidents exposed to Western civilization and Western interreligious traditions and have seen a flourishing of Islam in the West precisely under the conditions developed in these societies. They may be distrusted in part because of their exposure to the West, but they can also serve as interpreters of the Western interreligious norms back in Islamic societies.

Or time, perhaps?

Notes

1. Raul Hilberg, *The Destruction of the European Jews: Revised and Definitive Edition* (New York: Holmes & Meier, 1985), vol. I, p. 9.

2. Robert Wistrich, *Antisemitism: The Longest Hatred* (New York: Pantheon Books, 1991), p. 195.

3. Sura, 5:78/82.

4. Sura 3:63 .

5. This problem is also not alien to Judaism. Biblical tradition describes the stranger and sojourner as categories of people who dwell in the land of Israel. The Hebrew Bible did not know of citizens of a democracy, and since Jews lacked sovereignty between 70 CE and 1948, Jewish tradition was not forced to confront the discrepancy between its idealized vision of a Jewish state and the reality of non-Jews living in the state. For a few extremists, widely condemned by the rest of Israeli society, the solution was expulsion, ethnic cleansing. For religious messianists Israel's sovereignty was a religious imperative. Politically, Israeli leaders of the right and left have accepted partition time and again. And the religious justification for partition is the religious imperative of peace and of saving human lives.

6. Delay of fulfillment of a religious promise creates cognitive dissonance for the believer. Traditional theology manages that cognitive dissonance by a variety of strategies. Expectations can be deferred to another time; e.g., when Jesus did not return immediately as was the early Christian expectation, the return of the Christ was deferred until the end of days; the days of the Messiah serviced a similar role in Judaism. Sin is another explanation as to why the promise is not fulfilled; it calls forth a strategy of repentance, of more intense commitment to the tradition. Anger can also be a way of handling this cognitive dissonance, and the more imminent the expectation of the fulfillment, the more intense the anger.

SECTION III
The Migration of Discredited Myths

One must wonder how it is possible that at the beginning of the twenty-first century two entire chapters of a book on antisemitism must be devoted to the migration of discredited myths from the world of European Christendom to contemporary Islam. Yet it is imperative that we understand the trajectory of *The Protocols of the Elders of Zion*, both historically and within the contemporary world, as well as the significant differences between Islamic forms of Holocaust denial and their Western counterparts.

Richard S. Levy might have once imagined that his work on the *Protocols* would have been consigned to the dustbin of history; one could scarcely imagine the ongoing relevance of tracing of a universally rejected myth that had been repeatedly demonstrated and accepted as a fraud. Instead he finds himself in the unfortunate position of being relevant to contemporary events.

The Protocols, he contends, is the antisemitic myth most easily transferable to most varied languages and cultures; it is the most widely circulated antisemitic tract of all times, gaining vast exposure in places where Jews have lived such as Poland and Russia and where Jews have not lived such as Japan and China. In the early twenty-first century, it was the subject of a popular film on broadcast television and a multi-million-dollar, multipart series widely broadcast on Arab television.

Levy cautions that it is still not clear who has read the book; yet the Protocols is a book that is less read *by* the masses than *to* the masses.

He reviews for the reader all the basic research regarding the fact that the *Protocols* is a forgery that plagiarizes other material, but its repudiation by academic researches and enterprising journalists has done little to dampen its appeal. The work had its greatest appeal in the dislocation and confusion of the post–World War I period and again during the Great Depression. It serves as a tool for various—and often conflicting—political agendas, and rational tools of research and scholarship are dramatically inadequate to counteract its appeal. The *Protocols* have found a receptive audience among those attracted to conspiratorial theories and to those who in the words of Levy prefer "terrifying truths to gnawing uncertainties."

He cautions that the work has rarely been read by the mob and there is little evidence that it has incited mob violence, it has however been used to legitimate violence ex post facto.

What is different about the contemporary use of the *Protocols* within the Arab and Muslim world? The *Protocols* has migrated from the written word into the world of television and the Internet. Television is a major tool for reaching the masses and the Internet a New Age tool for mobilizing them. And, unlike other societies in which the *Protocols* have appeared, there is no publishing *debunking* of the Protocols by respected organs—the press, the media, scholars, and political leaders—in the Arabic language. No one, Levy argues, has felt honor bound to expose the fraud. Levy cautions that the *Protocols* may yet achieve in the Arab world the political potency that has been denied it elsewhere.

Holocaust denial in the Muslim world is another essential manifestation of the migration of the discredited myths rejected in the post-Holocaust world by Western Christendom, where they made cultural, theological, and historical sense, and imported to the Middle East, where they are alien and by all logic should not have gained a foothold but have proved peculiarly potent. Western deniers deny the Holocaust as a tool of the extreme right to rehabilitate the reputation of fascism, to recover the reputation of Germany, to restore the good name of its people, and to cleanse Hitler and his all-too-willing colleagues and the German nation of their crimes.

This is of little interest to Islamic deniers who are infuriated by the attention on Jewish victimization and by what they see as the consequences of the Holocaust. From their perspective Germans killed Jews and the Palestinians pay the price. They believe Europe exported its iniquities to the Jews. They have a three-point agenda in denying the Holocaust.

- They seek to delegitimize Europe, which perceives itself as the antithesis of the Nazis; pluralistic and tolerant, welcoming of the outsider, and deeply committed to human rights and human dignity.

- They seek to delegitimize the existence of Israel, which sees itself and is perceived by others as the legacy of the Nazis' victims and the antidote to another Holocaust.

- They inflict by words—and virtually without consequences—severe pain on Israel and Jews.

Holocaust denial in the Islamic world is an irresistible three-part triumph—proof that Europe is racist, and proof that if there was no Holocaust, there is no need for Israel to exist.

If the Islamic deniers confined themselves to a debate over the uses and abuses of Holocaust memory, the debate would have been far more legitimate and the support for such a debate would have attracted a better crowd than the David Dukes and the outer fringe of the Jewish groups—the six colorful Neturei Karta representatives who shamed themselves, their cause, and the Jewish people. They have been rightfully scorned even by their own political allies.

The clumsiness of Iran's president resorting to Holocaust denial has brought him much attention—perhaps even more attention than his nuclear aspiration. But with the attention has come derision in the West and even some criticism from the Muslim world and within his own country. The divisions he and his party created in Iran should not be overlooked. One should be grateful for such foolishness—grateful and scornful.

Robert Kahn, who has studied Holocaust denial and the law, suggests that one should differentiate between two forms of Holocaust denial, traditional Western Holocaust denial and its Islamic variation, and if his insights are to be heeded, one must be ever so cautious not to lump the two of them together and forge an alliance where none has been present.

There is a tension between the two forms of denial. Western denial is interested in rehabilitating Nazism and Hitler; they have repeated the lies so often such as the myth of the gas chamber and the challenge to the 6 million that Western deniers have an orthodoxy of their own to defend. In the West, Holocaust denial is opposed by governments and scorned by the elite, if not actually outlawed; it is a marginal phenomenon and one must aim to keep it that way. One cannot assess the depth of Holocaust denial in Islam for where the government does not permit freedom of expression, or only limited freedom of expression, there is no way to measure the problem. However, anecdotal evidence suggests that it is even present among the elite.

Islamic denial is consumed by Israel and to a lesser extent by the Jews less interested in Germany and in the orthodoxy of Western deniers. In Islam there are three different tendencies, which coexist uneasily with each other.

Soft-core denial of the Holocaust may be more prevalent and more lethal than hard-core denial. For some, Kahn contends, the Nazis were bad, the Israelis worse. Israel is depicted as the new Nazi Germany; the Jews the new Nazis. For such a perception to be taken seriously, one must presume that the Holocaust was a reality and the Nazis were its perpetrators. It is morally indicting of the Jews that the victims have now become the victimizers, according to the Arab narrative. The choice of Nazi imagery for depicting the Jews testifies to the potency of such imagery and the general acceptance of the crime.

There is a second tendency to use the Holocaust as a means of taunting the West. The response within Iran to the Danish cartoon controversy was to launch a Holocaust cartoon context as if the response to one demeaning cartoon was to invite a torrent of others.

A more extreme form of denial holds that the Jews and the Nazis collaborated, but even that version suggests the underlying criminality of the Nazi enterprise. As one moves toward hard-core denial, Kahn cautions that one should not exaggerate the alliance between deniers nor take action that would strengthen an uneasy commonality of cause. Instead, one should be mindful of the difference. There is some cause for optimism regarding Islamic Holocaust denial as segments of the Iranian population and others within the Arab world have seen its futility and the manner in which it is distracting from the Arab cause. It has also provoked an unusual solidarity in the West, including Holocaust commemoration by the United Nations.

10

The Migration of Discredited Myths:
The Wandering *Protocols*

Richard S. Levy

"Lies have short legs"—this is a proverb amusingly claimed as exclusively their property by the Germans, Danes, Italians, and Spaniards. Clearly, in the case of the *Protocols of the Elders of Zion*, such folk wisdom is just plain wrong. This may well be the longest-legged lie of modern times, the real and unkillable "hoax of the twentieth century"—and perhaps of the twenty-first. The history of its dissemination seems to invite hyperbole: It is certainly the antisemitic myth *most* easily transferable to the *most* varied languages and cultures and the *most* widely circulated piece of antisemitic literature of all time. It is also the carrier of the *most* potent negative representation of Jews in the modern era. In the twentieth century, the *Protocols* swallowed up the medieval concept of the Jew as deicide and the Jew as usurer and spat out a far more terrifying image: the Jew as remorseless, world-conquering conspirator. *The Protocols of the Elders of Zion* describes in astonishing detail, not the old accusation against Jews that they crucified Christ, and not a current form of alleged economic swindling, but something more chilling, an imminent disaster, a hovering menace, a catastrophe that can be foretold but may not be preventable. It thus feeds, and feeds upon, human anxieties and has flourished in an era sometimes called the Age of Anxiety.

Mixed in with these now familiar appraisals and breathless claims is a fair amount of truth. Such extreme summations, however, tend to overwhelm judicious examination of the document and its effects. This is the province of dispassionate analysis that risks the displeasure of those who prefer drama to detachment. The balanced approach I attempt here is more likely to result in open questions than satisfyingly neat answers.

True, the *Protocols* has been a mega-best-seller, circulating in hundreds of thousands of copies, multiple editions, and in two dozen languages. Yet, like that other best-seller, *Mein Kampf,* it is not the least bit clear that many have actually read the book, and it is still less clear what effects its reading has on human actions. For most of those who fear its power the book remains little more than a title and an evil reputation. Therefore, before examining the paradoxical nature of its reputed potency, its undoubted durability, and the ease with which it moves through the world, some basic information is necessary.

The Protocols of the Elders of Zion is a forgery *and* a plagiarism. It purports to be the verbatim record of a speech delivered in twenty-four sessions by the mythical "Chief Sage of Zion" to a secret meeting held during the first Zionist Congress in Basel, Switzerland, in 1897. Woven together, the twenty-four individual protocols comprise a Jewish plot to take over the world, reduce non-Jews to abject slavery, and destroy Christian states and peoples. Employing the world association of Freemasons, who are their slaves unto death, the Jews conspire by means of liberal institutions, modern culture, and both capitalism and communism gradually to undermine all nations, clearing the way for a Jewish world state, with a heartlessly cruel despot at its summit.

The fictitious origin of the document is a vital part of its claim to authority. Those who put the *Protocols* before the public always present it as originating from the innermost circles of powerful Jews, an absolutely authentic record of their deliberations, never meant to come before Gentile eyes. This is what makes it a forgery. In the last ten years, evidence gathered from archives in the former Soviet Union has clarified much about the document's true origins and has also put to rest some of the legends that still cling to its history.

The *Protocols* was created in Russia—not Paris as is often alleged—no earlier than 1902. There is no solid evidence that it was commissioned by a branch of the Okhrana, the Russian secret police, or any other tsarist state agency, or that the sinister Piotr Rachkovskii supervised its production. The thorough scoundrel Mathieu Golovinski, free-booting journalist and later a Bolshevik, may have done the writing—he has been suspect since 1934—but he may well have not. The best guess is that the document was composed by an as yet to be precisely identified group of reactionary antisemitic publicists. Why?

Here, we are still in the realm of speculation rather than certainty. Perhaps, to influence the tsar against reformers in his government, or perhaps to discredit the emergent Zionist movement, which could be deemed threatening to the multinational Russian empire, or perhaps to provide documentary proof of a Jewish world conspiracy—an idea that was already well established in the Russian empire.[1]

Establishing the true authorship, origins, and purpose of the forgery is important, but it is the political career and impact of the fraud that should command the most attention.[2] The work surfaced in Russia around 1902–3, first as a hastily compiled manuscript, then in 1905 as an appendix to a larger book prepared by the Russian mystic Sergei Nilus, who had nothing to do with writing it but much to do with its dissemination.[3] Thereafter, although published nearly twenty times before the revolution of 1917 under many different titles and with significant variations, the forgery retained its essential character as a slapdash patchwork cobbled together from several earlier and unrelated writings, namely: a French political satire[4] of the mid-nineteenth century that had nothing to do with Jews; a trashy German novel[5] of the same period; and a much older and well-developed strain of anti-Freemason literature.[6] That none of these sources were acknowledged is what qualifies the document as a plagiarism. The *Protocols* was eventually translated into French, German, English, Spanish, Italian, Swedish, Danish, Norwegian, Finnish, Romanian, Hungarian, Lithuanian, Polish, Bulgarian, Greek, Arabic, Chinese, Japanese, and Turkish. Despite its lowly pedigree, the book found its audience, especially in the turbulent times following World War I and then again during the Great Depression of the 1930s. The interwar era constituted its heyday, but the work continues to appear and reappear throughout the world; its basic proposition—that Jews control events that seemingly have other causes—is still with us, forming the essential basis for the widely and immediately circulated fable of the four thousand Jews who were mysteriously warned away from the World Trade Center on September 11.

Why has *The Protocols of the Elders of Zion*, a shameless fraud, seized the imagination and informed the political judgment of men and women for the past one hundred years? Reading the work does not in the least help answer this question. For example, what is one to make of this?

You can well imagine that the non-Jews, full of bitterness, will fall upon us with weapons in hand as soon as they discover how everything fits together. For this eventuality we have in hand a last, fearful means, before which even the bravest heart shall tremble. Soon all the capital cities of the world will be crisscrossed with tunnels and subways. In case of danger we shall, from these tunnels, blow up the whole city—government offices, courts, archives, and the non-Jews with all that they possess.[7]

Or this:

Observe the drunkards, befogged by alcohol. They believe themselves to possess the right to unlimited pleasure, which they confuse with the concept of freedom. From that idea we take leave for all time. The non-Jewish peoples are befogged with alcohol; their youths are infatuated with humanism and premature vices. To these they have been led by our agents, administrators, teachers, servants, governesses to the rich, educational institutions, etc., as well as by our women in pleasure resorts and public houses. Among these I also count the so-called "society ladies," who willfully ape the example of vice and ostentation.[8]

The patent nuttiness of the schemes described in the *Protocols* seems to have little or no bearing on its credibility for many who read it. Indeed, almost as soon as the *Protocols* assumed political significance in the 1920s, many careful analysts—Jews, Catholics, and Protestants, statesmen, priests, newspapermen, and private citizens—debunked the lie and libel. If ever there was a "discredited myth," this was—or should have been—it. Critics tracked down the book's plagiarized sources, exposed its faulty logic, laid bare its political motives, and condemned its defiance of common sense. Yet, eighty-five years of devastating judgments have failed to put an end to the fraud. In the last decade it has turned up in likely and unlikely places all over the world—Kirghizstan, Japan, India, New Zealand, Maylasia, and Indonesia.

In part, its portability has to do with its lack of specificity: It names few names (none of living people); it provides no dates and mentions no cities or countries. It appears timeless and spaceless and can be adapted to all manner of environments. Its promulgators do not hesitate to doctor the text or to translate "freely" to serve the needs of their particular audiences. Versions of the *Protocols* can now be downloaded effortlessly and cost-free from the Internet. Accompanied by all sorts of warnings and hand-wringing disavowals, the most popular English-language translation by Victor Marsden is for sale on Amazon.com. for twelve dollars; the Spanish edition of the French translation can be had for ten dollars. A Google search for "Protocols of Zion," taking .58 seconds, scores 59,200 hits. Even if two-thirds to three-fourths of the websites thus identified attempt to refute the document, the massive presence of the *Protocols* on the Internet remains an indisputable fact. It is more accessible today than at any time in its history.

Still, ubiquity does not automatically translate into significance. First, the thing has to be read and understood, and this is no easy task. I suspect not many will be swept away by the hair-raising depiction of a two-thousand-year-old, arcanely elaborated Jewish conspiracy, directed by a committee of nameless but bloodthirsty individuals immune to every decent human impulse. That the utterly fictitious and wholly anonymous "Elders of Zion" already stage manage world events and stand on the cusp of final victory will alarm few people open to reason. But, it may be countered, this misses the point. *The Protocols of the Elders of Zion* is not satire, and its durability and marketability have nothing to do with reasonableness. In any case, what is important is not the number of people who have read the book, but the type of people. Some have always been willing and some are still willing to find the work credible, and others gladly exploit that willingness. From its first actual publication in 1903, the myth was meant to serve a political function, to influence powerful individuals or mobilize large groups of people to think or act in particularly destructive and self-deluding ways. Over time, the specific political agendas of the promoters of the *Protocols* have varied, but the sowing of hatred against Jews and the undermining of liberal democracies, secular values, and rational politics by associating them with Jewish plotters have remained fairly constant purposes. Its inherent absurdity aside, the book and the nature of its appeal still need to be evaluated seriously.

The historical record is fairly clear that in the 1920s and 1930s, people from all social strata believed in the authenticity of the document and took its revelation of a worldwide Jewish conspiracy at face value. General Ludendorff, Henry Ford, and Kaiser Wilhelm II attested to its truth. Clemenceau, Churchill, and Wilson also subscribed to basic elements of the theory of a Jewish world conspiracy, at least for a time. Many lesser lights found in its pages a credible explanation of world events and both a familiar and accurate representation of Jewry. Such is still the case in certain areas of the world in the new millennium. Although just how many who are exposed to the *Protocols* find it believable is not easy to measure, there remains ample grounds for asking some difficult questions.

- Why has the book survived to the present day?
- What are the sources from which it draws strength?
- Does the *Protocols* have the potential for continuing political mischief?

The Protocols of the Elders of Zion combines two distinct motifs: the conspiratorial and the antisemitic. In our era both are familiar and both have peculiar appeal for particular, although not necessarily the same, audiences. The following analysis focuses on the conspiratorial facet rather than the antisemitic. This emphasis is justifiable in the case of the *Protocols*, because the text's thoroughly familiar antisemitic tropes are empowered by the conspiratorial framework in which they are lodged.[9]

Conspiracy thinking, we like to believe, has always appealed to the weak-minded, the deranged, or the semi-educated, but, to be honest, it has never been the exclusive property of dumbbells. The dark doings of secret societies figured in the great nineteenth-century novels of Goethe, Scott, Balzac, Dumas, Dickens, and Disraeli, in the grand operas of Mozart and Verdi, in the gothic romances, and in many other vehicles of popular and high culture. The fascination with conspiracy themes lives on in the modern thriller and the caper film, entertainments with their own broad appeal.

For most people conspiracy remains purely recreational or esthetic. But for reasons not altogether clear, on occasion and for even the highly intelligent and well educated, conspiracies acquire the power to explain the real world, and sometimes even to be seen as "the best explanation" of events. Not just Jews, but Jesuits and Jacobins, "wobblies" and "eastern bankers," suffragettes and misogynists have all, at one time or another, been endowed with both the power and motive to control the unfolding of history from behind the scenes. Such scenarios have been created by people intelligent enough to read and write books. Whatever the reasons behind the vulnerability of the intelligent, the idea that sinister, invisible forces could control our lives did not destroy but rather enhanced the credibility of the "Elders of Zion."

There is no need to exaggerate the intellectual gifts of those who actually read the *Protocols* and then choose to champion it.[10] Perhaps, would-be intellectuals is a better description of the true believers in the *Protocols*. For many who succumb to it, the least likely explanation of great events seems the best, because it is also the most effortless. Painstaking study of the data is not the strength of these people. Examining structural shifts in the economy, demographic trends, sociological changes, and making fine distinctions among life's complexities—all these demand serious work and rigorous thinking. Antisemitism in particular cannot survive such habits of thought. By contrast, accepting the existence of a conspiracy with Jews at its center provides the believer with a shortcut to "the cause" of the evil in question; he or she has but to fill in the details, make the obscure connections, expose the intricacies of the plot. This is a species of ingenuity many possess and almost everyone enjoys exercising, the sort of paranoia that Philip Roth aptly describes as "the organizing preconception of the shallow mind faced with chaotic phenomena, the unthinking man's intellectual life..."[11]

But the effectiveness of conspiracy thinking has not only to do with mental laziness or esthetic pleasure. At least one other factor ought to be considered in an explanation of the *Protocols'* credibility in certain circles. An investigation of disturbing public happenings carried out with respect for the laws of evidence often leads to no very satisfactory conclusions. To many caught up in the numerous crises of modern times such a lack of resolution is psychologically intolerable. Instead, they seize upon a simple and dramatic version of political realities because they prefer even truly terrifying "truths" to gnawing uncertainties. *The Protocols of the Elders of Zion* exploits this all-too-human need for certainty in an unoriginal, yet powerful, way. The very inadequacies of rational living and thinking seem to contribute to the prospering of the hoax. It takes a certain strength of character to live with ambivalence, and that strength is not in great supply. The flight into the fantastic has a greater emotional payoff. The uncertain, the incomplete, the unsatisfying truth cannot compete with this.

Typical of the conspiracy genre, the *Protocols* portrays a community unaware of the true laws of its own existence.[12] Thinking itself autonomous and self-regulating, it is, in fact, being ruled by a secret society of evil men with access to a global network of operatives. Although the society has a long history, it has never for a moment wavered in its basic aims of overthrowing the fundamental institutions, values, and traditions of the community. The cabal is infinitely flexible in the means it chooses and especially adept at recruiting unwitting agents from within the community itself to further the gradual process of destruction. Spreading discontent among the naive, sowing moral corruption in the young, turning class against class, the conspirators work their will on the hapless victims. All this transpires silently, nearly invisibly, to all except the initiated. Antisemites since Wilhelm Marr, at least, have whined that the Jews work their subversion without ever coming out in the open to confront their enemies in manly fashion.[13] The *Protocols* harps on the bloodless conquests of the incorrigibly sneaky Jews.

By making the victims of Jewish conspiracy privy to the ways Jews talk about them in private, the authors of the *Protocols* sought to goad them to rage and perhaps to violent retaliation against their oppressors. But the book appeals to its audience in more subtle ways as well. The promoters of the forgery wrote long, appreciative commentaries on the text, inviting at least the literate to join the elite of those "in the know." They are offered the single magical key which unlocks all the perplexing mysteries of the modern world. After being enlightened by this document, readers will rise above the helpless ignorance that characterizes the majority of their unsuspecting countrymen. Although this delicious sense of superiority comes at a high price—the horrifying prospect of imminent Jewish triumph—the *Protocols* offers the antidote against this terror, too. Knowledge of the Jews' conspiracy, as Hitler promised in *Mein Kampf*, renders it conquerable.[14] Part of the appeal of the *Protocols* is that it is ultimately empowering to this kind of reader.

When seen in this context, understanding how the *Protocols* gains access to the literate becomes somewhat clearer. Such an understanding is vital for students of this work and for those who would like to render it politically harmless. The *Protocols* almost always reaches a mass audience only through the mediation of intellectuals; it is a work rarely read by the mob but often read to it, cited, interpreted, or just waved in front of its face. Ordinary readers, those without intellectual pretensions or a compulsive need to "know all," would require extraordinary levels of patience to plow through the ramblings, repetitions, obscure allusions, and convolutions to be found in these pages. The literary qualities of the work are abysmal. If the thing is largely unreadable for ordinary people, then an obvious question needs to be asked: How dangerous can *The Protocols of the Elders of Zion* be?

The *Protocols is* dangerous historically and in the present, but not for the reasons most often mentioned.[15] Many authorities allege that the book has engendered mob violence, but they cite little or no proof. Admittedly, it would be difficult to prove or disprove that the *Protocols* ever actually functioned as a tool of mass political mobilization. But there is no evidence to suggest this in two of the most notorious instances where the *Protocols* was present. In Kishinev in 1903 and Buenos Aires in 1919, the tract arrived on the scene *after* acts of mob violence against Jews. Its main function seems to have been to justify the violence ex post facto and to attempt to inspire new outbreaks, which in these two episodes, however, never transpired. In another often cited case, Ukrainian peasants may have had the work read to them, as is sometimes claimed, but did they really need new or additional reasons to murder thousands of helpless Jews during the Russian Civil War? What they needed was the permission of their social superiors, the anti-Bolshevik army officers, priests, and tsarist bureaucrats who led them. *These* were the individuals who required the integrating myth of the Jewish world conspiracy and who may have extracted it from the *Protocols.* Argentinian and Japanese army officers of different epochs, the youths from good families who assassinated the Jewish foreign minister of Germany, Walther Rathenau, in 1922, a few African-American college students having a rough time with Jewish professors, quite articulate Holocaust deniers—these are the sorts of people who attest to the continuing power of the *Protocols.* To our justifiable dismay, we have not yet learned how to protect ourselves from those who find their truth in *The Protocols of the Elders of Zion.*

Unfortunately, they are with us still and still succumbing to the myth of the Jewish world conspiracy. For the first time in its century-long career, *The Protocols of the Elders of Zion* is more likely to be printed, quoted, and used in the Middle East and in the Islamic Diaspora than in Europe or America (the only country where it has been uninterruptedly present in ethnic and religious politics since the 1920s). In many respects, Arab and Muslim deployment of the document repeats the European and American pattern, with one notable exception. In the Arab world, the *Protocols* often appears with the imprimatur or under the open sponsorship of heads of state; such blatant official sanction was and is rare elsewhere in the world. The

Protocols has been used, distributed, produced, and promoted by the governmental leaders of Egypt, Kuwait, Jordan, Libya, Saudi Arabia, and many others since the 1950s. It makes frequent appearances in the state-controlled press, most obviously providing an alibi for those in need of one. Leaders conveniently explained their defeats at the hands of the Israelis and their numerous other policy failures as a product of the worldwide Jewish conspiracy. The Jews of the *Protocols* are the enemies of religion and morality, the manipulators of secularist and democratic values meant to befuddle the masses, a depiction that appeals to radical Islamists as well as the governing elite. It speaks to the state of the Arab world that this representation of Jewry is just as compelling there today as it was in the Russia of one hundred years ago. More current uses also follow familiar patterns. Whether the authors of Article 32 of the Hamas Charter, which cites the *Protocols* as proof of a Zionist imperialist plan, or Mullah Omar of the Taliban, who has called for an investigation of the "real perpetrators" of September 11, are cynical exploiters or true believers of the myth, they are attempting to mobilize masses of followers on its basis.[16] Will the *Protocols* be more successful mobilizing ordinary Arabs than ordinary Europeans, Japanese, or African-Americans? Will the book make more sense to those steeped in Islamic culture than the European Christians it was originally designed to enlighten? On the face of it, this seems unlikely.

But there are at least two things about the use and reception of the *Protocols* in the Arab world that are worrisome. First, to the best of my limited knowledge, Arabic is the only language in which there is no published debunking of the *Protocols*. Even in the days of its greatest popularity, the voices of non-Jews—many of them by no means favorably inclined toward Jews—have been raised against the fraud. With nothing much to gain, they felt honor-bound to speak out against lies. This may well have helped contain the damage the document can do among the educated. Philip Graves' exposé in the *Times* of London (1921) really did render the *Protocols* nearly useless in British politics. Almost everywhere else, the interventions of non-Jewish intellectuals have helped to move the *Protocols* out of mainstream political life— everywhere, that is, but in the Arab world. There are moderate and responsible Arab intellectuals willing to espouse unpopular causes and to adopt risky positions, people who surely recognize that combating an imaginary Jewish world conspiracy is not the solution to any real problem. They need to be heard from on the subject of the *Protocols*.

The second disturbing aspect of the *Protocols'* career in the Arab world is its penetration of popular culture through the mass media. Reading the thing has always been the biggest obstacle to its effectiveness as a tool of mass mobilization. The recent maxi-series, *Knight without a Horse*—forty-one episodes loosely based on the *Protocols*, shown during Ramadan of 2002 on twenty-two Arab-language TV stations—may change all this. It does not have to be read anymore. The myth can now gain direct access to Arab living rooms, make minimal demands on the staying power or intellect of the viewer, and exercise a dramatic, immediate impact on the consciousness of ordinary people. As modern propagandists have long known, the visual image can overcome the limitations of the printed word. The *Protocols* may yet achieve, in the Arab world, the political potency it has thus far been denied everywhere else.

Notes

1. The two leading authorities on the *Protocols* have "rewritten" the history of the document's origins on the basis of newly accessible archival sources. Cesare G. De Michelis, *The Non-Existent Manuscript: A Study of the Protocols of the Sages of Zion*, translated by Richard Newhouse (Lincoln, NE: University of Nebraska Press and SICSA, 2004), ignores the received wisdom and wildly conflicting testimonies concerning origins, concentrating instead on the many variants of the text that circulated before 1917. His close reading supersedes all that has gone before, including the standard studies of Norman Cohn, Henri Rollin, and Walter Laqueur. When it comes to the purposes, rather than the origins of the text, however, De Michelis presents his hypotheses as though they too were grounded in the text. I find more convincing and cautious in this realm the work of Michael Hagemeister, "Die 'Protokolle der Weisen von Zion' und der Basler Zionistenkongress von 1897," in *Der Traum von Israel. Die Ursprünge des modernen Zionismus*, edited by Heiko Haumann (Weinheim, 1998), 250–73; his "Die Protokolle der Weisen von Zion— eine Anti-Utopie oder der Große Plan in der Geschichte?" in Helmut Reinalter (ed.), *Verschwörungstheorien. Theorie—Geschichte—Wirkung* (Innsbruck, 2002), 45–57; and, especially, "Protocols of the Elders of Zion," in Richard S. Levy (ed.), *Antisemitism: Historical Encyclopedia of Prejudice and Persecution* (Santa Barbara, CA, 2005).

2. The following account relies on De Michelis, who, it should be said, disputes my position that impact and function are more important than authorship. Establishing the true origins, he argues, will help demystify and disempower the *Protocols*. De Michelis, *The Non-Existent Manuscript*, pp. 2, 51, 64.

3. Nilus is the subject of a number of erroneous claims. These are set right by Michael Hagemeister, "Nilus, Sergei Aleksandrovich," in Levy, *Historical Encyclopedia*.

4. Maurice Joly, *Dialogue aux Enfers entre Machiavel et Montesquieu, ou la Politique de Machaivel au XIXe Siècle. Par un Contemporain* (Brussels, 1864; Paris, 1987).

5. See Jeffrey L. Sammons, "*Biarritz*," and Henryk Baran, "Rabbi's Speech, The," in Levy, *Historical Encyclopedia*. These are the sources for the famous scene in the Jewish cemetery in Prague, often circulated with the text of the *Protocols* but not authentically a part of it. See also Volker Neuhaus, *Der zeitgeschichtliche Sensationsroman in Deutschland 1855–1878. 'Sir John Retcliffe' und seine Schule* (Berlin, 1980).

6. See Helmut Reinalter, *Die Freimauer* (Munich: C. H. Beck, 2000); and his "Freemasonry," in Levy, *Historical Encyclopedia*.

7. Gottfried zur Beek [Ludwig Müller], *Die Geheimnisse der Weisen von Zion* (4th ed., Charlottenburg, 1920), p. 94. Excerpt from the Ninth Protocol, my translation.

8. Beek, *Geheimnisse*, p. 72. Excerpt from the First Protocol, my translation.

9. The authors added nothing new to the list of anti-Jewish stereotypes already firmly part of the canon by 1902–3. The "genius" of the *Protocols* is that, once it was decided to present the book itself as the work of Jews, the Jews' control of money, sultry sensuality, political nihilism, yearning for revenge against Christians, and talent for conspiracy required not even the pro forma presentation of evidence. The book was meant to be read as an inadvertent confession—the Jews thus condemned themselves out of their own mouths. The antisemitism to be found in the *Protocols* was unusual in only one respect. Race and the well-developed vocabulary of racism are absent, a fact scarcely noted by the book's critics or admirers.

10. I am leaving entirely out of consideration here the many cynical exploiters of the myth, whose motives and psychology are transparently obvious.

11. Philip Roth, *Operation Shylock* (New York, 1993), p. 385. On the utility of conspiracy thinking in the modern era, see Hannah Arendt, *Antisemitism:*

Part One of The Origins of Totalitarianism (New York, 1968), p. 76.

12. On conspiracy literature in general, see Johannes Rogalla von Bieberstein, *Die These von der Verschwörung 1776-1945: Philosophen, Freimaurer, Juden, Liberale und Sozialisten als Verschwörer gegen die Sozialordnung* (Frankfurt, 1978); John M. Roberts, *The Mythology of the Secret Societies* (London, 1972).

13. See Wilhelm Marr, *The Victory of Jewry over Germandom* (1879) in Richard S. Levy (ed.), *Antisemitism in Modern Times: An Anthology of Texts* (Lexington, MA, 1991), pp. 74–93, especially pp. 79–80, 82, 84.

14. Adolf Hitler, *Mein Kampf*. Translated by Ralph Manheim (Boston, 1943), pp. 307–8. The influence of the *Protocols* on Hitler's thinking and actions has been much discussed. The Nazi renegade Hermann Rauschning reports Hitler as saying, after having read the book, "I saw at once that we would have to imitate this [the Elders]—in our own way, of course...." Rauschning, however, has been thoroughly discredited as a reliable source on Hitler, who has, in fact, left few verbal or written comments about the *Protocols*. See Binjamin Segel, *A Lie and a Libel: The History of the* Protocols of the Elders of Zion. Translated and edited by Richard S. Levy (Lincoln, NE, 1995), pp. 28–33.

15. I should say here that I have revised my views on the direct impact of the *Protocols* upon a mass audience. See Levy, *Antisemitism in the Modern World*. pp. 147–49; Segel, *A Lie and a Libel*, introduction, passim.

16. The use of antisemitic myth in the Islamic Diaspora, including the *Protocols*, is well documented in Pierre-André Taguieff, *Rising from the Muck: The New Anti-Semitism in Europe*. Translated by Patrick Camiller (Chicago, 2004).

11

Strange Bedfellows?
Western Deniers and the Arab World

Robert A. Kahn

This chapter looks at the efforts of Holocaust deniers in Western Europe and North America to win converts in the Arab world and Iran. Holocaust deniers have always dreamed of reaching the Arab world. For instance, in 1980, Ernst Zundel distributed a four-page mimeographed pamphlet entitled "The West, War and Islam," in which he argued that a conspiracy between communists, international bankers, freemasons, and Zionists was to blame for the Middle East conflict.[1] Around the same time, French Holocaust denier Robert Faurisson struck a similar tone when he included Palestinians among the victims of the Holocaust "myth."[2]

Meanwhile, Jews look at the growth of Holocaust denial in the Arab world with alarm for a variety of reasons. First, it serves as a reminder of the extent of antisemitism in the Arab world and the difficulties this poses for the establishment of a lasting peace between Israel and its neighbors. Second, it suggests that European and North American Holocaust deniers may be gaining a foothold in the Arab states from which, one day, they could launch a campaign to change world opinion about the Holocaust. This is troubling because over the past twenty years Jewish community groups, political leaders, and lawyers have worked very hard to create an environment in which Holocaust denial is repudiated or at least marginalized.[3] The emergence of Holocaust denial in the Arab world threatens to unravel these efforts, especially if migrants from Arab countries carry Holocaust denial into the heart of Europe and North America.

While Holocaust denial is widespread in the Arab world, Arab denial is different from denial seen in Western Europe and North America. In particular, while Western deniers use denial to legitimate Hitler and Nazis, Arab deniers are much more concerned with Israel and showing that Israelis are the "new Nazis." This, in turn, creates tension between Arab deniers (who claim that the Israelis were as bad as the Nazis) and Western deniers (who claim that the Nazis were not that bad).

This tension, in turn, poses problems for Western deniers as they seek converts in the Arab world. Sometimes these tensions are overcome, as for instance during Roger Gaurady's 1998 trip to Egypt. Gaurady, a former French communist who later converted to Islam, wrote a 1996 book *The Founding Myths of Modern Israel*, which denied the Holocaust. After being convicted under the French Gayssot Law, which makes it illegal to contest the Holocaust,[4] Gaurady traveled to Egypt where he was hailed as a hero.

At other times, the tensions are harder to surmount. For example, in March 2001 the Swiss group *Verite et Justice* and the California-based Institute for Historical Review (IHR) planned a conference in Beirut. The goal was to reach out to deniers in the Arab world. The Lebanese government banned the conference and although some Arab voices protested the ban (both on free speech and pro-denial grounds) many more distanced themselves from the conference organizers.

In what follows I will first lay out the differences between Arab deniers and their Western counterparts. Then I will show how these differences were largely overcome during Gaurady's visit but posed greater problems for the Beirut conference. I will conclude with some comments about what Gaurady's visit and the IHR conference say about the future of Holocaust denial in the Arab world.

Arab Denial vs. Western Denial

I have not seen any statistical studies about the extent of Holocaust denial in the Arab world. That said, denial has a higher profile there than in Western Europe and North America, where it is rejected out of hand (opinion polls put support for denial in the West in the low single digits).[5] One sees this in the articles in mainstream Arab newspapers, such as the Palestinian Authority's *Al Hayat* and Egypt's *Al-Ahram* denying the Holocaust.[6] The commonplace nature of the denial is striking. What would lead to a scandal if it appeared in the *New York Times* or *Le Monde* passes with little notice in *Al-Ahram*.

However, there are some caveats. First of all, the Middle East is very diverse. Some states, such as Iran and Syria, take a stand in favor of denial. Iran has given political asylum to Jurgen Graf, a leading Holocaust denier, and both states publish articles denying the Holocaust in state-run newspapers.[7] These articles draw chapter and verse from the deniers' hymnal—the gas chambers and the Holocaust are both presented as lies.

But here we are talking about government-supported denial in societies that have little or no freedom of expression. While the actions of Syria and Iran provide material support for Western deniers (in addition to Graf, Iran has opened its doors to Robert Faurisson, who took a weeklong holiday there in 2000), and provide a base for the conversion of the Arab world to denial, the authoritarian nature of these societies makes it difficult to draw direct conclusions about the level of support for denial among the general public in either country.

Once the focus turns to states that have greater freedom of the press—such as Egypt, Jordan, Lebanon, and the Palestinian Authority—a slightly different picture emerges. While the presses in these countries often run articles that deny some aspects of the Holocaust, other voices oppose denial. For example, `Abd al-Wahab al-Missiri, a noted Egyptian scholar, objects to Holocaust denial both because it is untrue and because it obscures the way that both the Nazis and Zionists act in ways that violate basic standards of humanity.[8] While this position, which recalls Hannah Arendt's "banality of evil" thesis, risks trivializing the Holocaust, it offers cold comfort to Faurisson and Zundel.[9]

Here one must keep in mind the goals of Western Holocaust deniers. In an age of increasing antisemitism, some of which takes the form of a "backlash" at the Jews' perceived exploitation of the Holocaust, one can easily forget how, for many deniers, the main goal is the rehabilitation of Hitler and Nazism. This clearly motivates Ernst Zundel, the anonymous author of *The Hitler We Loved and Why*. Faurisson is a more ambiguous figure. While he mentioned the Palestinians as a victim of "the Holocaust myth," the other victim he listed was the German people.

For Zundel and Faurisson it is not enough to trivialize the Holocaust; or to complain that Jews (or the state of Israel) make too much of the Holocaust; or to say that the Jews or Zionists are the "new" Nazis. Any formulation that leaves the Nazis in the role as global villain will not satisfy them in the long run. Moreover, after spending decades denying the truth, the deniers are deeply invested in their lies (whether they believe them is another story).[10] Therefore, any formulation that falls short of the key positions of the deniers' worldview—no planned extermination, no 6 million, no gas chambers—will not satisfy them, especially if it fails to mention that how the Zionists use the Holocaust lie to blackmail Germany.

This is significant because even those Arab writers who deny the Holocaust often fail to give the full-fledged Western version. The greatest area of overlap concerns the number of victims. Like their Western counterparts, Arab deniers will claim that the Jews have exaggerated their casualties and refer openly to the "six million lie." Some articles go further and refer to the "gas chamber lie." There are, however, almost no references to Jewish use of the Holocaust to blackmail Germany, in part because this line of argument does not advance the major goal of Arab deniers, which is to shift the victim role from Jews to themselves.

This role shifting takes three forms. A moderate version concedes that the Holocaust was bad, but insists the Israeli occupation is worse. Palestinians argue that the *nabka* ("catastrophe") of 1948, when they were forced from their homes, was worse than the Holocaust. Whatever one thinks of the occupation or *nabka*, statements like this clearly cross the line into denial because even the most extreme accounts of the Israeli violence against the Palestinians fall far short of the organized slaughter of millions.

This form of denial is "moderate" because many writers who take this line will readily admit to Jewish suffering, the better to argue that a people who suffered the Holocaust should know better.[11] (In fact, this position is taken by people who concede the uniqueness of the Holocaust, but use it as a model for how Israel—and the world—should view the *nabka*.)[12] Second, once they assert their point that the Palestinians suffered more, the people who make this argument focus their attention on the Middle East. Because their main goal is to show that the Palestinians suffered more than the Jews, they have little interest in exploring the more esoteric themes of Holocaust denial.[13]

A second, more extreme position explicitly compares Jews to Nazis. This is probably the most dominant trend in Arab Holocaust denial and it works on several levels. The first form—more trivialization than denial—is to refer to the Nazi methods of the Israeli occupation. This usage is ambiguous since in the West the term "Nazi" is often a code word for unsavory practices of the Hitler regime—such as for censorship—that do not directly relate to the Holocaust. However, this usage, even if it falls short of denial, is grossly insensitive to a nation made up, in part, of survivors of the Holocaust.[14]

Another form of the argument holds that Jews and Nazis collaborated during the Second World War. Some of the arguments have a basis—however tenuous—in fact. For instance, Arab deniers will argue that Jews served in the Wehrmacht, which is true—a very small number of Jews did serve in Hitler's armies as the film *Europa, Europa* movingly describes. They also argue that the Zionists and Nazis had a shared interest: namely to move Jews from Germany and Eastern Europe to the Middle East.

The most extreme position insists that Nazis and Jews are one and the same. While relatively rare, the argument reflects the common antisemitic trope of the powerful Jew expressed by *The Protocols of the Elders of Zion*, which has done well in the Arab world. The Holocaust is a stumbling block to those convinced of Jewish power: How can such a powerful group be the victims of mass murder? While many Western antisemites respond to this "contradiction" with traditional Holocaust denial (i.e., if there was no Holocaust, the Jews were never "weak"), a few responded by asserting that Hitler himself was a Jew.[15] This latter course has proven somewhat more popular in the Arab world.

What Arab deniers leave out is noteworthy. As we have seen, the gas chambers are a relatively minor theme and almost no one speaks of the Zionist blackmail against the Federal Republic of Germany. This should not be surprising. Just as the Western deniers view the Arabs instrumentally—as a way to spread denial; the converse is true. Arabs are interested in denial only insofar as it takes Israel and the Jews down a notch. Some Arab deniers are quite explicit about this, expressing disinterest in European history. While this itself can be a form of denial through trivialization (if Europe doesn't matter, neither does the Holocaust), it also presents problems for Zundel and Faurisson. If European history is truly irrelevant, then so is the deniers' alternative history. If Western deniers want to rewrite the history of Europe, Arab deniers just want Europe (and Israel) to go away. As we shall see, this can cause problems.

The Gaurady Affair

This returns us to the two examples I raised at the start of the paper: the 1998 Gaurady affair and the cancellation of the Beirut conference three years later. It is tempting to relate the success of Arab denial to the current state of the Arab-Israeli conflict. While in general this is a valid point, and an antidote to the tendency to downplay Arab antisemitism over the past few decades, an exclusive emphasis on the Arab-Israeli conflict does not tell the entire story.

If the strength of Arab denial depended solely on the current state of the Arab-Israeli conflict, one would have expected Gaurady, who visited Egypt at a time of relative calm, to have received a cooler reception than the IHR, which scheduled its conference during the middle of the Al-Aqsa intifada. But precisely the opposite occurred; while Gaurady was feted as a hero, Arab public opinion was far less favorable to the IHR. The reason for this difference was ideological: Gaurady had a better reception in the Arab world because his message was tailor-made for an Arab audience.

As we have seen, Gaurady was convicted under the French Gayssot Law for publishing *The Founding Myths of Modern Israel*. In the wake of his trial he went to Egypt. One of the most striking things about his visit was the broad level of support he received. An Egyptian lawyers' group offered to defend him. Another group paid his legal fees. Among his supporters numbered Nobel prize winner Nagib Mafouz.[16] By all accounts, Gaurady's visit was a success for the deniers. In addition to the kind words for Gaurady, many Egyptian papers printed articles denying the Holocaust.

Why did this happen? Why was Gaurady such an effective spokesperson for Holocaust denial? Part of the reason was biographical. Born in 1913, Gaurady was first a Catholic monk and then a hard-line communist who held a powerful position in the then-Stalinist French Communist Party. After he broke with the party, he became a steadfast supporter of Palestinian rights. In 1982 he converted to Islam, a decision some of his critics attribute to the Iranian revolution a few years earlier.[17] So when he was prosecuted under the Gayssot Law, he was viewed as a martyr for the Palestinian cause rather than as a Eurocentric neo-Nazi eager to rewrite history.

This perception was enhanced by his book—which focused on five separate "founding myths" of Israel, only one of which directly related to the Holocaust. (For example, the book also countered the "myth" that Israel was "a land with no people for a people with no land.") While some Arab intellectuals at the time, including Edward Said, warned his contemporaries of the dangers of defending Gaurady on the merits (rather than defending him on free speech grounds alone), they were in the minority.

However, some of Gaurady's supporters tried to separate his views on the Middle East from his views on the Holocaust. For example, Mohamed Hasanein Heikal, an Egyptian scholar who wrote the introduction to the Arabic version of Gaurady's book, said that he had wished the author had provided his own introduction and noted that only part of the book was about the Holocaust.[18] This is not to deny the larger significance of the Gaurady visit. For the first time, many in the Arab intellectual elite welcomed a Holocaust denier with open arms. But the reason for this success was, in part at least, that Gaurady was not just any denier. He was also strongly identified with the Palestinian cause.

The March 2001 Beirut Conference

The same could not be said for the IHR which, in conjunction with the Swiss group, *Verite et Justice*, scheduled a conference in Beirut for March 2001. In contrast to the Gaurady's visit, this story did not have a happy ending for the deniers. Word of the conference got out in advance and Jewish groups including the Simon Wiesenthal Center and several members of Congress from the United States asked the Lebanese government to cancel the conference.[19]

In late March then prime minister Rafik Hariri did just that. At first, he said that he canceled the conference because the promoters did not ask for a permit. Later he changed his position slightly and said that Lebanon was canceling the conference because it was not in the country's interest. At the time Lebanon was just recovering from over twenty years of civil war and there were fears that the proposed conference would lead to negative publicity at the very moment the state was seeking tourists.[20] In fact, Lebanese information minister Ghazi Aridi went so far to suggest that the proposed conference was a hoax designed to embarrass Lebanon.[21]

While the conference did have some supporters, most notably the Jordanian Writer's Association (more about them later), the support for the IHR was remarkably tame, especially given the appearance that the government had crumbled before international (read: Zionist) pressure. Instead, most of the press commentary on the conference took the IHR to task for a lack of concern about the Arab world. For example, the Lebanese paper *As-Safir* pointed out that the proposed list of conference speakers contained no Arabs, hardly a way to make friends in the Arab world.[22]

Equally important both to the way the affair played out (and possibly to the decision to ban the conference) was a letter appearing in *Le Monde* signed by fourteen Arab intellectuals, including Edward Said and Elias Khoury, denouncing the proposed conference.[23] The letter got extensive play in the Arab world and helped put some distance between Holocaust denial and support for the Palestinian cause.

This process, however, had its limits. For example, when the Israeli ambassador of France thanked the fourteen for their "courageous" letter, Elias Khoury felt compelled to refer to Israel as a racist, colonialist state that had no place giving anyone lessons about morality.[24] While the Holocaust was recognized, its lessons were reinterpreted to favor the Palestinian cause.

The experience of the Jordanian Writers Association tells a similar story. The JWA is a part of the antinormalization movement, which is opposed to Arab-Israeli peace. The JWA was a major critic of Lebanon for banning the banned IHR conference. In response, they decided to hold a "revisionist" conference of their own in Amman. While it was delayed for a few months by the Jordanian authorities (the first date had coincided with a state visit to the United States), the conference went off later that year. But the content of the conference was limited to the similarities between Zionism and Nazism and how Jews exploit the Holocaust. Conference organizers explicitly distanced themselves from the IHR conference.[25]

The IHR and its European allies failed where Gaurady succeeded in large part because they did not address the concerns of the Arab world. One sees this in the failure to have an Arab speaker at the conference. The text of speech Robert Faurisson planned to deliver at the conference conveys the same message.

The paper, available on the IHR's website, divides into two parts. How the Arabs deny the Holocaust (which he criticizes as ineffective) and how the Arabs should deny the Holocaust. Aside from the way Faurisson condescends to his Arab audience, the most striking aspect of his article is its Eurocentric focus. After warning his audience not to rely on theories, he prods them to speak up about the gas chambers. He then lists a string of martyrs to the cause including himself, Serge Thion, and Ernst Zundel. He then proclaims: "May the leaders of the

Muslim states hear the Palestinians—and the revisionists—appeals! Our ordeals are similar and our Intifadas identical."[26]

There is an irony here. Just as Arab deniers use comparison to trivialize the experiences of Jews and Holocaust survivors, Faurisson trivializes the experience of the Palestinians by comparing it to a few speech prosecutions in France and Germany. It is no wonder the same people who were willing to pay Gaurady's legal fees distanced themselves from Faurisson.

Nor were the organizers of the conference much more diplomatic. After the conference was banned, *Verite et Justice* sent a series of open letters. The first, issued right after the ban, managed to discuss the Holocaust almost without mentioning the Palestinians at all. Instead, after referring to the "financial blackmail" of Germany and its European neighbors, the author declares a refusal to compromise "with liars and oppressors," presumably including the Lebanese government.[27]

A second letter, a few days later, took a harsher tone. The letter writer claimed to be "frankly surprised" that the fourteen Arab intellectuals "who claim to oppose Zionism" would oppose the conference. The letter writer took them to task for not being familiar with the latest "revisionist" literature, including a dissertation written in 2000 from Alabama. The *Verite et Justice* representative added: "Anyone who claims to be anti-Zionist while at the same time condoning Zionist falsification of history, such as the 'six million' and 'gas chambers' tales, is simply a hypocrite...." who does "an appallingly bad service to the Palestinian people."[28]

Implications for the Future

What do the Gaurady and IHR affairs say about the state of Holocaust denial in the Arab world? The two events show the importance of the deniers' ideology. When deniers express sympathy with the Palestinian cause and restrict themselves to themes relating to Arab-Israeli conflict, they may make some headway. On the other hand, when Western deniers focus on the "gas chamber lie," the "Zionist blackmail of Germany," and, worse still, the sufferings of Faurisson, Zundel, and their ilk, they will be met with bemusement rather than sympathy.

Where does this leave the Jewish community? A few points are worth noting. First, a few sources have looked at the banning of the 2001 conference as a sign of hope. On one level they are right. It is a victory whenever deniers back down. But this time, the fault is as

much with the deniers themselves, rather than an outpouring of philosemitism in the Arab world.

This leads to a second point. The lesson of the two affairs is not
that the Arab denial is on the wane, but that it is different from the
European variety. In general, Arab deniers focus on reducing the scope
of Jewish suffering. There is far less interest in defending the extreme
right by whitewashing Nazi Germany's worst crimes. As I noted earlier
in the paper, Arab deniers do not want to give up the concept of the
evil Nazi, they want to graft it on the Zionist Jew.

While, in one respect, this is profoundly depressing, it offers a small
area of hope. The last twenty years has seen a growth of right-wing
extremism and neo-Nazi violence—especially in France, Germany,
and Austria, three countries critical for determining whether the post-
1945 antifascist consensus will last deep into this century. What role
will the Arab migrant communities play in this process? Will they join
forces with the neo-Nazis? Will they fight them as racists? Or will they
sit on the sidelines? The answers to these questions are open, but the
rejection of the hard-core deniers in Beirut is a comforting sign.

Postscript

Recent developments involving the president of Iran, Mahmoud
Ahmadinejad, demonstrate both the growth and limitations of
Holocaust denial in the Middle East. Ahmadinejad, the conservative
mayor of Teheran whose election as president in June 2005 came as
something as a political surprise, has made attacks on Israel, Jews, and
the Holocaust a staple of his public dialogue. In October 2005 he called
for Israel to be "wiped off the map."[29] Two months later he called the
Holocaust a "myth."[30]

The real fireworks began in February 2006 when, in the wake of
the controversy over the publication of the Danish cartoons insulting
the prophet Muhammad,[31] President Ahmadinejad called for a contest
for cartoons insulting the Holocaust.[32] Then, in a May 2006 interview
with the German newsmagazine *Der Spiegel*, he referred to Germans
as "prisoners of the Holocaust" adding that the subject required "more
research" from "impartial groups." In the same interview, he asked why
"among...60 million victims" of World War II "only the Jews are the
center of attention?"[33]

While President Ahmadinejad's repeated comments have given
Holocaust denial heightened visibility, his own denial is much closer

to the Middle Eastern version described earlier in the article. In particular, almost all of President Ahmadinejad's pronouncements on the Holocaust immediately bring in the Palestinians. He often does this by using the conditional: "If the Holocaust occurred, then Europe must draw the consequences and it is not Palestine that should pay the price for it."[34] Moreover, even though Ernst Zundel was on trial in Germany at the time of the *Der Spiegel* interview, Ahmadinejad did not refer to him or any other Holocaust denier by name, nor did he refer to the gas chamber hoax or any of the other markers of European Holocaust denial.[35]

Furthermore, not all the Iranian establishment shares President Ahmadinejad's position. Former president Muhammad Khatami referred to the Holocaust as a historical reality, albeit one misused by opponents of the Palestinians. He then referred to the "persecution of the Jews" and "Nazism" as "Western phenomena."[36] In other words, Khatami views the Holocaust as a European affair—one that is not the Palestinians' responsibility. The same perspective guides President Ahmadinejad and most of the Middle Eastern deniers. While this perspective overstates the connection between the Holocaust and the founding of Israel, and is often riddled with denial and other forms of antisemitism, it is not a message calculated to please the Faurissons and Zundels of the world.

Notes

1. For more on Zundel's activities at the time, see Stanley R. Barrett, *Is God A Racist? The Right Wing in Canada* (Toronto: University of Toronto Press, 1987).

2. Faurisson made these remarks in a 1979 radio broadcast. For more, see Pierre Vidal-Naquet, *Assassins of Memory: Essays on the Denial of the Holocaust.* Translated by Jeffrey Mehlman (New York: Columbia University Press, 1992).

3. I describe these efforts in my book, Robert A. Kahn, *Holocaust Denial and the Law: A Comparative Study* (New York: Palgrave-McMillan, 2004).

4. Gayssot was the first of a new generation of Holocaust-denial laws that punished the act of denial itself, rather than forcing the prosecution to show the defendants insulted the Jews or defamed the dead. This was a

great boon to the prosecution, but has led to opposition to the law on freedom of expression grounds. For more, see Kahn, *Holocaust Denial and the Law*, pp. 102–18.

5. See Tom Smith, *Holocaust Denial: What the Survey Data Reveal* (New York: American Jewish Congress, 1995).

6. See *Holocaust Denial in the Middle East: The Latest Anti-Israel, Anti-Semitic Propaganda Theme* (New York: Anti-Defamation League, 2001). This is an area where more research is needed. In addition to polling the general public in Arab countries on the Holocaust and denial, a content-analysis of the Arab press would be very helpful. In particular, it would be useful to know how often articles appear denying the Holocaust and to what extent, if any, letter writers and editorialists condemn denial. Without this type of information, one can say that Holocaust denial is part of the Arab mainstream, but it is harder to tell if denial is a majority opinion.

7. See *Holocaust Denial in the Middle East.*

8. Al-Missiri is the author of the Arabic language *Zionism, Nazism and the End of History* (1997). I draw my account of Al-Missiri's views from Goertz Nordbuch, "The Socio-Historical Background of Holocaust Denial in Arab Countries, Arab Reactions to Roger Gaurady's *The Founding Myths of Israeli Politics*" (available on the Internet at http://sisco.huji.ac.il/17.nordbuch.html).

9. Nordbuch, "Socio-Historical Background," takes a harder line on al-Missiri: "Despite his acceptance that anti-Jewish persecution and extermination did take place, al-Missiri's thesis represents a distorted and banal understanding of both Zionism and Nazism."

10. For an interesting discussion of the denier mind-set, see Nadine Fresco, "Negating the Dead" (Alan Sheridan, trans.) in Geoffrey H. Hartman, ed., *Holocaust Remembrance: The Shapes of Memory* (Oxford: Basil Blackwell, 1994), pp. 191–203.

11. See Ray Hanania, "Holocaust Denial is Wrong and Injures a Righteous Palestinian Cause," *Arab Media Syndicate*, September 24, 1998. While Hanania claims to oppose Holocaust denial—and significantly, given my thesis, distances himself from "neo-Nazi apologists"—he nevertheless questions whether the number of Holocaust victims is exaggerated.

12. See Nadim Rouhana, "The Holocaust and Psychological Dynamics of the Arab-Israeli Conflict," paper presented at the Northeastern University Symposium, Boston, April 18–20, 2001. Rouhana, an Israeli Arab, accepts the Holocaust and calls upon other Arabs to do so, but argues that the *nabka* should be treated the same way as the Holocaust. However, in

making this argument, he refrains from explicitly equating the *nabka* with the Holocaust.

13. The Anti-Defamation League report, *Holocaust Denial in the Middle East*, cites twelve examples of Middle Eastern Holocaust denial in its Appendix. Of these, only four mentioned the gas chambers, and only one raised the theme of the use of the Holocaust to "blackmail" Germany (although two other excerpts raised "blackmail" in a broader context). By contrast, nine of the twelve articles made explicit reference to the state of Israel or the Palestinian people.

14. The insult is independent of the appropriateness of the analogy itself. To put it another way, to refer to a particular practice of the Israeli government as "apartheid" may be unfair, but it lacks the insult carried by those who call Israel a "Nazi state."

15. During the 1950s German antisemite Friedrich Nieland made this claim. See Kahn, *Holocaust Denial and the Law*, pp. 66–69.

16. Nordbuch, "Socio-Historical Background," records that Mafouz supported Gaurady, but does not provide more detail. In particular, Nordbuch does not indicate whether Mafouz supported Gaurady's right to freedom of speech or defended him on the merits.

17. This, at least, is the claim made by Theodore J. O'Keefe in an article that ran in the IHR's *Journal of Historical Review*. See O'Keefe, "Origin and Enduring Impact of the 'Gaurady Affair,'" *Journal of Historical Review*, 18:4 (1998).

18. Muhammad Hasanein Heikal, "Foreword to the Arabic Edition of Gaurady's *The Founding Myths of Modern Israel*" (available on the Internet at: http://www.ihr.org/jhr/v19/v19n6p30_heikal.html).

19. *Holocaust Denial in the Middle East.*

20. Howard Schneider, "Jews, Arabs Join to Decry Holocaust Deniers," *Washington Post*, March 26, 2001.

21. Ibid.

22. Hisham Melhem, "Organizers of the 'Revisionism and Zionism' Conference Confirm That It Will Be Held in Beirut at the End of March, and Accuse Washington of Hypocrisy and a Double Standard," *As-Safir*, March 10, 2001.

23. "Arab Intellectuals Call on Lebanon to Cancel Revisionist Gathering," Agence France Presse, March 15, 2001.

24. Elias Khoury, "The Insolence of an Ambassador," March 2001 (Internet posting available at http://www.ihr.org/conference/beirutconf/eliasKhoury.hmtl).

25. "Dispute Over `Holocaust Denial' Conference in Jordan," *As-Safir*, April 20, 2001.

26. Robert Faurisson, "The Leaders of the Arab States Should Quit Their Silence on the Imposture of the 'Holocaust'," (available on the Internet at http://www.ihr.org/conference/beirutconf/010331faurisson.html).

27. Ver*ite et Justice* Statement on the Lebanese Government Ban of the 'Revisionism and Zionism' Conference, March 23, 2001 (available at http://www.ihr.org./conference/beirutconf/010323statement.html).

28. Second Ver*ite et Justice* Statement on the Lebanese Government Ban of the 'Revisionism and Zionism' Conference, March 27, 2001 (available at http://www.ihr.org./conference/beirutconf/010328statement.html).

29. "UN Raps Iran's Anti-Israel Rant," BBC News, October 28, 2005 (available on the Internet at http://news.bbc.co.uk/1/hi/world/middle_east/4387206.stm).

30. "Iranian Leader: Holocaust a 'Myth.' " CNN, December 14, 2005 (available on the Internet at http://www.cnn.com/2005/WORLD/meast/12/14/iran.israel/).

31. Another point of debate was raised as Muslims asked why European countries ban Holocaust denial but not cartoons defaming the Prophet Muhammad. For an early attempt to answer this question, see Abraham Cooper and Harold Brackman, "Punishing Religious Defamation and Holocaust Denial: Is There a Double Standard?" in *Equal Voices*, vol. 18, (June 2006).

32. In August 2006 a Teheran exhibit showed cartoons insulting the Holocaust. See Robert Tait, "Iran Cartoon Show Mocks Holocaust," *The Observer*, August 20, 2006 (available on the Internet at http://observer.guardian.co.uk/print/0,,329557472-119093,00.html).

33. *Der Spiegel*, interview with Iran's president Ahmadinejad (May 30, 2006), available on the Internet at http://service.spiegel.de/cache/international/0,1518,druck-418660,00.html (English translation).

34. Ibid.

35. Ibid.

36. "Ex-Iran Head Enters Holocaust Row," BBC News, March 1, 2006 (available on the Internet at http://news.bbc.co.uk/2/hi/middle_east/4763494.stm.)

SECTION IV

America Is Different

"Only in America" was the title of American Jewish humorist Harry Golden's warm tribute to the uniqueness of the Jewish experience in the United States. It was with those words that vice presidential nominee Joseph I. Lieberman concluded his 2000 acceptance speech at the Democratic National Convention, a moment that signified that being Jewish and even an observant Jew was no obstacle to holding the highest office in the land. These words have been echoed by many Jews, especially by Jewish immigrants to the American shores who have witnessed the differences between their native culture and their adopted homeland. For contemporary Jews born in the post–World War II period when there are seemingly no boundaries to Jewish participation in American life, the contemporary situation is taken for granted and regarded as a norm of Jewish experience, but historians and older Jews see the matter rather differently. They intuitively understand what has been termed American exceptionalism.

American historian Fred Cople Jaher and sociologist Jerome A. Chanes argue for American exceptionalism, the view that the experience of Jews within the United States has been so very different than the experience of Jews in Europe and elsewhere. For Jaher, Jewish political equality on American shores is organic, de facto not declarative; it emerged gradually and was not abrupt; and it took root independently of the American Revolution even as it was reinforced by the Revolution but not dependent upon it. In that sense the United States was the first postemancipatory society, one in which Jewish rights were a given from its inception and not an abrupt departure from the customs of generations.

Chanes argues that separation of church and state meant that Jews by definition were not living in a Christian society. They were however living in a frontier society, where new customs were possible and new arrivals determined the shape of the society or where in the words of Jaher, "circumstantial imperatives trumped ideological biases." In the frontier there were not yet "insiders" and "outsiders" but people thrown together by circumstances who had to forge bonds to survive. The United States became a nation of immigrants and in that context Jewish life was radically different than the established norms of European nationalism. Neither man argues that the experience of the Jews in what became the United States of America has been without hatred and prejudice, without discrimination and exclusion—or even without its dangers—yet each writer accounts for the vast differences between the American society and its European counterparts. Jaher further argues that the aversion to Jews within the United States has been of European derivation rather than America's distinctiveness.

Chanes maintains that American pluralism, which made room for the Jews, and included the Jews, has been an indispensable part of American exceptionalism. Still even Chanes must account for the dramatic imbalance between the findings of empirical research regarding the long-term decline of antisemitism and the widely held [*mis*]perception among American Jews that antisemitism is on the ascent. He cites the telling example of San Francisco Bay area where in 1985 more than one-third of those questioned said that Jewish candidates could not be elected to Congress from San Francisco, citing anti-Jewish bias or prejudice. Yet three out of the four congressional representatives from that area—as well as the two state senators and the mayor of San Francisco—were, in fact, well-identified Jews *at the time* the poll was conducted.

How to account for the imbalance, what Leon Wieseltier has termed the ethnic anxiety of contemporary American Jews?

Importantly, Chanes reviews the research that has been conducted tracing the behavioral and attitudinal decline of antisemitism over four decades. Jewish security is strong he argues. The legitimacy of antisemitism has been refuted, the studies yield strong evidence over a sustained period of time, they cannot be denied. He examines not only the research but the methodologies, most particularly the manner in which questions have been asked and problems have been posed and hence how we are to understand the answers. He also poses both a research agenda as well as as the outlines for a strategy for counteracting antisemitism.

The good new is that there is much good news and the bad news is that the bad news is not nearly as bad as it is perceived to be—even the in the contemporary climate—only in America.

12

The Experience of Jews in the United States and Europe Illuminates American Exceptionalism

Fred Cople Jaher

We begin with a routine but indispensable observation that a distinction between the United States and other countries can only be validated by comparative investigation. Accordingly, this study in national contrast examines encounters of Jews here and in their European lands of settlement, chiefly in France, where the largest concentration of Western European Jews have lived. Another obvious contention is that the modern Jewish experience was fundamentally defined and differentiated by those Western revolutions that transformed society and ushered in or shaped the nation-state. Jews were readmitted to England shortly after and appreciably due to the Puritan triumph; in France and Russia they were officially emancipated in 1791 and 1918. Across the Atlantic, however, this self-evident, even jejune, sequence abruptly disconnects. Neither revolution nor the emergence of the nation *seminally modified* the status of American Jewry. This difference illuminates American exceptionalism and ramifies into variance in the Jewish experience here from that in Europe. Viewed from this perspective, the apparently intuitive and puerile introductory perceptions become problematic and noteworthy.[1]

Revolutionary emancipation of Jews, in France and the Soviet Union for example, derived from abstract principles of natural rights or socialist comradeship. Liberation proceeded from modern state formation, a de jure conferral that abruptly transited Jews from semi-autonomous corporate communities to members of the national community, from outcasts to citizens. Comte de Clermont-Tonnerre proclaimed this development on December 23, 1789, when he urged emancipation in the National Assembly:

The Jews should be denied everything as a nation, but granted everything as individuals. They must be citizens....if they do not want this,
they must inform us and we shall then be compelled to expel them.
The existence of a nation within a nation a nation is unacceptable to
our country.[2]

Jew would forfeit their historic existence as a corporation ("a
nation with another nation") for equal rights (citizenship in the new
nation rising from the revolution).[3]

Political equality for American Jewry was organic not abstract, de
facto not declarative, gradual not abrupt, and not as embedded in larger
issues like a revolutionary transformation of society or the emergence of
a modern state. In this, as in other respects, America resembled its primary progenitor, a convergence suggesting an Anglo-American model
of Jewish emancipation in contrast to a European/Continental model.
In the United States and the United Kingdom attainment of equality
was incremental and organic. Anglo-American Jewish enclaves lived
in nations with greater denominational variety and pluralism than did
their European coreligionists. Catholics for extensive eras were deemed
the most dangerous sectarian foe. British and American Protestantism
was more philosemitic than French Catholicism, German Lutheranism,
or the Russian Orthodox Church. Neither America nor England (since
Jews returned in the seventeenth century) had enforced ghettoes and
semi-independent, legally recognized communities, trade restrictions,
special tolls and taxes on Jews, and antisemitic movements or political parties. American and British Jews entered their respective national
cultures earlier than did those in the Continent, except for Holland.
Perhaps the national context was more decisive. The U.S. and Britain
encountered weaker *volkish* urges and political tribulations than European countries. Comparatively free of foreign invasions and conquests,
insurrections, constitutional crises, and governmental turnovers, their
stability is mutually related to a sturdier national identity.[4]

Two colonial incidents involving Jews indicated the American
way. Governor Stuyvesant, an antisemite, wanted to remove twenty-
three Jews from Brazil who landed in New Amsterdam in 1654 (the
initial Jewish settlement in that country). The Dutch West India Company directors refused because the colony needed settlers and trade to
survive, and Dutch Jews had vital commercial connections and were
large shareholders in the nearly bankrupt company. Over the gover-

nor's objections, the company permitted the Jews to trade and, contrary to prevailing practice in Europe, to own real estate, live where they pleased, and become burghers.[5]

Fearing that their presence would discourage immigration, in 1733 the charter company of Georgia wanted to exclude Jews. Gov. James Oglethorpe, however, felt that Jewish immigrants would address the need for inhabitants and not inhibit other newcomers. Oglethorpe granted Jews land, and the company trustees, reconsidering their earlier protests, in 1737 gave a Jew a loan to grow grapes in order to procure a staple commodity.[6] Liberation in New Netherlands and Georgia did not reify concepts of natural rights or theories of citizenship associated with nation building. Instead, circumstantial imperatives trumped customary, ideological biases. Moreover, Jews arrived at the creation of these colonies; and, unlike their usual existence, were present in a semi-emancipated status not as ghettoized subjects of monarchical or feudal lordship.

Before 1775, America's Jews embarked on realizing the utopian universalisms, the emancipatory and egalitarian yearnings that helped impel (though imperfectly and in the end usually unsuccessfully) the Puritan, French, and Soviet revolutions and other Western insurgencies. What transpired for American Jews before independence, in contrast to their coreligionists in England before 1640, France in 1789, and Russia in 1917, conditioned the different trajectories of the Jewish experience in these nations. Plotting the course of this country's Jews begins with contextualizing it as a variety of what has become a truism, American exceptionalism (the consensus liberal paradigm), originally conceptualized by Alexis de Tocqueville in *Democracy in America* (1835, 1840) and elaborated by Louis Hartz in *The Liberal Tradition in America* (1955). Unlike other Western nations, the initial settlements of what became the United States emerged in the modern era, i.e., after the Middle Ages and at the conclusion of the wars of the Reformation and Counter-Reformation. Hence, American Jews were less liable to demonization, ghettoization, exclusion, submission, and other Old World torments.[7] New World conditions, absence of a feudal past, a legally enshrined nobility, and corporate organization of society, and a unitary intercolonial church establishment, and the necessity of attracting settlers promoted political, cultural, and ethnic diversity (American pluralism, currently called multiculturalism), that eventuated in inclusive nationalism, a cardinal tenet of the American creed. These ideological and situational developments early enhanced integration of Jews in America and differentiated them from coreligionists elsewhere.

Egalitarianism was fostered here and abroad by Enlightenment doctrines of natural rights and the faculty of reason as interrelated attributes inherent in humans. These principles were expressed in the Declaration of Independence and its partial clone, the Declaration of the Rights of Man and the Citizen, definitive documents of the rebellions of 1776 and 1789. Thomas Jefferson, America's premier *philosophe,* drafted the American declaration, and Benjamin Franklin, another Deist, was on the Continental Congress committee that prepared the document. A decade later Jefferson wrote Virginia's Bill for Religious Freedom, a vigorous defense of liberty of conscience.

American principles and practices, conventions, and exigencies, by the later provincial and revolutionary periods, yielded a unique magnitude of acceptance. At various times and in various colonies during the eighteenth century, Catholics, Presbyterians, Baptists, and Moravians were officially persecuted; after 1680 no such mistreatment befell Jews.[8] Avoidance of negative encounters was not the only measure of progress. Jews participated in American life in ways virtually non-extant across the Atlantic. They attended colleges and belonged to elite cultural and charitable organizations. Rhode Island Lopezes and the Levy-Franks clan in New York and Philadelphia belonged to the urban gentry and daughters of affluent Jewish families married well, as in the union between Philadelphia Franks and New York aristocrat Oliver DeLancey. A marker of parity was the service of Jews as Revolutionary army or militia officers up to the rank of colonel when their European brethren were generally excluded from the military.[9]

Although formally barred from public posts by the requirement of swearing to the divinity of the New Testament, a number of Jews held office. In the early provincial period they were constables in New Amsterdam and Boston. Later, Moses Lindo, the South's leading Jewish merchant, was inspector general of indigo for South Carolina, and Jews served as justices of the peace in Georgia. By the Revolution, Jews, particularly in the South, held offices of greater power and prestige, a result of their own social and economic distinction and of Jewish preference for the patriot cause due to less prejudice in America than England and to most Jews having few ties to the mother country or the imperial establishment. Merchant Moses Sheftall in 1774–75 headed the county government of metropolitan Savannah and became a brigade colonel and commissary general for South Carolina and Georgia. Another Jew sat in the South Carolina Provincial Congress, and after independence, when it became the General Assembly, became the first Jewish state legislator.[10]

Suffrage, like officeholding, was a function of citizenship inconsistently exercised by Jews. In some colonies Jews on occasion went to the polls and at other times were disenfranchised. They seemed to have exercised uninterrupted suffrage in Georgia, an apparently unique condition of equality in provincial America. Conversely, in several colonies Jews never voted and were not eligible for government posts. The New York Constitution of 1777 gave Jews political equality, but even in an age of revolutionary republicanism this was a unique conferral. The South Carolina Constitution of 1778, for example, excluded non-Protestants from the assembly despite Jews in the 1760s and '70s having regained voting and officeholding rights they lost in 1716.[11] As with so much else concerning American Jewry in the colonial and revolutionary epochs, assumption of civic rights was an incomplete process with advances and withdrawals dependent upon intracolonial conflicts and other circumstances. Nevertheless, Jews engaged in political activities of a type and on a scale denied them in other countries.

Although the War for Independence did not radically alter the status of American Jewry, revolutionary republicanism quickened the quest for equality. Jews faced two impediments, sectarian establishments and political hindrances. Starting in the Revolution and largely completed in the early national period, these disabilities gradually disappeared. Several colonies never had an established church and during the Revolution, New York, Virginia, and North Carolina ended public taxes for sectarian purposes. Although half the states still provided for public funds for religion, the trend was clear. The Northwest Ordinance (1787), U.S. Constitution, and the First Amendment of the Bill of Rights (1789) affirmed freedom of conscience and neither the federal government nor any states formed after nationhood provided for funding any creed.[12]

The other state constitutional impingement on civic rights was swearing to belief in Christianity in order to hold government posts. Many states felt that membership in the body of Christ was vital to the spiritual and social health of the commonwealth, and therefore a necessary condition of full membership in the body politic. Hence, test oaths for officeholding, even when, as in some revolutionary state constitutions, no provision was made for public support of religion. Eleven of the thirteen original states limited officeholders to Christians or Protestants.[13] The influence of the Virginia Bill for Religious Freedom, Article VI of the federal Constitution ("no religious test shall ever be required as a Qualification to any Office or public Trust under the United States"), the Northwest Ordinance, and the Bill of Rights helped ensure that new states did not require oaths and that older states dropped them.

Legal impositions upon full citizenship in the states were largely soon overcome, a momentum that owed much to the constitutional provision that Jews did not have to meet a religious test for holding federal office and thus made America the first nation to grant them civic equality. This break with the past, however, did not evoke the contention over emancipation present in the French National Assembly. Article VI stirred little discussion or dissent in the Constitutional Convention of 1787, only the North Carolina delegation opposed and Maryland divided over its passage. Nor did it arouse much controversy in state ratifying conventions or the widespread debate over the Constitution.[14]

A similar affirmative, brief, and dispassionate response greeted another departure from the past and other nations when Congress passed the Bill of Rights (1789). The First Amendment stated: "Congress shall make no law respecting an establishment of religion or prohibiting the free exercise thereof."[15] With ratification of the Bill of Rights (1791), the national constitution made America's Jews unprecedented unconditional citizens. De jure emancipation occurred a few months later in France, but it was temporary and incomplete.[16] In this respect the French and Soviet revolutions resembled each other and differed from the American, a variance partly due to religious sects in America not opposing the War for Independence. Organized religion resisted the communist uprising and the radical stages of the French Revolution, and communists and Jacobins persecuted all denominations when they seized power.

Ideology coalesced with policy to encourage emancipation. Renowned figures of the Revolution and the Age of Reason, Franklin, Benjamin Rush, Jefferson, and George Washington advocated religious liberty and civic equality for Jews. John Adams and James Madison as well defended Judaism and Jewish citizenship.[17] Deists or not, the foremost American leaders believed in natural rights and creedal diversity and, as a group, were unique among Western political leaders in approving Jews as a legitimate national enclave.

In the nineteenth century civic recognitions were renewed, enhanced, or introduced. Presidents (John Tyler) and eminent statesmen (Henry Clay) reiterated their predecessors' respectful and nondiscriminatory pledges to the Children of Abraham. By the 1840s, Jews sat in both houses of Congress and during the Civil War in the Confederate cabinet. And by 1842 only New Hampshire and North Carolina disqualified professing Jews from public office.[18]

Ascendance in politics related to amalgamation of Jew and nation, a cultural mutuality essential to the acquisition of unqualified citizenship. Unconditional acceptance in the American community would be a prolonged and problematic process rather than an immediate achievement. Before the Civil War, however, it seemed that total equality proceeded along an uninterrupted, if incremental, trajectory that made American Jewry globally unique and reflected the liberal exceptionalism of the United States. Absorption in the American civil religion was a fundamental avenue of attaining the goal desired by most Jews and many of their gentile compatriots.

Evidence abounded of progress in this dimension of the unity of Judaism and nationhood. In 1811 the New York state legislature granted the charity school run by Congregation Shearith Israel the same privileges accorded Protestant and Catholic parochial institutions, and the New York City Council made payments retroactive to the school's beginnings. Interfaith parity was an inclusive civic gesture exemplifying multiculturalism, and positive institutional interaction between Jewish and official, Gentile-dominated organizations endorsed Jews as citizens. Twenty-two years passed before France gave Jewish schools state funding equal to those of other denominations.[19]

Another sign of civic acceptance surfaced in 1829 when a Richmond rabbi voiced the invocation at the Virginia Constitutional Convention and twenty years later when a rabbi from the same congregation did so at a Virginia House of Delegates session, the first official blessing of a Jewish clergyman over a state legislature. In 1861 another spiritual leader from that congregation prayed before a House of Delegates meeting.[20]

Gershom Mendes Seixas, spiritual leader of Shearith Israel, America's oldest and largest Jewish congregation, epitomized, as symbol and creator, the integration of Judaism into the bourgeoning national civic cult. At the presidential inauguration process in New York City on April 30, 1789, Hazzan (cantor) Seixas marched alongside twelve other clergymen. On days designated by President John Adams and other officials for prayer, fasting, humiliation, or thanksgiving, Seixas sermonized and also consulted with other ministers to plan such events, thus forging ties between Jewish and Gentile sectarian communities, a role acknowledged by his being called "Reverend" and "minister." He preached in St. Paul's Episcopal Chapel and served as a Columbia College regent and trustee, a post unprecedented for a Jewish clergyman.[21]

Incorporation of Judaism in the civic cult was but one feature of the consolidation of American Jewry into national society; indeed civic affirmation of its creed reflected advancing comprehensive coalescence between the Jewish enclave and the national community. By midcentury American Jews commingled with citizens of other denominations in important business activities. General entrepreneurs in young, relatively undifferentiated communities like Santa Fe, San Francisco, and Los Angeles, they undertook ventures in trade, transportation, manufacturing, real estate, and banking. Even in older places, like Baltimore, Richmond, Charleston, Philadelphia, and New York, where social distinctions rigidified with time, Jews expanded their role as directors and officers of prestigious firms. Correlated with business and economic achievement, Jews won renown in law and medicine and attended prestigious colleges.[22]

Although social acceptance was more elusive than other types of advancement, voluntary associations of varying status and function, as in previous eras, admitted Jews. In Philadelphia, Richmond, Charleston, Los Angeles, Milwaukee, and other cities they belonged to elite clubs, charity, artistic, and scientific societies, and militia companies as well as to plebian volunteer fire companies. Preeminent antebellum and Civil War Jews, August Belmont and Judah P. Benjamin, respectively in 1848 and 1852, joined New York's premier social club, the Union Club, and the former celebrated the paramount intermarriage of the epoch (with the daughter of blue blood Matthew C. Perry) with the most fashionable wedding of the 1849 New York social season. Good repute of Jews also resonated in popular and high culture. For example, antebellum tragedians Junius Brutus Booth and Edwin Forest acted Shylock compassionately.[23]

* * *

I have highlighted the positive dimension of the Jewish encounter with this nation from colonial era to the Civil War because this time and aspect of the experience of American Jewry reflects American exceptionalism. Antisemitism was nonetheless a significant problem for Jews, as Leonard Dinnerstein and I have elsewhere noted.[24] Such aversion, however, evinced America's European derivation rather than its distinctiveness. Another reason for emphasizing the favorable reception of Jews was that America's pre-1861 existence was comparatively tranquil for them. Such good times would not come again for another century.

Modern antisemitism escalated dramatically in the United States, Germany, and France respectively in the 1860s, '70s, and '80s. While massive boycotts, antisemitic political parties, pogroms, and the Holocaust did not happen here, American Jews faced increasing hostility, triggered by the secession crisis, which brought them unprecedented public contempt. For a century after the Civil War outright exclusion or quotas were imposed on Jews in many schools, professions, neighborhoods, hotels, resorts, and social clubs. Some victims of bigotry were descendants of Jewish founders and members of the discriminating institutions. Climactic indicators of the intensification of prejudice were Gen. Ulysses S. Grant's infamous General Order No. 22 (December 17, 1862), which barred Jewish traders from the Department of the Tennessee (his military command) on the ground of nefarious business dealing; the trial and lynching of Leo Frank (1913–15), the only recorded lynching of a Jew in the history of this country; election of Thomas Watson to the U.S. Senate (1920), the singular episode of Jew hatred that catapulted a political figure into public office; and the advent of Father Charles Coughlin in the 1930s, America's foremost antisemitic demagogue. On both sides of the Atlantic, Jew hatred plunged to its nadir in the Great Depression and World War II.[25]

After 1945, Jews rose in esteem and acceptance in the West.[26] Whether this development resulted from an organic growth in humanity and multicultural respect that embraced other marginalized minorities as well or from guilt over the Holocaust, in which Western nations had considerable culpability, is still in open question. A 1947 French public opinion poll revealed that only 37 percent of the respondents felt that Jews were "French like all the rest" of the citizens; thirty-seven years later 94 percent agreed with this statement. In 1940, 63 percent of Americans thought Jews had objectionable qualities, by 1962, 22 percent held his view. Anti-Defamation League public opinion surveys in 1992 and 1998 showed that extreme antisemites (those agreeing to at least six of eleven negative statements, identical in both surveys, about Jews) declined from 20 percent to 12 percent and nonantisemites (those agreeing with one or none of the statements) rose from 39 percent to 53 percent. In the last ADL Survey (2002), however, the favorable trend was reversed; those holding pronounced antisemitic opinions climbed to 17 percent, while nonantisemites dropped to 18 percent.[27]

The ADL, also in 2002, conducted a Euroopean opinion poll containing four of the same statements. An important and intriguing finding was the percentages of Americans and Europeans agreeing with the statement: "Jews are more loyal to Israel than to this country." In the United States, it was phrased "than to America," and one-third of the respondents concurred. The statement addresses the historical contention of dual loyalty, a "nation within a nation" that defined the "Jewish Question" from the eighteenth century to the present in Europe. The agreement distributions in Europe were: Belgium (50%), Denmark (45%), France (42%), Germany (55%), United Kingdom (34%), Spain (72%), Italy (58%), Austria (54%), and The Netherlands (48%).[28] Except for the UK, the nation historically closest to the U.S. in many matters including its attitude and historical treatment of Jews, these percentages showed a sizable negative divergence from America. Presently, as in the past, it can be contended that the Anglo-American model of acceptance of Jews varies from its European/Continental counterpart.

Notes

1. These issues are elaborated in Frederic Cople Jaher, *The Jews and the Nation: Revolution, Emancipation, State Formation, and the Liberal Paradigm in American and France* (Princeton: Princeton University Press, 2002).

2. Speech of Count Stanislaus de Clermont-Tonnerre to the National Assembly, December 23, 1789, *Archives Parlementaires de 1787 à 1860,*

Premier Série (1789 à 1799) (Paris: Libraire Administratif de Paul Dupont, 1878), 10, pp. 754–56.

3. Fuller discussion of these issues is in Jaher, *Jews and the Nation,* chapters 2–3.

4. *Toward Modernity: The European Jewish Model,* ed. Jacob Katz (New Brunswick, NJ and Oxford: Transaction Books, 1987), pp. 226–42; Todd M. Endelman, *The Jews of Georgian England, 1774–1830: Tradition and Change in a Liberal Society* (Philadelphia: Jewish Publication Society of America, 1979), and idem., *Radical Assimilation in English-Jewish History, 1656–1945* (Bloomington and Indianapolis: Indiana University Press, 1990), pp. 21–22; Israel Finestein, "Jewish Emancipationists in Victorian England: Self-Imposed Limits to Emancipation," in *Assimilation and Community: The Jews in Nineteenth-Century Europe,* eds. Jonathan Franke and Steven Zipperstein (Cambridge and New York: Cambridge University Press, 1992), pp. 43–47; Geoffrey Alderman, "English Jews or Jews of English Persuasion? Reflections on the Emancipation of Anglo-Jewry," in *Paths of Emancipation: The Jews, States, and Citizenship,* ed. Pierre Bernbaum and Ira Katznelson (Princeton: Princeton University Press, 1991), pp. 128–37; M. C. N. Salbstein, *The Emancipation of the Jews in Britain: The Question of the Admission of the Jews to Parliament, 1828–1869* (Rutherford, NJ: Fairleigh Dickinson University Press; London and Toronto: Associated Universities Presses, 1982); David Cesarini, "Changing Character," in *Citizenship, Nationality and Migration,* ed. David Cesarini and Mary Fulbrook (London and New York: Routledge, 1996), pp. 57, 60–61.

5. The correspondence between Stuyvesant, the Jewish settlers, and the Dutch West India Company is in *A Documentary History of the United States: 1654–1875,* ed. Morris U. Schappes (New York: Schocken Books, 1971), pp. 1–14; see also Jacob Rader Marcus, *The Colonial American Jew: 1492–1776* (Detroit: Wayne State University Press, 1970), vol. 1, pp. 71–81, 175–79, 209-10, 218–43; Frederic Cople Jaher, *A Scapegoat in the New Wilderness: The Origins and Rise of Anti-Semitism in America* (Cambridge: Harvard University Press, 1994), pp. 89–91.

6. *The Colonial Records of the State of Georgia,* ed. Allen D. Candler (Atlanta: Franklin, 1904–16), vol. 1, pp. 98–99, 149–53; vol. 2, p. 62; "Journal of the Transactions of the Trustees for Establishing the Colony of Georgia in America," December 22, 1733; January 5, 1734, in *Documentary History,* ed. Schappes, pp. 24–25; Malcolm Stern, "New Light on the Jewish Settlement of Savannah," in *The Jewish Experience in America,* ed. Albert Karp (New York: KTAV, 1969), vol. 1, pp. 74, 84–85; Marcus, *Colonial American Jew,* vol. 1, p. 471; vol. 2, p. 888; vol. 3, p. 1130; Jaher, *Scapegoat,* pp. 111–12.

7. Fuller discussion of these matters is in Jaher, *Jews and the Nation*, pp. 9–56.

8. "The Charter of Georgia" (1732), in *The Federal and State Constitutions, Colonial Charters and other Organic Laws of the United States of America*, ed. Francis N. Thorpe (Washington, DC: U.S. Government Printing Office, 1909), vol. 7, p. 773; Abraham Goodman, *American Overture: Jewish Rights in Colonial Times* (Philadelphia: Jewish Publication Society of America, 1947), pp. 192–93, 195; Marcus, *Colonial American Jew*, vol. 2, pp. 421–22, 441, 443–47, 451, 454–55. 466–67, 485, 499–505, 507–08; and idem., *Early American Jewry: The Jews of Philadelphia and the South* (Philadelphia: Jewish Publication Society of America, 1951–53), vol. 2, pp. 330–31; *Jewish Experience*, ed. Karp, vol. 1, p. 74.

9. Goodman, *American Overture*, pp. 21, 108, 126–27; Marcus, *Colonial American Jew*, vol. 3, pp. 1148–52, 1199, 1206–7, 1307–9, and idem., *Early American Jewry*, vol. 2, pp. 8, 81, 244, 246-48, 265, 330, 348, 466–67, 495–98, 511; and idem., *American Jewry: Documents, Eighteenth Century* (Cincinnati: Hebrew Union College Press, 1959), p. 7; Leo Hershkowitz, "Some Aspects of the New York Jewish Merchant Community," *American Jewish Historical Quarterly* 66 (September 1976): 12, 25–27; *Jewish Life in Philadelphia: 1830–1940*, ed. Murray Friedman (Philadelphia: ISHI Publications, 1983), pp. 5, 291–92; Leon Huhner, *Jews in America in Colonial and Revolutionary Times* (New York: Gertz Bros., 1959), pp. 145, 149; Albert Ehrenfield, "A Chronicle of Boston Jewry: From Colonial Settlement to 1900" (mss., 1963, a copy is in the University of Illinois Library, Champaign-Urbana), p. 150.

10. "Minutes of the New York City Common Council," October 14, 1718; September 17, 1766, in *Documentary History*, ed. Schappes, pp. 19, 41: Hershowitz, "New York Jewish Community": 13; Goodman, *American Overture*, pp. 20, 199–200; Marcus, *Colonial American Jew*, vol. 1, p. 463; vol. 3, pp. 1261–62, 1276, 1279–80, 1307–9, and idem., *Early American*, vol. 2, pp. 160, 165, 229, 245, 344–48, 518–19, 527, and idem., *American Jewry*, p. 80; Huhner, *Jews in America*, pp. 147–49; Richard B. Morris, "Civil Liberties in the Jewish Tradition in Early America," in *Jewish Experience*, ed., Karp, p. 415; Jaher, *Scapegoat*, pp. 102–3.

11. Marcus, *Colonial American Jew*, vol. 1, pp. 405, 408–20, 422, 424, 436–37, 441, 444, 446–47, 462–65, 470, 510; vol. 3, p. 1282, and idem., *Early American Jewry*, vol. 2, pp. 56, 166, 229, 265, 330–31, 518–19, 522–26, 529–30; Goodman, *American Overture*, pp. 110–14; Morris, "Civil Liberties," p. 416; Hershowitz, "New York Merchant Community," 13; "The Constitution of New York" (1777), in *Federal*, ed. Thorpe, vol. 5, pp. 2630, 2632, 2636–38; "The Constitution of South Carolina" (1778), in ibid., vol. 6, p. 3250.

12. Jaher, *Jews and the Nation*, pp. 144–45. The best analysis of established religion in America is Leonard Levy, *The Establishment Clause: Religion and the First Amendment* (New York: Macmillan; London: Collier, Macmillan, 1986), pp. 1–63. Colonial charters and state constitutions are in *Federal*, ed. Thorpe.

13. *Federal*, ed. Thorpe, vol. 1, pp. 566, 568; vol. 5, pp. 2793, 3100; Jaher, *Jews and the Nation*, pp. 145–46; and idem., *Scapegoat*, p. 121.

14. A fuller discussion of Article VI is in Jaher, *Jews and the Nation*, pp. 141–44; for the vote in the constitutional convention see *The Records of the Federal Convention of 1787*, ed. Max Farrand (New Haven: Yale University Press, vol. 2, p. 468.

15. House of Representatives Debate, August 15, 1789, in Levy, *Establishment*, pp. 76–81. The Senate debate was not recorded.

16. Jaher, *Jews and the Nation*, pp. 66–102.

17. Ibid., pp. 165–68, and idem., *Scapegoat*, pp. 123–24; Benjamin Franklin, *The Autobiography of Benjamin Franklin* (New York: Vintage Books), p. 78; Franklin to Joseph Priestly, August 21, 1784, in *The Writings of Benjamin Franklin*, ed. Albert Henry Smyth (New York: Macmillan, 1906–7), vol. 9, p. 266; Thomas Jefferson to Mordecai Noah, May 28, 1818, in *Jewish Experience*, ed. Karp, p. 359; George Washington to the Hebrew Congregation in Newport, Rhode Island, August 17, 1790, in *Jews and the American Revolution: A Bicentennial Documentary*, ed. James Rader Marcus (Cincinnati: American Jewish Archives, 1975), p. 244; Paul F. Boller, *George Washington & Religion* (Dallas: Southern Methodist University, 1963), pp. 165, 167, 173, 175, 179–82, 192–94; John Adams to F. A. Vanderkamp, February 16, 1809, in *The Works of John Adams*, ed. Charles Francis Adams (Boston: Little, Brown, 1854), vol. 9, p. 609, and to Mordecai Noah, July 11, 1808, in *Jewish Experience*, ed. Karp, p. 362; James Madison to Jacob De La Motta, August 1802, and to Mordi[*sic*]cai Noah, August 15, 1818, in *James Madison on Religious Liberty*, ed. Robert S. Alley (Buffalo: Prometheus Books, 1985), pp. 80–81.

18. Henry Clay to Solomon Etting, July 16, 1832, in *The Jews of the United States, 1790–1840*, ed. Joseph l. Blau and Salo W. Baron (New York: Columbia University Press; Philadelphia: Jewish Publication Society of America, 1963), vol. 1, 58–59; John Tyler to Joseph Simpson, July 10, 1843, in *Publications of the American Jewish Historical Society* 11 (1903): 158–59, and to Jacob Ezekiel, April 19, 1841, in Herbert T. Ezekiel and Gaston Lichtenstein, *The History of the Jews of Richmond from 1769 to 1917* (Richmond: Herbert T. Ezekiel, 1917), p. 118; Jaher, *Scapegoat*, pp. 122, 125, 177.

19. "Memorial of the Trustees of the Congregation Shearith Israel to the New York State Legislature, drawn up by [New York City Mayor] De Witt Clinton (1811)," in *Jews of the United States*, ed. Blau and Baron, vol. 2, pp. 445–46; Jacob Hartstein, "The Polonies Talmud Torah of New York," in *Jewish Experience*, ed. Karp, vol. 2, pp. 45–63; Jaher, *Jews and the Nation*, p. 133.

20. Jaher, *Scapegoat*, pp. 125, 177.

21. N. Taylor Phillips, "Unwritten History: Reminiscences of N. Taylor Phillips," *American Jewish Archives*, 6 (June, 1954): 99; Rev. G. Seixas, "Discourse Delivered in the Synagogue in New-York. On the Ninth of May, 1798, Observed As A Day of Humiliation, &c. &c., Conformably to a Recommendation Of The President of The United States of America," facsimile in *Beginnings, Early American Judaica: A Collection of Ten Publications in Facsimile*, ed. Abraham J. Karp (Philadelphia: Jewish Publication Society of America, 1975), details on Seixas, the "Discourse" and Shearith Israel are on pp. 18–22; Eli Faber, *A Time for Planting: The First Migration, 1654-1820* (Baltimore and London: Johns Hopkins University Press, 1992), pp. 118–20.

22. Frederic Cople Jaher, *The Urban Establishment: Upper Strata in Boston, New York, Charleston, Chicago, and Los Angeles* (Urbana: University of Illinois Press, 1982), pp. 593–99, 601–3; Gunther Barth, *Instant Cities: Urbanization and the Rise of San Francisco and Denver* (New York: Oxford University Press, 1975), pp. 72–73; Peter Decker, *Fortunes and Failures: White Collar Mobility in Nineteenth-Century San Francisco* (Cambridge: Harvard University Press, 1978), pp. 116–18, 238–39; Max Vorspan and Lloyd P. Gartner, *History of the Jews of Los Angeles* (San Marino, CA: Huntington Library, 1970), pp. 34–35; Bertram Wallace Korn, *The Early Jews of New Orleans* (Waltham, MA: American Jewish Historical Society, 1969), pp. 96, 115–16, 125, 225–27; Isaac M. Fein, *The Making of a Jewish Community: The History of Baltimore Jewry from 1767 to 1820* (Philadelphia: Jewish Publication Society, 1971), pp. 17; 107; Myron Berman, *Richmond's Jewry, 1769-1976* (Charlottesville: University of Virginia Press, 1954), pp. 72, 127; Chares Reznikoff, *The Jews of Charleston: A History of an American Jewish Community* (Philadelphia: Jewish Publication Society of America, 1950), pp. 89–90; Barnett A. Elzas, *The Jews of South Carolina from the Earliest Times to the Present Day* (1902; Spartanburg, SC: Reprint Co., 1972), pp. 183, 188, 192, 196–97, 204; Henry Samuel Morais, *The Jews of Philadelphia* (Philadelphia: Levy-type, 1894), pp. 271, 417; Irving Katz, *August Belmont: A Political Biography* (New York: Columbia University Press, 1968), p. 7; Robert D. Meade, *Judah P. Benjamin: Confederate Statesman* (New York: Oxford University Press, 1943), pp. 107–23; Dan A. Oren, *Joining the Club: A History of Jews and Yale* (New Haven: Yale University Press, 1985), p. 10.

23. Morais, *Jews of Philadelphia*, pp. 33, 41, 272, 286-89, 298, 417; *Jewish Life in Philadelphia*, ed. Friedman, p. 5; Ezekiel and Lichtenstein, *Jews of Richmond*, pp. 35–36, 39–40, 62; Berman, *Richmond's Jewry*, pp. 18, 84, 128; Leopold Mayer, "Reminiscences of Early Chicago," in *Memoirs of American Jews, 1775–1865*, ed. Jacob Rader Marcus (Philadelphia: Jewish Publication Society of America, 1955), vol. 3, pp. 281–86; Morris A. Gutstein, *A Priceless Heritage: The Epic Growth of Nineteenth-Century Chicago Jewry* (New York: Bloch, 1953), pp. 51–64, 276–77, 312; Elzas, *Jews of South Carolina*, p. 243; Reznikoff, *Jews of Charleston*, pp. 94–97; Korn, *Jews of New Orleans*, pp. 96, 115–16, 125, 225–28; Louis Swichkow and Lloyd P. Gartner, *The History of the Jews of Milwaukee* (Philadelphia: Jewish Publication Society of America, 1963), pp. 55, 58–60; W. Gunther Plaut, *The Jews in Minnesota: The First Seventy-Five Years* (New York: American Jewish Historical Society, 1959), pp. 23–24; Harris Newmark, *Sixty Years in Southern California: 1852–1913* (New York: Knickerbocker Press, 1916), pp. 203, 283; Steven Hertzberg, *Strangers Within the Gate City: The Jews of Atlanta, 1845–1915* (Philadelphia: Jewish Publication Society of America, 1978), pp. 20, 68–69; Katz, *August Belmont*, pp. 1–2, 8–9; Toby Lelyveld, *Shylock on the Stage* (London: Routledge & Kegan Paul, 1961), pp. 63–65; Thomas R. Gould, *The Tragedian: An Essay on the Historical Genius of Junius Brutus Booth* (New York: Hurd and Houghton, 1868), pp. 73–81; Lisbeth Jane Roman, "The Acting Style and Career of Junius Brutus Booth" (PhD diss., University of Illinois, 1968), pp. 138–42. Further favorable regard for Jews in literature and the theater may be found in: Louis Harap, *The Image of the Jew in American Literature from Early Republic to Mass Migration* (Philadelphia: Jewish Publication Society of America, 1974), pp. 216–18; Augustin Daly, *Leah the Forsaken* (New York and London: S. French, n.d.); "Leah," *Harper's Weekly*, 7 (March 7, 1863): 146; Lafcadio Hearn, *Occidental Gleanings* (New York: Dodd, Mead 1925), vol. 2, pp. 179–89; *The Prose Writings of William Cullen Bryant*, ed. Parke Godwin (New York: D Appleton, 1901), vol. 2, p. 358; *Margaret Fuller, American Romantic: A Selection from Her Writings and Correspondence*, ed. Perry Miller (Ithaca: Cornell University Press, 1963), p. 202.

24. Jaher, *Scapegoat*; Leonard Dinnerstein, *Antisemitism in America* (New York: Oxford University Press, 1994), pp. 3–34.

25. Jaher, *Scapegoat*, pp, 170–250; and idem., *Jews and the Nation*, pp. 224–33; Dinnerstein, *Antisemitism in America*, pp. 35–149, 175–227.

26. Jaher, *Jews and the Nation*, pp. 220, 233–37; Dinnerstein, *Antisemitism in America*, pp. 150–74, 228–44.

27. Jaher, *Jews and the Nation*, pp. 220, 235; Dinnerstein, *Antisemitism in*

America, p.170; Anti-Defamation League, Anti-Semitism in America 2002, www.adl.org, p. 8.

28. CRIF (Conseil Représentatif des institutions juives de France), Dossiers (January 12, 2003), www.crif.org/index. pp. 2–3.

13

"America Is Different!"
Myths and Realities in the Study of Antisemitism in the United States

Jerome A. Chanes

*With regard to antisemitism, I don't really want to search for explana-
tions; I feel a strong inclination to surrender to my affects in this matter
and find myself confirmed in my wholly nonscientific belief that mankind on the average and taken by and large are a wretched lot.*

Are these the observations of a misanthrope? The rantings of a
malcontent? Nay, it is none other than Sigmund Freud, reflecting—
as have many—on the unpredictability, the utter irrationality, of
antisemitism. How is this phenomenon of Jew-hatred to be explained?
Is antisemitism just another form of group-prejudice, and therefore
explicable by the protocols of social science? Or is it *sui generis* an
eternal part of the *Jewish* experience, almost normative in nature: the
traditional Jewish rabbinic formulation: *"Halacha hi b'vadai: Eisav Sonei
es Ya'akov."*[1] "An established principle: Esau hates Jacob" is the classic
representation of antisemitism: Babylonia, Rome, Christendom as
"Edom"—the antisemitic descendants of Esau: antisemitism incarnate,
antisemitism universal, antisemitism unending, antisemitism eternal,
antisemitism immutable. Explorations into contemporary antisemitism
clearly implicate the questions of definition.

And perhaps this is a good place to begin, once again, after all of
many discussions of antisemitism. I have always liked David Berger's
workmanlike definition of antisemitism: "Antisemitism means either of
the following: (1) hostility toward Jews as a group that results from no
legitimate cause or greatly exceeds any reasonable, ethical response to
genuine provocation; or (2) a pejorative perception of Jewish physical

or moral traits that is either utterly groundless or a result of irrational generalization and exaggeration."[2] However one defines antisemitism, one point must be kept in mind: Antisemitism presupposes that the Jews are radically "other." This simple central point is a universal, timeless characteristic of antisemitism.

"America Is Different!"

America is different in two ways: First, the American condition—pluralism—is unique in history both in the contexts of time and place, and it is pluralism that informs and protects the security of any group and individual in American society; and second, different is the nature of antisemitism in the United States today, and the relationship of antisemitism to the security of Jews in America.

We begin with a seemingly counterintuitive assertion: The Jewish condition in 2004 is one of *security*. This assertion is made in full awareness—probably a greater awareness than most—of outbreaks of antisemitism in Europe in 2002 and earlier this year, of jihadist Jew-hating maniacs, of the current atmosphere in many corners of the academy, especially in Europe, in which anti-Zionism is quite the vogue. This assertion derives from a basic analysis of the verities of post–war Jewish history.

Let me take a step back. Historian Victor Tcherikover used to observe that very few phenomena in human history have a history of two thousand years. Antisemitism is one of them. And indeed, as analyst Leon Wieseltier has noted, in our own day the taxonomy of antisemitism yet includes religious and secular varieties, political and cultural varieties, theological and ideological. The antisemitism of the right still blames the Jews for modernity—I take this as a compliment!—the antisemitism of the left, seeking shelter, most recently, in antiglobalization, yet trots out old New Left dogmas of capitalism.

And anti-Zionism—not to be confused with criticism of Israel—the most dangerous, since it denies the legitimacy of a normal life for Jews.

My assertion of the fundamental security of Jews today is based on Wieseltier's important observation: The conclusion of the Second World War marked also the conclusion of the "European age" of Jewish history. The destiny of the Jewish people has at last left Europe, and the two-millennium European melodrama about "rights," which could be given, and therefore be taken away. The fate of the Jews is and will be determined elsewhere, in Israel and in the United States. There is a friendly competition between the Israeli reality, in which Jews enjoy the protections and privileges of *sovereignty*; and the American reality, in which Jews enjoy the protections and privileges of a *pluralist democracy*. Both of these realities regard the old European system of "rights" as inadequate, and obsolete. In Israel and America—very different from one another—the common characteristic is that rights are axiomatic.

American Jewish circumstances do not fit neatly into the classic Zionist construct, that of Jews running to a haven in order to escape from antisemitism. While Jews did emigrate to the United States for this reason, to limit our analysis of American Jewish life to this dynamic tells us nothing about the nature of Jewish security in America. America is not just another address for Jews on the run, another safe haven. America is in its philosophical foundations and political practices structurally hospitable to Jews.

There are four structural differences between the USA and Europe, which collectively account for American exceptionalism and uniqueness.

1. The separation of church and state tautologically meant that Jews were not living in a "Christian" society—or in any kind of religious society. It was church-state separation that lifted pluralism from being a conceptual or philosophical ideal and made it a *legal* obligation. In the United States, from the very beginning of the American polity, the public sphere was viewed, by legal fiat, as being a neutral place. Church-state separation therefore asserted that Jews (and other minorities and individuals) would not be merely tolerated but *accepted*. Maintaining a firm line of separation between church and state, therefore, is central to religious voluntarism and to religious freedom; by extension, it fosters the distinctive survival and creativity of religious groups, including Jews.

2. American society was a postemancipation society from its very beginnings. This reality was, in my view, most crucial in ensuring that political antisemitism of the kind that arose in nineteenth-century Europe did not come to be in the United States. Before the late eighteenth century, Jews everywhere in Europe were legally defined as outsiders in society, and therefore alien to the polity. The opening for Jews to become citizens came as a result of the Enlightenment—with the French Revolution acting as the engine for Enlightenment ideas—with

the result that Jews began entering the mainstream of European societies.

America did not carry the European pre-Enlightenment baggage—the bulk of American Jewish history begins after the Declaration of Independence and the Constitution were drafted—with the result that Jews no less than any others were entitled to equal status in the body politic.

3. The United States was a new nation—a frontier society—made up people of diverse backgrounds without "insiders" and "outsiders." In contrast, in Europe, Jews had to cope with the fact that the nation states in which they were citizens as a result of the emancipation had historical memories, deriving from a Christian context, going back centuries, and that they, the Jews, were not part of these memories except as aliens and enemies.

4. The United States, as a nation of immigrants, was inherently pluralist. Indeed, even when the ideology of choice was the "melting pot," the reality was always cultural and democratic pluralism, and pluralism became a uniquely American way of positioning oneself as a member of American society, even as that person (or group) retained religious and ethnic identity. An important by-product of a pluralist society was that it removed the onus under which Jews had been compelled to live in many other societies.

The sum result of these four dynamics is that antisemitism did not invade the formal institutions of power, as it did in Europe.

So how are we to understand the current state of antisemitism in America?

As we are well into the new millennium, antisemitism continues to confound and puzzle American Jews. There is a profound paradox—"the riddle of the defensive Jew"—that plays itself out within the American Jewish community when it comes to the question of antisemitism. On the one hand, Jews, when questioned in surveys, consistently aver that they feel "comfortable" in America. Yet some eight out of ten American Jews believe that antisemitism is a "serious" problem in the United States. In 1985, in the San Francisco Bay area, more than one-third of those questioned[3] said that Jewish candidates could not be elected to Congress from San Francisco, citing anti-Jewish bias or prejudice. Yet three out of the four congressional representatives from that area—as well as the two state senators and the mayor of San Francisco—were, in fact, well-identified Jews *at the time the poll was conducted.* (The population of San Francisco was approximately 97 percent non-Jewish, mirroring the national average.)

Antisemitism in the United States in 2006 is one of those areas that generate a high "head-scratching quotient," amongst social scientists and plain folks alike.

Conventional wisdom amongst most American Jews has it that the antisemites are at the gates; the next pogrom is about to begin. But we need to look at hard data and the rigorous interpretation of those data. Interpretation of data is often a Rashomon-like exercise. Here I do invoke Machiavelli: "Others will tell you how things should be; let me tell you how they *really* are."

A number of questions will guide our discussion:

First, what do we know? What are the current available data on the nature and extent of antisemitism in the United States? What is happening out there, and—just as important—what is *not* happening?

Second, and indeed salient, is how do we explain perceptions within the American Jewish community of a antisemitism ascendant, even as data along a broad range of evaluative criteria tell us that antisemitism in America has declined and continues in its decline? How can nine out of ten Jewish Americans in the 2000s say they "feel home in America"—as they in fact do—in a country they believe is rife with antisemitism?[4]

Jewish Perceptions of Antisemitism?

In 1983, in a survey conducted among American Jews by the American Jewish Committee, approximately one-half of the respondents disagreed with the statement "Antisemitism is currently not a serious problem for American Jews." By 1988, the proportion had risen to 76 percent. And National Jewish Population Surveys of 1990 and 2002 show 83-to-90 percent of American Jews either are "strongly" or "somewhat" agreeing that antisemitism is a serious problem in the USA. How can nine out of ten Jewish Americans say they "feel at home in America," in a country they think is rife with antisemitism?

What accounts for the perception among most Jewish people that antisemitism is a serious problem in America, and that the status and security of Jews is at risk? To paraphrase the political analyst Ben Watenberg, if things are so good out there, why do so many American Jews think that things are so bad?

Third, and related: When Jews say that antisemitism is a serious problem, what do they mean? What are they talking about? What do the attitudinal surveys show? How ought socialscientists be looking at the polls?

Fourth, what are the new realities of antisemitism? What more can we say about the "new antisemitism" other than "the Muslims hate us"?

Finally, what areas of study and research are indicated in those areas of antisemitism about which we know very little.

First, on the question of the nature and extent of antisemitism in the United States, there are some fairly concrete data. The good news is that the bad news isn't all bad.

There are two kinds of antisemitism—two kinds of anything, when it comes down to it, following the "Merton model"—behavioral and attitudinal. There is a crucial relationship between what people *think* and what people *do*, between *attitudinal* and *behavioral* antisemitism. Antisemitism of both kinds is assessed along a broad range of evaluative criteria.[5] The data on antisemitism, along these criteria, indicate that both behavioral and attitudinal antisemitism have declined in the United States over the past forty years, even as we must watch and concern ourselves with recurring danger signals. This finding, of course, is no great revelation, and is amply confirmed by evidence both anecdotal and research-generated, and fully explored by a number of essayists in this volume. Nonetheless, the finding calls for some analysis in terms of both behavioral and attitudinal manifestations.

Behavioral antisemitism is manifest, of course, in different ways, from swastika daubings to "JAP" jokes to political rhetoric. The reality is that behavioral antisemitism "where it counts" is simply no longer a factor in American life. Such behavioral antisemitism includes large-scale discrimination against Jews; the cynical use of antisemitism in political rhetoric in order to achieve political gains, arguably the most virulent form of antisemitism; and most important, the inability or reluctance of the Jewish community to express itself on issues of concern because of anti-Jewish animus. This kind of antisemitism— the kind that makes a difference in terms of the security and status of American Jews—has declined steadily and dramatically over the past four decades and more.[6]

A proposition, therefore: The issue for us is not antisemitism; it is *Jewish security*. In any analysis of antisemitism in the United States, a crucial distinction must be made. We need to distinguish between *antisemitism*, which does exist and must be monitored, repudiated, and counteracted; and *Jewish security*, which is strong. Jewish security—the ability of Jews, individually and collectively, to participate in the society without fear of antisemitic animus—is strong largely because of a history and tradition of constitutional protections and institutions that inform democratic pluralism, as noted above. While antisemitism and Jewish security are concentric circles and therefore obviously related, the distinction between them is important when discussing the issue in the context of contemporary America. This is the first time in history that the discussion of antisemitism is not the same as the discussion of Jewish security. The legitimacy of antisemitism has been all but repudiated. It is not Jews, but bigotry against Jews, that is the anomaly in the United States.

What about attitudinal antisemitism? Here is where the issue of data interpretation is best addressed, and some exploration is called for.[7]

It comes as a surprise to many that attitudinal antisemitism in the United States has been a relatively little-studied phenomenon over the past three decades. In an age when social scrutiny seems to extend into the most obscure corners of our experience, we learn that antisemitism—an enduring social phenomenon and one of special significance in our own time—has received scant attention from America's social scientists until recently. Most comprehensive, indeed landmark, studies were conducted during the 1960s. Notable among these were the Anti-Defamation League's "Patterns of American Prejudice" (the "Berkeley Studies"), which developed a scale of antisemitic beliefs of non-Jews and articulated the now-classic reverse correlation that the higher the education level, the less likely are non-Jews to hold antisemitic beliefs.[8]

The question is: What do Americans think about Jews? On this fairly narrow question there are fairly conclusive findings. The cumulative data of attitudinal surveys conducted by a range of researchers over the years have consistently substantiated the view that the level of conventional antisemitic beliefs has continued in its forty-year decline. Simply put, there are fewer Americans who profess unfavorable images of Jews.

The usual explanation for this transformation is generational. As analyst Earl Raab and others have put it, it is not that the antisemites are being converted, but that each succeeding age-group tends to display fewer antisemitic attitudes than the preceding generation of that age group. Committed antisemites are swayed to virtue neither by events nor by prejudice-reduction programs. Earl Raab says it best: antisemites do not fade away; they simply die. Research findings clearly, strongly, and consistently suggest that a younger, better educated, more affluent population is less antisemitic. This pattern, a negative correlation of education level and antisemitism, obtains across the board, including among blacks.[9]

While attitudinal surveys are always suspect (sometimes even for the right reasons!) the lack of a truly comprehensive study since the American Jewish Committee's 1981 Yankelovich poll has greatly hindered the examination of present-day antisemitism in America.

There have been five sets of studies in recent years: the University of Chicago's National Opinion Research Center (NORC) 1990 General Social Survey, a comprehensive survey of 58 ethnic groups commissioned by the American Jewish Committee and conducted by NORC's Tom W. Smith;[10] a 1992, 1998, and 2002 survey of American attitudes toward Jews conducted for the Anti-Defamation League by Marttila and Kiley and the Marttila Communications Group;[11] a 1992 intergroup relations study of New York City, done by the Roper Organization for the American Jewish Committee;[12] a 1993 ADL/Marttila and Kiley survey on racial attitudes in America;[13] and, most recently, a 1994 comprehensive study (commissioned by the American Jewish Committee) by NORC's Tom W. Smith confirming and synthesizing the findings of previous studies.[14]

It is instructive to analyze and compare the AJC/NORC and ADL/Marttila studies. (The American Jewish Committee Intergroup Relations Survey of New York, while containing valuable data, is a local study; and the Marttila racial-attitudes survey addresses the question of prejudice in America generally, and calls for its own discrete treatment.) The AJC studies have been broad surveys of ethnic attitudes; the ADL/Marttila studies have specifically assessed attitudes toward Jews.

The National Opinion Research Center 1990 General Social Survey provided data on 58 ethnic groups—including one fictitious group, the "Wissians"; NORC found that significant numbers of Americans hold negative attitudes toward the "Wissians"—were "massaged" by NORC's General Social Survey director Tom W. Smith for the American Jewish Committee in order to elicit specific information about anti-Jewish attitudes.

NORC analyzed data related to six areas.[15] Some of AJC/NORC's general findings: first, and most generally, antisemitism and negative attitudes are at a low point. Specifically, only few members of certain minority groups harbor some negative attitudes toward Jews, and that conflict between Jews and non-Jews is less serious than are clashes between many other ethnic groups. NORC tells us also that latent sources of antisemitism are not closely connected, and therefore are not likely to sustain one another. And the behavioral antisemitism that does exist in one area is almost always unconnected to that in another area. These are important findings. They suggest a pattern different from that which existed in America fifty years ago.

Particularly intriguing were AJC/NORC's findings on Israel and antisemitism. It has long been known that anti-Israel and antisemitic attitudes are linked, that antisemitic attitudes are more common among those with negative attitudes toward Israel, and that anti-Israel attitudes are stronger among those with antisemitic beliefs. According to NORC this linkage is not especially strong. Attitudes toward Israel may be related to causes other than antisemitic attitudes—oil, Arabs, a particular worldview, and so on.

Also instructive is the question of how Jews were perceived, in terms of social standing, relative to other groups. Among religions, Jews come in tenth of twenty religious groups, below "Protestants" and Catholics, but above Mormons, Greek Orthodox, Christian Scientists, Unitarians (!), Spiritualists, and Jehovah's Witnesses.

A most significant area of the AJC/NORC study—as in any poll of attitudes toward Jews—is that of perceived power and influence. The "Jewish-power" question is one to which significant import is given; it therefore merits some analysis. The way in which the question is asked makes a difference. If the question is open-ended—as in "Which groups have too much power?"—Jews will consistently come out low. If the question is closed-ended and contextual—"Which groups from the following list have too much power?"—Jews still come out relatively low. If the question is completely closed-ended—"Do Jews have too much power in the United States?"—the numbers are still higher.

The "Jewish-power" question was asked by NORC not as "Do Jews have too much power in the United States?"—it should never be asked like this, because the data do not tell us much. It was asked, however—as it should be asked—as a contextual question: "Which of the following groups (twenty-three were listed: Arab oil nations, the media, labor unions, Orientals, blacks, the Catholic Church, the banks) have too much influence and power?" The Jews come out way down; about the only ones lower than the Jews were the Hispanics.

Political scientist Seymour Martin Lipset suggests that with regard to this issue, people are not antisemitic, they are antipower.[16] That is, the issue is power, not Jews. People think that many groups have too much power in this society. But even this requires further nuance, which is illumined in the Marttila poll, discussed below.

Antisemitism in America is neither virulent nor growing, concluded the American Jewish Committee/NORC study, consistent with the data from earlier polls. But NORC cautioned that antisemitism in America is not a spent force, that Jews are yet recognized as an ethnic or religious out-group and are often accordingly judged and treated in a distinctive manner. Antisemitism has not disappeared; it has become dormant, and latent antisemitism does have the potential to become actualized. And antisemitic incidents do occur. Furthermore, antisemitic political groups may exist as isolated entities in the lunatic fringe. "Fringe" elements are tautologically "fringe," and rarely enter the mainstream. But lunatics can be dangerous.

While the American Jewish Committee/National Opinion Research Center study is more than a decade and a half old, it is hardly stale. The data are yet relevant and highly instructive.

Surveys conducted by the polling firm Marttila and Kiley for the Anti-Defamation League in 1992, 1998, and 2002 prove significant as well, but in a different way than the AJC/NORC study was. For NORC, Tom Smith massaged general data in order to generate information about attitudes toward Jews. The ADL/Marttila studies is the first comprehensive study, *specifically* of attitudes toward Jews, since the Yankelovich poll of 1981, and used once again as the criteria for antisemitism (the "index") first developed by the Berkeley Studies and used by Yankelovich, and the criteria are a problem. Moreover, Marttila's methodology suggests a number of significant questions about attitudinal surveys in general that are of import to social scientists.

ADL/Marttila's findings: 17 percent of Americans are "Most" or "Unquestionable Antisemitic." This number compares with 20 percent in 1998 and 12 percent in 1992.

ADL/Marttila generally corroborated everything that we have known for many years, and most things that we have suspected, about attitudinal antisemitism. Marttila's central investigative device consists of an eleven-item scale—the "Index of Antisemitic Beliefs"—made up of questions designed to detect antisemitism.[17] Six or more "Yes" answers make a person "most antisemitic"; two to five "Yes" answers result in a rating of "middle"; one or two "Yes" answers: "not antisemitic."

The survey results show a continuing pattern of decline—albeit a slow one—along a range of antisemitic beliefs. The negative correlation of "education and other social/economic indicators up, antisemitism down" holds for all groups in the society, including blacks. Age is a factor: Americans over 65 are twice as likely as those under 65 to fall into the "most antisemitic" category. Important data in ADL/Marttila were those linking antisemitism and racism. Individuals who are "most racist" are likely to be "most antisemitic," and vice versa.

Perhaps the most surprising finding in the ADL/Marttila survey was the refutation of conventional wisdom that the more contact a person has with Jews, the less antisemitic that person will be. It ain't so, says Marttila. This finding requires further study.

One other fascinating finding of the Marttila polls is that criticism of Israel is *no predictor* for antisemitic attitudes. Indeed, many critics of Israel are well educated and embrace tolerant, pluralistic attitudes.

The ADL/Marttila poll is valuable, even though it did not tell us that much that was new. (Indeed, arguably social scientist and Jewish "defense" agencies may wish to think about getting off the antisemitism-polling fix and explore other areas. Political scientist Seymour Martin Lipset, to cite one example, would prefer that social scientists study philosemitism; why do some people have an unusual affinity for—*like* or *love*—Jews?)[18] But with respect to data analysis and interpretation ADL/Marttila serves us well as a case study for data analysis. It is in this respect that I would suggest four questions about the ADL/Marttila poll, questions that illumine issues about the study of antisemitism in general:

The first question has less to do with the study and everything to do with the way in which data on antisemitism are presented and interpreted. "Twenty percent of Americans are strongly antisemitic," asserted an Anti-Defamation League press release when it released the Marttila findings in 1992. Was this bad news or good news? Although 20 percent is hardly a trivial number—30 million antisemites out there is nothing to be laughed at—it seems to me that the news was not all that bad. The first questions any social scientist asks about any such assertion is: "Compared to *when*, and compared to *what*?" The 20 percent reported was down from the 29 percent of the 1964 ADL/Berkeley Studies. Further, with respect to the "compared to what?" question, ample data exist from any number of sources that indicate that twenty percent—or more—of any group hates any other group. So: good news or bad?

Second, some of the questions in the index may not have been perceived by respondents as reflecting negatively on Jews; they indeed may not measure antisemitism. A classic example of this type of flaw in questioning is illustrated in the 1986 poll of evangelical Christians in America conducted by the Anti-Defamation League. At the height of what was known as the "Christianization of America," the ADL asked the question: Are fundamentalists more antisemitic than the general population? Is it antisemitism that informs their agenda? And—no great surprise—the ADL found that fundamentalists factor out in levels of antisemitism about the same as everyone else, approximately 20 percent.

In the course of the survey, the ADL in effect asked the following question: "Are Jews tight with their money?" A significant percentage of the respondents answered, "Yes, Jews are tight with their money." Antisemitism! But then, in a question that was brilliant in a post facto way, the follow-up question was asked: "Is this good?" Answer: "Yes, this is a good trait; Jews are thrifty, etc." Antisemitism? The lesson: A number of questions in the "Index of Antisemitic Beliefs" may not be measuring antisemitism, but some other beliefs or feelings that may indeed represent some anti-Jewish animus, or may in fact be reflective of positive attitudes toward Jews.

The problem is that the "Index of Antisemitic Beliefs," created in 1964 by the landmark "Berkeley Studies" commissioned by the ADL, may reflect the societal realities of that era, but surely does not reflect the realities of today. Some of the questions in the ADL/Marttila poll indeed do target antisemitic attitudes. But consider the following questions: "Jews stick together more than other Americans"; "Jews have too much power in the U.S. today"; "Jews have a lot of irritating faults"; "Jews don't care what happens to anyone but their own kind." Some of these questions are probably not perceived by respondents as reflecting negatively on Jews; they in fact may not measure antisemitism. Jews stick together? Jews care about "their own kind"? This is antisemitism?

Third: attitudes are much more nuanced than the three groupings "most antisemitic," "middle," "not antisemitic."[19] There is a basic ambiguity in most responses that needs to be noted. A respondent who answered "yes" to six or seven (some of which questions may in fact *not* measure antisemitism, as we just noted) has been just fine on four or five. (And even some of these questions may *not* measure antisemitism, as we have noted.) Even among the "Most antisemitic," therefore, there exist identifiable pro-Jewish attitudes. (Among the "Not antisemitic," the reverse is true: they may very well hold anti-Jewish attitudes.) A more sophisticated conceptual scheme is clearly needed, one that takes into account these ambiguities.

Fourth, and most troubling: ADL/Marttila—indeed, attitudinal surveys in general—are leading Jews toward a new definition of antisemitism: attitudes toward Jews that *Jews* find distasteful; attitudes that Jews wish "they," namely non-Jews, would not have; rather than the classic definition of antisemitism as expressed hostility toward Jews.

For example, the increase in numbers on the "Jewish-power" question is indeed troubling. But consider: Jews in America *are* a power group; is it unreasonable for some people to ask whether Jews have too much power? The question is: How do individuals who hold such views *act* on those views? The fundamental question in antisemitism anywhere, at any time: What is the relationship between *attitude* and *behavior*?

Mention ought be made of a two other studies. One, conducted by Louis Harris for the National Conference for Community and Justice (formerly the National Conference of Christians and Jews), released in 1994, evaluated the state of intergroup relations in the United States and provided a further context for the study of antisemitism.[20] With respect to prejudicial attitudes in general, the study found that members of minority groups are more likely than are whites to agree to negative stereotypes about other minority groups. In terms of antisemitism, the National Conference/Harris survey data revealed disturbingly high numbers in the responses to the "Jewish-power" and "dual-loyalty" questions, among both whites and minority-group members. Forty-three percent of blacks and 22 percent of whites said that Jews "have too much control over business and the media." Forty-seven percent of blacks and 24 percent of whites responded that Jews "are more loyal to Israel than to America."

Finally, *A Survey of the Religious Right: Views on Politics, Society, Jews and Other Minorities* was conducted by the Gallup International Institute and analyzed by Tom W. Smith of NORC for the American Jewish Committee, and was released in 1996 by AJC. Again, no surprises with respect to attitudes toward Jews: On the positive side, those aligned with the "religious right" are more supportive of Israel and the special biblical status of Jews than are other Americans; on the negative side, "religious-right" adherents are more likely to raise objections to Jews "on religious grounds." For example, 22 percent (as compared with 8 percent of other Americans) think that Jews must still answer for killing Christ. The interesting news from the AJC poll is that in terms of social and political acceptance, "religious-right" folks differ little from most Americans. Seventy-nine percent would vote for a Jew as president, and 88 percent do not believe that Jews have too much influence in American society.

There are, of course, inherent problems with any survey data. Respondents may be disingenuous: "I may *think* it; I can't *say* it." Or questions may be flawed, or not sufficiently probing, or without good follow-up. Recall if you will the ADL questions of the fundamentalists.

In sum: Notwithstanding the problems with comparing the two large surveys owing to the many differences between them, some conclusions with respect to broad trends are called for. There is a steady, albeit slow, lessening of expressed negativity toward Jews, with a possible exception of the stereotypes of Jewish power; a smaller percentage of the population scores as antisemitic; there is a more widespread acceptance of positive statements about Jews. The dual-loyalty numbers may have remained more or less constant over the years, but other statistics, exhibiting positive attitudes, have evidenced dramatic change: In 1958, 61 percent of Americans said they would vote for a Jew for president; in 1987, 89 percent of Americans said they would so vote. The number today is in the 90s.[21]

The "New Antisemitism"

There has been much discussion since 1992 about "The New Antisemitism," with a number of books having been authored. What, indeed, is "new" about the New Antisemitism? It is useful to set a historical context for this question. In order to be a "new" of anything, there has to be an "old." We can easily classify antisemitism historically as pointing to a half a dozen varieties. There was the pre-Christian antisemitism of the ancient world Greco-Roman world, most of which was not what we would call "antisemitism," but were part and parcel of the geopolitical conflicts attendant to the workings of monarchies and commonwealths.

There is the classic Christian antisemitism of antiquity and the Middle Ages—antisemitism that was in fact crucial to the shaping of a developing Christian theology in the early centuries of Christianity—extending into modern times. There is traditional Muslim antisemitism, which—at least in its classical form—is highly nuanced. There is the political, social, and economic antisemitism of Enlightenment and post-Enlightenment Europe. There is the racial antisemitism that arose in the nineteenth century out of Enlightenment thinking, and that culminated in Nazism and ultimately in the destruction of European Jewry.

Finally, there is the contemporary phenomenon of Israelophobia and "Zionism Equals Racism."

This catalog is cumbersome. I prefer to telescope these categories to three, and to say that if there is indeed any such thing as a "new antisemitism," it is "new" in the sense that it does not fit the pattern of ancient antisemitism, which was primarily *ethnic* or *cultural* in nature; Christian antisemitism, which was *religious*; or the *racial* antisemitism of the nineteenth and twentieth centuries.

So where does anti-Zionism and Israelophobia fit—if it does at all? And how do these fit into our definitional formulation?

The question, of course, goes to the nature of anti-Israel rhetoric and other expressions. Is this antisemitism? To refine the question: At what point does this activity become antisemitism? Indeed, there is a vigorous debate that is developing around this question.

Finally, how does all of this play out in America? Which "package" of criteria ought we be using in determining whether a particular expression is antisemitism in 2006?

First, there is the question that goes to the core of our definitional dilemma: At what point does anti-Israel rhetoric become antisemitism—if ever? How does our definition work with anti-Zionism? This is clearly a "threshold" question, and is therefore subjective. A reasonable threshold is as follows: Criticism of the policies of the government of the state of Israel—indeed harsh criticism—is entirely legitimate. The Israeli polity is itself deeply divided over the peace process; and beyond this, over its relations today and tomorrow with the Palestinians. The point at which such attacks become antisemitism is the point at which the *legitimacy* of the Zionist enterprise or the state of Israel is questioned, because it is at that point that the legitimacy of Jewish *peoplehood* is questioned. This, tautologically, is antisemitism.

What about that crucial clause in our definition of antisemitism, namely " …that results from no *legitimate cause*" (emphasis added)? Public affairs analyst Earl Raab—one of my mentors, and a person who taught many Jewish pros and academics how to articulate the vocabulary of analysis of antisemitism—indeed argues for the necessity of distinguishing Israelophobia (he calls it "anti-Israelism") and antisemitism. Let's not confuse these, argues Raab. Anti-Israelism is a concerted prejudice against Israel, birthed in large measure by leftist antiglobalist politics, but without a discernible hatred of Jews. Oppression and liberation, oppressors and oppressed—it's another riff on the political rivalries that characterized much of ancient anti-Judaism. Is there a specifically anti-Jewish bias here? Perhaps what motivates the Israelophobes *is* antisemitism. Perhaps it is not. But to unfairly tar all critics of Israel with the brush of antisemitism is unfair, so the argument goes, and may be counterproductive, in that it is the first principle of community relations that counteraction of an activity should be premised on what is the motivating factor of that activity.

(Parenthetically, I would note that one of the more important observations to be made about the recent flap over Tony Judt's *New York Review* screed, in which Judt called for a binational state—effectively for Israel's destruction—and the response to Judt in the pages of the *New Republic* and elsewhere, is that Judt does *not* come out of the academic "left," whence we expect his kind of analysis and rhetoric. Rather—as is clear from Judt's many writings on and about Europe—he is a centrist historian. This is once again the danger: the "mainstreaming" of anti-Zionism and Israelophobia: moving from its home in the left to perches elsewhere.)

Raab's view, by the way, is bolstered by the numbers: ADL's polls in Europe show a sharp fault line between attitudinal antisemitism—the numbers are way down—and anti-Zionism, which are up. To simplify: The ADL analysts say that these data tell us that Europeans are basically antisemitic; Raab and others suggest that it's more nuanced. These data call for further exploration.

The view that anti-Israelism needs to be distinguished from antisemitism, whatever the antisemitic motivation of some Israelophobes might be, may be consistent with, or may be *countered* by, a geopolitical analysis of the contemporary phenomenon.

A useful construct is one borrowed from the world of political science, and developed fully by Mark Lilla of the University of Chicago.

Using France as paradigmatic of Europe, Lilla in effect asks (and answers), "Why do the French hate us?" Antisemitism is historically linked to the political contours of each era, and of each country during a given era. The physiognomy of European antisemitism in any given era is a function of the primary political challenge facing Europeans in that time and place. (This, by-the-bye, is Hannah Arendt's unique insight in Volume I of *The Origins of Totalitarianism.*) Nationalism in the nineteenth century; racialist antisemitism. Augustine's anti-Aristotelian Christianity; religious antisemitism. And so on . . .

As the primary political challenge for Europe today is that of moving beyond the nation-state—that is, the problem of European integration— a problem that is framed in the clash between nationalism and postnationalism (with progressive or "good" opinion very much on the side of the latter)—it comes as no surprise that Israel (and America) are reviled for acting like the nation-states they are. Israel, as the product of nineteenth-century European nationalism, acts as the ideology of nationalism suggests sovereign states do and should act: It is ready to employ the force of arms to defend the nation's interest. This behavior is what drives the Europeans crazy. It strikes their postnationalist sensibilities (and it is important to note that the word "post" in its political and historical usage always means "contra") as retrograde and racist. Israel squares off against the Arabs in the same benighted manner as the French used to against the Germans, and so on. Hence, European antisemitism, and— *kal v'homer* [all the more so]—anti-Americanism as well.

I should add that Zionism, the darling of the left seventy years ago, became successful—created a nation-state—precisely at a time when the nation-state fell out of fashion.

What follows is what is maintained as being the "new" international/political antisemitism. "What's new" are three things: First, the collective expression of antisemitism, with Israel as a focal point, rather than the individual animus of the past. This leads, of course, to the claim of distinguishing between anti-Israelism and antisemitism; second: the center of gravity of antisemitism is now in the Islamic world. Finally, what's new is also very old: the "double-standard": the assertion that Jews may not defend themselves as may any other people or person. If this is the case, then—by extension—the legitimacy of a Jewish historical particularism is challenged. Deriving from this, of course, is the isolation of the state of Israel and the relegation of Israel to the status of "pariah state."

(I will parenthetically note that this view, historiographically, hearkens back to a forgotten reading of history, that of the Progressive historians, which emphasized class conflict, and which was itself replaced by the historiography of the 1950s and 1960s, "Consensus" historians—Richard Hofstadter, Arthur M. Schlesinger Jr., and David Potter—also a bit strange to the eyes and ears of scholars in recent decades, a historiography that stressed consensus over conflict, patterns of agreement and harmony over class struggle, and which was all the rage among liberals during the Cold War decades. The leitmotif of class struggle is clear in the "post-nation-state" analysis.)

So what's "new"? Nothing, really. The standard evaluative criteria for determining what is antisemitism and what isn't are not yet operative. The important new caution is for analysts to think about the "no legitimate cause" provision. Any geopolitical analysis leads us to either (1) the same old hatreds; or (2) a set of political animosities expressed by the leftist intelligentsia in Europe that may not be antisemitism.

Who Are the Antisemites?
Questions for Study and Research

All of the above suggests the question, not of "Who are the antisemites?"—who cares, really—but who are those who are *not* antisemites? There are three types of people: philosemites, non-antisemites, and anti-antisemites.[22] The security of Jews does not depend on people being non-antisemites; for most people in the United States, Jews are simply not an issue.

And indeed, in the 1991 gubernatorial campaign in Louisiana, 55 percent of the white vote went to former Klan leader David Duke not *because* of his racial views but *despite* those views; when self-interest is a factor, non-antisemites may ignore the antisemitism or racism of a candidate. According to exit-polling, 27 percent of voters supported Duke because of his views on the state's economy, 39 percent because of government corruption, and only 12 percent because of Duke's views on racial issues.[23] This response to Duke strongly suggests that many in the non-antisemitic group will support an antisemite if some other area of self-interest is invoked. A more recent—and more dramatic— example of this dynamic was the Million Man March convened by the Nation of Islam and its leader Louis Farrakhan on October 15, 1995. Most of the 800,000 or so blacks who gathered in Washington on that day were there not because of Farrakhan's virulent message, but despite that message.

There is a substantial number of people who do not care about the Jews one way or another, but who are unconstrained enough to support an antisemite if such support appears to serve their needs. These are the "non-antisemites." The dynamic at work in non-antisemitism lies at the interface of the social control and trigger mechanisms.

The real security of Jews lies in people being *anti*-antisemites, for whom antisemitism is totally illegitimate and must be repudiated. A relatively small number of people fall in the anti-antisemite category, and not much is known about the taboo that informs anti-antisemitism. It is clearly an area for study.

* * *

Finally, What *don't* we know about antisemitism in America? What ought to be our research agenda?

First: We need to know more about the taboos and controls surrounding expression of antisemitism, that cause non-antisemites to become anti-antisemites. With respect to triggers of antisemitism, it is not enough to mouth the simple formula of "bad times equals increased antisemitism." Bad economic times can be the background; they do not constitute the trigger. What is required is a combination and interaction of *background* and context; antisemitic *attitudes* of the population that are measured; and *trigger*.[24]

Second: There are forms of antisemitism that are difficult to observe and measure, namely hidden and latent antisemitism. Additionally, traditional, cruder forms of antisemitism may not have been eliminated, but may have been revamped and repackaged for a new generation. This "new" antisemitism, articulated in a different, perhaps less blatant manner, more subtle and nuanced, calls for study. The difficulty is that while new forms of antisemitism may be open and observable (as compared with hidden and latent antisemitism), they are often encrypted.[25]

Third: and related: the question of threshold. The different points at which individuals *perceive* antisemitism need to be probed. What yardstick are people using when they measure situations that they themselves perceive or experience as antisemitism? Should survivors of the Holocaust, on the one hand, and college students who never experienced behavioral antisemitism until they reached the campus, on the other, be categorized in the same manner? Both groups, from opposite ends of the spectrum, have very low thresholds for perceiving antisemitism.[26] This is a difficult and sensitive area.

Fourth: a new look at the surveys. The surveys, which may be either antiquated or irrelevant, need to be retooled.

Fifth: A hierarchy of antisemitism needs to be developed. This is extremely important. Not all forms of antisemitism carry equal weight. It is ridiculous to equate political antisemitism—a most virulent form of antisemitism—with an incident of antisemitic vandalism. No one would want to minimize any form of antisemitic expression—any person who is at the receiving end of such expression is an abused person—but until some serious weighting system is developed we will be at the mercy of those who would exploit antisemitism.

Sixth: the relationship of bigotry in general and antisemitism. The ADL/Marttila data are extremely valuable in this regard, and call for follow-up analysis.

Seventh: and most crucial: What is the relationship between attitude and behavior? This question has been around for decades, and has bedeviled the research psychologists as much as the sociologists.

And last: How do we assess, not antisemitism, but Jewish perceptions of antisemitism. My speculations and those of others in this area need more comprehensive analysis. What are the specific factors that influence or inform our perceptions? Why do American Jews respond more to the Jewish telegram than to realities? Why can't Jews take "yes" for an answer?

Until fifty years ago, antisemitism was perfectly normal—indeed normative—in Jewish history.[27] In our own day, however, one might say that Adolf Hitler gave antisemitism a bad name, as did Father Coughlin and Gerald L. K. Smith in the United States. But once again, taboos against expressions of antisemitism—against racism and bigotry in general—appear to be breaking down. Not many years ago, expression of antisemitism was not considered to be legitimate. But as the American Jewish Committee's David Singer has said, "Jesse Jackson was the first to show [in our day] that there is life after antisemitism."

Are there more negative dynamics at work today than there were ten years ago? Yes. Are there clouds in what five or ten years ago was a cloudless sky? Yes. Are they storm clouds? No, because the qualitative difference between a pluralistic America of 2006 and the Europe of 1926 and 1936 remains, and this is a very significant difference.

The Counteraction of Antisemitism

As a general proposition, the conditions for successful counteraction of antisemitism have never been better. The historical context in this regard is crucial: The destiny of the Jews has, after many centuries, left Europe. Throughout the history of Europe, Jews were traditionally at the mercy of "rights" granted by rulers, parliaments, and clerics. Jewish destiny is for the most part now in Israel, where Jews have sovereignty; and in America, where Jews enjoy with others the benefits of a pluralist democracy. The example of the United States, home of the world's largest Jewish community, is instructive. The United States is not just another "address" for Jews on the run from persecution, but is a place that is, because of its pluralist structure, fundamentally hospitable to Jews. It is a principle of pluralism that Jews can comfortably be "a state within a state" without fear of hostility. While antisemitism and other forms of bigotry can and do exist in a pluralist society, the conditions of pluralism are necessary for successful counteraction of antisemitism.

It is useful to place contemporary counteraction of antisemitism in the context of responses to antisemitism in history. There were three historical models of Jewish responses to antisemitism.[28]

First, in the "premodern" period, there was no concept of anti-semitism as humanly fashioned ideology or as political problem; anti-Judaism was a reflection of God's will and of divine "natural law," and it was "natural" that Jews (in the classic rabbinic formulation; see above, under "What Is Antisemitism?") were hated by non-Jews. Not only was there no point in trying to fight antisemitism, argued the rabbinic leadership, but there was something somewhat impious about any such effort. The overwhelming Jewish belief was that inordinate Jewish suf-fering—all of the many calamities of Jewish history going back to the destruction of the Temples and even further back in history, and for-ward: the Crusades, the Inquisition and expulsions, and so on—were the consequence of sinfulness.

This response—and response it was, not to be confused with the "quietism" that was the norm in the modern period—was primarily theological and rooted in orthopraxis: prayer and repentance, and awaiting divine salvation.

Second, during the period of the European Enlightenment, non-Jewish hatred of Jews was identified by Jews as a social and politi-cal problem to be addressed strategically by the Jewish community. Unfortunately, however, even though the diagnosis of the causes and nature of antisemitism was radically different from that of the classical rabbis—divine providence was no longer part of the equation—there was yet the tendency to "blame the victim." Many in the Jewish leadership in Western Europe—particularly those who were influenced by Enlightenment thinking—were convinced that non-Jewish hatred of Jews was the consequence of the behavior, dress, etiquette, and language of Jews. The prevalent view was that once Jews ceased to stand out among non-Jews, the problem of antisemitism would wither and ultimately disappear. This "quietist" approach expressed itself as well as Jewish dependence on "rights" being granted to Jews by sovereigns and parliaments in Europe.

The third historical response to antisemitism, that of the late nineteenth and twentieth centuries, emerged when it became clear that the first two responses were failures. In the late nineteenth century it was evident that neither a purely religious response to antisemitism, nor a quietistic program of Jewish "improvement," would alleviate Jew-hatred. On the contrary, antisemitism in Europe was growing in intensity, with new racialist ideologies and manifestations. A small group of Jewish political visionaries realized that the only solution to the deepening problem of European antisemitism was the removal of Jews from the lands in which antisemitism was rife and the creation of a Jewish state. This approach was proposed indeed by individuals who were mostly the products of an assimilationist approach to the problem. It was clear to these thinkers that antisemitism was an incurable spiritual disease of Europe, and that only the removal of the Jews themselves from the unhealthy and unnatural environment of Europe to their natural homeland could "cure" the hatred of them. The early Zionists were indeed convinced not so much that Israel would serve to protect Jews against the violent designs of their enemies, but that the very existence of a Jewish national homeland would dissolve antisemitism for once and all.

It is worth going into this level of detail on the history of the counteraction of antisemitism, because all contemporary Jewish approaches to counteraction (and for that matter, approaches to the counteraction of any prejudiced or racist activity) are informed by the premise that "blaming the victim" is not a legitimate approach to the problem; and, further, contemporary counteraction is influenced by the Zionist insistence that antisemitism must be dealt with aggressively and decisively, using *political* means. In short in the contemporary era—especially since the Holocaust—there is a consensus amongst Jews that the victims of this most vile and ancient hatred need neither apologize for their existence nor emasculate themselves in response to antisemitism, but must take action—be that action political, legislative, or judicial—against it.

The means of counteraction of antisemitism are many. We identify the most visible and efficacious.

Popular amongst Jewish "defense" agencies has been the use of a variety of prejudice-reduction programs (such as the "World of Difference" program of the Anti-Defamation League), although there are limited data that such programs result in the diminution of attitudinal antisemitism among members of the broad population. The weight of the data suggest that the lessening of prejudice is a result of generational changes in social, economic, and educational status rather than in the "conversion" of individual bigots. Nonetheless, prejudice-reduction programs are useful in that they demonstrate that populations that participate in the programs are committed to the diminution of prejudice.

Legislative and judicial remedies—"hate crimes" laws, for example—likewise are questionable in terms of their efficacy at reducing antisemitism; it is not clear that they prevent expressions of antisemitic bias. Such legislation is nevertheless extremely important (assuming that the laws are crafted in a way that do not inhibit legitimate freedom of expression, and thereby pass constitutional muster) in that the laws send the message that the central institutions of power in the society—in this case, government—will not tolerate bigoted behavior.[29]

The most efficacious counteraction of antisemitism, in the view of this author, is the improving of social and economic conditions. The data, without fail, assert that in any population, in any geographic area, at any time, in which the conditions of society are improved—primarily economic and educational conditions—bigotry and racism decrease.[30]

Transcending all of these—and this goes, not to the question of *antisemitism*, but to *Jewish security*—is the enhancement of the kinds of constitutional protections taken for granted in the United States and gaining currency in some other countries. In the USA, these protections are chiefly those embodied in the First Amendment to the United States Constitution, and most centrally the separation of church and state. For American Jews there is no surer guarantor of security than the strength of constitutional institutions. Any institutions in society that strengthen and thereby enhance pluralism will act as a preventive to antisemitism.

And last. The American Jewish community has been hypnotized by antisemitism. We monitor it, we measure it, we chase after antisemites. But ultimately the important issue is not antisemitism; it is Jewish security. There are any number of things in America that have nothing to do with antisemitism that are terribly destructive to Jews—noteworthy among these are attacks on church-state separation; and there are many things in this country that could be fairly characterized as antisemitism that are superficial, that pose little or no danger to the Jewish polity or to individual Jews. Why can't American Jews take "yes" for an answer? And more basic, how, ultimately, can we measure Jewish security?

Having based some of this chapter on judgments arising out of survey data, I close with a view that challenges this approach. The late historian Lucy Dawidowicz, writing in *Commentary* magazine in 1970, asked a simple question: "Can Antisemitism be measured?"[31] Dawidowicz suggested that survey analysis, which presents a picture frozen in a moment in time, is by its nature unequipped to investigate the historic images and themes that yet flourish, even in America; it is certainly unequipped to trace the passage of these themes from one culture to another. How much more difficult to locate a specific variety of antisemitism within a meaningful historical continuum, and translate this form of antisemitism in a responsible way for our communities? It is this last question that, ultimately, is our charge in interpreting antisemitism, and interpreting what we mean by Jewish security.

Notes

1.   Found in *Midrash Rabbah* (*Exodus*) and elsewhere.

2.   David Berger, "Antisemitism: An Overview," in David Berger, ed., *History and Hate: The Dimensions of Antisemitism*, p. 3.

3.   Jews affiliated in some manner with the Jewish community were surveyed.

4.   See Earl Raab, "Taking the Measure of Antisemitism in the in the 21st Century," p. 1, address to the 1992 Plenary Session of the National Jewish Community Relations Advisory Council.

5. Among the criteria for assessing antisemitism, developed by the National Jewish Community Relations Advisory Council (NJCRAC, now the Jewish Council for Public Affairs—JCPA), are: prevailing attitudes toward Jews; acts of aggression, covert or overt, toward Jews; discrimination against Jews; expressions of antisemitism by public figures; expressions of antisemitism by religious figures; response to conflict situations; official reactions to antisemitism; antisemitic "mass" movements; personal experience with antisemitism; anti-Zionist manifestations in which the legitimacy of the state of Israel—and therefore the legitimacy of the peoplehood of the Jews— is questioned. (This does not include criticism of the policies of the Israeli government.). *NJCRAC 1985-86 Joint Program Plan* (New York: NJCRAC, 1986).

6. Other behavioral manifestations are certainly present in the USA, some disturbingly so. For example, the number of incidents of antisemitic vandalism, as monitored by the Anti-Defamation League's annual Audit of Antisemitic Incidents, increased each year from 1987 to 1991, although the number of such incidents declined during the mid-1990s. Analysts suggest that the ADL's audit must be evaluated in the context of the total number of bias and prejudice-related incidents reported around the country, and assessed in terms of the nature of the incident and the identity of the perpetrator (for example, the skinhead who expresses hate against many groups, including Jews; the teenage swastika-dauber; and so on).

7. For a survey of the data, and a useful bibliography, on attitudinal antisemitism through 1995, see Renae Cohen, "What We Know, What We Don't Know, about Antisemitism: A Research Perspective," in Jerome A. Chanes, ed., *Antisemitism in America Today*, pp. 59–83.

8. "Patterns of American Prejudice" was published as a seven-volume series based on the University of California (Berkeley) Five-Year Study of Antisemitism in the United States, designed by the Survey Research Center at Berkeley and carried out by the University of Chicago's National Opinion Research Center under a grant from the Anti-Defamation League of B'nai B'rith. The eleven-item antisemitism "scale" developed by Gertrude Selznick and Stephen Steinberg for the Berkeley Studies was the model for subsequent surveys, including the 1981 Yankelovich, Skelly, and White poll commissioned by the American Jewish Committee and the 1992 Marttila and Kiley survey conducted for the Anti-Defamation League (see below). While there are numerous differences in the samples, study designs, and execution in the three surveys, the antisemitism scale used is substantially the same in all three. This has raised serious questions among researchers. See Tom W. Smith, "The Polls—a Review: Actual Trends or Measurement Artifacts? A Review of Three Studies of Antisemitism," *Public Opinion Quarterly* 57 (fall 1993): 380–93, for an exploration of these questions.

An earlier, landmark, study, *The Authoritarian Personality*, by T. W. Adorno, Else Frenkel-Brunswik, Daniel J. Levinson, and R. Nevitt Sanford (New York: Harper & Row, 1950), explored the personality of prejudice. In this American Jewish Committee study an earlier antisemitism scale was developed.

9. See, for example, the findings from the Anti-Defamation League/Marttila and Kiley survey.

10. *What do Americans Think About Jews?* (New York: American Jewish Committee, 1991).

11. "Highlights from an Anti-Defamation League Survey on Antisemitism and Prejudice in America" (New York: Anti-Defamation League, November 16, 1993).

12. Carolyn E. Setlow and Renae Cohen, *1992 New York City Intergroup Relations Survey* (New York: American Jewish Committee, 1992).

13. "Highlights from and Anti-Defamation League Survey on Racial Attitudes in America" (New York: Anti-Defamation League, June 1993).

14. *Antisemitism in Contemporary America* (New York: American Jewish Committee, 1994).

15. The six areas examined by NORC/AJC are (1) the perceived social standing of Jews compared to other ethnoreligious groups; (2) the images that people have of Jews compared to those of other ethnoreligious groups; (3) the perceived influence and power that Jews have compared to other groups; (4) the warmth or closeness that people feel toward Jews compared to other groups; (5) social interactions between Jews and non-Jews in the areas of friendship and intermarriage; and (6) the perceived loyalty of Jews and the connection between anti-Israel and antisemitic attitudes.

16. Personal conversation with the author.

17. The eleven items in the "index of antisemitic belief": Jews stick together more than other Americans; Jews always like to be at the head of things; Jews are more loyal to Israel than to America; Jews have too much power in the U.S. today; Jews have too much control and influence on Wall Street; Jews have too munch power in the business world; Jews have a lot of irritating faults; Jews are more willing than others to use shady practices to get what they want; Jewish business men are so shrewd that others don't have a fair chance in competition; Jews don't care what happens to anyone but their own kind; Jews are [not] just as honest as other businessmen.

18. Remarks to Plenary Session of the National Jewish Community Relations

Advisory Council, Washington, D.C., 20 February 1993, unpublished.

19. See on this issue Gary E. Rubin, "A No-Nonsense Look at Antisemitism," *Tikkun* (May–June 1993): 46–48, 79–81.

20. *Taking America's Pulse: The National Conference Survey on Inter-Group Relations* (New York: The National Conference, 1994).

21. The apparent contradiction between a decline in attitudinal antisemitism and an increase over a period of some of the years surveyed in the number of antisemitic incidents can be easily explained: Amongst those relatively few who profess antisemitic attitudes, there has been in recent years a greater propensity to "act out" their beliefs in various forms of expression, consistent with the general erosion of traditional societal taboos that has been noted in the USA.

22. The philosemitism phenomenon is a social-psychological phenomenon that calls for a discrete study.

23. *Exit Poll Cross Tabulations, Louisiana Runoff, 1991* (New York: Voter Research and Surveys, 1991), photocopied. The raw data were interpreted by Mark Mellman of Mellman and Lazarus, Washington. The question of whether there was receptivity to Duke's racist message even as his overt Klan connection was rejected or ignored is addressed by Mellman and others. Mellman points out that there are data to suggest that responses such as "reform the welfare system," conventionally considered to be code words for racism, are in fact nothing of the sort. Indeed, most Americans, when queried, respond that most people on "welfare" are white; and that welfare is an issue of being responsible for one's own actions, and not of race.

24. Earl Raab, "Taking the Measure of Antisemitism," explores this area.

25. For a comprehensive discussion of hidden, latent, and "new" antisemitism, see Tom W. Smith, *Antisemitism in Contemporary America*, pp. 19–22.

26. I thank Dr. David Singer of the American Jewish Committee for suggesting this example.

27. This is not to say that Jewish history is the history of antisemitism; it is not. What historians Cecil Roth and Salo Baron characterized as "the lachrymose theory of Jewish history" is a misrepresentation of the history of the Jews. Roth and Baron's point that antisemitism is but one aspect, albeit a significant aspect, of Jewish history is right on the mark.

28. The author acknowledges the work of historian Allan Nadler, who suggested this construct.

29. For a comprehensive review of the hate crimes arena, see Donald Altschiller, *Hate Crimes: A Reference Handbook*, Contemporary World Issues Series (Santa Barbara, CA: ABC-CLIO, 1999).

30. See, for example, data from studies conducted over the past two decades by the National Conference of Christians and Jews, Marttila and Kiley/ the Marttila Communications Group, Yankelovich, and the General Social Survey of the National Opinion Research Center of the University of Chicago. This inverse correlation—social conditions up, antisemitism down—holds true, contrary to conventional wisdom, across racial lines as well.

31. "Can Antisemitism Be Measured?" (July 1970): 36–43.

Section V

Antisemitism of the Right and of the Left

Mark Weitzman traces the migration of three major discredited myths: *The Protocols of the Elders of Zion*, the blood libel, and Holocaust denial from Western Christianity into Islam, which have developed a new potency and support from elites precisely at the moment when they are on the wane in the West and when they have been rejected by similar elites.

He also examines the use of new technologies to fuel ancient hatred. The Internet, he warns us, has revolutionized communication and makes it possible for potentially more than 1 billion people to be reached by this new form of global communication. Ancient stereotypes are now viewed in new social context and spurred on by globalized technology, which allows for cross-communication and cross-fertilization.

The extreme right has dressed its antisemitic venom in a new guise of anti-globalization. It has clothed anti-Zionism in the cloth of anti-imperialism and joined people of similar views throughout the world together in a global communication network. It has even embraced ecology as a mode of challenging the Jews and returned to themes present in Nazism such as blood and soil and the quest for ecological purity.

These themes are familiar not only on the extreme right but also on the extreme left. Sam Edelman has argued for a symbolic convergence between the extreme right and left regarding Jews and Judaism, Israel and Zionism. His examination, which concentrates of the left, examines five tracks that operate parallel to one another and reinforce one another.

- Opposition to Israel and Zionism and to the uses of Holocaust memory by Jews

245

- The remnant of the defunct communist world
- The United Nations
- Liberal church and university professors
- The contemporary antiwar movement

A thin line separates legitimate criticism from hate speech, and the two must never be confused. The damage done by the teachings of Voltaire and Marx regarding the Jews has not ended, nor has the enduring legacy of the Zionism-as-racism resolution of the United Nations, which on many occasions has provided an ongoing platform and infectious vocabulary of hate speech against Israel and to a lesser extent of Jews. It has reinforced structurally and rhetorically the abnormality of the Jewish state. Edelman also portrays antisemitism on the college campus, the place to which American Jews send nine out of ten of its college-age children, where many Jewish scholars call their home and where all barriers to full Jewish participation in the administration of the universities and its election to its boards has long passed. Like Weitzman, Edelman detects antisemitism within the ecological movement and the Green Party despite the prevalence of Jews within all environmental movements. Arab students and Islamic militants have joined forces with other student groups to attack Israel as a symbol of the West and Jews, now as the embodiment of the establishment.

14

Transmigration of Antisemitism: Old Myths; New Realities

Mark Weitzman

There really is no reason we should be surprised at the resilience and adaptability of antisemitic myths. Antisemitism has always reflected its times. The medieval period saw the flourishing of religious antisemitism, while the late nineteenth and early twentieth centuries reflected the growth in scientific knowledge with the establishment of what was called "racial science." And, the explosion of capitalism along with the revolutions of the early twentieth century gave life to the paranoid conspiracies of *The Protocols of the Elders of Zion*. Robert Chazan has already pointed out "every new stage in the evolution of anti-Jewish thought is marked by the dialectical interplay between a prior legacy of negative stereotypes and the reality of a new social context."[1] Thus the distinctions between "old" and "new" collapse, and we are left with an antisemitism that may take new forms, but is nonetheless dependent upon prior sources and manifestations.

Over the last half century, and certainly in our time, "the new social context" that Chazan describes actually reflects the dual and paradoxical poles of both the repudiation of traditional forms of antisemitism because of the Holocaust, and the embracing of anti-Zionism, which reflects the language of anti-imperialism, and even more currently, antiglobalization, thus appearing to legitimize antisemitism in political and social discourse. We shall show some examples of this current antisemitic discourse, as well as how current antisemitic tropes have been passed through different permutations before arriving at their present usage.

Chazan's "new social context" can also refer to the means of dissemination of this new antisemitic discourse, and not only to its content. In our time, the idea that the Internet has revolutionized communication has become commonplace; and while that is true, the implications of that revolution for the spreading of antisemitism have only been generally acknowledged recently. When we consider that approximately 1 billion people currently have access to the Internet throughout the world, its potential as a carrier and spreader of propaganda become apparent. It was this aspect of the Internet that the author Ian Buruma referred to when he described the Internet as "lack(ing) a superego that filters the monsters emerging from the lower depths"[2] since it encouraged the release of thoughts and emotions that had previously been inhibited.

The Simon Wiesenthal Center's database of extremist websites, which is, to the best of my knowledge, the largest in the world, illustrates this growth. It began in 1995 with one website, and now contains over 5,500 sites, with a surge in sites related to the Middle Eastern conflict, and in particular a huge jump in Islamist extremist sites, which were essentially invisible until about five years ago. These are sites that essentially reflect the combined ideologies of Islamist extremism, namely fierce and violent attitudes against Israel, the U.S., and by extension the West, and that are fueled by an extreme devotion to a radical fundamentalist and aggressive Islam.

Yet while the Internet is correctly perceived as presenting new challenges to those who are concerned about antisemitism,[3] there is one aspect of it that has scarcely been noted. This is the ability of the Internet to rescue from oblivion items that might otherwise be forgotten or ignored, referring to its power to disinter and revive material that had been discredited and discarded.[4] Simply posting an item on the Internet, dealing with any subject, no matter when it was written, gives it new life and potentially introduces it to over a billion people. And, while this applies to many different topics and themes, there is no question that in this manner, as with so much else online, antisemites have been in the forefront of Internet use.

Perhaps the most well known trope of recent antisemitic discourse is the theme of a Jewish cabal attempting to take over the world. And, of course, the Ur-text of that theme is the infamous *Protocols of the Elders of Zion*, a work that just saw its centennial.[5] The *Protocols*, purporting to describe in detail how a hidden group of Jewish leaders have plotted to take over the world, have not only been revived, but given birth to a dizzying host of new, updated versions, most of which can be found online.

While there are many sites that espouse some form of the *Protocols* online (including those that describe the terrorist attack of 9/11 as part of a Jewish/Israeli plot),[6] most of these are fairly basic and unsophisticated in their approach and outright antisemitism.[7] However, conspiratorial antisemitism does appear in some new and noteworthy forms. An example of this is the attempt by antisemites to use the anti-globalization movement as a conduit for recruitment. One needs only to return to the theme of the *Protocols*, or even the covers of some of the editions of *Protocols* that showed the Jewish plot as depicted by a Rothschild clasping the globe between his skeletal fingers to see how this theme was embodied. The fear engendered by that image is similar to the equation used by the antisemitic manipulators of antiglobalization. For them, it is fairly simple. Antiglobalization is a campaign against the large multinational corporations that threaten to blur national (and personal) identity. These corporations can easily be described with the terms "big business" or "Wall Street," terms with pejorative meaning in traditional antisemitic discourse, where they represent a Jewish economic plot for world domination. The late William Pierce, founder of the National Alliance, and until his death in 2002 the most important U.S. neo-Nazi, in his tract "Who Runs America," answered that question by pointing to Jewish (or assumed Jewish) financial success.[8] Thus, when perceived correctly, antiglobalization is really a campaign against "Jewish world domination." In a 1998 broadcast (ostensibly relating to India's detonation of nuclear weapons), Pierce spelled out this idea openly, saying: "The prospect of a nuclear arms race between India, China and Pakistan may not seem very encouraging, but it is a far brighter prospect than a continuation of the process of globalization being promoted by the Jews and their allies, whether international capitalists or deranged liberals."[9]

Pierce was not the only U.S. extremist to take that position. David Duke weighed in on the issue in 2002. In two separate Internet radio reports that year, one of which was entitled "The Lies of Globalization," Duke described the press as the "same media that is in lockstep for Israel is also in lockstep for the New World Order and the Globalism that it represents." Then Duke went on to identify those who are behind this "New World Order." "The Jewish supremacists are the... hypocrites, the racial supremacists. They and their New World Order seek to destroy every nation, every culture, every heritage but their own. They seek a global supremacy over media, economics and governments."[10]

At the time Duke was making these pronouncements (2002), he was spending time in Russia and addressing an international audience. While he had left the U.S. to avoid legal problems (which resulted in a jail sentence upon his return), he was also using the opportunity to begin the process of recreating himself as a figure of importance on the international extremist scene. Duke found Russia to be a congenial and vital home away from home, and despite visiting other prominent European extremists like Jean-Marie Le Pen and Bruno Gollnisch (of the National Front) in France, it was Russia that he described as being the possible "Key to White Survival."[11] While in Russia, Duke took part in a January 2002 international conference that was held in Moscow and called the Anti-Globalist Leaders Conference. The list of speakers at this conference makes it clear that this was nothing more than an international gathering of professional Holocaust deniers and antisemites mixed with prominent Eastern European antisemites. The titles of some of the major addresses at the conference spelled out the main themes. They included "Globalization and Education" (by the rector of the Moscow Social-Humanitarian Academy, Igor Ilyinsky), "Globalization and Christianity" (Oleg Platonov, editor-in-chief of the *Russian Encyclopedia* and conference co-chair), "Globalization: The Last Stage of the Colonization of the Orthodox Front" (Volen Sidorov, a Bulgarian journalist), "The Influence of Globalization on the Policies of the Russian Government" (Boris Mironov, who was Boris Yeltsin's minister of press and information from 1993–94, when he was fired for extreme nationalistic statements), "Globalization and Russia" (Igor Froyanov, then Dean of the History Department of St. Petersburg University, who was subsequently dismissed from his position), and finally, "Globalization's New Phase" (former dissident Alexander Zinoviev. Zinoviev, who was unable to attend due to illness, sent in his paper, as did Borislav Milosevic, brother of Slobodan Milosevic, the former Yugoslav president who was indicted a war criminal. Borislav Milosevic served as Yugoslavia's ambassador to Russia during his brother's rule).

Along with the concentration on globalization delineated above, conference attendees also had talks with titles like "Treblinka: A Critical Analysis of the Official Version" (Jurgen Graf, a Swiss Holocaust denier who fled to Iran to avoid prosecution), "The Influence of Zionism in Western Europe" (Ahmed Rami, who runs the notorious Radio Islam website out of Sweden), "The Blackmailing of Sweden" (Rene Berclaz, a Swiss Holocaust denier), and David Duke's own talk on "The

Zionist Factor in America." Finally, mention should be made of the presentation entitled "Globalization and Zionism" (by what the conference identified as the "well-known researcher into the *Protocols of the Elders of Zion*, Yuri Begunov), which makes explicit the link between globalization, antisemitism, and the *Protocols.*

The conference was cosponsored by Willis Carto's *Barnes Review*[12] and attracted participants from Australia, Sweden, Belarus, Bulgaria, Switzerland, the U.S., and Russia. Here, however, we must clarify their use of the term "globalization." While they certainly used globalization in the commonly understood sense of the growth of multinational corporations that destroy national boundaries and individual identity in an insatiable search for profits, they also added their own definition, namely looking at "global problems in world history." This enabled the conference participants to lay title to use the term antiglobalists, even as they spoke of the Holocaust and Zionism. Their use of the phrase "antiglobalists" thus resembles their earlier appropriation of the term "revisionism" to legitimize their efforts at Holocaust denial.[13] And, even as they acknowledged that their numbers are presently few, the hope that they have for increasing their international presence and for gaining in legitimacy and strength rests, in great part, on how successful they are in presenting themselves as socially committed activists and thinkers.[14]

So far, we have discussed the efforts of the extreme right wing to be identified as members in good standing of the antiglobalization movement. But this is only one aspect of the picture. The extent of the problem was identified in an article by Mark Strauss in *Foreign Policy* as "Antiglobalization's Jewish Problem."[15] In this article, Strauss describes the antisemitism evident at the 2003 World Social Forum in Brazil, where the swastika joined the peace sign, the rainbow flag, and the blue-and-white UN symbol as visible images. In this vein, the ideas expressed by former Malaysian prime minister Mahathir Mohammad, about "Jews who determine our currency levels and bring about the collapse of our currency,"[16] are viewed as reality, and are believed to explain all the issues and problems that exist for those outside the global economy. Thus the Frenchman Jean Bove, who made his reputation leading protests against McDonald's, could travel to Ramallah and stand with Yasser Arafat, because "Israel is trying to impose an apartheid system on both the occupied territories and the Arab population in the rest of Israel. They are also putting into place—with the support of the World Bank—a series of neoliberal measures intended to integrate the Middle East into globalized production circuits, through the exploitation of cheap Palestinian labor."[17] For these theorists, conspiracy becomes reality, and as the Palestinian paper *Al-Ayyam* wrote, they can then praise Osama bin Laden as "the man who says no to the dominization of globalization."[18]

Other voices are also unabashed about attempting to manipulate the antiglobalization movement. As noted above, before his death in 2002, William Pierce embraced antiglobalization and created a (now defunct) website for an organization called the Anti-Globalization Action Network. This front featured the writings of a Jewish (sounding) activist named David Finkel and defended its links to the National Alliance as an attempt to "broaden the base of their support."[19]

Antiglobalization is a theme that has great resonance among the many in the world who feel left out of the promised riches, exploited by faceless corporations and cast adrift from their familiar institutions. They are joined by political opponents of the West, especially of the U.S. and Israel; and finally it provides an opportunity for those who seek to exploit the antiestablishment feelings of youth who are looking for a cause to believe in, and an activity that will define their behavior against that of the adults who make the rules.

The role of *The Protocols of the Elders of Zion*, as referred to above, is both important and instructive in this regard. The *Protocols* have been steadily growing in importance in the Middle East, as the *New York Times* reported, "Stay in a five-star hotel anywhere from Jordan to Iran, and you can buy the infamous forgery, the *Protocols of the Elders of Zion*,"[20] and used by authoritative papers such as Egypt's semiofficial *Al-Ahram*, which answered the question: "What exactly do the Jews want? Read what the 9th Protocol of *The Protocols of the Elders of Zion* says."[21] And they have even become official elements of policy, as witnessed by Article 32 of the *Hamas Charter*, which claims, "Their (the Jews') plan is embodied in *The Protocols of the Elders of Zion*.[22]

But the *Protocols* are not a Muslim document. Like so many other antisemitic myths, they have migrated across time and cultures. Originating in Eastern Europe about one hundred years ago, the *Protocols* were essentially a tool of the oppressive tsarist regime.[23] Like many other antisemitic images they were brought to the Middle East by Western sources. Bernard Lewis has described this general process, writing, "The real penetration of modem style anti-Semitism, how ever, dates from the nineteenth century. It began with the Christian Arab minorities ... It was actively encouraged by Western emissaries of various kinds, including consular and commercial representatives on the one hand, and priests and missionaries on the other."[24] Lewis later turns to the *Protocols,* and notes

> *The Protocols of the Elders of Zion* is occasionally mentioned in Arab polemics linking Zionism and Bolshevism in the early 1920s. The first Arab translation of the Protocols, made from the French, was ... published in Jerusalem ... on January 15, 1926.[25]

The effects were soon felt. In his *A Century of Jewish Life,* the supplemental volume to Heinrich Graetz's monumental *History of the Jews* published in 1944, Ismar Elbogen wrote that in August 1929 the British mandate authorities "tolerated the incitement in the Arab press which used excerpts from the *Protocols*" to help stir up the Arab riots of that summer.[26] These riots culminated in the massacre of the Jewish population of Hebron, where almost 70 Jews were murdered and about another 60 were wounded.

The same pattern applied to the charge of ritual murder. Although there appeared to be cases of ritual murder earlier in the Muslim world, it was the Damascus Affair of 1840 that really put the theme into the Middle Eastern landscape.[27] And, perhaps even more important, for their own reasons, Western authorities, including the Vatican, essentially validated the idea. "With the publication of the *Protocols,* the Damascus affair was given a new lease on life. Here, after all, for the entire world to see was an account of human sacrifice not in the Middle Ages, but in the present day, authenticated by the representatives of a modern European state and 'volunteered' down to the most horrifying details by the self-confessed murderers themselves."[28] This meant that the medieval antisemitic stereotypes of Europe were now being planted in new soil, in the Middle East, and were supported by the leading Western institutions operating there. In effect, the impulse was to empower this new form of antisemitic discourse, with little regard to its consequences for both Jews and the rest of society.

David Kertzer has shown how the Catholic Church was convinced of Jewish guilt in Damascus, and kept the case alive.[29] Kertzer concluded that the popes, in the decades leading to the end of the nineteenth century, "regulated the anti-Semitic campaigns conducted in the Catholic press" that featured ritual murder and conspiracy charges against the Jews.[30] The antisemitic tropes introduced into the Middle East in this manner have horrible resonance today. For example, in 1882, Father Giuseppe Oreglia published a pamphlet that Jews kidnapped a Muslim boy, baptized him, and, after slitting his throat, used his blood for Passover ritual purposes.[31] Today we can find longtime former Syrian defense minister Mustafa Tlas's 1983 book *The Matza of Zion*, in its eighth printing and being highlighted at the 2002 Damascus Book Fair.[32] In an interview that he gave in 2003 to an Arabic newspaper published in London, Tlas explained his book as being "set in Damascus. I did not invent it, and it is backed up by documents. It shows some Jewish rituals. How can the Zionists deny this reality? They want no one to know about their hostile morality."[33] This authentication of the blood libel did not only appear in Syria; Egypt's semiofficial newspaper, Al-Ahram, published a lengthy story in October 2000 that drew on some of the Damascus Affair's documents to conclude that "the bestial drive to knead Passover Matzahs with the blood of non-Jews is [confirmed]."[34] And, in March 2002, a Saudi government paper extended the Jewish use of blood to the holiday of Purim by asserting that "for this holiday, the Jewish people must obtain human blood so that their clerics can prepare the holiday pastries."[35]

The form of antisemitism known as Holocaust denial also reflects this transmission from West to East. Although there were prior manifestations of denial in the Arab world, a significant shift occurred with a conference that was proposed for Beirut in June 2001. This conference was planned to bring Western figures like William Pierce, Jurgen Graf of Switzerland, and Horst Mahler of Germany together with Arab Holocaust deniers in the first major effort to use this theme as a united focus against Jews and Israel. The conference was canceled by the Lebanese government due to the international outcry raised by Jewish organizations and foreign governments, but a follow-up conference, with a lower profile, was held shortly after in Amman. And, to help strengthen this connection, Holocaust denial groups in the U.S. began reaching out to the Arab and Muslim world, featuring speakers on "Palestinian" issues at their conferences and articles and speeches on that subject in their outreach.[36]

While we have explored the way some Western antisemitic themes have entered Islamic antisemitic discourse above, the traditional antisemitic discourse in the West also shows some unforeseen growth. The attempt by extreme rightist groups to use unexpected themes or ideas can be seen in, for example, the growth of what has been called "eco-fascism." Although, to the popular perception, ecological issues are almost invariably associated with liberal to left-wing beliefs, the past few years have seen a concerted effort on the part of the extreme right wing to co-opt the issue, to claim it as their own, and to use it to reach a wider, younger, and more mainstream audience. The basic approach was succinctly summed up by the late William Pierce of the National Alliance. In a radio broadcast aired on July 27, 2002, he said: "There are, in fact, several issues on which we are closer to what would ordinarily be considered the left-wing or liberal position than we are to the conservative or right-wing position. One of these issues is the ecology issue: the protection of our natural environment, the elimination of pollution, and the protection of wildlife."[37] Pierce was not the only theoretician of the movement to express such views. David Duke explains how this idea is consistent with his other beliefs; his goal is "to preserve the character and beauty of my people the same way that, as an ecology minded individual, I desire the preservation of the Blue whale or the great African Elephant." [38]

Tom Metzger, the founder and leader of WAR (White Aryan Resistance) also drew the same lesson. For Metzger, the belief that native species need protection from foreign invaders just illustrates how, in nature, species need to be separated. This then is a lesson to be applied to human society, especially in regard to racial issues. In other words, for Metzger, it is nature that commands segregation. Metzger also uses ecology as an opening to attack financial interests (which, in the scarcely coded language of a neo-Nazi, always stands for Jews) and describes the efforts of those who are cleaning up the mess in racial terms. For Metzger, the task of the committed white person is to care for, and to clean up, the environment. In Metzger's own words: "Those who buy into Economic Determinism, the fast buck and the maximization of profits by any means possible, have sold their heritage for greed and power. On the other hand, many White people are in the advance guard of turning to technology to aid in recovering clean air, clean water, and rich soil. White men and women are even in the far-flung nations of the world, working to improve the environment. Racial and Cultural Determinists care about our environmental future. The White race cannot be strong if our environment is polluted."[39]

This usage of environmental issues by far right groups is not limited to the United States. Groups like the Swiss Schweizer Demokraten

(Swiss Democrats) or the Russian Pamyat, have also made ecological issues into a prominent part of their platform. Pamyat's protests about various Russian environmental difficulties included putting the blame for these problems on "pernicious Western influences, Jews and cosmopolitanism."[40]

These brief examples serve to illustrate how right-wing extremists are using ecological issues today, but to fully understand and appreciate the depth of their commitment to the language of environmentalism, we need to go back to the Nazi period and even before. The Nazi idea of "blood and soil" was an expression of ecological purity. As one scholar of ecological movements wrote: "This environmental ideology extolled purity of race, purity of the Fatherland, purity of the German forests, and yes, purity of food. Strict vegetarians, both Hitler and Rudolf Hess championed organic foods and converting biotech farms to organic ones. Nazi intellectuals championed *Blut und Boden,* the mystical connectedness of Germans to their land, crops, and food. German racial theorist (Walther) Richard Darre, arguing in *Blut und Boden,* said Jews were "weeds."[41] Online, we can even find a National Socialist Library website that has a section devoted to environmentalism that maintains, "To be a Nazi means that one is a nationalist, or one who believes that a nation should be delineated by genetic familiarity, and that within that nation one advocates 'socialism' or the collective support of individuals in society There are other beliefs including environmental standards that we uphold, and these are integration with the national socialist belief as part of our concept of nature: Nature is everything, including ourselves, and in nature, race, family and environmental system as a whole are most important. We reject morality in all its forms as unnatural."[42] The attempt to create a Brown-Green alliance is one that has deep roots and connections, and must be recognized for what it is. Precisely because of these roots, some of which have been spelled out for us by scholars such as Leon Poliakov or George Mosse,[43] the usage of the language of ecology is authentic and not artificial and thus can become powerful and more appealing than expected. Further, because of the image we generally have of people concerned with the environment as being kinder and more caring, by stressing these ecological issues, especially to younger listeners, the extremist can, in effect, disarm some of the suspicions that might arise should they immediately begin with racial, religious or other red flag issues.

Together with the use of themes not usually associated in the popular mind with extremism, such as antiglobalization or ecological concerns, the revival, or better yet the transmigration of antisemitic myths have now become a staple of antisemitic discourse. This revival of discredited myths is nothing new. After all, this sense of revival is at the center of at least one modern definition of the word (myth)—the meaning as given in the writings of Mircea Eliade and Joseph Campbell. As Steven Wasserstrom has pointed out, "The historical myth of world cycles" was at the center of their belief, and this myth "made law evaporate."[44] According to Wasserstrom, those who followed this reading of history saw a "Judaism almost wholly without law," and a world in which "historic, legal and sexual constraints are, in principle, no longer binding."[45] The effect of this mythological view is first of all to create a world in which Judaism is, in effect, de-Judaized, by removing the vital, and defining characteristic of the *Halakhah,* of law. It secondly allows the mythologizer to create an own alternate reality, a reality that explodes conventional historical, legal, and social realities. Thus, for example, the *Protocols* can become what one antisemitic musician could call "The News behind the News."[46] However, to stop at this recognition of the revival of old myths is to ignore another aspect of today's antisemitism, one that might not be new, but is certainly novel to most of us. As I tried to describe above, the union of unexpected allies, of opposites (such as neo-Nazis and ecologists, antisemites and antiglobalist activists, Muslim terrorists and Western intellectual elites) requires another look. And, while the scope of this collaboration appears to be unprecedented, the reality is that it is not new. Historians such as Saul Friedlander, George Mosse, Jeffrey Herf, and Wasserstrom have all noted it. Friedlander described "the ... magical logic of the marriage of opposites" "the coincidence ... of themes from the radical right and radical left, that is the most fundamental feature of fascism."[47] For Mosse it was summed up in the words of Alfred Rosenberg that "death and life are not contraries, but (are) linked to one another,"[48] and Herf has described how this theme reverberates even in the terminology they choose to use (National Socialism, Conservative Revolution, Reactionary Modernism).[49] And, as Wasserstrom shows, leading ideologues of the fascist and neofascist movement, and their intellectual collaborators, have thought and written about this idea. But, as we have seen, they are not alone; as the Spanish journalist Pilar Rahola wrote last spring, "The new antisemitism is leftist, it is an antisemitism of the elite and it is unconscious. But it exists."[50]

Conclusion

Where we go from here is of course, not totally in our own hands. Yet there are certain considerations that I would suggest. First, we have to accept the reality of these new versions of a deadly serious political antisemitism that uses the forms of the older varieties. We made a mistake in believing that the Shoah had dealt a death blow to the mainstreaming of antisemitism in the Western world, and we were wrong.

Also, we must accept that the idea of migration of these myths must be taken literally. Islam did not create *The Protocols of the Elders of Zion*, ritual murder or Holocaust denial. Part, in some cases, a significant part, of the Muslim world has adopted these beliefs and made them into articles of faith and policy. They have sometimes recast them into their own language (figuratively as well as literally), and made them part of the international political scene. This means that since antisemitism has become globalized, our responses have to be flexible enough to respond in a similar manner. Thus we need to be actively engaged in the international arena. When I spoke at last June's UN conference on antisemitism, the prevailing reaction that I got from the Jewish community was one of suspicion and cynicism about the UN, and why we should even bother with that institution. While it might be understandable, it is self-defeating. If we give up the field without a fight, we cannot complain if the results are unfavorable.

I would also like to suggest a proposal that might be somewhat more hopeful than realistic. If, as I noted above, the Christian churches bear a great deal of responsibility for the injection of traditional Western antisemitic themes in the Middle East, perhaps, as part of the ongoing dialogue between Jews and Christians we can urge the churches to acknowledge their responsibility, just as they have acknowledged it in a European context. And, just as they have done in Europe, after acknowledging their responsibility, they can begin to work toward reversing those teachings and to eradicating these forms of antisemitism from the Middle East. This work is as much a religious as it is a political and social imperative.

Finally, we also have to have respect for history. To claim that we are living through a reenactment of the 1930s is, I believe, false. First of all, and most important, the existence of the state of Israel fundamentally challenges these claims. Second, the experience of the Shoah has altered the internal Jewish response to antisemitism. Despite what I said above, we still are better organized, more influential, and more willing to use these attributes to protect them. Third, I do believe that the Shoah has created a core group in Western society who recognize the potential for further genocide that does exist, and so are committed to its prevention.

A more appropriate comparison is, I believe, with the period of the 1970s and '80s. Just as a quick reminder, that was the period of the Yom Kippur War of 1973–74, when a surprise Arab attack threatened Israel's very survival, the UN's infamous Resolution 3379 of 1975 which by defining Zionism as a form of racism legitimized Israel's definition as a pariah state,[51] bombings of Jewish institutions and stores throughout Europe, and a series of armed terrorist attacks and hijackings aimed at Israel and Jews. At the same time, antisemitism was also then a matter of public policy, nurtured and exploited by both the Arab states and the Soviet bloc. Yet we lived through it, and came out into better times. Having done so once, I believe that with a great deal of effort, we can do so again.

Notes

1. Robert Chazan, *Medieval Stereotypes and Modern Antisemitism*, University of California Press, Berkeley, 1997, p. 135.

2. Ian Buruma, "China in Cyberspace," *New York Review of Books*, vol. 46, no. 17, November 4, 1999.

3. For perspectives on online antisemitism see Mark Weitzman, "The Internet Is Our Sword," in *Remembering for the Future: The Holocaust in an Age of Genocide*, ed. John Roth, Palgrave, 2001, vol. I, pp. 911–25, and Simon Schama, "Virtual Annihilation," in *Those Who Forget the Past: The Question of Anti-Semitism*, Random House, New York, 2004, pp. 353–64.

4. I had noted this capability of the Internet in "Antisemitism and Holocaust Denial in Right-Wing Extremism" in Thomas Greven and Thomas Grumke, *Globalisierter Rechtsextremismus? Die extremischer Rechte in der Ara Globalisierung*, VS Verlag, Wiesbaden, 2006.

5. The bibliography on the *Protocols* is enormous. While Norman Cohn's *Warrant for Genocide* (New York, 1967) has long been the prime analysis

of the *Protocols*, Cesar DeMichelis, *The Non-Existent Manuscript: A Study of the Protocols of the Sages of Zion* (Nebraska, 2004) has recently examined the origins of the *Protocols*, Hadassah Ben Itto (*The Lie That Wouldn't Die: The Protocols of the Elders of Zion*, London, 2005) has discussed the legal proceedings involving the *Protocols*, Neil Baldwin's *Henry Ford and the Jews* (New York, 2001) describes the *Protocols'* dissemination in the U.S. by the great industrialist, and Steven L. Jacobs and Mark Weitzman have written the first point-by-point refutation of the contents of the *Protocols* in *Dismantling the Big Lie: The Protocols of the Elders of Zion* (Ktav, New York, 2003). *The Protocols of the Sages of Zion: A Selected Bibliography* (Jerusalem, 2006) is a book-length bibliography published by the Vidal Sassoon Center for the Study of Antisemitism at the Hebrew University in Jerusalem to mark the centennial of the *Protocols*.

6. See the report by Harold Brackman, *9/11 Digital Lies: A Survey of Online Apologists for Global Terrorism,* www.wiesenthal.com/atf/cf/%7BDFD2AAC1-2ADE-428A-9263-35234229D8D8%.

7. In my article "The Protocols and the Propaganda of Liberalism" in the forthcoming memorial volume for Simon Wiesenthal, I have examined how the *Protocols* have begun to filter into some left/liberal discourse.

8. http://www.natall.com/who-rules-america/.

9. William Pierce, *Nationalism vs. the New World Order: Free Speech,* vol. IV, no. 5, May 1998, online at http://www.natvan.com/free-speech/fs985c.html.

10. David Duke, *The Lies of Globalism,* http://www.davidduke.com/radio/transcripts/globalism09042002.htm.

11. Duke, *Is Russia the Key to White Survival,* http://www.duke.org/dukereport/10-000.html.

12. Carto was described by the ADL as "one of the most influential American anti-Semitic propagandists of the past 50 years... (controlling such groups as) Liberty and Property, Western Destiny, the Noontide Press, American Mercury, National Youth Alliance, the Institute for Historical Review, the Populist Party, and, most notably, the Liberty Lobby. http://www.adl.org/learn/Ext_U.S./carto.asp?xpicked=2&item=carto.

13. See Holocaust denial conference, Tehran, Iran, December 12, 2006.

14. Information about the conference can be found at http://oag.ru/reports/revisionists.html.

15. Mark Strauss, "Antiglobalization's Jewish Problem," *Foreign Policy,* (November/December 2003).

16. Ibid. For the full text of Mahathir's speech, see http://www.adl.org/Anti_semitism/malaysian.asp

17. Strauss, *Antiglobalization.*

18. Ibid.

19. http://www.g8activist.com

20. *New York Times,* April 30, 2002.

21. *Al-Ahram,* July 8, 2001, as found on the MEMRI website, Special Dispatch Series, Number 238, http://www.memri.org/bin/articles.cgi?Page=countries&Area=egypt&ID=SP23801

22. English translation, http://www.library.cornell.edu/colldev/mideast/hamas.htm. The translation is "a verbatim reproduction of the Palestinian Hamas Movement's own English version of its covenant."

23. See note 5 above

24. Bernard Lewis, *Semites and Anti-Semites: An Inquiry into Conflict and Prejudice,* Norton, 1986, p. 132.

25. Ibid., p. 199.

26. Ismar Elbogen, *A Century of Jewish Life,* Philadelphia, Jewish Publication Society, 1944, p. 619.

27. For some earlier examples of the blood libel in Muslim lands see Jacob Barnai, "Blood Libels in the Ottoman Empire of the Fifteenth to Nineteenth Centuries," in Shmuel Almog, ed., *Antisemitism Through the Ages* (Oxford 1988), pp. 190–92.

28. Jonathan Frankel, *The Damascus Affair: "Ritual Murder," Politics, and the Jews in 1840,* Cambridge, Cambridge University Press, 1997, p. 416.

29. David Kertzer, *The Popes Against the Jews: The Vatican's Role in the Rise of Modern Anti-Semitism,* N.Y., Random House, 2002, pp. 104–5

30. Ibid., pp. 213–14.

31. Ibid., pp. 159–60.

32. Tlas served as Syria's defense minister from 1972 until 2004. For its popularity at the book fair, see http://www.memri.org/bin/articles.cgi?Area=sd&ID=SP43202

33. http://www.memri.org/bin/articles.cgi?Page=countries&Area=syria&ID=SP56603.

34. http://www.memri.org/bin/articles.cgi?Area=sd&ID=SP15000.

35. http://memri.org/bin/articles.cgi?Page=archives&Area=sd&ID=SP35402.

36. For the Beirut conference, see http://www.tau.ac.il/Anti-Semitism/updates.htm, March 23, 2001. For the Amman conference see ibid., May 23, 2001. For an example of U.S. Holocaust denial use of this theme, see http://www.ihr.org/conference/14thconf/speakers.html where at least two of the featured talks at the 2002 Institute of Historical Review conference (the last regularly held conference of the IHR) dealt with Israel and/or Palestinian themes. I have not discussed the recent notorious Holocaust denial conferences in Teheran and Cairo here as this paper was presented a few years earlier.

37. *American Dissident Voices*, broadcast of July 27, 2002, at http://www.natvan.com/pub/2002/072702.txt.

38. David Duke, *America at the Crossroads*, http:llwww.duke.org/writings/crossroads.html.

39. Tom Metzger, *The Environment*, http://www.resist.com/home.htm.

40. Jonathan Olson, "The Global Rise of Right-Wing Ecology," *Earth Island Journal* (summer 2000), vol. 15, no. 2, www.earthisland.org/eijournal/sum2000/fe-sum2000rightwingeco.html.

41. Gregory Pence, http://www.philosophers.co.uk/portal article.php?id=5 82.

42. http://www.nazi.org/libra[y/faq.

43. Poliakov, Leon, *The Aryan Myth: A History of Racist and Nationalist Ideas in Europe*, New York, New American Library, 1977. George Mosse, *The Crisis of German Ideology: Intellectual Origins of the Third Reich* (New York, Fertig, 1998, p. 211) discusses the German philosopher Ludwig Klages, who anticipated much of current "green" thinking and describes him as an "an intellectual pacemaker for the Third Reich."

44. Steven Wasserstrom, *Religion after Religion: Gershom Scholem, Mircea Eliade, and Henry Corbin at Eranos,* Princeton, Princeton University Press, 1999, p. 141.

45. Ibid.

46. Carl Klang, who describes himself as "America's #1 Christian Patriot Musician," http://www.klang.com/ew14.html.

47. Saul Friedlander, *Reflections of Nazism: An Essay on Kitsch and Death*, New York, Harper & Row, 1984, p. 131.

48. George Mosse, *Masses and Man: Nationalist and Fascist Perceptions of Reality*, Detroit, Wayne State University Press, 1987, p. 74.

49. Jeffrey Herf, *Reactionary Modernism: Technology, Culture and Politics in Weimar and the Third Reich*, Cambridge, Cambridge University Press, 1984. Wasserstrom (above, n. 44, cites Friedlander, Mosse, and Herf). The point has been made by others, including recently Enzo Traverso, "Intellectuals and Anti-Fascism: For a Critical Historization," *New Politics*, vol. 9, no. 4 (new series), whole no. 36 (winter 2004), who described fascism as a "a nebulous assemblage in which conservatism and eugenics, futurism and neoclassicism, cultural pessimism and conservative revolution, spiritualism and anti-Semitism, regressive romanticism and technocratic totalitarianism all cohabit."

50. Pilar Rahola, *Spanish Antisemitism Is Alive in the Left*, http://www.pilarrahola.com/ (originally published in *Diario El Mundo*, Madrid).

51. The resolution, adopted on November 10, 1975 (the thirty-seventh anniversary of *Kristallnacht*), was revoked by U.N. Resolution 4686 on December 16, 1991.

15

Antisemitism and the New/Old Left

Samuel Edelman

A few years ago San Francisco State University was the site of one of the most egregious antisemitic incidents during an anti-Israel demonstration in a series of incidents across the state of California. The poster which was at the heart of the accusation of antisemitism was a mockup of a can of food with the top of the label reading "Made in Israel," the next line "Palestinian Children Meat" surrounding the word "Sharon" with a blood drop hovering over the picture of an infant, with the word "Trademark" along the side and the phrase, "Slaughtered under Jewish Rites under American License." In talking with a number of the Jewish students after the event, I was told that this anti-Jewish image from the medieval Christian accusation of "blood libel" was carried by known leftist students as well as Palestinians.

The people who embrace this developing form of antisemitism are the standard-bearers of an anti-Jewish tradition beginning with the liberal ideology of Voltaire, the socialist vision of Karl Marx, the paranoia of Stalin, the pre-WWII peace movement, the antiauthority rhetoric of the French, German and British student revolts, the convergence of radical environmentalists with antiworld trade movement, antireligion and anti-Jewish radical feminists and radical trade unionists, and the left-leaning World Council of Churches, all of whom have used the Palestinians' status as underdogs in the Arab-Israeli conflict to launch a new form of Judeophobia couched in the cloth of opposition to Israel and Zionism.

I am going to argue in this chapter that these varied and different political, economic, social, and ideological strains that hither-to have not interacted well with each other are showing signs of coming together in a kind of "symbolic convergence" regarding Jews, Judaism, Israel, and Zionism. The field of rhetorical studies has developed a critical form of analysis for social movements called "fantasy theme analysis." Bormann, Craigan, and Shields have written extensively in communication journals that groups often form bonds of common interest and sometimes begin to share common fantasies in what they call a form of symbolic convergence. Examples of shared fantasies and symbolic convergence include the suffrage movement out of the abolitionist and temperance movements, the antiabortion movement bringing Catholic and Protestant fundamentalists together in a shared vision in response to abortion, and the civil rights movement out of the voting rights movement and civil disobedience program of groups connected to Dr. Martin Luther King.

In the case of the new antisemitism from the left, we can see a number of parallel tracks that seem to be converging with regard to Jews and Israel. Track one includes the writings and speeches of Jews opposed to Israel and Zionism as well as to the current uses of the Holocaust. The work of these Jewish writers and speakers has been used as a justification for the new antisemitism of the left. Track two involves the residue of the now defunct communist world. Track three includes the UN Racism Conference in Durban, South Africa, and the Zionism-as-racism resolution of the UN in the seventies. Track four includes both the liberal churches and a core of college professors who embrace the political vision of Noam Chomsky and other Jews referred to in track one who have embraced the divestment movement against Israel. Track five includes the current antiwar movement. Track six includes many of the groups involved in the antiglobalization, antiworld trade movement, including many farm and labor populist groups. Track seven includes environmentalist, green, and antivivisectionist groups.

We will be exploring how the following groups have come together to share a common fantasy about Jews, Israel, and Zionism:

- Anti-Zionist anti-Israeli Jews
- Communist attacks on Zionism and Israel (Stalinist shift after 1948) as antinationalism
- UN racism conference in South Africa
- Antiwar movement

- Antisemitism on the campus
- Anti-WTO and World Bank movement
- Environmental/Green

Anti-Zionist Anti-Israeli Jews

The first track includes some Jews, referred to in a recently published paper from the American Jewish Committee by Alvin Rosenfeld, who even question Israel's right to exist. These groups are as varied as the Neturei Karta, an ultra-orthodox group of *haredi* who recently participated in Iran's Holocaust Denial Conference, not to deny the Holocaust, but to deny the right of the state of Israel to exist, to those, who in the words of David Harris, executive director of the AJC, are "ultra-leftists who find a territory-based Jewish existence to be antithetical to their own self-referential definitions of Judaism."[1]

One of the most prolific and effective of the anti-Israel Jewish writers is of course Noam Chomsky. Yet, accusing Chomsky of being an anti-Jewish Jew is a bit of a stretch; nevertheless, his writings on Israel have enabled an army of leftist antisemites with a Jewish argument in support of their prejudice and hate. The core of Chomsky's attack on Israel is that the Jews of Israel and America have permitted Israel to become a pawn of American imperialism in the Middle East.

Leftist and liberal Jewish writers have viewed themselves as expressing an alternative to the Jewish nationalism of Zionism. Their efforts became the core of the political ideology of the Jewish socialist and labor Bund. The Bundists and their descendants are the second group of Jewish anti-Zionists after the ultra-orthodox haredi, Neturei Karta, and the equally anti-Zionist movement made up of Reform Jews who opposed Herzl and Zionism as early as the late nineteenth century. These groups represent a small core of anti-Zionist, anti-Israel Jews whose writings and speeches, as well those of their symbolic offspring, have become the supporting evidence of the justification of the new antisemitism of many non-Jewish groups for whom antisemitism has become fashionable.

These Jewish anti-Zionist, anti-Israel individuals and groups have found commonality and a shared vision with many leftists who have moved from legitimate criticism of Israel to out and out hate speech.

Communist Attacks on Zionism and Israel (Stalinist Shift after 1948) as Anti-Nationalism

The second track of liberal and leftist antisemitism is at the core of the Socialist Marxist vision of a utopian world where workers rule. In this utopian vision all discrimination disappears in the rule of the proletariat. We see the core of liberal antisemitism in Voltaire's' anti-Judaism.

> They are all of them, born with raging fanaticism in their hearts, just as the Bretons and the Germans are born with blond hair. I would not be in the least bit surprised if these people would not someday become deadly to the human race.

Voltaire went on to condemn Jews for "their stubbornness, their new superstitions, and their hallowed usury." Addressing the Jews directly, Voltaire wrote, "You have surpassed all nations in impertinent fables, in bad conduct, and in barbarism. You deserve to be punished, for this is your destiny."[2] Karl Marx also felt the need to excoriate the Jews of Europe:

> The monotheism of the Jew, therefore, is in reality the polytheism of the many needs, a polytheism which makes even the lavatory an object of divine law. *Practical need, egoism,* is the principle of *civil society,* and as such appears in pure form as soon as civil society has fully given birth to the political state. The god of *practical need and self-interest* is *money.*
>
> Money is the jealous god of Israel, in face of which no other god may exist. Money degrades all the gods of man—and turns them into commodities. Money is the universal self-established *value* of all things. It has, therefore, robbed the whole world—both the world of men and nature—of its specific value. Money is the estranged essence of man's work and man's existence, and this alien essence dominates him, and he worships it.
>
> The god of the Jews has become secularized and has become the god of the world. The bill of exchange is the real god of the Jew. His god is only an illusory bill of exchange.

The view of nature attained under the domination of private property and money is a real contempt for, and practical debasement of, nature; in the Jewish religion, nature exists, it is true, but it exists only in imagination.

Once society has succeeded in abolishing the *empirical* essence of Judaism—huckstering and its preconditions—the Jew will have become *impossible*, because his consciousness no longer has an object, because the subjective basis of Judaism, practical need, has been humanized, and because the conflict between man's individual-sensuous existence and his species-existence has been abolished.

The *social* emancipation of the Jew is the *emancipation of society from Judaism*.[3]

Voltaire and Marx represent the liberal and the socialist-communist tracks of the new antisemitism. Marxist, socialist, communist representations of antisemitism have waxed and waned as the political world of the Soviet Union changed. When it suited Stalin to be antisemitic in his battle with Trotsky, he was. When it suited Stalin to be pro-Zionist to help push Britain out of the Middle East, he was. During the years following the death of Lenin, Stalin ramped up his antisemitic campaign by reconfiguring the old tsarist secret police's forgery called *The Protocols of the Elders of Zion*. The Soviet Union also embarked on a three-part campaign to malign Trotsky, to go after Jewish bourgeoisies, and to attack the new socialist-oriented Zionism that had become a greater force among Eastern European Jewry in the years before and just after WWI. The antisemitic campaign sponsored by the Soviet Union was carried out by a variety of surrogates from labor leaders to communist ideologues, referring to Jews as cosmopolitans or Trotskyites. Jews were portrayed in the press and in a variety of other publications as either traitors to socialist ideals or as greedy capitalists hell bent on taking over the world and thwarting the will of the proletarian revolution.

Zionism as Racism in the UN, and the UN Racism Conference in Durban

In the years following the death of Stalin, successive Soviet administrations used antisemitism as a means of pushing their Cold War agenda out to their Arab client states with their arms and economic aid. It was critical for the Soviet Union to portray Israel as a foil for American imperialism in the Middle East and therefore continuing the antagonism toward the Jewish state by the Arab surrogates of the Soviet Union was critical. So the Soviet Union continued to distribute *The Protocols of the Elders of Zion* and other anti-Jewish works across the Middle East to "keep the pot boiling."

This growth of antisemitism in the Soviet Union had implications both internationally and domestically. Internationally it enabled the Soviets to gain greater inroads into the Arab world, and domestically it enabled Soviet leaders to deflect internal criticism. It also fit nicely into their oft argued idea that nationalism was bad, especially Jewish nationalism. According to Eliyahu Biletsky it was the Soviet Union's efforts that stimulated the original accusation in the UN and Arab world that Zionism = racism.

Biletsky notes that according to *Caution—Zionism!* by Yuri Ivanov published in 1969, "Modern Zionism is the ideology and ramified set of political organizations and activities of the extensive Jewish bourgeoisie, which has combined with monopolistic circles in the United States and other imperialist powers. The essence of Zionism is chauvinism and anti-communism."[4] He goes on to write:

The family weekly, *Ogonyok*, describes Zionist organizations as gangster mobs encompassing the whole capitalist world, characterized by mutual loyalty, the liquidation of doubters, and total subjection to the leaders. Since at the end of the nineteenth century, most of the world's wealth and industrial power passed into the hands of the Jewish bourgeoisie, the Zionist Organization has exerted its influence over all Jews everywhere to gain support in a struggle for power and money. The concept embedded in the notion of the Jews as the chosen people—a concept constantly examined and discussed in Judaism throughout the generations—is, according to the Soviet propaganda mill, the basis of Zionism, i.e., a religious basis. It is used to further expansionism, reaction and imperialism. This technique exploits all the elements of Czarist antisemitic propaganda, with the addition of a few modern gimmicks: it depicts the Jews as ugly, base, dirty, degraded and mindless, or as secret intriguers, aggressors, masters, and the spearhead of rampant imperialism. Anthologies, weeklies and other periodicals described entire Arab communities mercilessly wiped off the map, little girls raped, and senseless Arabs forced to crawl. There are maps of Israel's expansion encompassing Lebanon, Syria, all of the Arabian Peninsula, as well as other Arab territories. The term, world domination, written by the Russian priest in 1903 serves as the heritage and "spiritual value" upon which the superstructure of modern antisemitism in the form of "Zionism=racism is being erected.[5]

According to Biletsky, the subject of Judaism and Jews and Zionism

has been elevated in the Soviet Union to the status of the faith stuffed down the throats of all sectors of the public. In Western Europe, North and South America, the Jews are three times as rich as the Christians, claims Soviet propaganda, and in southern and western Russia, the Jewish population engages exclusively in trade and refuses to work. In all countries wealth, science, heavy industry and essential services are controlled by the Jewish bourgeoisie. South Africa is an example of Israel's identification with racism. In Latin America, Jewry and Zionism are sucking the marrow out of the bones of the people. The Soviet agency Tass announced the publication of *Zionism—Theory and Reality*, a book containing the contributions of dozens of writers in an attempt to present a "scientific" rather than a publicistic image. The book appeared in 1973 and was translated into several languages, aimed not only at Russia's allies. Following Lenin's conception of Jewish nationalism, the book denies the existence of Jews as a people. That is just "an invention of the Zionists" that, of course, represents the regressive elements in Jewish communities eager to assimilate with their environments. Excerpts from the book that appeared in the world press indicate that it adds nothing to medieval or modern antisemitic literature. Many paragraphs could very well have been taken from *Mein Kampf* or *The Protocols of the Elders of Zion* or the speeches of the attorneys handling blood libels against Jews.[6]

The antisemitism of the Soviet Union went beyond the issues of the Arab Israeli conflict and even Zionism itself to attack the very "essence" of Judaism, characterizing it as "a source of hatred and hypocrisy." Soviet scholars of varying types attempted to prove that "there is a close connection between Zionism and the Jewish religion." Because of this connection they argued that, "Judaism isolates the Jews from other people and teaches them to scorn the Gentile world."[7]

In May 1977, on the twenty-ninth anniversary of the creation of the state of Israel, the journal of the Soviet army *Red Star* published an article entitled "Zionism's Subversive Strategy":

> It described Zionism as exemplifying the main features of reactionary imperialism: expansionism, racism, and uncompromising hostility to peace and progress. "Zionism is a danger not only to the Arab peoples, but to mankind as a whole."[8]

> The UN resolution dealing with Zionism as a form of racism poured oil on the fires of hatred and antisemitism blazing in Russia from Czarist times down to the present. Editorials on the resolution of the Soviet press seem to be attacking only Israel and Zionism. The Soviet propaganda machine and media gained mass support, and in TF swastikas were up a bit on the doors of Jewish apartments. If Zionism is racist-fascism, something must be done to combat it (*Caution—Zionism!*).

> At the World Congress to Combat Racism, which met on August 20, 1978, Soviet Russia and other Communist countries (with the exception of Romania) called for the condemnation of Israel as a racist country, declaring "we emphasize the great moral and political contribution of all the resolutions passed by the UN General Assembly against racism, including the resolution stating that Zionism is a form of racism and racial discrimination."[9]

Even though the Zionism-as-racism resolution was eventually withdrawn by the United Nations in the 1990s, its legacy continues within the UN and without. All of the antisemitic, anti-Zionist, anti-Israel canards embodied in the rejected UN resolution continue to be trotted out at any opportunity. They continue to be used in a variety of college courses both in the United States and in Europe and continue to be referred to on numerous Internet sites. It is in the leftist community where they have found greatest salience, especially regarding the continued charge that Israeli policy toward the Palestinians is apartheid-like. The origin of this accusation is clearly in the ex–Soviet Union's anti-Zionism propaganda. Unfortunately, even former United States president Jimmy Carter in his latest book on Israel and the Palestinians has resurrected this inaccurate and prejudicial accusation.

The most vicious use of the rejected Zionism-as-racism UN resolution came in August-September 2001. It is ironic that the 9/11 attack came just three days after the end of the United Nations World Conference against Racism, Racial Discrimination, Xenophobia and Related Intolerance held in Durban, South Africa, from August 31 to September 8, 2001. The UN General Assembly goal for the conference was to "explore effective methods to eradicate racial discrimination and to promote awareness in the global struggle against intolerance."[10]

The conference was co-opted by a strange coalition of leftist groups, Arab and Muslim NGOs, Palestinian groups, and African groups, etc., all intent on proving over and over again that there was no other racism in the globe except for the racism of Jews, Israel, and the Zionists, and by definition those nations that supported Israel, such as the U.S.

American and Israeli government officials and representatives of a variety of Jewish NGOs such as Hadassah and the American Jewish Joint Distribution Fund all began to get an idea of what was going to happen a few months before the conference. The U.S. threatened to withdraw from the conference unless the antisemitic nature of the conference was altered. It was not and on September 3, U.S. secretary of state Colin Powell read:

> Today I have instructed our representatives at the World Conference Against Racism to return home. I have taken this decision with regret, because of the importance of the international fight against racism and the contribution that the Conference could have made to it. But, following discussions today by our team in Durban and others who are working for a successful conference, I am convinced that will not be possible. I know that you do not combat racism by conferences that produce declarations containing hateful language, some of which is a throwback to the days of "Zionism equals racism"; or supports the idea that we have made too much of the Holocaust; or suggests that apartheid exists in Israel; or that singles out only one country in the world—Israel—for censure and abuse.[11]

Elihai Braun noted that:

> Copies of the antisemitic work, *The Protocols of the Elders of Zion*, were sold on conference grounds; anti-Israel protesters jeered participants chanting "Zionism is racism, Israel is apartheid," and "You have Palestinian blood on your hands"; fliers depicting Hitler with the question, "What if I had won?" circulated among conference attendees. The answer: "There would be NO Israel and NO Palestinian bloodshed."[12]

On September 3, the Israeli official proclamation proclaimed:

> Racism, in all its forms, is one of the most widespread and perni-
> cious evils, depriving millions of hope and fundamental rights. It
> might have been hoped that this first Conference of the 21st cen-
> tury would have taken up the challenge of, if not eradicating racism,
> at least disarming it. But instead humanity is being sacrificed to a
> political agenda. ... Can there be a greater irony than the fact that a
> conference convened to combat the scourge of racism should give
> rise to the most racist declaration in a major international organiza-
> tion since the Second World War?[13]

In the parallel NGO conference, Jewish representatives were
harassed and treated very badly. Any attempts by Jewish delegates to
get references to antisemitism into the documents of the conference
were thwarted. In fact, the one key paragraph in the document referring to antisemitism was removed by unanimous vote. The Jewish representatives walked out. The removed paragraph read:

> We are concerned with the prevalence of anti-Zionism and attempts
> to delegitimize the State of Israel through wildly inaccurate charges
> of genocide, war crimes, crimes against humanity, ethnic cleansing
> and apartheid, as a virulent contemporary form of antisemitism
> leading to firebombing of synagogues, armed assaults against Jews,
> incitements to killing, and the murder of innocent Jews, for their
> support for the existence of the State of Israel, the assertion of the
> right to self determination of the Jewish people and the attempts,
> through the State of Israel, to preserve their cultural and religious
> identity.[14]

In the end, the NGO conference called Israel "a racist apartheid
state." The final report accused Israel of being guilty of the "systematic
perpetration of racist crimes including war crimes, acts of genocide
and ethnic cleansing." Finally, the document accused Israel of perpe-
trating "state terror against the Palestinian people."[15]

The UN high commissioner for human rights was upset about
the conflict but never rejected either the NGO document or the conference document. High-profile human rights organizations such as
Human Rights Watch, Lawyers for Human Rights, Amnesty International, Physicians for Human Rights, and a host of other organizations

endorsed the resolution of the NGO group and two days after the conference ended voiced concerns as an afterthought. Amnesty International said, "Although not accepting or condoning some of the language used within the NGO Declaration, Amnesty International accepts the declaration as a largely positive document which gives a voice to all the victims of racism wherever it occurs."[16]

Elihai Braun in a web-based review noted that the final declaration of the World Conference against Racism, Racial Discrimination, Xenophobia and Related Intolerance included the following passages relevant to Israel:

> 63. We are concerned about the plight of the Palestinian people under foreign occupation. We recognize the inalienable right of the Palestinian people to self-determination and to the establishment of an independent State and we recognize the right to security for all States in the region, including Israel, and call upon all States to support the peace process and bring it to an early conclusion;

> 64. We call for a just, comprehensive and lasting peace in the region in which all peoples shall co-exist and enjoy equality, justice and internationally recognized human rights, and security;

> 65. We recognize the right of refugees to return voluntarily to their homes and properties in dignity and safety, and urge all States to facilitate such return;

> 151. As for the situation in the Middle East, calls for the end of violence and the swift resumption of negotiations, respect for international human rights and humanitarian law, respect for the principle of self-determination and the end of all suffering, thus allowing Israel and the Palestinians to resume the peace process, and to develop and prosper in security and freedom.[17]

Anti-War Movement

In the late winter of 2003, Michael Lerner, peace activist and editor of *Tikkun* magazine, was asked not to speak at a peace rally in San Francisco because of his support for Israel. Lerner has been a lifelong supporter of the antiwar movement and a significant critic of Israeli policies regarding the Palestinians, nevertheless his rejection by the organizers of the rally was symptomatic of the growing antisemitism among the antiwar movement both in the United States and in Europe. Lerner's experience was not isolated.

Aurélie Filipetti, of the Parisian Green Party, criticized French antiwar demonstrators for creating atmosphere that encourages anit-semitism in demonstrations she helped organize in Paris. She said:

> I felt we should stop putting our head in the sand, saying that these are only fringe effects and therefore "none of our concern," which leads us to just condemn them and do nothing more.... They explained to me that the slogan "Bush and Sharon are murderers" is not antisemitism but anti-Zionism. But for me, when you burn the flag of Israel, it is antisemitism. The meaning is the delegitimation of Israel's right to exist.[18]

Recently, Professor Amnon Rubinstein wrote that the French Left is in an ironic position of trying to oppose right-wing neo-Nazism, especially from Le Pen and the National Front while at the same time not condemning it when it comes from the "oppressed world" of the Arabs. He called that "the big treason of the French Left, which came as a shock to the Jews who used to see the Left as their true friend."[19]

Cindy Sheehan, the famous mother of a young soldier killed in Iraq while he served in the U.S. armed forces, became an iconic rep-resentative of Americans opposed to the war. Camped out near Presi-dent George Bush's ranch she quickly became the darling of the media. After appearing on *Nightline* with Ted Koppel on March 14, 2005, she wrote on an Internet bulletin board the following:

> Am I emotional? Yes, my first born was murdered. Am I angry? Yes, he was killed for lies and for a PNAC Neo-Con agenda to benefit Israel. My son joined the Army to protect America, not Israel.[20]

So alarmed was a group of left-wing British academics, jour-nalists, and activists that they met at a pub across from the British Museum on Euston Road and wrote the Euston Manifesto in April 2006. Their goal was to end the growing antisemitism of the left by writing a new statement of principles for the democratic left. The Euston Manifesto says that: " 'Anti-Zionism' has now developed to a point where supposed organizations of the Left are willing to enter-tain openly antisemitic speakers and to form alliances with antisemitic groups. Amongst educated and affluent people are to be found individuals unembarrassed to claim that the Iraq war was fought on behalf of Jewish interests, or to make other 'polite' and subtle allusions to the harmful effect of Jewish influence in international or national politics — remarks of a kind that for more than fifty years after the Holocaust no one would have been able to make without publicly disgracing themselves."[21]

The Anti-Defamation League (ADL) has identified ANSWER (Act Now to Stop War and End Racism) Coalition, founded by the New York–based International Action Center (IAC) in 2001, as having played a central role in getting antisemitic, anti-Zionist, and anti-Israel sentiment into the antiwar movement.

As the ADL noted:

> In addition to claims that Israel is guilty of "war crimes" against Palestinians and that Israel is a "racist state," ANSWER events, which often attract protestors by the tens of thousands, have openly supported terror groups targeting Israelis, as well as the "resistance" fighting American forces in Iraq. This environment has led to displays of antisemitic sentiments, such as signs comparing Israeli leaders to Nazis or equating the Jewish Star of David with the Nazi swastika.

> ANSWER, which considers Israel a capitalist outpost for Western powers, has supported anyone that counters the spread of capitalism around the world, including genocidal dictators such as Saddam Hussein and Slobodan Milosovic. ANSWER sees Hezbollah and the Palestinian terror organizations as being at the forefront of the war against capitalism and American imperialism. During a July 31, 2006 interview with FOX News, ANSWER's national coordinator, Brian Becker, said: "Do I consider Hezbollah a terrorist organization? The answer is no."[22]

Antisemitism on Campus

Whether it is an Ivy League campus or state university or community college or junior college, there is a rise of anti-Jewish attacks and demonstrations taking place in the U.S., Britain, and in Europe. The irony of this rise is amazing, that at the place where ideas are sacrosanct, antisemitism is couched in terms of a critique of Israel or

Zionism or as an exposé of alternative histories or even out-and-out Holocaust denial. I have personally witnessed colleagues at a number of institutions across the United States involved in a variety of efforts that are beyond the pale. Growing use of *The Protocols of the Elders of Zion* on the campus with the accusation of Jewish involvement in global economics and world trade coupled with the accusation of Jewish involvement in the slave trade (pushed by the Nation of Islam) and Jewish control of the entertainment industry and Jewish control of banking have become the grist of courses on a number of campuses. What began as an aberrant effort in a few Departments of Ethnic Studies or African-American Studies of materials produced by Farrakhan's Nation of Islam has generated into core concepts for a number of African-American scholars who speak about the genocide of African-Americans sponsored by the Jewish community. Conspiracy theories abound on campus, with Jews, Zionists, and Israel at the heart of the conspiracy. Accusations of Jewish control of Washington have found strained legitimacy with publication of *The Israel Lobby* by John Mearsheimer and Stephen Walt in 2006.

Paid announcements in college papers denying the Holocaust from Nation of Islam speakers on campus ended the twentieth century. The twenty-first century began with anti-Israel, anti-Zionist activities on campuses which exploded exponentially after 9/11 and the U.S. attack on Iraq. Just one example—Amiri Baraka in his poem *Somebody Blew Up America* alleges that Jews blew up the World Trade Center buildings to put the blame on the Arabs. This 9/11 conspiracy has been promoted on campuses where Baraka has been an invited speaker by faculty and students.

Who is at the core of this disturbing trend, which moves from coast to coast and south to north and includes Canada, Mexico, and most of Europe as well? The core group of anti-Israel, antisemitic efforts is in part derived from faculty who grew up and were educated during the student revolts of the sixties and seventies in the United States and Europe. Having cut their teeth on Marxist ideology and Soviet antisemitic propaganda, including the canard of Zionism-as-racism, many of these faculty members have without thought regurgitated old ideas from the seventies and connected them to their interpretation of the Arab-Israeli conflict. Interestingly enough, there has been a confluence of ideas between old Marxists and old fascists centered on the issues of the Arab-Israeli conflict.

We therefore see at the heart of much of the ideologically based oratory expressed on many campuses the return of the Zionism-as-racism" debate of the seventies and the old ex-Soviet campaign attacking Zionism and the State of Israel as an apartheid state referred to earlier in this chapter. Legitimate criticism of Israel has been sidestepped by vitriolic, *ad hominum, ad populum* and quasi-logical arguments, emotionally placing the interests of downtrodden Palestinians over other discriminated groups whose only fault for not making it big on the campus is that they were not being "persecuted by Jews."

The second major force on campus for antisemitic activity are the various Arab, Islamic, and Palestinian groups that have found commonality with leftist and progressive-oriented student groups as well as some African-American and Latino student organizations. Demonstrations connected to the antiwar movement and demonstrations and speakers who solely focus on the Arab-Israeli conflict have become both forums for hate as well as catalysts for hate acts against Jewish students and campus Jewish institutions. The photograph contained in this chapter is a representation of the kind of material that often appears at these events. The impact of these student groups when coupled with the impact of a cadre of anti-Israel, anti-Zionist faculty forms a critical mass which often leads to antisemitic excesses.

The third force on the campus is the movement of college students, faculty, Arab and Muslim student groups, leftist labor groups, and outside liberal Christian groups at the forefront of the twin issues of divestiture and the anti-Israel boycott. Lessons learned from the anti-apartheid movement on the campus twenty years ago have been put into place by the organizers of the anti-Israel boycott and divestiture. Boycotts began in Great Britain with the efforts of Britain's National Association of Teachers in Further and Higher Education (NATFHE) which has approved an academic boycott on Israeli higher education institutions that do not condemn Israel's "apartheid policy." NAFTHE, which with a membership of 67,000 educators is one of the UK's largest teachers' unions, voted 106 to 71, with 21 abstentions, in favor of the boycott during a Blackpool convention.[23]

The American Association of University Professors had a major debate concerning boycotts. Its response was as follows:

> In spring 2005, the Association's Committee on Academic Freedom and Tenure, in response to a controversy that was roiling the British

academic community, approved a statement condemning academic boycotts. The statement declared that:

Since its founding in 1915, the AAUP has been committed to preserving and advancing the free exchange of ideas among academics irrespective of governmental policies and however unpalatable those policies may be viewed. We reject proposals that curtail the freedom of teachers and researchers to engage in work with academic colleagues, and we reaffirm the paramount importance of the freest possible international movement of scholars and ideas.[24]

We affirm these core principles but provide further comment on the complexities of academic boycotts and the rationale for opposing them, and we recommend responses to future proposals to participate in them.[25]

In addition, the divestiture movement on campus specifically and among a number of mainstream Protestant liberal churches shows an interesting convergence of social movements derived from the older antiapartheid movement co-opted by the quasi-logical leap of these disparate groups looking at maps of Jewish settlements used in the failed Clinton Camp David process that showed a hodgepodge of Jewish settlements interspersed among the West Bank and Gazan Palestinian villages and cities. The divestiture movement ignored the fact that Ehud Barak and the Israeli bargaining team had already recommended consolidating many of these settlements and moving Jewish populations of the West Bank and Gaza closer to defensible areas nearer to the 1948 and 1967 armistice lines and trading some Israel territory for Jewish settled Palestinian territory. These proposals from the Israeli side were rejected by Arafat in favor of a new intifada. For these campus groups and liberal churches, nothing short of full Israeli withdrawal to the 1948 lines no matter their indefensibility was critical.

Inspired in part by the activities of the Sabeel ("the way") Ecumenical Liberation Theology Center, and Arab/Christian think tank based on the antisemitic ideas of Palestinian Anglican priest, Rev. Naim Ateek, the former canon of St. George's Cathedral in Jerusalem, has become an advocate of liberation theology for the Arab world. Ateek has been accused by some of pushing a new version of the older Christian doctrine of the "teaching of contempt" rejected by Vatican II. Ateek wrote in 2000 that the Israeli government was equal to "modern-day Herods." He went on in his 2001 Easter message to say that "in this season of Lent, it seems to many of us that Jesus is on the cross again with thousands of crucified Palestinians around Him....The Israeli government crucifixion system is operating daily." In February 2001 he went on to say that Israeli occupation is like "stone placed on the entrance of Jesus' tomb. ... This boulder has shut in the Palestinians within and built structures of domination to keep them in. We have a name for this boulder. It is called the occupation."[26]

Members of the Sabeel organization have at times tried to resurrect ancient Christian anti-Jewish images in their oratory including showing Israel as a nation of baby killers and Christ killers who "block humanity's salvation."

Sabeel's efforts as well as those of a variety of leftist, liberal, and progressive student groups supported by Muslim, Arab, and Palestinian student organizations to build coalitions between liberal churches and campus groups was briefly successful, leading to attempts at divestiture at UC Berkeley, Harvard, MIT, Princeton, Cornell, the University of Michigan, the University of Illinois, and others. To date, these efforts on campuses have more or less been unsuccessful. Former Harvard president Lawrence Summers argued that the so-called divestiture campaigns were "antisemitic in effect, if not in intent."[27]

Yet at the same time the campuses were being asked to embrace divestiture and failed to do so, liberal churches were succeeding in their own divestiture movement. With the support of Nobel Peace prize winner Desmond Tutu, Sabeel, and others mentioned above, the Presbyterian USA Church voted in 2004 to divest in Israel, asserting that the "occupation" was "at the root of evil acts." The World Council of Churches followed in 2005, and the United Church of Christ and the New England Conference of the United Methodist Church followed in 2005. The Methodists voted to divest funds in a resolution that said:

- Whereas the United Methodist Church should not profit from the illegal Israeli occupation of Palestinian land or the destruction of Palestinian homes, orchards, and lives,

- Whereas we are committed to ensuring that our denomination's money is used in a manner consistent with our beliefs, with international law, and with Christ's teaching.[28]

Antisemitism from the left on campus is showing signs of a convergence of heretofore competing and conflicting groups, including

Marxist faculty looking for a cause, faculty who became politically active during the seventies student revolts either in Europe or the United States, students who formed early bonds with the Nation of Islam or with Arab and Palestinian student groups, and left-leaning church groups embracing the apartheid issues regarding Israel and the growing anti-war movement on campuses.

In November 2005, after a briefing hearing before the United States Commission on Civil Rights, the following report was released. Based on the record, the commission adopted findings and recommendations on April 3, 2006. The commission found that:

> Many college campuses throughout the United States continue to experience incidents of antisemitism, a serious problem warranting further attention.
>
> - When severe, persistent, or pervasive, this behavior may constitute a hostile environment for students in violation of Title VI of the Civil Rights Act of 1964.
>
> - Anti-Israeli or anti-Zionist propaganda has been disseminated on many campuses that include traditional antisemitic elements, including age-old anti-Jewish stereotypes and defamation.
>
> - Antisemitic bigotry is no less morally deplorable when camouflaged as anti-Israelism or anti-Zionism.
>
> - Substantial evidence suggests that many university departments of Middle East studies provide one-sided, highly polemical academic presentations and some may repress legitimate debate concerning Israel.
>
> - Many college students do not know what rights and protections they have against antisemitic behavior.
>
> - More data are required to determine the full extent of this problem. While the Department of Education's Office of Postsecondary Education (OPE) requires recipient institutions to report hate crimes involving bodily injury, these institutions are not currently required to report many crimes that do not involve bodily injury.

Based on these findings, the commission recommended that:

> - OCR should protect college students from antisemitic and other discriminatory harassment by vigorously enforcing Title VI against recipients that deny equal educational opportunities to all students.

- University leadership should ensure that all academic departments, including departments of Middle East studies, maintain academic standards, respect intellectual diversity, and ensure that the rights of all students are fully protected.

- Federal grant-making institutions should exercise appropriate oversight to ensure that federal funds are not used in a manner that supports discriminatory conduct.

- OCR should conduct a public education campaign to inform college students of the rights and protections afforded to them under federal civil rights laws, including the right of Jewish students to be free from antisemitic harassment.

- Congress should direct OPE to collect and report data on a broader range of antisemitic and other hate crimes that take place at postsecondary institutions consistent with the hate crime categories reported by the Federal Bureau of Investigation under the Hate Crimes Statistics Act.

- OPE should collect and report data by category of prejudice as well as category of crime.

- Congress should amend Title VI to make clear that discrimination on the basis of Jewish heritage constitutes prohibited national origin discrimination.[29]

Finally, the commission agreed to undertake a public education campaign to inform students of the protections available to them against antisemitic harassment or intimidation.

The findings of the U.S. Commission echo the findings of the various EEC commissions on antisemitism and represent a significant indictment of universities in the both the United States and Europe. Hate on campus, whether from the left or from the right, is an egregious violation of what should be an environment of ideas and openness.

Anti-World Trade Organization, Anti–Free Trade, and Anti–World Bank Movement and the Environmental/Green Movement

Again, convergence of disparate groups from both the left and the right, from extremists of all shades, is coming together over free trade, the World Trade Organization, the World Bank, and a variety of environmental issues to form a loosely configured social movement tied by a common hatred of Jews, Zionism, and Israel. Groups as widely distributed as Nathan Hales' World Church of the Creator, an antisemitic group connected to the murder and wounding of a number of Jewish Americans and other minorities of color who said of the 1999 anti-WTO protests in Seattle that they were shutting down "the talks of the Jew World Order,"[30] to a number of extreme anti-vivisectionist groups who target kashrut [kosher] organizations over the issue of ritual slaughter of animals, have found common ground in attacking Jews, Judaism, Zionism, and Israel.[31]

The green parties in much of the ex–Soviet Union are made up of retrograde Communist Party members. According to a recent Rand Corporation report, many of these green party organizations have become a central flash point for antisemitic activities in the guise of environmental concerns or out of sympathy with the plight of Palestinians.[32] Antisemitism has not only been the *bete noir* of the ex–Soviet Union green parties but also of a number of Western European and even U.S. green party political organizations. The German Green Party has over the last decade been involved in a number of instances where environmental and poverty issues have been co-opted by unreflective Green Party support for Palestinian causes where Israel and Jews are often connected to the Nazis. In essence, Israel, Zionism, and Jews in general are lumped together as evil and Palestinians are viewed as only good. This kind of simplistic generalization is based on an *allness error* that is often at the heart of prejudice and hate.

In the last presidential election, independent presidential candidate and former Green Party presidential candidate Ralph Nader echoed *The Protocols of the Elders of Zion* and numerous anti-Jewish cartoons in the Arab press by saying on C-Span at a conference, The Muslim Vote in Election 2004, that:

> What has been happening over the years is a predictable routine of foreign visitation from the head of the Israeli government. The Israeli puppeteer travels to Washington. The Israeli puppeteer meets with the puppet in the White House, and then moves down Pennsylvania Avenue, and meets with the puppets in Congress. And then takes back billions of taxpayer dollars. It is time for the Washington puppet show to be replaced by the Washington peace show.[33]

This accusation of Israel being the puppet master is vintage antisemitic oratory which clearly says that Israel and the Jewish community control the United States. This idea is at the core of much of anti-Jewish imagery and activity globally. That it is acceptable to a presidential candidate is disturbing. It also echoes the antisemitic words of the Malaysian prime minister, Mahathir Mohamad, in his speech to the tenth Islamic summit in October 2003.

It is true that although Nader no longer represented the Green Party when he spoke those words, they nevertheless represent a portion of the environmental movement and the anti–free trade movement in the U.S. Nader in fact represents the cojoining of the environmentalists and the anti–free trade social movements.

While it must be said that antisemitism represents only a fraction of the people who support both the environmental and the anti-free trade movements. Generally, both movements and their potential convergence are based on issues which are not in any way related to antisemitism. Nevertheless, a strong and vocal minority with spokespersons such as Ralph Nader represent a growing and alarming trend.

In conclusion, I have attempted to show in this chapter that there indeed is a growing symbolic convergence within the left of an anti-Jewish, anti-Zionist, anti-Israel perspective based on innuendo, half truth, and outright falsehood. There are groups that would not have spoken to each other in decades past now meeting and talking and even forming public policy based on such forgeries as *The Protocols of the Elders of Zion*; who form opinions about Jews, Jewish Israelis, and Jewish nationalism based on the thinnest of evidence.

Eric Hoffer in his work on mass movements, *The True Believer*, noted that hate is one of the truest unifiers of mass movements.

> Mass movements can rise and spread without belief in a God, but never without belief in a devil. Usually the strength of a mass movement is proportionate to the vividness and tangibility of its devil. When Hitler was asked whether he thought the Jew must be destroyed, he answered: "No....We should have then to invent him. It is essential to have a tangible enemy, not merely an abstract one."[34]

One aspect of the left continues to follow in the footsteps of the ex–Soviet Union in choosing Israel and Zionism as its devil. For the Jewish community this choice is painful because many in the Jewish community would like to continue to support the issues important for the left. Nevertheless, there is evidence as I point out that there is now a symbolic convergence of disparate groups coalescing around the idea that Israel, Zionism, and the Jews are the devil and are antithetical to the values and motivations of the left. Movements can be changed by countermovements. It is time for those of us who have been in the left or who are currently in the left to fight against this growing trend to unify based on the hatred of Jews and Israel.

Notes

1. Forward to Alvin Rosenfeld, *Progressive Jewish Thought and the New Antisemitism* (New York: American Jewish Committee, December 2006).

2. Chaim Potok, *Wanderings* (New York: Fawcett Crest, 1978), pp. 482–83.

3. "On the Jewish Question Karl Marx, February, 1844," in *Deutsch-Französische Jahrbücher*; http://www.marxists.org/archive/marx/works/1844/jewish-question/

4. Eliyahu Biletsky, *Libel: Zionism =Racism* (Tel Aviv: Amal Publishing, 1979), p. 63.

5. Ibid., pp. 64–65.

6. Ibid., p. 66.

7. Ibid., p. 69.

8. Ibid., pp. 70–71

9. Ibid., pp. 71–72.

10. Elihai Braun, an editor of the Jewish Virtual Library: http://www.jewishvirtuallibrary.org/jsource/UN/durban1.html

11. Statement by Secretary of State Colin L. Powell, World Conference against Racism, U.S. State Department, Washington, DC, September 3, 2001.

12. Jewish Virtual Library: http://www.jewishvirtuallibrary.org/jsource/UN/durban1.html

13. Statement by Rabbi Michael Melchior, deputy foreign minister of the state of Israel, Israel Ministry of Foreign Affairs, Durban, September 2001.

14. ADL http://www.adl.org/durban/durban_090401d.asp

15. Ibid.

16. Ibid.

17. Declaration, UN World Conference against Racism, Racial Discrimination, Xenophobia and Related Intolerance, September 8, 2001.

18. http://www.nrg.co.il/online/archive/ART/466/162.html

19. http://www.nrg.co.il/online/1/ART/768/168.html

20. http://groups.google.com/group/bullyard/msg/7f523b1a73be1a36?hl=en

21. http://en.wikipedia.org/wiki/New_antisemitism#_note-euston#_note-euston

22. http://www.adl.org/Israel/answer.asp

23. http://www.zionism-israel.com/log/archives/00000081.html

24. http://www.aaup.org/AAUP/pubsres/academe/2006/SO/Boycott/OnAcademicBoycotts.htm#1

25. http://www.aaup.org/AAUP/pubsres/academe/2006/SO/Boycott/OnAcademicBoycotts.htm

26. http://www.juf.org/news_public_affairs/article.asp?key=6398

27. Ibid.

28. http://www.neumc.org/news_detail.asp?TableName=oNews_PJAYMY&PKValue=60

29. http://www.usccr.gov/pubs/081506campusantibrief07.pdf

30. http://www.sourcewatch.org/index.php?title=New_World_Order; http://forum.skadi.net/hates_jews_now6284.html?s=0deb7966b717f6245030c96aeafb168b&p=65753

31. http://www.adl.org/Anti_semitism/holocaust_imagery_ar.asp

32. http://www.rand.org/pubs/commercial_books/CB367/chap7.pdf

33. http://www.cnionline.org/hearings/muslims/transcript.htm

34. Eric Hoffer, *The True Believer* (New York: Harper & Row, 1951), p. 91

Section VI
Israel and Contemporary Antisemitism

No issue is quite as complex or as problematic as the contemporary relationship between criticism of the state of Israel and antisemitism. What precisely is the dividing line between legitimate criticism warranted as it may be and antisemitism. Defenders of Israel flounder when they cannot distinguish between the two, and many of Israel's most ardent supporters hurl this accusation at anyone with whose criticism they take issue They consider all or most criticisms of Israel by non-Jews as antisemitic and criticism offered by Jews, especially on the left, as a manifestation of self-hatred, which is often pathological.

In the two essays that follow two veteran Zionist thinkers grapple with this issue from very different perspectives. We would do well to remember the definition of antisemitism offered by David Berger, as quoted by Jerome Chanes:

> Antisemitism means either of the following: (1) hostility toward Jews as a group that results from no legitimate cause or greatly exceeds any reasonable, ethical response to genuine provocation; or (2) a pejorative perception of Jewish physical or moral traits that is either utterly groundless or a result of irrational generalization and exaggeration." However one defines antisemitism, one point must be kept in mind: antisemitism presupposes that the Jews are radically "other." This simple central point is a universal, timeless characteristic of antisemitism.[1]

Richard L. Rubenstein rejects the notion that opposition to contemporary Israel can be explained merely by antisemitism. He writes that "Explaining hostility to Jews or Israel by means of a term connoting hostility is tautologous." Hatred is explained by hatred. Instead he advocates that to understand the response to contemporary Israel, one must address the enduring power of religion and myth to shape the opinions of even the most secularized of men and women. Borrowing Stephen R. Haynes is concept of Jews as the "witness people," those who must endure to bear witness to Jesus Christ, he argues, "constitutes a singularly important component in the hostile, emotionally charged response of a number of contemporary Europeans and their government officials to Israel and to the Jews." Rubenstein also reintroduces the concept of "cognitive dissonance" that has been central to his understanding of the role of Jews in the world. The ongoing presence of Jews challenges the Christian narrative, but since Paul of Tarsus, the Jews, or at least a remnant thereof, must remain to bear witness that Christ is the savior, Rubenstein argues. Dissonance reduction is one strategy for dealing with such cognitive dissonance; elimination of the disconfirming other is a more radical strategy. Jewish defeat, Rubenstein argues, was seen in Christian thought as a manifestation of divine disfavor. How then was the Christian world, even in its most secularized form, to deal with Jewish victory?

The focus on Israel, the disproportionate interest and accusations against Israel, Rubenstein argues is "certainly evident in the response of the Christian West to Israel. Unfortunately, it also often involves the ascription of demonological qualities to Israel that arouses anger and a distaste of a deeper sort than that felt against other nations and groups whose policies are looked upon with disfavor."

The Muslim world, long accustomed to Jews as *dhimmis,* resident aliens, also has no theological way of coming to terms with a victorious Israel. Muslim rage is fueled by defeat. It is joined by those who have "pre-critically and unconsciously," to use Haynes's term, internalized the "witness myth." Rubenstein cautions that even Israel's most ardent Christian supporters manifestly link their support to the Jews' role as witnesses in the end of days to the Savior. "Only Israel's determination may enable them to craft an alternative narrative."

Manfred Gerstenfeld argues as well for the continuity between antisemitism and anti-Zionism and the prevalence of antisemitism in some—but by no means all—critiques of Israeli policy. Borrowing from former Soviet prisoner and Israeli politician Natan Sharansky, Gerstenfeld suggests that the dividing line between antisemitism and opposition to the policies of the state of Israel—legitimate or illegitimate as they may be—is demonization, double standards, and delegimization.

He briefly sketches the post-Holocaust history of antisemitism. Reviled at the manifestations of antisemitism in the Holocaust, Europe imposed a taboo regarding the expression of antisemitism within Europe, and a taboo on expressing the feeling of antagonism toward the Jew. The taboo was on expressions of antisemitism and on expressions of antisemitic feelings. Naturally, no one could declare the actual feelings taboo and one can debate the degree to which antisemitic feelings vanished or were merely suppressed. The latent hatred, Gerstenfeld argues, remained but could not quite be expressed.

In the immediate aftermath of the Holocaust, the image of the Jew had been transformed into the victim par excellence, but this transformation was shattered by Israel's great victory in the Six-Day War and one gradually saw the emergence of a new image, the victim as victimizer.

Gerstenfeld stresses the continuity between classical antisemitism and its contemporary manifestations. In an age of acute nationalism, the Jews were regarded as an alien element; in an age of racism, the Jews as racially inferior, and in an age, such as ours of universalism, the Jews have been portrayed as particularistic. Consistent throughout the various garbs of anti-Jewish hatred has been the process of demonization, isolation, and elimination.

Cartoons, Gerstenfeld maintains, are a popular form of characterization that depend for their effectiveness on the immediacy by which their content can be grasped and the speed at which audience can identify with the images. Thus, Gerstenfeld's analysis of contemporary cartoons presents manifold instances in which the Jew is portrayed as the embodiment of evil, the devil incarnate. One even observes within the Muslim community, where the themes should be alien, the image of Jew as deicide and the suggestion that Israel is behind all disasters from poisoning children to the AIDS epidemic, from responsibility for the 9/11 bombings to the attacks on the Shiite mosque in Samarra. Familiar images from an earlier time reappear regarding the Jewish quest for world domination and their ferocious lust for money.

Notes

1.   David Berger, "Antisemitism: An Overview," in David Berger, ed., *History and Hate: The Dimensions of Antisemitism*, p. 3.

16

The Witness-People Myth, Israel, and Anti-Zionism in the Western World

Richard L. Rubenstein

In May 2003 the YIVO Institute for Jewish Research sponsored an international conference in New York City on the topic of Old Demons, New Debates: Antisemitism in the West. More than thirty internationally recognized "scholars, journalists and public intellectuals from Europe, Israel and North America" offered their views on the revival of antisemitism, especially in Europe, that has accompanied the conflict in the Middle East.[1] The stellar group offered much insight into the renewal of an ancient hatred. Nevertheless, one subject was largely absent, namely, the continuing power of *religion and myth* to shape the opinions of many men and women of Christian inheritance on Israel and Zionism. There was some discussion of the Christian right's support of Israel, but little discussion of the power of the traditional Christian narrative to shape thinking and decision-making about Jews and Israel even among secularized persons of Christian inheritance.

If I may begin with a personal note, I explored that issue in my first published book, *After Auschwitz,* and have continued the pursuit of that subject throughout my career.[2] However, in this essay I have chosen to use the findings of a Protestant theologian, Stephen R. Haynes, who has insightfully explored the question in his book, *Reluctant Witnesses: Jews and the Christian Imagination.*[3] Haynes has written about the "witness-people myth" and its derivatives, "witness-people thinking, doctrine, theory, and theology." Haynes has described the myth as "the belief that whatever happens to the Jews, for good or ill, is an expression of God's providential justice and, as such, is a sign 'for God's church.'"[4] According to Haynes, the witness-people myth is "a deep

293

structure in the Christian imagination...a complex of ideas and symbols that, often *pre-critically* and *unconsciously*, informs ideas about Jews among persons who share a cultural heritage."[5] Admittedly, the term "Christian imagination" is an abstraction. Nevertheless, Haynes employs it and similar terms, such as the "Christian mind," quite legitimately to convey the persistence, durability, and universality of the myth. According to Haynes, "Jews must always be special cases in products of the Christian imagination, because of the uniquely ambivalent place which the Jewish people inhabit there."[6] Haynes also notes that this is also true of Israel as a nation among nations. As we shall see, this insight goes a long way to explain Christian attitudes toward contemporary Israel. In agreement with Haynes, it is my thesis that the witness-people thinking constitutes a singularly important component in the hostile, emotionally charged response of large numbers of contemporary Europeans and their government officials to the conflict between Israel and the Palestinians.

Among the ideas Haynes identifies as characteristic of "witness-people thinking" are the following:

(a) *Jews are an important sign* because of the extent to which "their fate is profoundly significant for Christians."[7]

(b) Nevertheless, *the Jews are an ambivalent sign.* Although sometimes obscured by bitterly hostile Christian rhetoric, Christianity never rejected belief in the election of Israel or its role as heir of divine promises. The theological dispute between Christianity and Judaism has always been over the role of Christ in determining which community could rightfully claim to be the elect community and, as such, heir to the divine promises.[8]

(c) *The witness-people myth gives rise to a diversity of thought-forms.* While the witness-people myth may predispose Christians to scapegoat Jews and embrace beliefs such as the blood-libel or the notion that Jews conspire to undermine or destroy Christendom, especially in times of social crisis, the same myth is also the source of "positive" mythic conceptions of the Jewish people.

(d) *The witness-people myth and Christian anti-Judaism are inseparable but not identical.* Haynes insists on the *ambivalent* character of the "witness-people myth" as distinguished from outright, unmitigated antisemitism that regards Jews as a danger so unrelieved of redeeming characteristics that they must be eliminated either by expulsion or extermination. While fully cognizant of the Christian religious roots of antisemitism, Haynes argues that both preservationist and eliminationist components co-exist within the myth. It is for that reason that the Jews, alone among the Roman Empire's non-Christians, survived within Christendom until the French Revolution. Nevertheless, Haynes insists that the myth is "... more ambivalent and more subtle in its pernicious effects than pure Jew-hatred."[9] Haynes takes issue with theologian Rosemary Ruether's insistence on the essential continuity of medieval and modern antisemitism and agrees with scholars such as Yosef Yerushalmi, Eugene Fisher and others that Ruether's position fails to account for the millennial survival of Jews within Christendom. Their criticism seems fully justified to me. The descendants of Europe's Jews are alive today largely because the Christian Church, however grudgingly, permitted their ancestors to survive.

(e) Hence, under certain conditions the witness-people myth places a positive value on Jewish survival. According to the myth, the Jews still have a role to play in world history. Whatever tribulations the Jews have endured or will endure are but a prelude to their ultimate affirmation of the Christian narrative that Christ is Lord. In reality, that is their *raison d'être*.

The roots of the myth are to be found in the biblical belief that God has chosen Israel as his people, bestowing upon her a covenant and stipulating that fidelity to the covenant would be rewarded by divine protection, as surely as infidelity would be harshly punished. The early Christians did not reject belief in the election of Israel. They did, however, claim that election had passed to the infant church rather than the synagogue and that they, rather than the rabbis and Pharisees, truly understood what constituted fidelity to the covenant. Nevertheless, the early Christians could not ignore Jewish "unbelief" and felt compelled to offer reasons for rejecting the older Jewish claims of election. If the Jews could not be convinced of the error of their ways, it was important that a credible account of their refusal be offered.

This writer has long held that the *theory of cognitive dissonance* in social psychology sheds much light on the ways in which each of the religious communities dealt with rival claims.[10] The theory also illuminates the necessity of the witness-people myth for Christianity and the difficulty of doing away with it. Both Judaism and Christianity have historically regarded their distinct narratives of God's action in history as indispensable for group existence and survival. Nonetheless, all historical events rely for their credibility on the slender reed of testimony and memory. Any group whose existence is founded upon a narrative of God's action in history will regard as dangerous those who explicitly or implicitly challenge that narrative. According to cognitive dissonance theory, if a person or a group has an important stake in an item of information, such as the report of an historical event, that does not fit together psychologically with a second item of information, such as a plausible denial of the same event, the person or group will attempt to make the dissonant items consistent with each other, a process known as *dissonance reduction*.[11]

Dissonance reduction is one of the theologian's most important tasks. An obvious method of dissonance reduction is to discredit or defame the source of disconfirmation. An even more radical method would be to eliminate the *disconfirming other* altogether. As is well known, such methods have been employed in the history of religion. Nevertheless, one must bear in mind that the fundamental motive for even the most abusive attempts at dissonance reduction has been the defense of values or beliefs perceived to be indispensable to the survival of one's own community.

It is my belief that in its formative stages, the witness-people myth played an important role in teachings of Paul of Tarsus. Consider the situation of the early church less than a generation after the departure of Jesus of Nazareth. The infant church was united in the belief that the crucifixion of a charismatic Galilean Jewish religious leader was the prelude to his resurrection and ascension to heaven as humanity's Savior. Although this belief was fervently held by the Christians of his time, Paul frankly acknowledged that it stretched the limits of credibility for those upon whom the Christian faith had not been bestowed. Thus, he wrote:

> For the message about the cross is foolishness to those who are perishing but to us who are being saved it is the power of God....For the Jews demand signs and Greeks desire wisdom, but we proclaim Christ crucified, *a stumbling block to Jews and foolishness to Gentiles*. (I Cor. 1: 19–24, italics added)

Moreover, as firm as was their belief, the early Christians were a mis-sionizing minority in an overwhelmingly non-Christian world. If they were to convert outsiders and prevent their own flock from apostasy, they could not entirely ignore that world or what was being said about their beliefs in it. In either case, dissonance reduction was called for.

Of all the unbelievers, none were as important as the Jews. By their kinship with Jesus and their scripturally validated credentials, Jews were, unfortunately, Christianity's most important *disconfirming others*. Jews could argue that their understanding of Scripture was author-itative, that Jesus was one of them, and that they knew him better than those Gentiles who claimed him as their savior. They could also reject as spurious the claim of Gentile Christians to be the new Israel and they could appeal to the inherent skepticism of ordinary people by casting doubt on the resurrection narrative.

It was therefore necessary for the infant Church to rebut any pos-sible Jewish arguments. Since the disagreement was about events that God was purported to have brought about on the stage of history, the most potent Christian argument was the painful historical fate of the Jews. Paul could not use that argument as effectively as could his suc-cessors because he passed from the scene before the fall of Jerusalem and the destruction of the Temple in 70 CE. We can, however, discern an early Christian use of the fall of Jerusalem to rebut Jewish claims of election and divine favor in the parable of the Great Supper (Matt. 22:1–14), in all likelihood written ca. 90 CE. In the parable, a king is depicted as sending servants to invite guests to "a marriage feast for his son." When the guests refuse to come, the king sends other servants to repeat the invitation. They are abused and murdered, whereupon the "king was angry and sent his troops and destroyed those murderers and burned their city." The parable is clearly an allegory reflecting the Christian view of the Judeo-Roman War of 66–70 CE in which the fall of Jerusalem is depicted as divine punishment of the Jews' rejection of Jesus and their alleged responsibility for his crucifixion. Indeed, what better argument could Christians offer for the claim that Christ was the *telos,* the end, of the Law, than the destruction of the very Temple in which the sacrifices stipulated in the Torah were carried out? Was not the destruction of the Temple, they argued, a sign that the Law had been fulfilled in Christ?

Ironically, the survival of Jews and Judaism in Christendom for two millennia, dangerous, harsh, and degrading as it was at times, owes much to Paul of Tarsus. Had Christians regarded the destruction of the Temple unambiguously as divine punishment meted out to an allegedly deicidal people, Jews might have disappeared as did the Cathari or Albigensians, heretics of the first decades of the thirteenth century. Jews would have survived only as an object lesson of the fate of sinners in Christian memory. In Paul's interpretation, Jewish "unbelief" is seen as part of God's redemptive plan for humanity. He argued that sooner or later, Israel will see the light and her conversion will be a supreme event in humanity's salvation. Once Israel is "saved," at least representationally, the final sequence of eschatological events will commence: Christ will return. The dead will be resurrected and Christ will then hand over the kingdom to God the Father, "having done away with every sovereignty, authority and power" (1 Cor. 15:25). (One can discern echoes of Paul's explanation in the contemporary Christian right's motives for supporting Israel.)

With Paul's explanation of Israel's "unbelief," witness-people thinking became an inescapable and ineradicable part of Christian thinking and some measure of Jewish survival became a theological imperative for Christianity. There was, however, a price to be paid, one that Jews continue to pay to this day. An important element in that price is that in the perennial Christian narrative, unbelieving Jews are always destined to lose *unless and until* they accept Christ as their Savior. As noted above, from the time of the fall of Jerusalem, Jewish defeat has historically been understood in Christian thought as supremely important *evidence* that Christ is Lord and Savior. Whenever Jews openly or implicitly challenged Christian belief, Christians could and did make the claim that Jewish suffering and defeat is both divinely inflicted punishment and proof that Christ is the Messiah and Redeemer.

We see this, for example, in the dialogue of Justin Martyr (ca. 100–160 CE) with a rabbinic Jew that has been preserved in his *Dialogue With Trypho*, written shortly after the Roman victory in the Judeo-Roman War of 132–35 CE. Referring to circumcision, Justin says to his Jewish interlocutor:

> [It] was given for a sign . . . that you alone suffer what you now justly suffer; and that your land may be desolate, and your cities burned with fire; and that strangers may eat your fruit in your presence, and not one of you may go up to Jerusalem.[12]

A harsher version of the same argument is found in Martin Luther's "Concerning the Jews and Their Lies" (1543) in which Luther counseled Christians who enter into dialogue with Jews to offer the following proof of Jewish "error":

> ...do not say any more than this: "Listen, Jew, are you aware that Jerusalem and your sovereignty, together with your temple and priesthood, have been destroyed for over 1,460 years?" ... *For such ruthless wrath of God is sufficient evidence that they assuredly have gone astray*.... this work of wrath is proof that the Jews, surely rejected by God, are no longer his people, and neither is he any longer their God....[13]

The Holocaust was the supreme example of Jewish defeat. It eventually led to a rethinking but not necessarily to an abandonment of the witness-people myth among Christian thinkers. In the early postwar years, some Christian leaders saw the Holocaust as yet another example of divine punishment.[14] Even Karl Barth, arguably the greatest Protestant theologian of the twentieth century and a consistent opponent of both antisemitism and National Socialism, interpreted the Holocaust through the prism of the witness-people myth. In 1942, Barth reproved a stricken Jewish community for failing to understand the Holocaust as divinely inflicted for its *willful* refusal to believe in the lordship of Christ. He wrote, "There is no doubt that Israel hears; now less than ever, can it shelter behind the pretext of ignorance and inability to understand. But Israel hears—and does not believe."[15] Barth clearly saw the Holocaust as a divine visitation that had stripped the Jews of any possible excuse for "unbelief." Barth was well informed about what was happening to Europe's Jews and wrote neither in malice nor ignorance.[16] Four years after the Nazi surrender, Barth continued to suggest that the evil that came to the Jewish people was "a result of their unfaithfulness," that the Jew "pays for the fact that he is the elect of God," and that the Jewish people are "no more than the shadow of a nation, the reluctant witnesses of the Son of God and the Son of Man."[17]

Barth's interpretation of the Holocaust was no different than that of the overwhelming majority of German religious leaders. Nor could they or most European churchmen regard as legitimate the Zionist project of creating a Jewish homeland. As is well known, the Zionist project arose out of desperation in the face of the increasingly apparent failure of the civic emancipation of the Jews and their assimilation within their host countries in Europe. As a skilled journalistic observer and an assimilated Jew, Theodor Herzl, the father of political Zionism, came to understand long before the rise of National Socialism that the Jews of Europe were fated for elimination. Partly as a result of reporting on the 1894 trial of Capt. Alfred Dreyfus and witnessing his subsequent degradation on January 5, 1895, accompanied by the shouts of the Parisian mob, "Death to the Jews," Herzl became convinced that only mass emigration and resettlement in a territory of their own could save Europe's Jews. He devoted the rest of his life to the realization of that objective.

There was much that was problematic in Herzl's thinking, but his prescience concerning the impending doom awaiting Europe's Jews is undeniable.[18] Herzl's analysis of the Jewish situation was political and social rather than theological. Although he recognized the desirability of Palestine as the location of his proposed Jewish state, he briefly considered part of Argentina or Canada and even Uganda. By contrast, both the Orthodox Jewish and Christian responses to his proposed state were overwhelmingly theological. Agudat Israel, the most important Orthodox group, opposed any attempt to revive Jewish nationhood in the land of Israel through human agency.

The influence of the witness-people myth is especially evident in one of the earliest authoritative Roman Catholic responses to Zionism. In 1897, four months before the First Zionist Conference was held in Basel, Switzerland, the authoritative Jesuit journal *Civiltà Cattolica* published its first comment on the Zionist project:

> 1827 years have passed since the prediction of Jesus of Nazareth was fulfilled, namely that Jerusalem would be destroyed...that the Jews would be led away to be slaves among all the nations, and that they would remain in the dispersion till the end of the world...According to Sacred Scriptures, the Jewish people must always live dispersed and wandering among the other nations, so that they may render witness not only by the Scriptures...but by their very existence. As for a rebuilt Jerusalem, which would become the center of a reconstituted state of Israel, we must add that this is contrary to the prediction of Christ Himself.[19]

Articles and editorials of *Civiltà Cattolica* were vetted by the cardinal secretary of state before publication and reflected official Vatican opinion. The editorial remains one of the most succinct statements of conservative Catholic position on the subject. At the time, the journal published numerous articles testifying to the "veracity" of the blood libel, the accusation that Jews murdered Christian children in order to use their blood in their Passover rites, a hideous parody on the sacrament of Holy Communion.[20]

On January 25, 1904, Pope Pius X granted Theodor Herzl an audience in which he sought the pope's support for Zionism. The pope replied:

> We are unable to favor this movement. We cannot prevent the Jews from going to Jerusalem—but we could never sanction it. The ground of Jerusalem, if it were not always sacred, has been sanctified by the life of Jesus Christ. As the head of the Church I cannot answer you otherwise. The Jews have not recognized our Lord, therefore we cannot recognize the Jewish people.[21]

The pope then mentioned his friendly personal relations with Jews in his home city of Mantua. He told Herzl: "There are other bonds than those of religion: social intercourse, for example, and philanthropy. Such bonds we do not refuse to maintain with the Jews." Nevertheless, he was not prepared to compromise on his tradition, the Church's view of what it regarded as the divinely ordained fate of the Jews.

The prospect of a Jewish state in Palestine struck an ancient and sensitive chord in Vatican circles. When Pope Urban II summoned the First Crusade in 1095, the idea was prevalent that Palestine was Christ's patrimony. In addition to summoning the knights of Western Europe to a Holy War, the pope summoned the Crusaders to a vendetta, a very familiar enterprise for knights of the period, to avenge Christ, who had been crucified and "banished from his estates" and who still cried out "desolate and begging for aid."[22] When on November 2, 1917, Arthur James Balfour, the British foreign secretary, wrote to Baron Lionel Walter Rothschild that the British government looked with favor on "the establishment in Palestine of a national home for the Jewish people," the Vatican was fearful that control of "Christ's patrimony" would revert to the Jews.[23] That fear was intensified when British troops led by Gen. Edmund Allenby captured Jerusalem on December 9, 1917.

Over the centuries the Christian churches, both Orthodox and Latin, had achieved a *modus vivendi* concerning Palestine with the Ottoman Empire. The conquest of Palestine by Protestant England, which had made a qualified promise to the Jews of a "national home," did not sit well in Rome.

British control of Palestine as the mandatory power required the approval of the League of Nations, and the Vatican began a vigorous diplomatic campaign to prevent the creation of an organized Zionist community in Palestine. Typical of the Vatican opposition to a Zionist establishment was the speech delivered by Pope Benedict XV on March 10, 1919: Referring to the holy places, it read in part:

> Who can ever tell the full story of the efforts of Our Predecessors to free them from the dominion of the infidels, the heroic deeds and blood shed by the Christians of the West through the centuries? And now that, amid the rejoicing of all good men, they have finally returned into the hands of Christians, Our anxiety is most keen as to the decisions which the Peace Congress at Paris is soon to take concerning them. For surely it would be a terrible grief for US and for all the Christian faithful if infidels were placed in a privileged and prominent position; much more if these most holy sanctuaries of the Christian religion were given into the charge of non-Christians.[24]

Several days later, Pietro Cardinal Gaspari, papal secretary of state and mentor of Eugenio Pacelli, who succeeded to the papacy in 1939 as Pope Pius XII, explained the pope's words to a Belgian diplomat: "The danger we most fear is the establishment of a Jewish state in Palestine. We would have found nothing wrong in Jews entering that country, and setting up agricultural colonies. But that they have been given rule over the Holy Places is intolerable for Christians."[25]

The Vatican's antipathy to a Jewish settlement in Palestine continued throughout World War II. In March 1943, Archbishop Angelo Roncalli, apostolic delegate to Turkey and later Pope John XXIII, transmitted a request from the Jewish Agency for Palestine that the Vatican intervene with the Slovak government to permit one thousand Jewish children to emigrate to Palestine. The archbishop indicated that the British were willing to let the children enter Palestine. Archbishop William Godfrey, apostolic delegate to the United Kingdom, sent a similar message the same day, but referred to the settlement of Jewish children from all of Europe. The requests were handled by Mgr. Domenico Tardini, who exhibited some interest in the proposal to rescue the Jewish children from Slovakia, but the idea of endorsing the settlement of Jews in Palestine gave him pause. Tardini wrote:

> The Holy See has never approved the project of making Palestine a Jewish home. But unfortunately England does not yield....And the question of the Holy Places? Palestine is by this time more sacred for Catholics than... for Jews.[26]

In his response to Archbishop Godfrey, Luigi Cardinal Maglione, cardinal secretary of state, also expressed strong opposition to a Jewish majority in Palestine. He repeated the claim that the land of Palestine was sacred to Catholics because it was the land of Christ. If Palestine were to become predominantly Jewish, Maglione maintained, Catholic piety would be offended. Maglione also instructed Archbishop Amleto Cicognani, the apostolic delegate in Washington, to communicate his views to President Roosevelt. As one of wartime Europe's best-informed foreign secretaries, Maglione had no illusions concerning the fate of Jewish children under Nazi control. Clearly, the Vatican in the twentieth century continued to take a political stand on Palestine on the basis of a religious position at least as old as the First Crusade, namely, the idea that Palestine was Christ's patrimony.

In opposing the establishment of a Jewish state, the Vatican's leaders were fully cognizant of the extent to which their views were theologically motivated. The same cannot be said of the endemic bias against Israel that characterizes mainstream public opinion and official policy in contemporary Europe. Much has been written of late concerning the revival of antisemitism in France, but that country is by no means alone. Extreme expressions of hostility toward Israel and support of the Palestinian cause are pervasive in the media throughout Western and Central Europe. Elsewhere in this volume, some of the many obscenely antisemitic cartoons that have become commonplace in so-called "respectable" European newspapers and journals are cited.[27] Indeed, in their ability to oversimplify, mass media cartoons have long been one of the most effective means of demonizing Jews and fostering antisemitism.

Most European diplomats and political leaders usually express their distaste for Israel with greater finesse than the cartoonists, but the effects of their hostility are potentially deadlier. In the essay to which I allude above, I also cite the incident in which the late Daniel

Bernard, ambassador of France to the United Kingdom, referred to Israel as "that shitty little country" that has put "the world in danger of World War Three."[28] Nor was Barnard the only diplomat who suggested that Israel or at least its leader was responsible for the crisis. Two weeks after 9/11, a "senior British Foreign Office source" was quoted in a front-page story in *The Guardian* as declaring that Ariel Sharon was "the cancer at the center of the Middle East crisis." That official may very well have been Jack Straw, British foreign secretary, who commented during his official visit to Iran at the very same time, "I understand that one of the factors that help breed terrorism is the anger many people in this region feel over events in Palestine."[29] While the French government did not see fit to offer even a *pro forma* retraction, after visiting Teheran, Straw called on Ariel Sharon in Israel and he and Tony Blair tried to patch things up. Unfortunately, in spite of the oft-employed rhetoric of two states living side by side in security, it is highly likely that most West European governments, with the possible exception of Germany, would regard Israel's demise as a welcome solution to the Middle Eastern crisis.

European impatience with Israel was especially evident in the response to Operation Defensive Shield, Israel's answer to the escalating terror attacks that culminated in the killing of more than 130 Israelis during March 2002, the worst attack being the suicide bombing of the Park Hotel in Natanya on March 27. A Palestinian from nearby Tulkarm blew himself up, killing 29 Israelis and wounding more than 170 as they gathered to celebrate the Passover Seder. The assault was designed indiscriminately to kill and injure as many ordinary citizens as possible.

Hamas proudly claimed responsibility. *New York Times* correspondent Joel Brinkley reported that Hamas leader Mahmoud al-Zahar told him with much satisfaction, "Forty were killed and 200 injured—in just two operations."[30] The late Yasser Arafat and the Palestine Authority were deeply implicated in the attacks in spite of *pro forma* disavowals. In a *New York Times* op-ed piece on Sunday, February 3, 2002, Arafat denounced "murderers who had spilled innocent blood," but on January 27, 2002, he addressed a mass rally in Ramallah in Arabic in which he announced that "a million martyrs are on their way to Jerusalem." Inspired by their leader's words, the Palestinians commenced perhaps the bloodiest period of terror attacks of the intifada. In all probability, there was no conflict in the mind of Arafat or others like him when they claimed that they oppose the shedding of *innocent* blood. Unlike Osama bin Laden, who issued a *fatwa* on February 23, 1998, declaring that it is "an individual duty for every Muslim who can do it in any country" to kill "Americans and their allies," Arafat and his followers are less than candid concerning whom they consider innocent.

Until recently, terrorist attacks were normally restricted to the political, military, or religious leaders of the targeted community. Terrorists wanted "a lot of people watching, not a lot of people dead." That is no longer the case. Contemporary terrorist groups seek to challenge the legitimacy of the state and/or its governing elite by demonstrating that the state cannot fulfill its most fundamental responsibility, guaranteeing the safety and security of its citizens. Moreover, by characterizing their struggle against Israel as a *jihad*, Israel's adversaries make explicit the nonnegotiable character of their objectives and their refusal to settle for any political or territorial compromise.

No responsible government could tolerate so sustained an assault on its unarmed citizens without a forceful response. Hampered by a pledge to President Bush not to harm Arafat, Ariel Sharon sent twenty thousand troops into the West Bank to limit, if not prevent, further outrages. He sought to deny to would-be suicide bombers, weapons-makers, and other extremists the sanctuary of the narrow streets and passageways of the West Bank's ancient towns, villages, and refugee camps. The Palestinians resisted what they regarded as an invasion. They also sought with considerable success to focus world attention on the inevitable bloodshed of urban warfare while ignoring the context that mandated military action in the first case.

Gruesome media images of Palestinian victims, combined with the kind of malicious, stereotypical cartoons cited above, aroused enormous indignation over Israel's alleged "abuse" of innocent Palestinians. Images of Israeli civilians blown apart by bombs packed with poisoned nails elicited no comparable sympathy. Biographies of suicide bombers, extolled as martyrs for a noble cause, appeared regularly in both the print and electronic media. While Europeans recognized 9/11 for the terrorist assault that it was, they tended to regard terrorist attacks against Israelis as legitimate acts of national resistance by Third World victims of a Jewish version of Western imperialism and colonialism. That view was supported by a convenient forgetfulness concerning the reasons why Europe's Jews were compelled to take the risks inherent in creating their own state in so hostile an environment the first place.

For a very long time, the major western European powers refused to acknowledge that Hamas, Hezbollah and Islamic Jihad were terrorist organizations.

In the nineteen months before Israel's occupation of the West Bank in 2002, more than half of the suicide bombers responsible for killing hundreds of Israelis came from a single town, Jenin, that had become an armed camp and a haven for the most embittered, hard-core Palestinian extremists. Jenin was a veritable breeding ground for terrorists. Suicide bombers were glorified and offered as role models to the young in schools. The Natanya bombers came from Jenin. Moreover, it is hardly likely that the UN officials in charge of Jenin's refugee camp were ignorant of the terror networks and weapons-making shops active in them.

Jenin's narrow, winding streets as well as its booby-trapped roads and buildings offered the defenders ideal conditions for ambush. To minimize their own casualties, the Israelis could have bombed Jenin from the air, as the Americans had done in Afghanistan. Instead, they chose to limit Palestinian casualties by sending its citizen-soldiers into the heart of the town. As always in bitter urban combat, there was bloodshed and death, but the angry, indignant reaction of UN officials, church leaders, and the media was altogether different than the muted reaction to far greater recent bloodshed and ethnic cleansing in Bosnia, Kosovo and Chechnya, as well as genocide in Rwanda. Nor did the Israeli political mainstream emulate the enforced population transfers and expulsions that took place in Europe after World War II. The transformation of Europe's ethnic map began with Nazi Germany's monumental plan to "resettle" ethnic Germans in a German *Lebensraum* mercilessly enlarged by military conquest and the expulsion or, in the case of the Jews and Gypsies, extermination, of the indigenous population. When the war was over, the policy of population "resettlement" initiated by the Germans was continued by the victorious Allies, who sought to create a new order based on homogeneous national states.[31] The ethnic Germans of Eastern and Southern Europe were held collectively responsible for the crimes of a regime they had largely supported during the war. 11.5 million of their number either fled before the advancing Red Army or were expelled, but they were by no means the only expellees. Several million Hungarians, Ukrainians, Finns, and "Yugoslavs," as they were then called, were also expelled in the cause of national homogeneity.

The Czechs expelled 3.5 million Sudeten Germans, 40,000 of whom died during the transfer.

These expulsions have occasioned little, if any, regret among the Czechs. During the elections of 2002, Milos Zeman, prime minister of the Czech Republic, called the expelled Germans "Hitler's fifth column" and "traitors" because of their role in facilitating the Nazi takeover of Czechoslovakia in 1938 and 1939.[32] He also counseled the Israelis to follow the Czech example. According to Radio Prague, during a visit to Israel in February 2002, Zeman, told the Israelis to expel the Palestinians as Czechoslovakia had expelled the Germans. With the exception of the ultranationalist Kakh Party founded by Rabbi Meir Kahane, no responsible Israeli group of either the right or the left has advocated the expulsion of the Palestinians even though a critical mass of Palestinians is committed to the destruction of the state of Israel and the expulsion of its Jewish citizens.

Nabil Shaath, the Palestine Authority's minister for planning and international cooperation, claimed that the Israelis had massacred five hundred people in Jenin. Terje Roed-Larsen, the UN special coordinator in Jenin, declared that the place smelled of "the stench of death" and that the destruction was "horrific beyond belief." In an overheated lead editorial on April 17, 2002, *The Guardian* (UK) described Jenin as "the scene of a crime" reminiscent of Osama bin Laden's 9/11 attack on New York, one that was "no less distressing, and every bit as manmade." In the same issue, Suzanne Goldenberg, *The Guardian's* correspondent in Jerusalem, accused the Israelis of "contempt for the Geneva convention" and of having committed "war crimes" in its campaign in the occupied areas. Janine di Giovanni reported in *The Times* (UK) on April 16, "Rarely in more than a decade of war reporting from Bosnia, Chechnya, Sierra Leone, Kosovo, have I seen such deliberate destruction, such destruction of human life."

In spite of the Yasser Arafat's complicity in the terror attacks on Israel, Europe's political leaders were unanimous in reaffirming their support for him and their extreme distaste for Ariel Sharon. European leaders let it be known that they would continue to aid him as the leader of the Palestine Authority. Anna Lindh, foreign minister of Sweden, declared that "any attempt to crush the Palestinian leadership is unacceptable to the international community and will only lead to greater losses and insecurity for Israel." She also declared that she was "horrified" to hear Sharon refer to Arafat as his "enemy."[33] Belgium's foreign minister Louis Michel proposed that the EU "reconsider its trade ties with Israel."[34] Shortly after Jenin, Javier Solana, the European Union's foreign policy chief, noted that a European Union summit meeting in Barcelona had reaffirmed the organization's faith in Arafat as "the legitimate authority."

L'Osservatore Romano, the official Vatican newspaper, was especially intemperate in its rush to judgment. Ignoring the Passover bombing of March 27, the journal published a front-page editorial denouncing the Israeli countermeasures:

> Rarely has history been violated with such savagery and contempt, with such clear intention to offend and trample upon the dignity of a people. We witness an unbridled attack against persons, territories and holy places: the land of the Resurrected Lord is profanated [sic] with fire and iron and continues to be the daily victim of an aggression that has become an extermination.[35]

With little regard for fact or context, *L'Osservatore Romano,* in effect, accused the Israeli forces of practicing extermination. As a student of genocide over many decades, I cannot recall so passionate a denunciation by *L'Osservatore Romano* of the *real* extermination of Europe's Jews, the Nazi attack on Poland, France, Belgium, the Netherlands, or, more recently, genocide in Rwanda.

About the same time *L'Osservatore Romano's* editorial appeared, about two hundred armed Palestinians took sanctuary in the Church of the Nativity, one of the oldest and most sacred sites in Christendom. The media-savvy gunmen deliberately violated the holy place, knowing that armed Israelis would not stage a shootout in the church and that international pressure would compel the Israelis to permit their escape. The gunmen took refuge in the section of the basilica controlled by the Roman Catholics rather than the Greek Orthodox or the Armenians because of the Vatican's greater diplomatic clout. Although the Israelis were denounced for besieging the church, neither the Vatican nor any Western government protested the gross violation of the holy place by the Palestinians. It is not difficult to imagine international reaction had Jews instead of Muslims invaded the sanctuary and taken its priests and nuns hostage.

The Vatican has long favored the Palestinians over the Israelis, and its reaction to the siege was consistent with *L'Osservatore Romano's* April 3 editorial.[36] There was little, if any, difference between the Vatican responses and that of most Europeans. Arab oil, Muslim numbers worldwide, and, most especially, the presence of millions of Muslims in Western Europe were among the motives. Many observers also pointed to the return of European "antisemitism" in the form of anti-Zionism, but the term "antisemitism" explains little or nothing. The term connotes extreme hostility to Jews and Judaism. Explaining hostility to Jews or Israel by means of a term connoting hostility is tautologous. As we shall see, the witness-people myth goes a long way toward explaining the *underlying basis* for the hostility.

Insofar as any attempt was made to maintain a pretense of "even-handedness," the Israelis were told that only negotiation and dialogue could bring about lasting peace. Jacques Chirac and the U.S. State Department were at one on this issue. However, no one explained how "dialogue" or "negotiations" is possible with Hamas, an organization unconditionally committed by *religious belief* to the destruction of the state of Israel and to the expulsion of its Jewish population.

We have already noted that according to the witness-people myth, a portion of Israel will be redeemed after it accepts the lordship of Jesus Christ. There is another darker side to the myth in which continual Jewish suffering and defeat are depicted as wholly consistent with divine providence. We have also noted that the myth was influential in the formation of the Vatican's opposition both to the early Zionist movement in 1897 and to the settlement of Jewish children in Palestine during the Holocaust. An even harsher version of the myth is to be found in the current revival of Christian *replacement theology* which holds that Christians have replaced Jews in God's favor. Hence, God's promises to the Jews, including settlement in the land of Israel, have been inherited by Christians who are "the true Israel," and the state of Israel has no right to exist nor do Jews have any right to dwell in the land.[37]

The classic claim of Christian theology that the Church has super-seded Israel as the New (and true) Israel provides the theological basis for replacement theology. Not surprisingly, Palestinian Christians, especially Anglicans, have been in the forefront of the revival of replacement theology and have had a powerful influence on some of their coreligionists in the Anglican Church in the United Kingdom. Replacement theology plays easily into the image of the Jew as Judas and Christ-killer and serves as a very useful tool for advancing the cause of those who seek religious legitimation for Israel's total destruction.

For the so-called true believer, the potentially genocidal implications of this theology are no impediment. After all, if deicide and failure to believe in Jesus as Savior are unforgivable sins, there can be no imputation of injustice to a God who once again causes the Jews apocalyptic calamity. One ultra right-wing Catholic group has expressed such supercessionary claims on its website. Its discussion of the Israeli siege begins by citing John 8:42–45 in which Jesus is depicted as telling the Pharisees why they cannot "hear" him:

> You are of your father the devil and you want to do the desires of your father. He was a murderer from the beginning, and does not stand in the truth, because there is no truth in him.

In the text that follows, the Israeli soldiers at the church are called "the children of Satan."[38]

Whatever the theological differences that divide adherents of replacement theology from radical Islamists, they are in agreement concerning the fate of Israel and its Jews.

The systematic boycott of Israeli goods and services is hardly new and has become widespread. It was originally employed by the Arab League, a confederation of twenty nations, as a form of economic warfare, but that effort has been only partly successful and may actually have served as a stimulant to Israel's economic development. With the renewal of the intifada, the boycott of Israeli goods and services became popular among numerous non-Muslim groups, some Christian, others partisans of the left including Jews and even some Israelis, and still others "human rights" advocates. In addition to the commercial boycott, there have been cultural, academic, and scientific boycotts and an ongoing campaign to compel colleges and universities to divest themselves of their investments in Israeli corporations and financial institutions.

The earlier anti-apartheid campaign against South Africa has served as a model for both the boycott and divestiture campaigns. Boycott and divestiture advocates allege that Israel is a racist, apartheid state that has violated the human rights of the Palestinians by their continuing occupation of Arab land and their alleged treatment of the Palestinians. Some go so far as to assert that Israel has been violating the rights of Palestinians from its inception as a nation in May 1948. Opinion varies among the boycotters concerning what constitutes "Arab land." Is it *all* of pre-1948 Palestine, the Arab territories after the

War of Independence, or the areas occupied by Israel after the 1967 war? In any event, for Muslim activists, the campaigns are useful tools in their war against Israel.

By 2001, an unofficial but effective boycott of Israeli goods and service was in place throughout much of Europe. Some supermarket chains placed special identification labels on Israeli goods instead of outright boycott. The result was the same. A well-organized and highly effective boycott has been organized and led by Boikott Israel, a Norwegian group, with the cooperation of similar groups in Iceland, Denmark, and Sweden. One has only to key in "Boikott Israel" and follow its links on the web to discover how extensive boycott activities have become in the Nordic countries. With no regard for the history of the conflict, Boikott Israel asserts that "Israel occupies and oppresses the Palestinians...breaks International Law, UN resolutions and Human Rights during the occupation."[39] In answer to the question, "Do you support Palestinian suicide bombers," Boikott Israel states that they are against "any form of terrorism against civilians" and go on to assert that they "see terror from the Israeli state as one of the most serious and bloody form [sic] of collective punishment of a whole people."[40] Their stated goal is to end Israel's "50-year occupation of and the return of all refugees to a free Palestine." As of this writing, this remains the goal of the Palestinians. Its implementation would, of course, spell the end of Israel as a Jewish state and would leave the Jews of Israel subject to the tender mercies of a Palestinian population thirsting for revenge for its prior defeats. As one journalist wrote about the Norwegian boycott, "In 1941, the grafitti on Jewish businesses in Oslo read 'Jews go to Palestine.' Now, 'the campaign is to get them out of Palestine.'"[41]

The call for a cultural and an academic boycott of Israel has been equally widespread. The first call was issued by Hilary and Stephen Rose in April 2002, UK academics of Jewish origin long active in left-wing causes, in the form of a letter to *The Guardian* calling on Europeans to suspend scientific grants and contracts "until Israelis abide by UN resolutions and open serious negotiations with the Palestinians... including...that sponsored by the Saudis and the Arab League." The letter was signed by 120 academics from the UK, Europe, the United States, and even a few from Israel. The Roses' letter was followed by a second signed by 286 academics worldwide. The signatories declared that "they could no longer in good conscience cooperate with official Israeli institutions, including universities." They also pledged not to attend scientific conferences in Israel but would continue "to collaborate and host Israeli scientific colleagues on an individual basis."[42]

The boycott call spread rapidly and gained enthusiastic adherents throughout the European scientific and academic communities. In the same month that the Roses issued their first letter, the National Association of Teachers in Further and Higher Education called on "all UK institutions of higher and further education" to sever "any academic links" they may have with Israel, and in May 2002 the Association of University Teachers of the UK called for a cessation of EU funding of cultural and research links with Israel. In June, Mona Baker, an Egyptian and professor of translation studies at the University of Manchester Institute of Science and Technology (Umist), fired Gideon Toury and Miriam Shlesinger, two liberal Israeli academics who were on the boards respectively of *Translator* and *Translation Studies Abstracts*, both owned and edited by Baker. Baker had signed the Roses letter, as did ten Israeli scholars, and decided to go one step farther, boycotting *individual* Israeli scholars no matter what their politics.

Dr. Eitan Galun, head of the Gene Therapy Institute at Jerusalem's Hadassah Hospital, had a somewhat similar experience. Hadassah Hospital treats Arabs and Jews alike, 10 percent of the staff are Israeli Arabs, and there are ten Palestinian doctors on the staff.[43] Dr. Galun has been engaged in research at the hospital to cure a blood disease prevalent among Palestinians. Nevertheless, feelings are so strong among some European researchers that they refuse to cooperate with their Israeli counterparts. Recently, Galun requested assistance from a Norwegian colleague. The Norwegian researcher responded by e-mail: "Due to the present situation in the Middle East. I will not deliver any material to an Israeli institution." [44]

Dr. Oren Yiftachel, an Israeli scholar with very strong pro-Palestinian feelings, also felt the force of the boycott. When he submitted a paper coauthored by an Arab colleague, Dr. Asad Ghanem of Haifa University, to *Political Geography*, a left-leaning periodical, the paper was returned unopened by David Slater, the editor, with a note appended stating that the journal could not accept a submission from Israel. The paper itself was decidedly pro-Palestinian, describing Israel as "a state dedicated to the expansion and control of one ethnic group" and concluding that such societies "cannot be classified as democracies in a substantive sense." After considerable negotiations from May to November 2002, Slater informed Yiftachel that the paper might be considered if Yiftachel included a comparison between Israel and apartheid South Africa.[45]

As stated, these incidents are by no means isolated. Throughout Europe there have been both formal and informal attempts to exclude Israeli institutions, scholars, and students. Since the start of Intifada II, few Western scholars attend conferences in Israel partly because of the violence but also because of the kind of subtle and not-so-subtle pressure that influences academic appointments and encourages academics to play it safe and stay away. For example, when a young British lecturer who had been working at the University of Tel Aviv decided to seek employment at home, he was told, "We don't accept any applicants from a Nazi state."[46] There is no way to quantify the number of situations in which academics were excluded from appointment in the UK and elsewhere in Europe by officials with similar prejudices but with a greater sense of discretion about revealing them. In all likelihood there were others.

Israel's most important capital is its intellectual and scientific capital. As journalist Andy Beckett has pointed out, lacking natural resources, science and technology have assumed far greater importance in Israel than in most countries. Israel excels in such fields as physiology, neuroscience, physics, and computer science. Its agriculture, industries, and military establishment have been technology-driven to a far greater extent than its neighbors and most other nations its size, making it especially vulnerable to academic boycott. About 40 percent of the papers published in Israel have involved international cooperation. Unable to establish cooperative links with Arab universities, Israel has long cultivated relations with European and other Western universities and has received some subsidies from the EU for scientific research.

Steven and Hillary Rose were aware of Israel's vulnerability and determined to take advantage of it in order eventually to compel Israel to pursue policies more to their liking. Convinced that the boycott against Israel would eventually be successful, Steven Rose told *The Guardian's* Andy Beckett, "It's water on stone—in the end the stone wears out."[47]

In reading the boycott material, one is struck by its relentlessly one-sided character. Greta Duisenberg, wife of Wim Duisenberg, head of the European Central Bank, went so far as to say that Israel's occupation of the West Bank was worse than the German occupation of

Holland, ignoring the murder of 105,000 Dutch Jews. She is a leader of a Dutch group, United Civilians for Peace, that wants the EU to "persuade" Israel to end occupation, if necessary by curtailing trade benefits. Her husband has said that he supports his wife's activities. The Joint Nordic Boycott Israel Resolution makes a similar demand: The Israeli occupying power must be forced to leave the occupied territories NOW! Israel's war crimes against the Palestinian people must be put to an end![48]

Understandably, the divestiture and boycott campaigns are ardently supported by European Islamic groups as well as most Muslims and Arab nationalists worldwide. Most Muslim nations are at least technically in a state of war with Israel and see such campaigns as tools to defeat the enemy. Academics and human-rights advocates use a different language to justify the boycott and divestiture campaigns. The Roses, by no means Israel's harshest critics, see the boycott as a "non-violent weapon open to civil society to express its *moral outrage*."[49] They praise the negative responses of academics, scientists, and artists to Israeli invitations as "individual ethical refusals." They inform us that "the only prospect for a just and lasting peace lies in Israel's recognition of the legitimacy of a Palestinian state and the Arab world's acceptance of a secure Israel behind its 1967 borders," but like almost all boycott supporters, they make no demands on the Palestinians to end acts of terrorism again Israeli civilians, such as suicide bombers who target civilians in crowded squares, buses, hotels, or wherever casualties can be maximized. When Palestinian militants, such as the al-Aqsa Martyrs Brigade, claimed "credit" for the deliberate killing of seven-year-old Noam Leibowitz and for seriously injuring her three-year-old sister in a shooting attack on her family's car June 17, 2003, boycott advocates have nothing to say. By contrast, the unintentional shooting death of twelve-year-old Muhammad al-Dura during a shooting exchange between armed Palestinians and Israeli troops at Netzarim in October 2000 became a *cause célèbre* throughout Europe and was repeatedly broadcast on French TV and elsewhere as evidence of extreme Israeli brutality and indifference to Palestinian life.

The reason for the silence is clear. Palestinian attacks on civilians and suicide bombings are widely viewed as a legitimate weapon of an oppressed people seeking to end the oppression of its colonial overlords. When the Group of Eight (G8) met for their annual summit in Evian, June 1–3, 2003, and issued a consensus document on "Building

International Political Will and Capacity to Combat Terrorism," the document listed terrorist incidents "over the past year" in "Morocco, Pakistan, the Philippines, Russia, Saudi Arabia, Tunis, and Yemen" but ignored terrorist incidents in Israel. Some of the G8 nations refuse to recognize Hamas, Hezbollah, and the al-Aqsa Martyrs Brigade suicide bombers as terrorists, a recognition that came slowly and reluctantly even to the U.S. State Department.

Moreover, the boycotters have a simplistic notion of the legitimacy of UN resolutions and actions. For years the UN had been a forum for unrelenting attacks on Israel and Zionism, culminating in the General Assembly's Resolution 3379 on November 10, 1975, declaring "that Zionism is a form of racism and racial ideology." Resolution 3379 took notice of the declaration proclaimed by the World Conference of the International Women's Year, held at Mexico City June 19–July 2, 1975, stating that among other things "international peace and cooperation" required the elimination of "Zionism, apartheid and racial discrimination in all its forms." The document also cited the resolution adapted at the Conference of Ministers for Foreign Affairs of Non-Aligned Nations held at Lima August 25–30 1975, "which most severely condemned Zionism as a threat to world peace and called upon all countries to oppose this racist and imperialist ideology..."

In his address to the United Nations on September 23, 1991, President George H. W. Bush commented on Resolution 3379:

> ...to equate Zionism with the intolerable sin of racism is to twist history and forget the terrible plight of the Jews in World War II and indeed throughout history.

Sen. Daniel Patrick Moynihan, American ambassador to the UN under President Gerald Ford, denounced the Zionism-is-racism resolution as "a criminal resolution" and quoted the UN delegate from Costa Rica who called it "an invitation to genocide against the Jewish people."[50] Nevertheless, Resolution 3379 remained in force until December 16, 1991, when it was finally revoked by the General Assembly. In an address in Jerusalem to the Israel Council on Foreign Relations and the United Nations Association of Israel on March 25, 1998, UN Secretary General Kofi Annan declared:

> We must use the occasion to denounce antisemitism in all its manifestations. This brings me to the lamentable resolution adopted by

the General Assembly in 1975, equating Zionism with racism and with racial discrimination. That was the lowest point in our relations; its negative resonance even today is difficult to overestimate. Fortunately, the General Assembly rescinded the resolution in 1991.

Unfortunately that was hardly the end of the matter. The UN-sponsored World Conference against Racism that met in Durban, South Africa, August 28–September 7, 2001, turned into a veritable cesspool of antisemitic, anti-Israel, and anti-American bile.[51] The language and propaganda were so unrelievedly hostile to Zionism and Israel and, at times, to all things Jewish, that the United States joined Israel in walking out. The twin accusations that Israel is an apartheid state and that "Zionism is racism" were repeated *ad nauseum*. Attempts by Jewish speakers to bring some balance into the proceedings were shouted down, with no attempt by conference officials to restore order and decorum. After the withdrawal of the United States, France and representatives of the European Union indicated that they too would leave the conference if no acceptable compromise could be found. The Arab and Muslim delegates sought to include a condemnation of Zionism as racism in the conference's final declaration but did not prevail. The final declaration recognized the Palestinians "right to return," but contained no charge of racism against Israel.

The conference itself was preceded by four regional conferences for Europe, Africa, Latin America, and Asia. The latter was hosted by Ayattolah Ali Khamenei's Islamic Republic of Iran in Teheran and began February 19, 2001. As was the case with many of the participating governments, the record of the Teheran regime in human rights is replete with human rights abuses. According to the U.S. Department of State:

> Systematic abuses include summary executions, disappearances, widespread use of torture and other degrading treatment, reportedly including rape, severe stoning such as stoning and flogging, harsh prison conditions, arbitrary arrest and detention, and prolonged incommunicado detention.[52]

Both Israel and Jewish NGOs were barred from participation. Israel's "occupation" was referred to as a "crime against humanity, a new form of apartheid," and a "threat to international peace and security." As Irving Cotler has pointed out, UN Resolution 1373 had characterized terrorism as a "threat to international peace and security." By so characterizing Israel and by identifying the state as intrinsically apartheid, the document was in effect giving its approval to Palestinian terrorism as a legitimate response on behalf of "international peace and security."

Among the many instances of consistent UN bias against Israel was the election on January 20, 2003, of Libya to the chairmanship of the United Nations Human Rights Commission. Thirty-three nations voted in favor, three against, with seventeen abstentions. Given the endorsement Libya received from the overwhelming majority of the commission's member nations, none of whom could claim ignorance of that country's unwavering commitment to the destruction of Israel and its own record of financing and carrying out acts of terrorism, the commission can hardly be regarded as trustworthy or impartial in its dealings with Israel. In spite of the UN's dreary history vis à vis Israel, boycott calls, such as those of the Roses, fault Israel for its "defiance of United Nations Resolutions" and demand that the boycott continue "until Israel abides by UN resolutions."

In elevating the UN to the role of impartial arbiter of national legitimacy and international justice, the boycotters either deliberately ignore or are ignorant of history and context. Apart from the record of consistent blatant bias in the UN's dealings with Israel, over the years that organization has been used as a forum for the expression of some of the worst antisemitic diatribes since the defeat of the Third Reich. As of January 2005, the UN had a membership of 191 nations of which at least 36 are predominantly Muslim. Together with sympathetic Third World nations, they constitute a powerful bloc within the UN. Unable to achieve their stated object of defeating Israel militarily, they use the UN as a principal weapon to accomplish the same objective diplomatically.

Clearly, the Israeli settlements on the West Bank and in Gaza constitute one of the most serious stumbling blocks to ending the conflict, and Israel is regularly faulted for fostering their growth. Here again, context and history are ignored. At the end of Six-Day War, the Israeli government declared on June 17, 1967, that it was prepared to return the recently occupied Golan Heights to Syria, the Sinai Peninsula to Egypt, and most of the West Bank to Jordan in exchange for a normalization of relations. The Arab response came from the eight Arab heads of state meeting at the Arab Summit Conference in Khartoum, Sudan, on September 1, 1967. The leaders announced the "three no" policy: there would be "no peace with Israel, no recognition of Israel and no negotiations with Israel." Israel's antagonists remained at war, pledged to compel Israel to withdraw.

Israelis were understandably unwilling to oblige. They had not forgotten that on May 23, 1967, Egyptian president Gamal Abdel Nasser had announced a blockade of all Israeli shipping passing through the Gulf of Aqaba, an act of war, and that on May 26, 1967, he had declared to Arab trade unionists that in the coming battle with Israel "our basic objective will be to destroy Israel." Jordan had been the de facto ruler of the West Bank. Absent a credible peace treaty, no responsible government would have voluntarily surrendered territory to its enemies, especially in view of the fact that before 1967 the West Bank was only nine miles from the Mediterranean at one point. Had the armed conflict resumed, Israel's adversaries would have attempted to split the nation in two at its narrowest point. Nor could the Israelis have turned over the occupied territories to the Palestinians, whose stated objective was the destruction of Israel and the return of the refugees to their original domiciles, a privilege enjoyed by none of the displaced Germans at the end of World War II. In command of a hostile population committed to its undoing, the Israelis had no alternative but to take control.

How much does one people owe another that is committed to its undoing? After Adolf Hitler and the Holocaust, Jews have no choice but to *believe* those who promise to destroy them. Nor could they take seriously the idea, so favored among left intellectuals, of a single multiethnic, democratic, secular state. As has happened so often elsewhere, religio-ethnic loyalty would speedily trump state loyalty. The fundamental issue would come down to control of the state's instruments of coercion. In the light of current demographic trends, a predictable international demand for "democracy" and majority rule in such a state would sooner or later assure Palestinians of that control. In such a case, it is hardly likely that victorious Palestinians would even give Israelis the option of "the suitcase or the coffin" that the victorious Algerians granted to the pieds noirs.

The settlements do constitute an obstacle to peace, but so too does the stated objective of Palestinian militants to eliminate Israel altogether, an issue never seriously raised by the boycotters, high-minded clerical moralists, or the pro-Palestinian media. Even if a goodly number of Palestinians were willing to accept a two-state solution, genuine peace would not be possible unless those who favor such a step proved capable of controlling the violence of the militants. Nor is it likely that the militants' objective would be abandoned even if Israel dismantled the settlements unilaterally. On the contrary, those who seek Israel's demise would interpret dismantling as evidence of Israeli weakness and a way station on the road map to Israel's demise. Moreover, Israelis fully understand that were *their* territory occupied, there would be no international outcry about "illegal" settlements or outraged academics calling for a boycott of the Palestinians and their partners.

Under the circumstances, the question of the settlements must be seen as a *political* rather than a *moral* issue to be resolved, if at all, by a mutually-agreed-upon compromise. It is very likely that the best that can be hoped for is an extended truce. If both parties can find the outlines of such a truce credible, it might be prudent for Israel to abandon those settlements that do not compromise its strategic situation, never forgetting that verbal promises can easily be retracted while territory can only be regained at the cost of much blood. In any event, no responsible Israeli government could return to the 1967 borders with its nine-mile corridor between the West Bank.

The conflict between the Israelis and the Palestinians has a profoundly tragic character. Two peoples, deeply attached to the same land by historical memory, religion, and political necessity yet unable fully to trust each other, are condemned precariously to live together with the never-ending possibility that the day may come when one side drives out the other or both succumb to an apocalyptic nuclear finale.

That, of course, is not the way the situation is viewed by the boycotters or by those who fault only the Israelis in the conflict. They apply pressure and make one-sided demands for which, unlike the Israelis, they need pay no price in blood or treasure. Inevitably, innocents die when peoples are at war and hostile populations must be kept under control, if necessary by compulsion. Nevertheless, there is a level of atavistic animus directed at the Israelis that is without parallel among the responses to perceived injustices and abuse anywhere else in the world. Atavistic images that have been dredged up from the slime of genocidal antisemitism are intended to transform a difficult territorial dispute between two peoples into a cosmic struggle between the oppressed and innocent on the one hand and the forces of absolute evil on the other. We cite these images in my other essay in this volume. What greater evil can there be than one so radical that schoolchildren can be instructed that if they blow themselves up and take the enemy with them, God will bless them in paradise, and for Europeans to characterize such behavior as a legitimate response to Israeli "colonialism"? To repeat, there is a level of anger and indignation in the propaganda against Israel both in the Muslim world and much of Europe unmatched by anything else in the contemporary world.

In his analysis of the witness-people myth, Stephen Haynes notes "the incommensurate scrutiny Israel seems to receive in the news media" and claims that it is due to the fact that "Jews actually have held a position of unique prominence in the collective imagination of the Christian West for centuries."[53] That "incommensurate scrutiny" and position of "unique prominence" is certainly evident in the response of the Christian West to Israel. Unfortunately, it often involves the ascription of demonological qualities to Israel that arouses anger and a distaste of a deeper sort than that felt against other nations and groups whose policies are looked upon with disfavor. Muslim demonization of Israel can perhaps be explained by the fact that hatred and resentment of an enemy is most overpowering in defeat, especially when defeat is not decisive. Historically, Islam has known Jews primarily as *dhimmis*, resident aliens tolerated under conditions of strict subordination. There may be a readily available explanation of Muslim rage: The experience of Jews uncharacteristically defeating Muslims militarily on what Muslims consider their territory (*dar al-Islam*) has been a profound affront religiously as well as politically. But why would so many Christians demonize Israel and Israelis and be so strongly pro-Palestinian? A possible answer is that there are far more Muslims than Jews and more is to be gained from favoring the Palestinians, but that would hardly explain the transformation of an ostensibly military and political conflict into something approaching a cosmic conflict.

The cosmic-eschatological interpretation of the conflict is also evident in the support given to Israel by those on the Christian right who see "the rebirth of the state of Israel" as "by far the greatest biblical event of the twentieth century" and "a portent of the triumphal return of Christ."[54] The religious dimension is also present in replacement theology. Nor can the influence of the religious dimension of Zionism be denied even among secular supporters of Israel. When, in desperation over the Kishinev massacres of April 6–7, 1903, Theodor Herzl announced at the Sixth Zionist Congress (August 1903) that he was considering the suggestion of Joseph Chamberlain, the British foreign

secretary, that the young Zionist Organization establish a Jewish settlement in British-controlled East Africa, he was met with furious opposition especially from Jews from the tsarist empire. As an assimilated
Jew, Herzl understood the political and economic conditions that were
rendering European Jewish life untenable. He was willing to settle Jews
anywhere a refuge could be found. By contrast, no matter how des-
perate the situation, for most contemporary secular Zionists, the religious basis of the idea of a return of the "exiles" to Zion was too deeply
rooted for any other place of settlement to be acceptable.

Nevertheless, there is another idea deeply rooted in the Christian
religious consciousness to which we refer above that presents a darker
vision of the Jewish return to Zion. If, as Christian thinkers have held
throughout the centuries, the destruction of the Temple and the exile
of the Jews from their homeland was divine punishment for their failure to accept Christ, it follows that the alleged "punishment" can only
be revoked if and when the Jews accept Christ. God in his mercy may
gather them up and give them yet another chance to accept Christ,
but their inability or failure to do so can only have the direst of entail-
ments. Put differently, in the Christian narrative, unconverted Jews are
always fated to lose, especially in "Christ's patrimony." This scenario is
altogether consistent with the witness-people myth as described and
analyzed by Haynes.

Let us recall that Haynes characterizes the witness-people myth as
"a deep structure in the Christian imagination" and holds that it operates "often pre-critically and unconsciously" in forming "ideas about
Jews among persons who share a cultural heritage or world view."[55]
According to Haynes there is profound irony in the Zionist project. He
observes that "many Jews have perceived a national existence as the
symbol and guarantor of Jewish normalcy, and as an implicit rejection
of the theological role assigned to the Jews by the Christian imagination." Ironically, "the emergence of the Jewish state has only revivified
the witness-people tradition among many influential Christians." Let
us also recall that Haynes does *not* restrict the influence of the witness-people myth to believers but insists that it operates unconsciously
and without critical scrutiny among those who share a Christian cultural heritage. Moreover, Haynes concludes that the "the witness-people myth in all its modern and pre-modern versions spells danger for
the Jewish people." Nor does he offer much hope that the mystification of the Jew in the Christian imagination can be demystified. The

mystification is too deeply rooted in Christian texts, liturgy, tradition and theology.[56]

When account is taken of all the reasons for the widespread European sympathy for the Palestinians, there remains a need to understand the immoderate and, in all too many instances, hateful response to Israel by the European mainstream, as well as by left and right-wing fringe groups, as Israel seeks a measure of security in the midst of bitterly hostile and resentful neighbors. What are we to make of the comments of British novelist and historian A. N. Wilson and Oxford professor and poet Tom Paulin? In October 2002, Wilson wrote in his weekly column:

> The logic of supporting the Palestinians is to question the very right of the State of Israel to exist.... Of course, we do not want the Israelis to be "driven into the sea." But the 1948 experiment, claiming the "Israelis" had a right to exist as a state just because a few brave terrorists such as Menachem Begin killed some British army officers—this was lazy thinking.[57]

Apparently, Wilson sees no link between the Holocaust and the creation of the state of Israel. It is, however, comforting do know that he doesn't want Israelis "driven into the sea," even though he holds that the only institution fully committed to their protection has no right to exist.

Poets are capable of expressing raw, naked emotion, and Tom Paulin is no exception. On February 18, 2001, his poem characterizing the IDF as the "Zionist SS" appeared in the Sunday edition of *The Observer*. He introduced the poem by quoting Victor Klemperer (1881–1960) on the Zionists. Klemperer is best known for the diary of his experiences during the Third Reich.[58] Married to a non-Jewish woman, himself a convert to Christianity, a Marxist, and wholly alienated from Judaism, he chose to live in the German Democratic Republic after the war. On June 13, 1934, he wrote:

> To me the Zionists, who want to go back to the Jewish state of 70 AD (destruction of Jerusalem by Titus) are just as offensive as the Nazis. With their nosing after blood, their ancient "cultural roots," their partly canting, partly obtuse winding back of the world, they are altogether a match for the National Socialists.

Paulin's poem follows:

> We've fed this inert
> this lying phrase
> like comfort food
> as another little Palestinian boy
> in trainer jeans and a white teeshirt
> is gunned down by the Zionist SS
> whose initials we should
> —but don't—dumb goys—
> clock in that weasel word *crossfire*

Calling Israelis Nazis, or even worse, SS, after the Holocaust is the ultimate obscenity. Nevertheless, the editors of *The Observer*, part of *The Guardian* newspaper chain, believed it was fit to print.

So too did the editors of *al-Ahram*, Egypt's most prestigious newspaper, whose correspondent interviewed Paulin and reprinted his poem in its English-language weekly April 4–10, 2002. In the interview the poet called Israeli behavior in Palestine "an historical obscenity" and declared "I never believed that Israel had the right to exist at all." He reserved his special venom for "Brooklyn-born Jewish settlers." According to *al-Ahram*'s report, Paulin said forcefully, "They should be shot dead. I think they are Nazis, racists. I feel nothing but hatred for them."[59]

The poet and the novelist give the game away. The witness-people myth is alive and well. In their scenario, the Jews are destined to fail, especially in the Holy Land. If one objects that these are wild rantings, let us recall that these men are *Salonfähig*.[60] Both are regularly featured on BBC; Wilson is a world-class novelist and historian who writes a regular column for a respectable newspaper. They say what others in the mainstream churches, the academy, the media, and the professions prefer to couch in more discrete language, speaking of Israel's right to exist but putting one-sided pressure on Israel absent any serious consideration of Israel's security requirements. We see this in the boycotter's one-sided, monodimensional criticisms of Israel, their demand that Israel withdraw unilaterally from the occupied territories and abide by UN resolutions without a *credible* Palestinian assurance of a genuine end to terrorism. If taken seriously, such rhetoric would have the practical effect of the step-by-step dismantling of the state.

The analogy to pre–World War II Czechoslovakia is all too appropriate. Hoping for "peace in our times," Neville Chamberlain agreed to Germany's takeover of the Sudetenland, thereby depriving the Czechs of any possibility of a viable defense against German aggression. A few months later Hitler took over all of Czechoslovakia. This will not happen in Israel for the simple reason that in one respect Israel's situation remains what it was in 1947. Then Israel's Jews declared, *"Ayn lanu b'raira"* (We have no choice). Save for the exceptionally gifted, there was almost no place in the world where they were welcome. They may be scripted for defeat in the witness-people myth. Hopefully, by their determination they can write an alternative narrative.

Notes

1. The conference took place May 11–14, 2003. Among those who presented their views were Alain Finkielkraut, Simon Schama, Leon Wieseltier, Jehudah Reinharz, Pierre Birnbaum, Hillel Halkin, Tony Judt, David Remnick, Henry Louis Gates Jr., Nathan Glazer, Paul Berman, Josef Joffe, Roger Cohen, Ian Baruma, Jane Kramer, Anthony Julius, Mark Lilla, Konstanty Gebert, David Harris, Mortimer B. Zuckerman, Daniel Jonah Goldhagen, David Kertzer, Deborah Lipstadt, Martin Peretz, Irving Cotler, Fiamma Nirenstein, David Pryce-Jones, and Robert Wistrich.

2. For example, in a lecture in Recklinghausen, Germany at a conference sponsored by the German Evangelical Church in February 1963, I commented that ".... the Christian will always encounter the Jew as myth rather than real person unless some way can be found to demythologize their conception of Israel." See, "Person and Myth in the Judaeo-Christian Encounter," in Richard L. Rubenstein, *After Auschwitz: Radical Theology and Contemporary Judaism*, 1st ed., (Indianapolis: Bobbs-Merrill, 1966), p. 71. See also the chapters on "Religion and the Origins of Death Camps," "The Dean and the Chosen People," as well as "Person and Myth in the Judaeo-Christian Encounter," in *After Auschwitz*, 1st ed., pp. 1-82.

3. Stephen R. Haynes, *Reluctant the Witnesses: Jews and the Christian Imagination* (Louisville, KY: Westminster John Knox Press, 1995). On a more personal side, although he did not take any of my courses, I am pleased that one of Professor Haynes's graduate degrees is from Florida State University, where I taught for twenty-five years.

4. Ibid., pp. 8ff.

5. Ibid., italics added.

6. Ibid., p. 3.

7. Ibid., p. 12.

8. Ibid., p. 13.

9. Ibid., p. 7.

10. See, for example, Richard L. Rubenstein, *After Auschwitz: History, Theology and Contemporary Judaism*, 2nd ed. (Baltimore: Johns Hopkins University Press, 1992), pp. 84–86, 91-95; Rubenstein and John K. Roth, *Approaches to Auschwitz: The Holocaust and Its Legacy*, rev. ed. (Louisville, KY: Westminster John Knox Press, 2003), pp. 41–45, 63, 329, 385, n. 18.

11. See Leon Festinger, Henry W. Riecken, and Stanley Schacter, *When Prophecy Fails* (Minneapolis: University of Minnesota Press, 1956); Leon Festinger, "Cognitive Dissonance," *Scientific American* 207 (October 1962): 93–102; and Elliot Aronson, "The Rationalizing Animal," *Psychology Today*, May 1973, 46-52.

12. Justin Martyr, *Dialogue with Trypho*, in *The Ante-Nicene Fathers*, ed. Alexander Roberts and James Donaldson (Grand Rapids, MI: Eerdmans, 1950), vol. 1, p. 202.

13. Martin Luther, "On the Jews and Their Lies," trans. Martin H. Bertram, in *Luther's Works*, ed. Franklin Sherman and Helmut T. Lehman (Philadelphia: Fortress Press, 1971), 47: 139.

14. See Rubenstein, "Antisemitism and the Contemporary Jewish Condition," p. 10 and p. 14, notes 48 and 49.

15. Karl Barth, *Church Dogmatics*, trans. G. Bromiley et al. (Edinburgh: T. & T. Clark, 1957), II, 2, p. 235.

16. See Eberhard Busch, *Karl Barth: His Life from Letters and Autobiographical Texts*, trans. John Bowden (Philadelphia: Fortress Press, 1976), p. 223.

17. Karl Barth, "The Jewish Problem and the Christian Answer," in *Against the Stream* (London: S.C.M. Press, 1954), pp. 196, 198. We are indebted to Emil Fackenheim, *To Mend the World: Foundations of Future Jewish Thought* (New York: Schocken, 1982), p. 133. In that book, Fackenheim, one of the twentieth century's most important Jewish thinkers, describes Barth as "the last great Christian supersessionist thinker" (p. 284).

18. Herzl, for example, sought a top-down solution to the Jewish problem, seeking, for example, the support of Kaiser Wilhelm II and Sultan Abdul Hamid II as well as such Jewish notables as Baron Maurice de Hirsch.

Moreover, he offered no realistic assessment of the possible response of the Islamic world to the establishment of a Jewish state in Palestine.

19. *Civiltà Cattolica*, May 1, 1897, cited by Sergio I. Minerbi, *The Vatican and Zionism: Conflict in the Holy Land 1895–1925*, trans. by Arnold Schwarz (New York: Oxford University Press, 1990) p. 96.

20. On *Civiltà Cattolica'*s use of the blood libel, see David Kertzer, *The Popes Against the Jews: The Vatican's Role in the Rise of Modern Antisemitism* (New York: Alfred A. Knopf, 2001), pp. 152–65.

21. Theodor Herzl, *The Diaries of Theodor Herzl*, trans. and ed. Marven Lowenthal (New York: Grosset and Dunlap, 1962), p. 428.

22. Baldric of Bourgeuil, "Historia Jerosolimitana," in *Recueil des Historiens des Croisades, Historiens occidentaux* (1844-95), vol. 4, p. 101, cited by John Riley-Smith, *The Crusades: A Short History* (New Haven: Yale University Press, 1987) p. 16.

23. "The Balfour Declaration," in Paul Mendes-Flohr and Jehuda Reinharz, eds., *The Jew in the Modern World: A Documentary History* (New York: Oxford University Press, 1980), p. 458.

24. *Osservatore Romano*, March 21, 1919.

25. Pierre van Zuylen (Rome) to Foreign Minister Hymans, March 16, 1919, no. 57/26, Archives du Ministère des Rélations Extérieures, Brussels, St. Siège, 1919–20.

26. *Actes et Documents du Saint Siège relatif à la seconde guerre mondiale* (Vatican City: Liberia editrice Vaticana, 1967), vol. IX, no. 272; John Morley, *Vatican Diplomacy and the Jews During the Holocaust, 1939–1943*, (New York: KTAV Publishing House, 1980), p. 92.

27. See Rubenstein, "Antisemitism and the Contemporary Jewish Condition," pp. 23–25.

28. Ibid., p. 25.

29. Anton LaGuardia and Patrick Bishop, "Straw's Trip to Teheran Infuriates Teheran," *Daily Telegraph* (UK), September 25, 2001.

30. Joel Brinkley, "Bombers Gloating in Gaza as They See Goal within Reach: No More Israel," *New York Times*, April 4, 2002.

31. This issue is discussed in Richard G. Plaschka, Horst Haselsteiner, Arnold Suppan, and Anna M. Drabnek, eds., *Nationale Frage und Vertreibung in der Tschechoslowakei und Ungarn 1938–1948, Aktuelle Forschungen,*

Zentraleuropa-Studien, vol. 3, Vienna: Verlag der österreichischen Akademie der Wissenschaften, 1997.

32. Askold Krusheinycky, "Czechs in Poll Row over Expulsion of Sudeten Germans," *Daily Telegraph* (UK), June 14, 2002.

33. Warren Hoge, "European Leaders Are Alarmed by Rising Turmoil in the Mideast, *New York Times,* March 29, 2002.

34. "Belgium FM: EU Should Reconsider Trade Ties with Israel," *Haaretz*, April 7, 2002.

35. "The Profanation of the Holy Land, the Violation of History," *L'Osservatore Romano*, April 3, 2002.

36. For an informed discussion of the siege of the Church of the Nativity, see Ron Dreher, "Held Up in Bethlehem: What's Really Going on Inside the Church of the Nativity," *National Review Online,* April 9, 2002.

37. For an informed overview of the influence of replacement theology, especially in England, see Melanie Phillips, "Christians Who Hate Jews: Palestinian Christian Has Revived Replacement Theology," *Spectator*, February 16, 2002.

38. http://servus.christusrex.org/www1/icons/palestine-index.html.

39. http://www.boikottisrael.no/eng_views.html. See also the "Joint Nordic Boycott Israel Resolution" of September 14, 2002 (Nordic Boycott Israel Day), http://www.apk2000.dk/netavisen/artikler/synspunkt/2002-na0912-joint_nordic_boycott_israel.htm.

40. http://www.boikottisrael.no/eng_faq.html.

41. Sol Liebgott, "Nattering Norwegians," *Jerusalem Post*, June 13, 2002.

42. See Hilary Rose and Steven Rose, "The Choice Is to Do Nothing or to Try to Bring about Change," *The Guardian*, July 15, 2002.

43. See Matt Rees, "Amid the Killing, E.R. Is an Oasis," *Time,* June 16, 2003.

44. Report by Dr. Benjamin Sachs, Harold H. Rosenfeld Professor of Obstretics, Gynecology and Reproduction Biology at Harvard Medical School, January 26, 2003.

45. Andy Beckett, "It's Water on the Stone—in the End the Stone Wears Out," *The Guardian*, December 12, 2002.http://education.guardian.co.uk/higher/worldwide/story/0,9959,858544,00.html.

46. Rod Liddle, "Watch Who You Call Nazis," *The Guardian*, July 17, 2002.

47. Beckett, "It's Water on the Stone."

48. Joint Nordic Boycott Israel Resolution, http://www.apk2000.dk/netavisen/artikler/synspunkt/2002-na0912-joint_nordic_boycott_israel.htm

49. Hilary Rose and Steven Rose, *The Guardian*, July 15, 2002 (italics added).

50. Daniel Patrick Moynihan, introduction to Jacques Givet, *The Anti-Zionist Complex*, trans. Evelyn Abel (Englewood, NJ: SBS Publishing, 1982).

51. NGOs met August 28–31; the official meeting of government representatives took place from September 1–7.

52. United States Department of State, "Iran-Country Reports on Human Rights Practices-2001," March 4, 2002.

53. Haynes, *Reluctant Witnesses*, p. 1.

54. Advertisement for the Billy Graham film, *His Land*, cited by ibid., p. 141.

55. Ibid., p. 1 and p. 8.

56. Ibid., pp. 182–83.

57. See the response of Jonathan Sack, "Israel Has a Right to Live without Fear and Terror," *Evening Standard* (UK), October 24, 2001. Professor Sack is chief rabbi of Great Britain and the Commonwealth. His essay was in response to Wilson's column on October 22, 2001, denying the right of Israel to exist. Wilson's column is no longer available on the *Evening Standard* website, although most of his other columns are.

58. Victor Klemperer, *I Will Bear Witness: The Diaries of Victor Klemperer* (New York: Random House, 1998).

59. "That Weasel Word," *al-Ahram Weekly*, April 4–10, 2002.

60. *Salonfähig* can be understood to mean "fit to be received in respectable circles," originally "worthy of being received in the salons of respectable circles."

17

Anti-Israelism and Antisemitism: Common Characteristics and Motifs

Manfred Gerstenfeld

Antisemitism's core theme is that Jews embody absolute evil. It has been propagated intensely for many centuries. This extreme fallacy and its principal submotifs have remained largely the same during the ages. Their representation, however, has evolved according to the circumstances. The three main permutations of the core theme are religious antisemitism—one might call it more exactly anti-Judaism—ethnic (racist) antisemitism, and anti-Israelism or anti-Zionism.

Large parts of Christianity have propagated hatred of the Jews for close to two millennia. In the last decades this has changed even though until today there are still substantial parts of the Christian world that continue their demonization of the Jews. When powerful institutions or elites promote ideas over a very long period, they usually become an integral part of societies' culture.[1]

The Christian Theological Foundations of Jew Hatred

In the 1960s, James Parkes analyzed the conflict between Christians and Jews during the first eight centuries of the Christian era. Concerning that period he concluded: "There was far more reason for the Jew to hate the Christian than for the Christian to hate the Jew—and this on the evidence of Christian sources alone."

Parkes also came to the conclusion that the Christian theological conceptions of the first three centuries created the foundations for the hatred, on which an "awful superstructure" was constructed. The first stones for this were laid "the very moment the Church had the power to do so, in the legislation of Constantine and his successors."

Parkes referred to modern antisemitism, saying: "If on the ground so carefully prepared, modern antisemites have reared a structure of racial and economic propaganda, the full responsibility still rests with those who prepared the soil, created the deformation of the people and so made these ineptitudes credible."[2]

The ongoing diffusion of this extreme loathing of Jews by Christian churches made it very powerful. The latter kept defining absolute evil in theological terms, suggesting that as supposedly tens of generations ago, some forefathers of Jews had killed God's son, Jews were capable of everything wicked. The degree of severity of the propaganda of antisemitic hatred differed between various countries.

The infrastructure laid by Catholicism, Lutheranism, etc., was responsible for a large part of the European mind-set, which made the Holocaust possible. European national movements in the nineteenth century adopted the same core motif of the Jews' ultimate wickedness. Hand in hand with the religious variant, ethnic antisemitism developed as a second major form of extreme Jew hatred. German and Austrian Nazism and their many supporters elsewhere took this antisemitic worldview to its genocidal consequence.

The Holocaust Changes the Jew's Image

The Holocaust led to a gradual modification of the negative image of the Jews. This now partly mutated little by little into the symbol of the ultimate victim. It led for several decades to a taboo in many, but not all democratic European countries concerning public antisemitism. This taboo was particularly strong in Germany, even though there it is also fading away in recent years.[3] In its latent form, antisemitism, however, remained present in all European countries.

Many continue to hold classic antisemitic stereotypes.[4] Several opinion surveys show that currently tens of millions of Europeans are hard-core antisemites. A 2002 poll carried out on behalf of the Anti-Defamation League in five countries, Austria, Switzerland, Spain, Italy, and the Netherlands, found that one out of five respondents "harbor strong antisemitic views."[5]

Mainly starting from the Six-Day War—when the magnitude of the Israeli victory shattered the image of Jew as victim—and intensifying after the Lebanon War in 1982, a third category of antisemitism strengthened that targeted Israel as a Jewish collective. In recent years it has augmented rapidly as it does not encounter the resistance of the two previous types, which are considered by many to be politically incorrect.

Common Elements

The three main permutations of antisemitism have a number of common characteristics. These include:

1) There is a powerful ongoing promotion of a discourse of hatred of the Jews. This demonization has developed central subthemes over the years, which repeat themselves in various disguises. They gradually permeate society's narrative. Over the years the accusations become increasingly complex and difficult to disentangle. On this substrate the Jews' enemies build further whenever circumstances are suitable, when they wish to attack a specific person or group, or seek a scapegoat in a given situation.

2) The main motif of the Jew being absolute evil expresses itself according to the prevailing worldviews at a given time. The Jew is denounced as the quintessential other as perceived at that moment in time. When Christianity dominated the mind-set, the Jew was presented as the killer of God, the anti-Christ, and Satan. In periods of strong nationalism Jews are presented as extreme alien elements. When the societal emphasis is on race, the Jewish one is called a greatly inferior one. When ideological currents promote universalism, the state of Israel is demonized as nationalist, racist, and postcolonialist.

3) The core accusation of the Jew being evil splits into submotifs. A central one is desire for power. One finds this first and foremost in the promotion of conspiracy theories—the prime one being *The Protocols of the Elders of Zion*—but also in many other variants. Other permutations include thirst for blood, infanticide, having a subhuman nature, and lust for money. These originated in the worlds of Christian or racist antisemitism—and many have been rejected and discredited but not disappeared in the West—but nevertheless recur concerning Israel nowadays.

4) One recurring fundamental accusation is that Jews have a severe genetic deficiency. Christian teachings said that the Jew was born guilty because the forefathers of some Jews were reputedly responsible for the death of their religion's originator. In Christian antisemitism there was an escape clause: One could convert and by that, if all went well, rid oneself of the birth defect.

Yet when Jews converted massively in medieval Spain, a new genetic criterion to discriminate against the converts and their children was introduced: the purity of blood. Nazism went further and said that the genetic defects of the Jewish race, born extremely inferior and pathologically dangerous, could not be repaired. The logical conclusion of this hate propaganda was that Jews had to be eliminated. The "Final Solution" envisioned the mass murder of all Jews, which was the Holocaust.

In our days the genetic motif has mutated further. Mainly in Arab and Western left-wing circles, one hears the antisemitic accusation that Israel was born in sin. Israeli political scientist Shlomo Avineri remarked ironically: "This is in contrast to the Arab states having been immaculately conceived."[6] The antisemitic character of the accusation becomes clearer if one considers that if there will be a second Palestinian state in addition to Jordan, its origins will be in genocidal propaganda, terrorism, war crimes, and corruption.

The motif also regularly recurs that some Jews or Israelis can escape condemnation provided they publicly oppose Israeli politics. This sometimes happens in proposed selective academic and similar boycott campaigns against Israel, where those Israelis who are willing to come out against their government are sometimes excluded from the boycott.[7]

An example of the latter occurred when in March 2006 a British dance magazine, *Dance Europe*, refused to publish an article on Israeli choreographer Sally Ann Freeland. The editor said she would publish the article only if Freedland condemned "the occupation." She refused and the article was not published.[8] Economic boycott campaigns against Israel on the other hand have no exceptions.

5) As circumstances change, the main antisemitic motifs are dressed up in different ways, over the centuries, often according to local circumstances. As time passes, the central subthemes fragment and mutate, yet rarely new major ones are added. In postmodern times, antisemitic mutations and fragmentations increase rapidly. This makes contemporary antisemitism so many-sided and complicated to combat.

6) Verbal or physical attacks on Jews and Israelis are often combined. This merging of both targets is the strongest among many current proofs for the major overlap of anti-Israelism and antisemitism. It came to the fore again in many European reactions during the summer 2006 war in Lebanon.

7) Jews and nowadays Israel are measured by standards applied to them but not to others. As former Canadian justice minister Irwin Cotler observed: "Traditional antisemitism denied Jews the right to live as equal members of society, but the new anti-Jewishness denies the right of the Jewish people to live as an equal member of the family of nations."[9]

Former Swedish deputy prime minister Per Ahlmark pointed out:

> Anti-Zionism today has become very similar to antisemitism.
> Anti-Zionists accept the right of other peoples to national feelings and a defensible state. But they reject the right of the Jewish people to have its national consciousness expressed in the State of Israel and to make that state secure. Thus, they are not judging Israel with the values used to judge other countries. Such discrimination against Jews is called antisemitism.[10]

A typical, more recent example of such double standards is the new UN Human Rights Council which, according to the Israeli ambassador to the United Nations in Geneva, Itzhak Levanon, "has focused on Israel to the exclusion of other pressing human rights needs."[11] The council, for instance, has not passed a resolution condemning the more than 200,000 deaths in Darfur, nor has it dealt with major human rights offenses in countries such as China, for instance.

8) While currently the world's main demonizing forces of Israel and the Jews come from the Arab and Muslim world, the motifs and semantics used are also expressed in extreme left- and right-wing Western circles. The same is true—be it in lesser intensity—in the Western mainstream. This can best be demonstrated by analyzing antisemitic cartoons, which rely upon generally known and immediately grasped stereotypes for their effectiveness.

9) In its extreme form the antisemitic process has three stages:

- Demonization,
- Isolation, and
- Elimination.

The latter can be done by expulsion or destruction.

10) Spreading antisemitism worldwide in all its permutations has accelerated in the last decades due to improvements in communications. The Internet has added a new, fast means of communicating

prejudice, including antisemitism.[12] This is termed "cyberhate." It plays a major role in the postmodern global war against Israel and the Jews.[13] Nazism used mass media in an effective way when demonizing the Jews. The Internet plays a similar and much faster role.

The impact of contemporary communication was recognized by the British All-Party Parliamentary Inquiry into Anti-Semitism in its report, published in September 2006: "Anti-Semitism can now [be] disseminated faster and further than ever before. Egyptian and Syrian state television broadcast anti-Jewish propaganda to millions of homes, including in the UK, and far right and radical Islamist organizations are using the Internet as a key component in their campaigns of hatred."[14]

Anti-Israelism

The late twentieth and early twenty-first century explosion of anti-Israelism, a hate phenomenon that had existed for decades at much lower levels, caught the Jewish world and Israel by surprise. Yet several aspects of the anti-Zionist permutation of antisemitism had already been described much earlier by some authors.

Jacques Givet wrote in 1979 in the original French version of his book *The Anti-Zionist Complex*: "The anti-Zionist becomes an overt anti-Semite as soon as he goes beyond criticism of the policies of the Jerusalem government (a favorite activity of the Israelis themselves) and challenges the very existence of the State of Israel."[15]

In France—where new mutations of antisemitism are frequently pioneered—the overlap of antisemitism and anti-Israelism happened early. It was partly linked to the large number of communist intellectuals. One occasion when this came to the fore was during the so-called doctors' plot in 1953. Jewish doctors in the Soviet Union were accused of having caused the death of leading political figures by incorrect diagnoses and treatment. This was accompanied by a campaign against cosmopolitanism and Zionism.

French communist intellectuals organized a major solidarity meeting in Paris. Many of the speakers explained that this was normal practice to suspect doctors of poisoning people, like Mengele had done in Auschwitz. A Jewish physician publicly said, using German behavior during the Second World War, that one could not exclude that Jews or Zionists had decided to poison Soviet personalities.[16]

A retired Israeli diplomat, stationed in the early 1980s at the Israeli embassy in Oslo, related how he had been invited to speak at the general headquarters of the Norwegian army on Israel's military strategy. In question time, one of the generals asked why the Jews "crucified our Lord." The Israeli diplomat asked the questioner what that had to do with the topic. The questioner answered that he took this opportunity for the question because the diplomat was the first Jew he had ever met and presumably could give an answer because his ancestors were probably responsible. The diplomat then suggested that he call upon the ambassador of Italy, as he was likely to be a descendant of the Romans who had pronounced the verdict.[17]

It took many years until it was more widely accepted, with many provisos, that antisemitism and anti-Israelism overlap. In a 2004 report prepared for the French interior minister, the author, human rights expert Jean-Christophe Ruffin, explicitly linked antisemitism to the anti-Israeli mood prevailing in the country: "It is not conceivable today to fight actively in France against anti-Semitism in its new mutations without going all-out to try and balance anew the public's view of the situation in the Middle East."[18]

The U.S. Commission on Civil Rights found *inter alia* in a 2006 report titled *Campus Anti-Semitism* that "Anti-Israeli or anti-Zionist propaganda has been disseminated on many campuses that include traditional antisemitic elements, including age-old anti-Jewish stereotypes and defamation." A second finding was that "anti-Semitic bigotry is no less morally deplorable when camouflaged as anti-Israelism or anti-Zionism." It was also found that "substantial evidence suggests that many university departments of Middle East studies provide one-sided, highly polemical academic presentations and some may repress legitimate debate concerning Israel."[19]

The 2006 British All-Party Parliamentary Inquiry into Antisemitism wrote in its report: "Anti-Zionist discourse can be polluted with anti-Semitic themes in different ways and with different levels of intent. It can be used deliberately as a way to mask or articulate prejudice against Jews. It is difficult to counter because one must first identify and explain the antisemitism behind the language and imagery. For instance, a far right party may use the terms of 'Zionist' and 'Zionism' instead of 'Jews' and 'Jewish.' "[20]

A major handicap in exposing the racist anti-Zionist permutation was the lack of a generally accepted contemporary definition of antisemitism. An important attempt to define the "new" antisemitism was made by Cotler. He already drew attention to several of the points later included in the EUMC definition of antisemitism, such as those who call for the destruction of Israel and the Jewish people, the Nazification of Israel, and the discriminatory treatment of Israel through denial of equality before the law.[21]

A Rapid Test

Nathan Sharansky, when he was the Israeli minister of Jerusalem and diaspora affairs, developed a simple formula, which he called the "3D" test to help distinguish legitimate criticism of Israel from antisemitism—demonization, double standards, and delegitimization.

He wrote: "The first 'D' " is the test of demonization. When the Jewish state is being demonized; when Israel's actions are blown out of all sensible proportion; when comparisons are made between Israelis and Nazis and between Palestinian refugee camps and Auschwitz—this is antisemitism, not legitimate criticism of Israel.

"The second 'D' is the test of double standards. When criticism of Israel is applied selectively; when Israel is singled out by the United Nations for human rights abuses while the behavior of known and major abusers, such as China, Iran, Cuba, and Syria, is ignored; when Israel's Magen David Adom, alone among the world's ambulance services, is denied admission to the International Red Cross—this is antisemitism.

"The third 'D' is the test of delegitimization. When Israel's fundamental right to exist is denied—alone among all peoples in the world—this too is antisemitism."[22]

After several years of a high incidence of antisemitic incidents, the Organization for Security and Cooperation in Europe (OSCE) adopted the Berlin Declaration in April 2004. This document recognized that antisemitism "following its most devastating manifestation during the Holocaust has assumed new forms and expressions." The document also declared "unambiguously that international developments or political issues, including those in Israel or elsewhere in the Middle East, never justify anti-Semitism."[23]

The EUMC Working Definition

The European Monitoring Centre on Racism and Xenophobia (EUMC) in its 2004 report on antisemitism noted the lack of a common definition for this term.[24] It requested a small group of Jewish NGOs to prepare one. Subsequently this detailed text has been increasingly accepted. One example of this acceptance came when the delegates to the OSCE Cordoba Conference in May 2005 constantly referred to it. Another example was when the Report of the British All-Party Parliamentary Inquiry into Anti-Semitism recommended that "the EUMC Working Definition of anti-Semitism is adopted and promoted by the Government and law enforcement agencies."[25]

The working definition reads:

> Anti-Semitism is a certain perception of Jews, which may be expressed as hatred toward Jews. Rhetorical and physical manifestations of antisemitism are directed toward Jewish or non-Jewish individuals and/or their property, toward Jewish community institutions and religious facilities.

> In addition, such manifestations could also target the state of Israel, conceived as a Jewish collectivity. Anti-Semitism frequently charges Jews with conspiring to harm humanity, and it is often used to blame Jews for "why things go wrong." It is expressed in speech, writing, visual forms and action, and employs sinister stereotypes and negative character traits.

The document that contains the working definition gives a series of contemporary examples of antisemitism. One of these is: "Accusing the Jews as a people, or Israel as a state, of inventing or exaggerating the Holocaust."[26]

The document also states that "criticism of Israel similar to that leveled against any other country cannot be regarded as anti-Semitic." It lists a series of examples of how antisemitism can manifest itself concerning Israel.

- Denying the Jewish people their right to self-determination, e.g., by claiming that the existence of a state of Israel is a racist endeavor.

- Applying double standards by requiring of it a behavior not expected or demanded of any other democratic nation.

- Using the symbols and images associated with classic antisemitism (e.g., claims of Jews killing Jesus or blood libel) to characterize Israel.

- Drawing comparisons of contemporary Israeli policy to that of the Nazis.

- Holding Jews collectively responsible for actions of the state of Israel."[27]

Cartoons

The EUMC definition is gradually becoming a significant tool in identifying the antisemitic character of anti-Israelism. Yet the complex manifestations remain difficult to analyze due to their almost limitless permutations. The most efficient way to show how anti-Israelism not only uses the same core and submotifs as religious and racist antisemitism is by analyzing contemporary anti-Israeli cartoons.

Those who create cartoons for the mass media must appeal to widely existing and easily recognizable stereotypes in their society among their drawings' viewers. (At the same time they strengthen these typecasts further.) As the mass audience is unsophisticated, this limits the number of subthemes the cartoonist can use to depict Israel, Israelis, and Jews as the absolute evil to a few recurrent ones. These are then packaged in many diverse ways. By analyzing such cartoons one can identify systematically these basic themes. Once this has been clarified one can point to the same antisemitic motifs appearing elsewhere in society.

Arieh Stav has undertaken an important analysis of antisemitic imagery in cartoons. He mentions that he mainly focused on "how Israel and the peace process have been reflected in the mirror of Arab caricature, which is a direct, authentic and highly influential expression of views in the Arab world, where nearly half the population is illiterate."[28]

The Illness of the Century

Analyzing antisemitic cartoons after many thousands of additional antisemitic Arab caricatures were published has been developed further by the Belgian political scientist Joël Kotek, in a book so far only available in French.[29]

The core motif of the Jew embodying absolute evil is expressed, for instance, in a cartoon published before the second Palestinian uprising, in December 1999, by *Al-Hayat al-Jadida*, the official Palestinian

Authority journal.[30] Kotek describes it: "It depicted an old man in a *djel-laba*, symbolizing the twentieth century, taking leave of a young man wearing a tee-shirt symbolizing the twenty-first century. In between them stood a small Jew with a Star of David on his breast, above which an arrow pointed to him saying, 'the illness of the century.'"[31]

A contemporary permutation of the Christian deicide motif returned in a cartoon in *La Stampa*, a leading Italian liberal daily—at the time of the siege of Bethlehem—by the well-known cartoonist Giorgio Forattini. He drew a tank with a Star of David on it standing outside the Church of the Nativity, and inside the child Jesus, with a halo, saying, "Are they going to kill me a second time?" The cartoonist's evil intentions, however, misfired as his caricature was even more insulting to Christians than to the Jews. It can easily lend itself to the interpretation that the Palestinian murderers, who had sought refuge in the Church of the Nativity, were the contemporary equivalents of the founder of Christianity.

Another example depicting a similar idea was when in 1991, a Jordanian cartoon showed Jesus on the cross, the nails through his hands dripping with blood forming the Star of David.[32] Somewhat surprisingly, the deicide motif recurrently appears also in the Arab world, which is overwhelmingly Muslim, to whom Jesus is a prophet but not the son of God.

The Devil

The Jew depicted as the devil is yet another incarnation of absolute evil. In a Syrian paper the Zionist devil is presented as a hairy being with a tail. He has a black *kippa* [skullcap] on his head and a black beard, which are Jewish stereotypes and not Israeli ones. On his forehead he has a Star of David. In his hand he holds a pole with a seven-branch candelabra.[33] It is one of many examples of how anti-Jewish and anti-Israeli themes are mixed.

In today's secularized European society, God-killers and the hairy devil are considered old-fashioned images. Nazi images are the contemporary representation of absolute evil. A cartoon in the Greek daily *Ethnos* in 2002, close to the then-ruling Pasok socialist party, showed two Israeli soldiers dressed as Nazis with Stars of David on their helmets, stabbing Arabs. The text read: "Do not feel yourself guilty, my brother. We were not in Auschwitz and Dachau to suffer, but to learn."[34]

It is one among many examples of how anti-Israelism and antisemitism overlap or merge.

The image of the Jew as a Nazi recurs frequently in Arab and other antisemitic drawings. A cartoon in the Egyptian *Al-Akhbar* shows then Israeli prime minister Ehud Barak dressed as a Nazi with a Hitler moustache, blood dripping from his hands.[35] In the third-largest Norwegian daily, *Dagbladet,* both Israeli prime ministers Ariel Sharon and Ehud Olmert have been depicted as Nazis.[36]

In the beginning of 2006 the largest Iranian newspaper *Hamshahri* launched a competition of the "best" Holocaust cartoons.[37] The cartoons thus collected also cover most of the above motifs.

Jews and Israel behind All Disasters

The core motif of the Jews and Israel being extreme evil manifests itself also in writing and declarations in many other ways. The Jew and nowadays Israel are made responsible for all disasters in the world. The Jews were blamed for the transmission of various plagues such as the Black Death in the fourteenth century. From the Christian to the nationalist world the core motif mutated. Germans invented the "stab in the back" (*Dolchstoss*) legend, which held the Jews responsible for Germany's defeat in World War I. It was subsequently used by the National Socialists in their murderous antisemitic campaigns.

On a local level, when Christian children disappeared and were found dead, Jews were regularly accused of having murdered them, often out of religious motives. This was the classic antisemitic version. A modern anti-Israeli variant occurred when mass hysteria broke out in the northern West Bank in March 1983. A number of girls at a middle school in the village of Arrabeh fell sick. The symptoms included fainting, drowsiness, nausea, headaches, stomachaches, and vision disturbances. Almost immediately afterward, Palestinians, in a modern variant of the blood-libel motif, accused Israel of being responsible.

During the following weeks the number of patients, mostly young women, rose to nearly a thousand in the West Bank. Investigations carried out by both Palestinians and Israelis did not find any traces of poison. Gradually, it came to light that many of the later "patients" had faked their illnesses, often at the prompting of Palestinian leaders.

In one of its initial articles on the event, the Israeli daily *Haaretz* implied that there were indications Israel had used nerve gas. The secretary-general of the Arab League accused Israel of using poison gas against Palestinian pupils. The Israeli authorities called in experts from the Centers for Disease Control and Prevention (CDC) in Atlanta, a world leader in epidemiology. They concluded that most of the patients' illnesses were of "psychogenic origin and induced by stress."[38]

The Murderers of 9/11

The mass murderers of September 11, 2001 were Arabs, belonging to Al Qaeda. The organization has also claimed these mass killings. Yet perhaps a majority of the Arabs and other Muslims in the world believes that the Israeli secret service Mossad was responsible for the attack. The prejudice in its various forms is much wider spread. Twenty seven percent of all Canadians outside Quebec and 38 percent of Quebecers think "Israel's actions were a 'primary cause' of 9/11."[39]

Also on this matter, accusations against Jews and Israel are interwoven. The chairman of the British All-Party Parliamentary Inquiry into Antisemitism mentions that he "held a meeting with prominent Muslims in Yorkshire shortly after the 9/11 attacks. He recalled his surprise at hearing professionals of high status claiming that 'no Jews reported for work in the Twin Towers on 11th September' and that 'Mossad faked the attack to cast Muslims in bad light.' "[40]

A Pew poll found that 56 percent of British Muslims do not think Arabs carried out the attack, and only 17 percent think they did. The respective figures for Muslims in France are 46 percent and 48 percent; for those in Germany, 44 percent and 35 percent; and for Spanish Muslims, 35 percent and 33 percent.[41]

Other recent versions of Israel being behind all evil derive from Iranian president Mahmoud Ahmadinejad, one of the world's leading genocidal antisemites. He said the Jews were behind the Danish cartoons satirizing Muhammad, and declared: "They [who insult the founder of Islam] are hostages of the Zionists. And the people of the U.S. and Europe should pay a heavy price for becoming hostages of Zionism."[42]

In February 2006, the Syrian state-controlled paper *al-Tawhra* asserted that Israel was responsible for the expanding bird flu phenomenon. It said Israel had spread the virus in the Far East to mislead the world while aiming to attack the Arabs.[43]

Later that month, Iran's supreme leader Ayatollah Khameini claimed that Zionists and foreign forces were behind the bombing of the gold-domed Shiite mosque in Samarra, Iraq, on February 22. His words were echoed by Ahmadinejad, who said that "these heinous acts are committed by a group of Zionists and occupiers that have failed. They have failed in the face of Islam's logic and justice."[44]

The mutations of the core motif are almost endless. Rory Miller, an academic who has studied Irish attitudes toward Israel, mentions that Aengus Ó Snodaigh, the Sinn Fein party's international affairs and human rights spokesperson in the Irish Parliament, described Israel as "one of the most abhorrent and despicable regimes on the planet."[45]

The facts on free and unfree regimes can be found in the *Freedom in the World* publication of Freedom House, which every year lists countries according to their political rights and civil liberties. In 2005, Israel was in the upper third and among the 89 free countries. Eight countries were in the lowest category of un-free countries. Five were Muslim ones: Libya, Saudi Arabia, Sudan, Syria, and Turkmenistan. (The three others were Cuba, Myanmar, and North Korea.)[46]

Dominating the World

The core theme of the Jews and Israel being the world's main evil branches out into partly overlapping principal submotifs. One is that the forces of evil, i.e., the Jews and Israel, seek to dominate the world.

Again an Arab cartoon expresses the motif succinctly. The American caricaturist of Algerian origin Bendib "designed a monkey with a Star of David on its breast sitting on top of the globe on which small figures of the Pope and an Arab are drawn. The monkey [i.e., Israel] says: "Jerusalem: from New York City to Kuala Lumpur, undivided eternal capital of Israel; everything else is negotiable."[47]

The conspiracy theory found its culmination in the tsarist falsification of *The Protocols of the Elders of Zion*. It recurs in Arab television programs, a mode of communication far more effective and encompassing than the written book. This fraud is widely reprinted in the Arab world. But it has also been published in recent years in many Western countries, Norway once again being one of the examples.[48] The truth is different. As far as contemporary conspiracy is concerned: Now that Nazism and communism have failed, the *jihadi* current of Islam is the only major movement that actively conspires to rule the world.

Lust for Money

The second submotif—a derivative of the first—is that the Jews have a lust for money and through it corrupt the world. Kotek says: "Bendib draws God holding a fat bag of dollars. On it the names of major Jewish organizations are written: 'ADL, AIPAC, ZOA.' God outstretches his hand to [President George W.] Bush who slaughters a child on the altar of the Holyland Foundation for needy Muslim children. The caption reads:

> And the Almighty dollar [represented by God] said: "Sacrifice me, a Muslim son, or else."

> And George W. said: "You've got it Lord, if this improves my chances for a second term."[49]

In other contexts the Jews, however, are regarded as mean and miserly.

The conspiracy motif appears as well in multiple forms and in many circles. This came to the fore in an incident in September 2006 (shortly after publication of the report of the British All-Party Parliamentary Inquiry into Antisemitism in which was written, "We were told that Jewish conspiracy theories have been applied to many contemporary issues").[50]

At a meeting of the Liberal Democrat Party Conference, Baroness Tonge said: "The pro-Israel lobby has got its grips on the Western world, its financial grips. I think they have probably got a certain grip on our party." She also repeated her earlier comments of sympathy for Palestinian suicide bombers. More than twenty members of the House of Lords of the major parties condemned her language as "irresponsible and inappropriate."[51]

Jews and Israel as Subhuman: Zoomorphism

Often cartoons embody more than one principal antisemitic submotif. This is the case with the aforementioned cartoon of Bendib, which shows Israel as a monkey. In addition to the conspiracy motif, it also expresses a second one that Israel or the Jews are subhuman. Kotek mentions that Jews are often represented as spiders, bloodthirsty vampires, and octopuses. He relates that he has not found any other nation besides the Jews being depicted systematically as vampires.

He adds: "Zoomorphism is a very common theme throughout the world. To abuse one's adversaries, one dehumanizes them by turning them into animals. In Nazi, Soviet and Romanian caricatures, the Jew is often depicted as a spider interrupting the peace process. [The Lebanese cartoonist] Stavro portrays [former prime minister Ehud] Barak, with a star of David on his breast, as a spider interrupting the peace process."

Nazi propagandists often claimed that Jews were like rats and cockroaches. This demonization was the first step on the road to extermination, the word that is applied to vermin and was used by the Nazis as a euphemism for systematic murder. These dehumanizing semantics comparing people to insects are deeply rooted in contemporary German culture also where non-Jews are concerned.

For instance, in 2005, Franz Muentefering, then chairman of the German Socialist party (SPD) and currently the country's deputy chancellor, called some foreign financial investors "locusts" who graze companies bare and move on.[52] Oskar Lafontaine, a former SPD chairman and now leader of the Left-wing party agreed, adding that Chancellor Schroeder and Muentefering were also "locusts" since they had demolished the German welfare state.[53] Around the same time, the major German metalworkers trade union (IG Metall) published a cartoon on the cover of its monthly *Metall* comparing American investors to [bloodsucking] mosquitoes.[54]

The Lust for Blood, Killing Children

A fourth permutation of the core motif of Jews and Israelis being evil is that of the lust for cannibalism and blood. Though often its origins are seen in the blood libel, the Dutch scholar Pieter van der Horst, in his 2006 farewell lecture, censored by Utrecht University, has pointed out that there is a straight line from Greek pre-Christian antisemitism to current Muslim antisemitism.[55] The Christian libel that Jews use the blood of Gentile children for religious purposes originated in England during the Middle Ages.

In 1994, the Jordanian *A-Dastur* showed a caricature of how the late Israeli prime minister Yitzchak Rabin pours blood on the carpet of peace.[56] The "lust for blood" motif also returned in a drawing of *Guardian* cartoonist Steve Bell of Conservative leader candidate Michael Howard—a Jew—with a glass of blood in his hand, saying, "Do you drink what I drink, vote Conservative."[57]

This submotif overlaps with a fifth one, the Jew as child killer. This motif remerged in its anti-Israeli form in a cartoon in the British daily *The Independent* by Dave Brown, showing then Israeli prime minister Sharon as a child-eater. When solicited, the UK Press Complaints Commission cleared the drawing. Subsequently it won the Political Cartoon of the Year Award for 2003 of the Political Cartoon Society. The competition was held on November 25, 2003, on *The Economist* weekly's premises, and the award was presented to Brown by Labour MP and former minister for overseas aid Claire Short.[58]

This infanticide motif comes back in the accusation that the Israel Defense Forces intentionally kill Palestinian children. Its symbol in Palestinian society is the death of Muhammad Al-Dura, which according to many was probably the result of Palestinian shooting.

Scientific Approach and Polls

Cartoons lay a structural basis for the analysis of the major overlap of anti-Israelism and antisemitism. There are also tools for a more precise assessment of this. Researchers at Yale University analyzed an Anti-Defamation League opinion survey of 500 citizens in each of ten European countries. They found that anti-Israel sentiment "consistently predicts the probability that an individual is antisemitic, with the likelihood of measured antisemitism increasing with the extent of anti-Israel sentiment observed."[59]

This also becomes clear from various opinion surveys. A major poll, interviewing over 2,600 Germans, was undertaken in 2004 by the University of Bielefeld. Thirty-two percent of those interviewed agreed, or largely agreed, with the statement: "Because of Israel's policies, I have increasing antipathy toward Jews." Sixty-eight percent agreed with the allegation: "Israel undertakes a war of destruction against the Palestinians." Fifty-one percent shared the opinion: "The way the state of Israel acts toward the Palestinians is in principle no different from the Nazis' behavior in the Third Reich toward the Jews."[60]

An Italian poll conducted in the fall of 2003 by Paola Merulla showed that only 43 percent of Italians have sympathy for Israel. Seventeen percent of those polled consider that it would be better if Israel did not exist. Twenty percent of those polled think Jews are not real Italians; 10 percent think Jews lie when they maintain that Nazism murdered millions of Jews.[61]

Even more telling was a major opinion survey undertaken in 2003 covering about 2,200 Italian youngsters between the ages of 14 and 18. Broadly speaking, one-third of these youngsters considers that the Jews control the financial power. Twenty to twenty-five percent see as negative items concerning the Jews that they are the leading racists, feel themselves superior to everyone else, are too attached to money, and one can never trust them completely. About 20 percent believe that the Jews exaggerate when speaking about the Holocaust and close to 20 percent think that the Jews should "return to Israel." The latter proves once again how hard-core antisemitism and anti-Israelism are linked.[62]

The semantics of anti-Israelism often reveal references with an antisemitic undertone. Israeli policies are defined as "eye for eye," an expression rarely if ever used for far more severe actions by other countries. The word "revenge" is another expression associated much more with the Israel Defense Forces than with other armies, such as the American or British in Iraq.

Georges Elia-Sarfati, a professor of linguistics in France, has researched how anti-Zionism emerged as an ideology. He points out that the word did not appear in dictionaries until the 1970s. He adds: "Anti-Zionism's major 'canonic' texts are first and foremost Soviet fabrications. One of the Supreme Soviet's ideologists, Trofim Kitchko, published several antisemitic books between 1963 and the beginning of the 1980s. His first one, *Judaism Unembellished,* was sponsored by the Academy of Sciences."[63]

The Tip of the Iceberg

Cartoons, scientific analysis, polls and semantics demonstrate in detail that anti-Zionism is a new permutation of antisemitism. The behavior of anti-Israelis provides many additional proofs. In 2003, Richard Ingrams wrote in the British weekly *Observer*: "I have developed a habit when confronted by a letter to the editor in support of the Israeli government to look at the signature to see if the writer has a Jewish name; if so, I tend not to read it." He also argued that those who side with Israeli policy should say whether they are Jewish in order to make this transparent. The British Press Complaints Commission considered Ingrams' position legitimate.[65]

A few more examples from several countries may further illustrate how anti-Israelism and antisemitism overlap. On May 7, 2002, Jewish students at San Francisco State University—where antisemitism has now been rife for several years—organized a rally in support of Israel. Pro-Palestinians heckled them with slogans like "F...the Jews," and "Jews go back to Russia," as well as "Too bad Hitler didn't finish the job."[65]

Patrick Klugman, then president of the French Union of Jewish Students, observed:

> "On some university campuses like Nanterre, Villetaneuse and Jussieu, the climate has become very difficult for Jews. In the name of the Palestinian cause, they are castigated as if they were Israeli soldiers! We hear "death to the Jews" during demonstrations which are supposed to defend the Palestinian cause. Last April [in 2002], our office was the target of a Molotov cocktail. As a condition for condemning this attack, the lecturers demanded that the UEJF declare a principled position against Israel!"[66]

In the Netherlands many years ago, thousands of fans of the Feijenoord soccer club sung from their stands, when Ajax from Amsterdam played against them: "Gas the Jews."[67] The same chants occur elsewhere as well on Dutch football fields. In recent years the more frequent version has a Middle Eastern hate element in it: "Hamas, Hamas, Jews to the gas." Ajax is not a Jewish club but has a group of fervent non-Jewish supporters who partly as a reaction to the racist attacks call themselves "Jews." Somewhat similar antisemitic chants are also sung on other European football fields, for instance, in the UK, by the opponents of Tottenham Hotspur, a London club with many Jewish supporters.[68]

Two Dutch authors relate another example of how anti-Israelism and antisemitism mingle: "On 13 April 2002 a pro-Palestinian demonstration on the Dam [Amsterdam's main square], degenerated. American and Israeli flags were burned. Banners dominated the picture with: texts like 'Sharon is Hitler,' and 'the lie of the six million' dominated the streets. In front of Hotel Krasnapolsky a man with a kippah was beaten up. The police let it happen."[69]

One regularly finds in marches of antiglobalists and antiwar demonstrations extreme antisemitic and anti-Israeli banners, often carried by Muslims. Frequently these are tolerated by the organizers.

The Lebanon 2006 War

The Lebanon 2006 summer war brought further proof in a concentrated way that antisemitism and anti-Israelism go hand in hand. During the war, at a demonstration "attended by many Moroccan youngsters in Amsterdam one could read texts like: 'Jews, the army of the Prophet Muhammad is marching.' "[70]

After the war, the European Jewish Congress published a document titled *Antisemitic Incidents and Discourse in Europe During the Israeli-Hezbollah War.*[71] A few examples from it underline the overlap between antisemitism and anti-Israelism.

Gerald Grosz, leader of the right-wing Alliance for the Future of Austria party (BZÖ) led by Jörg Haider requested that the Jewish communities of Vienna and Graz "publicly issue a condemnation of the 'cruel and cowardly murder.'"[72]

Dan Kantor, executive secretary of the Central Council of Jewish Communities in Finland, noted that: "Marginal extreme-left groups, often in co-operation with Islamic groups in a so-called 'Peace Movement' held weekly small marches, where signs were observed equating the Star of David with Nazi symbols. Such groups make little distinction between Israel and local Finnish Jews, Kantor stated, although this also is 'nothing new.' "[73]

In France, the representative council of French Jewry, CRIF, reported that: "Demonstrations in support of Lebanon took place in different cities through France, with antisemitic placards visible reading 'Death to the Jews—Death to Israel,' stars of David emblazoned with swastikas."

A tract sent to a synagogue reads: "Wake up France, and join us in refusing that 'Jewry' massacres the Palestinians in their own homeland.... In France, your duty as well is to combat the Jew. The enemy is the Jew, and they need to be chased from the media, finance, institutions."[74]

In Germany, over three hundred letters were received by the Zentralrat der Juden in Deutschland, (the Jewish umbrella body) "directly attacking both the organization and German Jews for both blindly supporting Israel and spending state money to support a 'fascist state' in the Middle East." Stephan Kramer, the executive director, "called the amount of antisemitic letters received 'mind-boggling.' Complaints from Jewish students of harassment by Muslim and non-Muslim schoolmates were received by the Berlin Jewish Community."[75]

In the Netherlands in July 2006 the chairman of the extreme left-wing Socialist Party, Jan Marijnissen, "compared Islamic terrorism in the Middle East to the actions of the Dutch resistance against the Nazi German occupiers in World War Two." Marijnissen eventually apologized, having received major criticism. He still claims that the Islamist terrorist groups exist "because of Israel's occupation of Palestine, the American presence in the Middle East and the West's support to undemocratic regimes."[77]

In Spain, an article "that appeared in *El Mundo* [a leading daily], entitled *Cauchemar Estival*, made a link between Nazi Germany and Israel, accusing Israel of using the same arguments made by the Nazi leaders to justify "its aggression." The article continues, "Now the victims of this period (the 1930s) have become the executioners.... The victims of today are systematically taken hostage, reduced to live in ghettos, and closed in by a horrible wall.'"[77]

Double Standards

Governmental double standards toward Israel were demonstrated in a major way in the Lebanese war.[78] Though commonly hidden under the title of political opinions, one can apply the EUMC definition to the statements of, for instance, leading European politicians. Many of these meet this definition of antisemitism.

British author Frederic Forsyth wondered how European politicians could dare to call the Israeli response to the Hezbollah attacks disproportionate, when their own countries had behaved far worse in the Yugoslav war: "Why did the accusers not mention Serbia?... In 1999 five NATO air forces—US, British, French, Italian and German—began to plaster Yugoslavia, effectively bombing the tiny and defenceless province of Serbia. We were not at war with the Serbs, we had no reason to hate them, they had not attacked us and no Serbian rockets were falling on us."[79]

There are also similarities between the reaction of Jews during outbursts of Christian antisemitism and those of Jews now in Muslim countries. Kalman Sultanik, a long-term member of the Board of the Jewish Agency, recalls how as a young man in his Polish home town "on Christmas Eve our Christian neighbours were worked into a frenzy by the Church clerics who preached about the crucifixion of Jesus and the Jewish responsibility for his death. We did not dare emerge from our homes for fear of being beaten up or worse."[80] Nowadays, Jewish visitors to Morocco are frequently told by local Jews how they keep a very low profile during periods of tension between Israel and the Palestinians or other Arab communities.

Conclusion

There is overwhelming evidence that anti-Israelism is a major new mutation of antisemitism. The two often overlap and frequently, though not always, appear together. Much progress has been made in exposing the similarity in characteristics and motifs of anti-Israelism and the two earlier major types of antisemitism, the religious and the racist variants.

Yet while many books and much detailed literature exist on these earlier forms of antisemitism, the newer anti-Israelism requires much more detailed investigation, all the more so as its postmodern expressions often are covered with thick layers of pseudo-humanism and political correctness. They are thus much more complicated to analyze and expose than the types long familiar to the public at large.

Notes

1. I am grateful to Michael Berenbaum and Ashley Perry for their comments on this chapter.

2. James Parkes, *The Conflict of the Church and the Synagogue* (Cleveland, New York: Meridian Books, 1961), pp. 375–76.

3. Andrei S. Markovits, "A New (or Perhaps Revived) 'Uninhibitedness' toward Jews in Germany," *Jewish Political Studies Review,* vol. 18, nos. 1 & 2 (spring 2006): 57–70.

4. Manfred Gerstenfeld, *Europe's Crumbling Myths: The Post-Holocaust Origins of Today's Anti-Semitism* (Jerusalem: Jerusalem Center for Political Affairs, Yad Vashem, World Jewish Congress, 2003).

5. Anti-Defamation League, Press Release, "ADL Survey of Five European Countries Finds One in Five Hold Strong Antisemitic Sentiments; Majority Believes Canard of Jewish Disloyalty" (New York), October 31, 2002.

6. Remark made in broadcast and confirmed in personal communication with this author.

7. Manfred Gerstenfeld, "How to Fight Anti-Israeli Campaigns on Campus," *Post-Holocaust and Anti-Semitism,* 51, December 1, 2006.

8. Jonny Paul, "The Emergence of a Silent Academic Boycott of Israel," *EJPress*, May 28, 2006.

9. Robert Fife, "UN Promotes Systemic Hatred of Jews, MP Says," *National Post,* April 2, 2002.

10. Per Ahlmark, *Det ar demokratin, dumbom!* (Timbro, 2004), p. 307 [Swedish].

11. Tovah Lazaroff, "UN Human Rights Council Singles Out Israel Again," *Jerusalem Post*, November 28, 2006.

12. Manfred Gerstenfeld, interview with Rabbi Abraham Cooper, "Antisemitism and Terrorism on the Internet: New Threats," *Post-Holocaust and Anti-Semitism*, 20-A, May 16, 2004, www.jcpa.org/phas/ phas-20a.htm; and Michael Whine, "Cyberhate, Antisemitism and Counterlegislation," *Post-Holocaust and Anti-Semitism* 47, August 1, 2006, www.jcpa.org/phas/phas-047-whine.htm.

13. Manfred Gerstenfeld, "The Twenty-First-Century Total War against Israel and the Jews," *Post-Holocaust and Anti-Semitism* 38, November 1, 2005, 39, December 1, 2005.

14. *Report of the British All-Party Parliamentary Inquiry into Antisemitism,* para 20.

15. Jacques Givet, *The Anti-Zionist Complex* (Englewood, NJ: SBS Publishing, 1982), p. 39.

16. Manfred Gerstenfeld, interview with Simon Epstein, "Fifty Years of French Intellectual Bias against Israel," *Post-Holocaust and Anti-Semitism* 4, January 1, 2003.

17. Personal communication, David Zohar.

18. Jean-Christophe Ruffin, "Chantier sur la Lutte contre le Racisme et l'antisémitisme," Ministère de l'interieur, de la sécurité interieure, et des libertés locales, October 30, 2004 [French].

19. "Campus Anti-Semitism," Briefing Report by the United States Commission on Civil Rights (Washington, USCCR, July 2006).

20. *Report of the British All-Party Parliamentary Inquiry into Antisemitism,* para. 89.

21. www.jafi.org.il/agenda/2001/english/wk3-22/6.asp.

22. Nathan Sharansky, foreword, *Jewish Political Studies Review* 16, nos. 3 & 4, (fall 2004): 5–8.

23. Michael Whine, "Progress in the Struggle Against Antisemitism in Europe: The Berlin Declaration and the European Union Monitoring Centre on Racism and Xenophobia's Working Definition of Antisemitism," *Post-Holocaust and Anti-Semitism* 41, February 1, 2006.

24. "Manifestations of Antisemitism in the EU 2002-2003," European Monitoring Centre on Racism and Xenophobia, Vienna. For background on the process, see Michael Whine, "International Organizations: Combating Antisemitism in Europe," *Jewish Political Studies Review*, vol. 16, nos. 3–4 (fall 2004).

25. *Report of the British All-Party Parliamentary Inquiry into Antisemitism* (London: Stationery Office Ltd., September 2006), para. 26.

26. Michael Whine, "Progress in the Struggle Against Antisemitism in Europe."

27. Ibid.

28. Arie Stav, *Peace, the Arabian Caricature: A Study in Antisemitic Imagery* (Tel Aviv: Gefen Books, 1999), p. 18.

29. Joël et Dan Kotek, *Au nom de l'antisionisme : L'image des Juifs et d'Israël dans la caricature depuis la seconde Intifada*, (Brussels, Édition Complexe, 2003) [French].

30. *Al-Hayat al-Jadida*, December 28, 1999; p. 53.

31. Manfred Gerstenfeld, interview with Joël Kotek, "Major Antisemitic Motifs in Arab Cartoons," *Post-Holocaust and Anti-Semitism* 21, June 1, 2004.

32. *A-Rai*, Jordan, December 26, 1991, Stav, *Peace*, p. 161.

33. *A-Thawra*, Syria, March 4, 1993, Stav, *Peace*, p. 202.

34. *Ethnos*, April 7, 2002 [Greek].

35. *Al Akhbar*, October 3, 2000, Kotek, *Au nom*, p. 60.

36. Erez Uriely, "Jew Hatred in Contemporary Norwegian Caricatures," *Post-Holocaust and Anti-Semitism* 50, November 1, 2006.

37. Simon Freeman and Agencies, "Iranian Paper Launches Holocaust Cartoon Competition," *Times online*, February 6, 2006.

38. Raphael Israeli, *Poison: Modern Manifestations of a Blood Libel* (Lanham, MD: Lexington Books, 2002).

39. Janice Arnold, "1 in 3 Canadians Blame Israel for 9/11," *Canadian Jewish News*, September 14, 2006.

40. *Report of the British All-Party Parliamentary Inquiry into Antisemitism*, para. 96.

41. Pew Global Attitudes Project, "The Great Divide: How Westerners and Muslims View Each Other," June 22, 2006, p. 4.

42. AP, "Iran Blames U.S., Europe in Cartoon Crisis," *New York Times*, February 12, 2006.

43. Roee Nahmias, "Syrian Paper Accuses Israel of Having Spread Bird Flu to Kill Arabs," *Ynet News*, February 9, 2006.

44. "Ahmadinejad Warns West over Shrine Blast," Reuters, February 23, 2006.

45. Rory Miller, "Irish Attitudes Toward Israel," *Post-Holocaust and Anti-Semitism* 49, October 1, 2006.

46. www.infoplease.com/ipa/A0930918.html

47. Manfred Gerstenfeld, interview with Joël Kotek; also Kotek, *Au nom*, p. 69.

48. Erez Uriely, "Jew Hatred in Contemporary Norwegian Caricatures."

49. Joel et Dan Kotek, *Au nom*, p. 71.

50. *Report of the British All-Party Parliamentary Inquiry into Antisemitism*, para. 96.

51. http://www.timesonline.co.uk/article/0,,59-2370675,00.html

52. Manfred Gerstenfeld, "Rewriting Germany's Nazi Past—A Society in Moral Decline," *Jerusalem Viewpoints* 530, May 1, 2005.

53. "Lafontaine giftet wieder gegen Parteifreunde," *Spiegel Online*, April 22, 2005 [German].

54. www.igmetall.de/metall/mai05/titel_voll.html

55. Pieter W. van der Horst, "De Mythe van het joodse kannibalisme (De ongecensureerde versie)," CIDI, Den Haag, 2006 [Dutch].

56. *A-Dastur*, Jordan, April 4, 1994, Stav, *Peace*, p. 146.

57. Steve Bell, "Are You Drinking What We Are Drinking? Vote Conservative," *Guardian*, April 7, 2005.

58. www.politicalcartoon.co.uk/html/exhibition.html

59. Edward H. Kaplan, Charles A. Small, "Anti-Israel Sentiment Predicts

Antisemitism in Europe," *Journal of Conflict Resolution* 50/4 (August 2006): 548–61.

60. Wilhelm Heitmeyer (ed.), *Deutsche Zustände* (Frankfurt am Main: Suhrkamp, 2005) [German].

61. Renato Mannheimer, "E antisemita quasi un italiano su cinque," *Corriere de la Sera,* November 10, 2003 [Italian].

62. Enzo Campelli, *Figli di un dio locale, Giovani e differenze culturali in Italia* (Milan: Franco Angeli, 2004), p. 147 [Italian].

63. Manfred Gerstenfeld, interview with Georges Elia-Sarfati "Language as a Tool against Jews and Israel," *Post-Holocaust and Anti-Semitism* 17, February 1, 2004, www.jcpa.org/phas/phas-17.htm.

64. Sharon Sadeh, "UK Watchdog Backs Writer Who Won't Read Mail from Jews," *Haaretz,* August 5, 2003.

65. Yair Sheleg, "A Campaign of Hatred," *Haaretz,* May 5, 2002.

66. Ori Golan, "Same Word, Same Meaning," *Jerusalem Post Magazine,* January 17, 2003.

67. Simon Kuper, "Ajax, de joden, Nederland," *Hard Gras* 22 (Amsterdam: March 2000), p. 141 [Dutch].

68. Oliver Bradley, Anti-Semitism or Endearment?" *EJPress,* June 26, 2006.

69. Margalith Kleywegt, Max van Weezel, *Het Land van Haat en Nijd* (Amsterdam: Balans, 2006) 226 [Dutch].

70. Ibid., p. 214.

71. Ilan Moss, *Antisemitic Incidents and Discourse in Europe during the Israel-Hezbollah War* (Paris: European Jewish Congress, 2006).

72. Ibid., pp. 9, 10.

73. Ibid., p. 19.

74. Ibid., pp. 20, 21.

75. Ibid., p. 23.

76. Ibid., p. 33.

77. Ibid.,.p. 43.

78. Manfred Gerstenfeld, "Europe's Mindset Toward Israel as Accentuated by

the Lebanon War," *Jerusalem Viewpoints* 547, October 1, 2006.

79. Frederic Forsyth, *Daily Express*, August 11, 2006.

80. Kalman Sultanik, "The New Antisemitism," *Midstream* (November/ December 2004).

About the Authors

Mehnaz M. Afridi has a BA and MA in Religious Studies from Syracuse University and has studied at the Hebrew University in Jerusalem. Her PhD was on "Mahfouz and Modern Egypt" from the University of South Africa in Religious Studies. As a Muslim, she has had a deep interest in Judaism and the modern jewish diaspora that has led her to numerous exciting interfaith conferences and invitations by non-Muslims to expound on the intellectual and theological similarities between Jews and Muslims. Her extensive background in both Jewish and Islamic thought and culture has led to numerous prestigious research grants and fostered the development of courses in Jewish and Islamic Studies programs. Her recent research projects are focused in Italy, Muslims and Jews in Italian culture; she taught in Rome and recently received a grant from the National Endowment of Humanities to attend a seminar in Venice, Italy.

She is involved in interfaith initiatives in Los Angeles with the Raoul Wallenberg Institute of ethics in conjunction with the Islamic Center of Southern California. She is the lead Muslim Participant and Presenter at the annual face-to face dialogues. In addition, she is presently on the board of directors for the International Education and Welfare Society, and Progressive Muslim Union to direct and plan educational bridges between Americans, Pakistanis, and interfaith conferences. She is currently teaching Islam and Judaism, Cultural Diversity, and Humanities at Antioch University, National University, and the Mary & Joseph Center in Palos Verdes, California.

She has taught at Syracuse University, Hamilton College, American Intercontinental University, and Loyola Marymount University. She has had several publications and papers presented; "The Middle East in Religious Perspective: A Study Guide for Instructional Development," 1991; "Religious Diversity, Walking and the City of Ruins," Academic Exchange Extra, May 2005; "Contemporary Readings of the

Qur'an: Cruel/Compassionate?" Journal of Sacred Tropes, University Press of Duke, 2006; "Islam and its Forgotten Neighbors," Journal of Textual Reasoning, UCLA Press, November 2005; Annual Humanitarian Conference: International Education and Welfare Society, Pakistan Link, February 2006. In addition, she has appeared in two documentaries on the History Channel and PBS, 2006. Born in Pakistan, raised in Europe, educated in the United States, Professor Afridi brings a global perspective to exploring the images of Islam in the modern world. Her goal is to develop an American Islamic Learning Foundation (ALIF), where all of her many goals can be met in an educational and nurturing environment.

Michael Berenbaum is director of the Sigi Ziering Institute: Exploring the Ethical and Religious Implications of the Holocaust, and a Professor of Jewish Studies at the American Jewish University (formerly the University of Judaism). He served as Executive Editor of the *Encyclopaedia Judaica*'s second edition. He is former President and Chief Executive Officer of the Survivors of the Shoah Visual History Foundation. He was the Director of the United States Holocaust Research Institute at the U.S. Holocaust Memorial Museum and the Hymen Goldman Adjunct Professor of Theology at Georgetown University in Washington, D.C. From 1988–93 he served as Project Director of the United States Holocaust Memorial Museum, overseeing its creation. He has written and edited seventeen books on the Holocaust, most recently *A Promise to Remember: The Holocaust in the Words and the Voices of Its Survivors.*

Jerome Chanes, author of the award-winning *A Dark Side of History: Antisemitism through the Ages* and editor of *A Portrait of the American Jewish Community*, has taught at Barnard College and at Yeshiva University, and is a Faculty Scholar at Brandeis University's Cohen Center for Modern Jewish Studies. Chanes is the author as well of the widely used *A Primer on the American Jewish Community* and the comprehensive *Antisemitism: A Reference Handbook*, the first reference work on antisemitism. He has authored some seventy-five articles, papers, reviews, encyclopedia entries, and book chapters.

Samuel M. Edelman is Dean of the College of Arts and Sciences at the American Jewish University (formerly the University of Judaism) in Los Angeles. He has been a Professor of Jewish and Holocaust Studies as well as Rhetoric and Communication Studies. He was the founder of the program in Modern Jewish and Israel Studies at the California State University Chico in Northern California. Edelman was also the coordinator of the California State University Statewide Modern Jewish Studies BA Degree. He recently was Scholar-in-Residence at Haifa University in Jewish Education. Edelman is also Codirector of the California State Center of Excellence in Holocaust, Genocide, Human Rights and Tolerance Education and Chief Liaison to the State Taskforce on Holocaust, Genocide, Human Rights and Tolerance Education.

Reuven Firestone is Professor of Medieval Jewish and Islamic Studies, HUC-JIR/Los Angeles. He served for eight years as Director of HUC-JIR's Edgar F. Magnin School of Graduate Studies and the Jerome Louchheim School of Undergraduate Jewish Studies at the University of Southern California, which offers degrees in cooperation with HUC-JIR. Prior to joining the HUC-JIR faculty, he taught at Boston University and was Yad Hanadiv Research Fellow at the Hebrew University. He received a Center for Arabic Study Abroad (CASA) III research fellowship for the spring 2006 semester for study at the American University of Cairo, funded by the Fulbright Binational Committee in Egypt and the U.S. Department of Education. In 2000, Professor Firestone was awarded a fellowship for independent research from the National Endowment for the Humanities, and was chosen to be a fellow of the Institute for Advanced Jewish Studies at the University of Pennsylvania in 2002. His specialties are early Islam and its relationship with Jews and Judaism, scriptural interpretation of the Bible and Qur'an, and the phenomenon of holy war.

Manfred Gerstenfeld is Chairman of the Board of Fellows of the Jerusalem Center for Public Affairs. He is an international business strategist who has been a consultant to governments, international agencies, and boards of some of the world's largest corporations. He is editor of the *Jewish Political Studies Review* and copublisher of *Post-Holocaust and Anti-Semitism*. Among his ten books are *Europe's Crumbling Myths: The Post-Holocaust Origins of Today's Anti-Semitism* (JCPA, Yad Vashem, WJC, 2003); *American Jewry's Challenge: Conversations Confronting the 21st Century* (Rowman & Littlefield, 2005); and *Israel and Europe: An Expanding Abyss?* (JCPA and Konrad Adenauer Stiftung, 2005).

Frederic Cople Jaher is an Emeritus Professor of History at the University of Illinois, Champaign-Urbana. He received his PhD from Harvard University and specializes in American social and intellectual history and the study of Jews in America. His publications in the history of American Jewry include: *A Scapegoat in the New Wilderness: The Origins and Rise of Anti-Semitism in America* (Harvard University Press, 1994), which was chosen by the Gustavus Myers Center as an outstanding book on the subject of human rights in North America, and *The Jews and the Nation: Revolution, Emancipation, State Formation and the Liberal Paradigm in America and France* (Princeton, 2003). In addition, he has published several articles on Jewish-American subjects and was a Fulbright visiting professor in American Civilization at Hebrew University in Jeruaslem in 1986–87.

Robert A. Kahn is an Assistant Professor of Legal Writing at Brooklyn Law School. He has a PhD in Political Science from Johns Hopkins University and a JD from NYU Law School. He is the author of *Holocaust Denial and the Law: A Comparative Study* (New York: Palgrave-Macmillan, 2004), which covers Canada, France, Germany, and the United States. His other interests include the legal regulation of cross burning and the response of American and European courts to the free speech and free exercise claims of Muslims.

John Kelsay is Distinguished Research Professor and Richard L. Rubenstein Professor of Religion at Florida State University. His work in the comparative study of religious ethics focuses on political and military aspects of Christianity and Islam. Publications include *Islam and War: A Study in Comparative Ethics* (1993). More recently, Professor Kelsay is working on two books, the working titles of which are *Islam and the Political Future: The New Jihad and the Crisis of Shari`a Reasoning*, and *Religion and the Imperatives of Justice: The Islamic Law of War and Peace*. In connection with these projects, he received fellowships from the John Simon Guggenheim Foundation and the Princeton University Center for Human Values in 2002–3.

Richard S. Levy has taught German history since 1971 at the University of Illinois in Chicago. He is author of *The Downfall of the Antisemitic Political Parties in Imperial Germany* (Yale Press, 1975), editor of *Antisemitism in the Modern World: An Anthology of Texts* (Houghton

Mifflin, 1991), and editor, translator, and annotator of Binjamin Segel, *A Lie and A Libel: The History of the Protocols of the Elders of Zion* (University of Nebraska Press, 1995). He recently completed editing a two-volume encyclopedia: *Antisemitism: Historical Encyclopedia of Prejudice and Persecution*, 2 vols. (Santa Barbara, CA: ABC-Clio, 2005).

Richard L. Rubenstein is President Emeritus of the University of Bridgeport and Robert O. Lawton Distinguished Professor Emeritus at Florida State University. A student of genocide for some five decades, he is the author of *After Auschwitz: Radical Theology and Contemporary Judaism* [first edition, 1966], and *After Auschwitz: History, Theology and Contemporary Judaism* [second edition, 1992] as well as *The Cunning of History, the Age of Triage: Fear and Hope in an Overcrowded World* along with *Approaches to Auschwitz,* coauthored with John K. Roth, and numerous other books.

Mark Weitzman is Director of the Task Force against Hate and Terrorism and Chief Representative of the Center to the United Nations in New York, as well as founding director of the SWC's New York Tolerance Center. Mr. Weitzman is a member of the official US delegation to the Task Force for International Cooperation on Holocaust Education, Remembrance and Research, and a board member and former Vice President of the Association of Holocaust Organizations. In June 1999, Mr. Weitzman was honored with the Distinguished Service Award by the Center of Hate and Extremism at the Richard Stockton College of New Jersey.

His publications include editing and contributing to *Kristallnacht: A Resource Book and Program Guide* (1988), *Dignity and Defiance: Confronting Life and Death in the the Warsaw Ghetto* (1993), and *The New Lexicon of Hate* (3rd edition, 2004) as well as the annual CD, *Digital Hate and Terrorism* (2000–2005). He has published numerous scholarly articles in the fields of Holocaust studies, antisemitism, and extremism, most recently as a contributor to the *Encyclopedia of Genocide and Crimes against Humanity* (Macmillan), His book (coauthored with Steven L. Jacobs) *Dismantling the Big Lie: The Protocols of the Elders of Zion*, which is the first full refutation of the infamous protocols, was published in the fall of 2003, has been translated into Arabic, and is in the process of being translated into Turkish.

Efraim Zuroff is director of the Israel office of the Simon Wiesenthal Center and coordinator of Nazi war crimes research (worldwide) for the center. He is the leading Nazi hunter of his generation, insisting that the perpetrators of the Holocaust be brought to justice. Zuroff is the author of *The Response of Orthodox Jewry to the Holocaust in the United States.*

Index